Issues In Evolutionary Ethics

SUNY Series in
Philosophy and Biology

David Edward Shaner, Editor

Issues in Evolutionary Ethics

Edited by
Paul Thompson

STATE UNIVERSITY OF NEW YORK PRESS

Production by Ruth Fisher
Marketing by Fran Keneston

Published by
State University of New York Press, Albany

For information, address the State University of New York Press,
State University Plaza, Albany, NY 12246

Library of Congress Cataloging-in-Publication Data

Issues in evolutionary ethics /   edited by Paul Thompson.
    p.   cm. — (SUNY series in philosophy and biology)
    Includes bibliographical references and index.
    ISBN 0-7914-2027-2 (alk. paper). — ISBN 0-7914-2028-0 (pbk.   :
alk. paper)
    1. Ethics, Evolutionary.   2. Sociobiology—Moral and ethical
aspects.   I. Thompson, Paul, 1947– .   II. Series.
BJ1311.I88   1995
170—dc20   93-37841
                                                                  CIP

10 9 8 7 6 5 4 3 2 1

For
Lewis Thompson,
with love and gratitude

Contents

Preface

In selecting the material for this collection I have attempted to capture the excitement, controversy, and promise of the endeavor to bring together evolutionary theory and ethics. The name most frequently used to refer to this endeavor is *evolutionary ethics*. Two watershed dates in this endeavor are 1859 and 1975.

In 1859 Charles Darwin's revolutionary book *The Origin of Species* was published. Although Darwin did not speculate on human origins or ethics in this work, it fundamentally changed the framework within which discussions by others of the relation between evolution and ethics took place. Darwin waited more than a decade before reporting his views on the relation of evolution and morality in *The Descent of Man*. An excerpt from this latter work is reprinted in this collection. The collection also contains excerpts from the works of two other leading figures in the early discussions of evolutionary ethics: Herbert Spencer and Thomas Henry Huxley. The work of all three individuals has had a profound effect on the development of evolutionary ethics during this century and has permeated the contemporary discussion.

In 1975, evolutionary ethics received renewed attention. The impetus for this was the publication of Edward O. Wilson's ground-breaking book *Sociobiology: The New Synthesis*. The importance of this book resides in its bringing together a massive amount of research in different fields of inquiry and unifying it under the general category of sociobiology (the evolutionary biology of social behavior). Wilson drew on, and integrated, research in anthropology, sociology, ethnology, ecology, genetics, evolutionary biology, physiology, and psychology. The most controversial parts of the book were those dealing with humans. A storm of protest emerged shortly after publication. The protests came from a cross section of the population ranging across evolutionary biologists, anthropologists, sociologists, philosophers, and political activists.

In the introduction, I have provided an account of some of the central concepts that play a role in the contemporary debate and are taken for granted by many of the authors in this volume as background knowledge. In addition, for Darwin, Spencer, and Huxley, I have provided a sketch of their lives and views. There are two reasons for this. First, Darwin, Spencer, and Huxley died around a century ago and the corpus of their work, therefore, is complete and no longer unfolding and developing. As a result, there is a substantial body of commentary on the works, and their importance is widely accepted. The same is not true of the contemporary material in the collection. It reflects the buzz of active controversy and I have selected widely from the ongoing debate. Second, and more important, the reader's cultural distance from Victorian Britain as well as the fact that the selections from Darwin, Spencer, and Huxley are but a fragment of the authors' comprehensive views as expressed in a large integrated body of work, complicates the reader's task of understanding the material.

The General Bibliography contains entries for all the works cited in the Introduction as well as a large number of other works that have emerged as having an important role in discussions of evolutionary ethics. Where a selection contained its own bibliography, that bibliography has been printed with the selection. Although there is considerable overlap, no attempt has been made in the General Bibliography to duplicate the bibliographies contained within the selections.

I am grateful to numerous colleagues and anonymous reviewers who commented on various aspects of the collection and, although our disagreements are many, I am especially grateful to Michael Ruse. I am also indebted to Robert Richards, who, through his book, *Darwin and the Emergence of Evolutionary Theories of Mind and Behavior,* changed, from negative to positive, my assessment of the nature and importance of the views of Herbert Spencer. Kerry Max and Jonathan Thompson assisted me in obtaining and computer scanning the articles for the collection. Jennifer McShane proofread numerous versions of the Introduction and provided useful feedback on the intelligibility of the explanations contained in it.

Introduction

With the publication in 1859 of Charles Darwin's *The Origin of Species*, thinking about humans was transformed. Although the theory expounded and defended in *The Origin of Species* was ostensibly about the origin of various physical forms of organisms, few failed to see the implications for theories about human origins and about the nature of mind and morality. Realizing that it would attract undue attention and controversy, Darwin was careful in *The Origin of Species* to avoid speculation about humans. His caution was later abandoned, and in *The Descent of Man and Selection in Relation to Sex,* he provides a detailed and thoughtful account of the origin and nature of humans, including mind and morality.

Although Darwin transformed the discussion of the evolution of humans and of its implications for ethics, speculation about the relation of evolution to ethics predates *The Origin of Species*. Indeed, through much of the nineteenth century the relation of evolution to morality was widely discussed. For example, evolution, as expounded by Jean-Baptiste de Lamarck, Erasmus Darwin (Charles Darwin's grandfather), and Robert Chambers, was clearly seen to be relevant to morality. Indeed, the negative implications of these evolutionary views for morality constituted strong grounds for rejection of such evolutionary thinking. For many in Britain (especially the clergy), evolution was a false and pernicious view that, if accepted, would undermine the moral fabric of civilized society.

The change that *The Origin of Species* brought about was the elevation of the status of evolutionary theorizing. Darwin achieved this by providing a wealth of evidence for his theory of evolution. In addition, he presented his theory from a position of personal strength. He was a highly re-spected naturalist and geologist, and was well connected within the scientific community and within high society. As a result, evolution was taken seriously and became more widely accepted. Hence, by the time Darwin wrote on hu-mans in *The Descent of Man*, the idea of evolution was more widely tolerated. This more open attitude toward evolution, however, in no way protected Darwin from severe criticism regarding his views on evolution and morality. Indeed, many supporters of his theory of evolution criticized his views on morality.

Understandably, the stronger is the case for evolution, the more pernicious become the views of evolutionists on morality. In this light, it is not surprising that the reaction to Darwin's theory and his writings on humans was at the time, and has continued to be, intense and often extreme: a great deal is perceived to be at stake. Given the wide-spread acceptance of evolution within the scientific (and wider academic) community during the past forty or so years, the preferred strategy of opponents of evolutionary ethics has been the marginalization of the importance of evolu-tion for ethics. The most powerful tool in the arsenal of opponents has been the logical principle that moral state-ments cannot be derived from factual statements alone (com-monly referred to as the *naturalistic fallacy*).

In 1975, the appearance of *Sociobiology: The New Synthe-sis* by Edward O. Wilson sparked renewed and heated debate about the relevance of evolutionary theory to human social behavior. Of special concern was the relevance of evolution-ary theory to morality. Wilson quite clearly threw down the gauntlet by claiming:

> Camus said that the only serious philosophical question is suicide. That is wrong even in the strict sense intended. The biologist, who is concerned with questions of physiology and evolutionary history, realizes that self-knowledge is constrained and shaped by the emotional control centers in the hypothala-mus and limbic system of the brain. These centers flood our consciousness with all the emotions—hate, love, guilt, fear, and others—that are consulted by ethical philosophers who wish to

intuit the standards of good and evil. What, we are then compelled to ask, made the hypothalamus and limbic system? They evolved by natural selection. That simple biological statement must be pursued to explain ethics and ethical philosophers, if not epistemology and epistemologists, at all depths. Self-existence, or the suicide that terminates it, is not the central question of philosophy. (p. 3)

Most of the articles in this collection have been written against the background of Wilson's challenge and sociobiology as a field of investigation. Sociobiology is, in essence, the application of modern evolutionary theory to the investigation and explanation of, as well as the integration of knowledge about, the social behavior of animals including humans. Modern evolutionary theory is a descendent of Darwin's evolutionary theory. It brings together theories of selection, the sources of variation, and heredity. Darwin's major contribution was the development of the concept of selection. Since Darwin first introduced it, theoretical work on selection has advanced in significant ways but the underlying idea is still the one Darwin put forward.

In what follows, I provide in Part I a brief description of the life and views of Darwin, Spencer and Huxley and in Part II an introduction to four major issues in the contemporary debate over evolutionary ethics. The motivation for the latter is clear: these four permeate the articles in the collection. The motivation for the former is set out in the Preface. Briefly stated, I am attempting to offset the disadvantage of the cultural and temporal distance of these authors from present readers as well as the fact that the selections are excerpts from larger works.

Part I. Darwin, Spencer, and Huxley

1. Charles Darwin (1809–1882)

Charles Darwin was born on February 12, 1809, and received his early education at Dr. Butler's School in Shrewsbury (1818–1825). After this he went to Edinburgh University to study medicine as his father (Robert Darwin) and his grandfather (Erasmus Darwin) before him had done. His performance at Dr. Butler's school was at best mediocre. It was a largely classical-based education, for which Darwin showed no talent or interest. Edinburgh was no better. He found the lectures dull (except for chemistry) and dissection revolting. He did not apply himself to his studies but did become involved in extracurricular activities in science. He left Edinburgh in 1827, having given up on a medical career. His father determined that if medicine was not for Charles, an Anglican clerical career was a good second choice. Darwin attended Cambridge University for three years (1828–1831) and received his bachelors degree in 1831. He did not find his studies at Cambridge any more exciting than those at Edinburgh, he again found his main interest in science: particularly geology, botany, and beetles (he was part of a collecting craze that swept England). His contact with John Henslow (professor of botany) and interest in science resulted in Henslow arranging for Darwin to travel on *H.M.S. Beagle* as a gentleman companion for the captain, Robert Fitzroy, and to engage in naturalist activities. Specifically, he was to carry out a geological survey and collect specimens of animals and plants for shipment to England.

    H.M.S. Beagle, after a couple of false starts, set sail from Plymouth Harbour on December 27, 1831, and returned to England in October 1836, docking at Falmouth Harbour. Darwin had collected an enormous number of specimens and had recorded a wealth of geological information. During the voyage he had come to accept Charles Lyle's gradualist and actualist views as set out in Lyle's two-volume *Principles of Geology*. The *Beagle* voyage was a crucial element in the development of Darwin's evolutionary views. In addition, his naturalist activities during the voyage secured for him a strong reputation in natural science. As a result, his reputation was solid long before the publication of *The Origin of Species* and before his evolutionary speculations were widely known. His evolutionary speculations go back to the final period on the *Beagle* and are contained in a series of notebooks (the *Transmutation Notebooks* were begun in the summer of 1837).

In 1839 he married Emma Wedgewood and they had ten children. Darwin was independently wealthy as a result of his inheritance from his father and the Wedgewood dowry. He suffered from sporadic bouts of a mysterious illness. In spite of this, however, he produced a large corpus of writings on a wide array of different topics in natural science.

The work that most people associate with Darwin is *The Origin of Species* (hereafter *The Origin*). In it, he provides an argument for the mutability of species (one species can change over time into a different species) and for a causal mechanism that governs these changes. There is considerable controversy over what Darwin meant by *species* in *The Origin*, because he claims to be explaining their origin and yet appears to argue that there is no reality to the concept "species." Instead, it is portrayed as an artificial human construct. This artificial character of species explains clearly why species are mutable. If there is no such thing in reality as a *species*, then there can be no reason why what we call *species* cannot undergo changes that will result in an organism sufficiently different that trained authoritative naturalists are prepared to call it a new species. There are no real boundaries between species because there are no real species. Organisms blend into one another in an insensible grade of differences: just like the development of a tree from a seed or an animal from an embryo. There are no real breaks in the development and terms like *seedling, sapling, infant, toddler, teenager,* and so on, are artificial ways of breaking up the continuous development.

The causal mechanism that brings about change in the organic world is natural selection. In the organic world there is variation among organisms. Characteristics possessed by some organisms make them better able to survive to reproduce and better able to engage in the activity of reproduction. Under circumstance where not all organisms will survive, those with a characteristic that enhances their ability to survive and reproduce, on average, will leave more offspring than others. Hence, there will be proportionally more organisms with the genetic characteristic that enhances survival in the next generation than in the previous generation. Over many generations organisms with that characteristic will become dominant. The situation is, of course, far more complex than this description conveys. Just as Newton's laws can be simply stated although how they work in nature is complex, so the actual working of the causal mechanism of natural selection in nature is exceptionally complex. For example, changes in the environment (climate, food sources and types, predators) will affect the characteristics that enhance survival and reproduction. Also, a matrix of characteristics will enhance survival and reproduction. Hence, it is a gross simplification to imagine that a particular characteristic is identifiable as enhancing survival in isolation from other characteristics and from a dynamic environment. Nonetheless, the causal mechanism itself is accurately captured in the above description.

In his autobiography Darwin credits his reading of Thomas Robert Malthus's *An Essay on the Principle of Population* with providing the key insight into the causal mechanism of evolution. The views of Malthus (1766–1834) on population was first published anonymously in 1798 and had a profound effect on the political and legal thinking of England. In 1803 Malthus wrote what in name was a second edition of *An Essay on the Principle of Population;* in actual fact it was a new work on the same topic (as Malthus acknowledges in the Preface to this work). In 1830 Malthus's *A Summary View of the Principle of Population* was published.

Darwin applied Malthus's conceptual framework of "a struggle," developed by Malthus as a framework for understanding human economic and social structures, to the organic world. In simple terms Malthus argued that population growth, when unchecked, was geometric (with a doubling occurring every twenty-five years), whereas resources to support a population grew arithmetically. Hence, a point would be reached, quite rapidly, at which the size of a population would outstrip the resources available to support it. At that point, without checks on population growth, there would be a struggle for existence within the population. For Darwin, "the struggle for existence," in a more general form, was the basis for natural selection.

After the publication of *The Origin* a storm of contro-versy broke out. Few failed to see the implications of its thesis for human origins even though Darwin avoided stat-ing those implications. Others were less cautious and the controversy about the implications for human origins, mo-rality and destiny took off. In 1871, Darwin's views on the implications of his evolutionary theory for human origins and morality were published in *The Descent of Man, and Selection in Relation to Sex* (a second edition was published in 1874). The selection in this collection is from the first edition of this work.

Darwin's moral theory is based on conscience, social instinct, intelligence, and group selection. The evolution of morality is the evolution of conscience. The evolution of conscience is underpinned by the evolution of social instinct, which causes organisms to behave in ways that benefit the social group to which they belong. Social instinct alone, however, is only the basis on which morals are built. True moral action requires intellect, which allows one to reason about the best ways to achieve the ends toward which social instinct impels one and also enables one to reflect on desires that compete with the social instinct. Social instinct and intellect are products of evolution. Hence, morality is a prod-uct of evolution.

One of the challenges for a theory of morality based on evolution is to explain how a propensity for behaviors that are detrimental to the individual performing them can be a product of evolution; for example, altruism. Darwin, like Spencer and contemporary sociobiologists, employed recip-rocal altruism (discussed in Part II) as one model of expla-nation. Darwin also explained the evolution of social instincts that are detrimental to the survival of the individuals per-forming them in terms of group selection (also discussed in Part II). Some social instincts benefit the group to which the individual belongs and as a result, the more individuals with those instincts in a group the more likely the group is to survive relative to other groups. Darwin argues for group selection in these cases of social instinct by drawing on the social behavior of insects like honeybees. In this respect,

Darwin's explanation is very close to the contemporary sociobiological explanation. There are even hints that Darwin understood the need for members of a group to be closely related in order for the social instincts of individuals that are of benefit to the group to be passed to the next generation. These, however, are only hints and far from forming the basis for the modern explanation of altruism in terms of a concept known as inclusive fitness.

Darwin's moral theory was criticized by his contemporaries because they took it either to be a morality of self-interest or a form of utilitarian moral theory. Utilitarianism is the view that morally right actions are those that result in the greatest amount of happiness. Utilitarianism was in its formative stages during the nineteenth century and some versions seemed to be based on selfishness or self-interest. Hence, some critics of Darwin charge him with supporting a self-interested utilitarianism. Darwin was aware that, by the time *The Descent of Man* was published, utilitarians no longer cast their theory in terms of selfishness or self-interest.

Such criticisms of Darwin's moral theory miss the mark. Darwin is quite clear that he rejects self-interest as the motivation for moral action. Individuals do not act out of self-interest but from social instinct, which is sometimes directed toward the benefit of the group to which the individual belongs. In addition, contrary to the utilitarian view, individuals act morally because they have an evolved propensity to do so and not because they calculate the balance of pleasure (happiness) over pain.

2. Herbert Spencer (1820–1903)

Herbert Spencer was born on April 27, 1820, in Derby, England. His early education was unstructured and unfocused. From 1830 to 1833, he was educated by his uncle William Spencer. From 1833–1837, he was educated by another uncle, Thomas Spencer, who had received honors at Cambridge. At age 17, and after a brief stint as assistant schoolmaster at Derby, Spencer was offered a job as an engineer with the London and Birmingham Railway. He remained in this position until 1841, at which time he left to work with his father on the development of an electric engine. After a year he abandoned the project (deeming it uneconomical) and went to live with his Uncle Thomas. Spencer spent this period reading widely, and writing a number of letters on "The Proper Sphere of Government." After a brief period in 1844 as subeditor of the newspaper *Pilot*, he returned to the London and Birmingham Railway as an engineer. In 1848 he became the managing editor of the newspaper *Economist*. It was in this year that he began his first major work, *Social Statics*, which was published three years later. In the following year (1849) he wrote a paper, "A Theory of Population," which embodies Lamarkian evolutionary thinking but also contains hints of natural selection. This was a watershed for Spencer. The essay received considerable attention (some positive, some negative) and became the vehicle that brought him into prominent circles in England, including the beginning of a deep friendship with Thomas Huxley.

Spencer was a prolific writer and advocate of an evolutionary conception of knowledge, society, and morality. For much of this century, however, he has been regarded with derision as the father of social Darwinism in its ugliest, meanest forms. As a result, he is often cited as an example of all that is wrong with many programs of evolutionary ethics. He is cast as a hardline advocate of the principle of the survival of the fittest within a laissez-faire social structure. (The expression *survival of the fittest* was coined by Spencer and used by Darwin in the fifth and sixth editions of *The Origin* as a cognate for Natural Selection.) This characterization, however, is extremely unfair to Spencer and is largely a result of isolating some of his claims from his overall view and also of removing him from the social context that his writings were addressing and which informed his thinking. Without doubt, his prose, especially in his later works, does nothing to create excitement about, and interest in, his views. And there is much in Spencer with which a late-twentieth century reader can disagree. This, however, is true of almost all historical figures, including Darwin. For some reason, however, Spencer is especially targeted for holding biological views commonly held by his contemporaries. For example, Spencer is often brushed aside because of his commitment to the inheritance of acquired characteristics. With inconsistency, Darwin's acceptance of the inheritance of acquired characteristics and a "pangenesis" theory of inheritance does not result in the same dismissive attitude. Some take refuge in the fact that Darwin got the picture of evolution largely right whereas Spencer got almost nothing right. This will not do. Much in late-twentieth century thinking bears the marks of Spencer, and notwithstanding the existence of points of disagreement, his views are far richer and more complicated than the standard characterization conveys. Indeed, there is good reason to believe that he was one of the most important, influential, and creative thinkers of the second half of the nineteenth century.

A sense of his importance in the nineteenth and early twentieth century can be gained by considering the use made of his books. The *Principles of Biology* was used as a text at Oxford University; the *Principles of Psychology*, at Harvard University; and the *Study of Sociology*, at Yale University. His *Study of Sociology* was the text for the first course offered in the United States on sociology.

Spencer's opposition to the poor laws is a striking example of the misunderstanding of Spencer's views that arise from isolating a few of his claims from the body of his works and the social and intellectual context of his time. Like many of the professional upper-class in nineteenth century Britain, Spencer was vigorously opposed to the poor laws. The poor laws imposed a tax on parishes to generate funds for relief and welfare payments. Originating with legislation in 1572 that permitted each parish to tax its citizens when charitable donations were inadequate to meet the needs of the poor, these laws in different forms persisted until 1929 with the passing of the Local Government Act. In 1834, the Poor Law Amendment Act was passed with the intent of removing support from those who were deemed unwilling to work. Only those who demonstrably could not work were to receive support: those with a physical impediment, the elderly, and so on.

For Spencer poor laws of any kind were unacceptable. This opposition is often cited as evidence of Spencer's lack of compassion for those less fortunate than himself. According to this view of Spencer, his supposed lack of compassion is rooted in his principle of the survival of the fittest. This view of Spencer, however, is seriously in error. He was not opposed to individual charity—indeed he championed it— rather, he opposed state intervention as a means of resolving the problems of poverty. His views were anything but lacking in compassion when placed within the context of nineteenth century British society and within his own larger philosophical framework. Much was wrong with the administration of the poor laws in the nineteenth century. Parishes were permitted but not mandated to impose a certain level of tax, and the actual administration of the tax and its disbursement was governed by central government policy not local parish circumstances. The result was wide variation from parish to parish in the treatment of the poor. Frequently the support offered was inadequate and the policies for disbursement caused regressive behavior in the poor (e.g., women bearing numerous children to increase support payments). It is unlikely that anyone today who investigated the workings of the poor laws in Spencer's time would support this system. This alone was reason enough for compassionate people to oppose the poor laws, but Spencer has at least two other reasons, one connected to the effect of the poor laws, the other connected to his philosophical system.

In Spencer's mind, the poor laws repressed social progress by suppressing the desire of the working poor to rise up against the social conditions of the time. Certainly prior to the reforms of 1834 and to a significant extent afterwards, the poor law taxes were used to supplement the below-subsistence wages paid by wealthy landowners and manufacturers to the working poor. For Spencer, this had the effect of perpetuating a system that held a large portion of working people in poverty and allowed landowners and manufacturers to pay unreasonably low wages. The potential for the working poor to press for change (which in other parts of Europe had erupted in violent upheaval) was muted by this state supplement through the poor laws, which made life just barely tolerable for the working poor.

These two reasons for his opposition were practical reasons. They exemplify considerable compassion and desire for change in the lot in life of the working poor. Indeed, it was through the work of social reformers who had the same concerns about the plight of the poor under the poor laws that they were abolished in the early twentieth century.

Spencer also had a more philosophical and theoretical reason for opposing the poor laws, which goes to the heart of his evolutionary ethics. He was vehemently opposed to government intervention in society save for the purpose of securing and maintaining the maximum freedom of all citizens. The sole function of government should be to protect the maximum possible freedom of each citizen from encroachment by the behaviors of others: limitations on individual freedom are acceptable only insofar as they are necessary to secure and maintain an equal freedom for all.

Spencer believed in social as well as organic evolution. Indeed, they were intimately interconnected. Social evolution would lead to a society of socially perfected individuals (those morally and physically adapted to social interaction) in which land would be held in common, the dignity of each person's labor would be respected and appropriately rewarded, the greatest happiness for the greatest number would be achieved, and the maximum freedom possible would be had by everyone. This was Spencer's social utopia. Government intervention not only diminishes individual freedom (and with it responsibility) but it impedes the evolution of society toward this utopia by creating artificial social environments that ultimately delay the social adaptations necessary to bring about the utopia. In other words, just as intervention in a stable ecosystem disrupts the system and can result in its demise, intervention by governments in the dynamics of society disrupts the society, which impedes its improvement and can result in its demise.

One may still harbor doubts about Spencer's views and, with a century of hindsight, might reject any notions of the perfectibility of humans or achievable utopias—even Spencer, in his later years, came to doubt these notions. However, placed in context, Spencer can be seen to be striving for the same goals that many strive to achieve today. His views may rest on some mistaken ideas about how to achieve the goals but his position is far from morally bankrupt or repugnant. And it is not at all clear that his general conception of the evolution of society and of the evolutionary basis of morality are entirely without credibility.

As indicated, Spencer believed in the perfectibility of humans and in an eventual utopian society. These ideals play a large role in his *Social Statics*, *First Principles*, and *The Principles of Ethics*. In his later years he came to doubt whether perfection or social utopia was achievable but retained his commitment to progress toward them. Even without these features, there is plenty of vitality to Spencer's evolutionary ethics of which I now shall provide a brief account.

Spencer's moral theory centered around the greatest happiness principle (the greatest happiness for the greatest number). Although this principle is also the foundation of utilitarianism, Spencer rejected utilitarianism. According to the utilitarianism espoused by Spencer's contemporaries (e.g., John Stuart Mill), the rightness or wrongness of one's actions is determined by whether they contribute to or detract from the realization of the greatest happiness for the greatest number. Spencer rejected the idea that anyone did, could, or should attempt to calculate the amount of happiness each behavior or class of behaviors would produce. To him, it was absurd that a decision about the rightness or wrongness of a behavior depended upon a calculation in terms of units of happiness. He accepted the goal of the greatest happiness for the greatest number but rejected the view that its assessment and achievement were to be found in a calculation for each behavior. Instead, he argued that social evolution is the means of achieving it.

The achievement of the greatest happiness for the greatest number is dependent upon the social environment within which individuals function and on inherited behavioral dispositions. The social environment that brings about the greatest happiness is one in which individuals have the maximum freedom consistent with equal freedom for all. This social environment will result from a social evolution during which individuals will become more and more adapted to living in a society and, by so adapting, will come to have the requisite behavioral dispositions. In this way morality is linked to social evolution. In effect, the laws of social evolution and the principles of morality are the same because the goal of both morality and social evolution is the greatest happiness for the greatest number.

Two important refinements of this characterization are required to give Spencer's view more substance. First, even though Spencer himself speaks a great deal about happiness, happiness is not the most useful way to characterize the grounding of his position. For Spencer, happiness is equated with justice. And in the end, social evolution is best thought of as resulting in justice and the goal of morality is best construed as justice. This is important because happiness can be diminished by regarding it as an emotional state that seems inappropriate as a goal of morality. Justice is a richer concept that involves human social relationships and not just an emotional state-of-mind of individuals. Justice is a more appropriate description of what Spencer was striving to achieve.

Second, a key step in Spencer's argument is the move from maximal freedom to greatest happiness or justice. Because a great deal rests on the acceptance of this step, elaboration seems in order. A key element in this step is altruism which will result from the social struggle for survival. Maximal freedom is a requisite for the occurrence of a social struggle for survival and, hence, the exercise of altruism.

Spencer's arguments in support of his claim that altruism will result from the social struggle are strikingly similar to the explanations of the evolution of altruism proffered by sociobiologists today. Spencer in the *Principles of Ethics* distinguishes between altruism toward members of one's own family and altruism toward members of one's society. The former he explains by referring to the negative results of too much selfishness in parents. If parents do not behave altruistically toward their children, the survival of the children is compromised, and hence, these families will reproduce in lower numbers, if at all. In the end, such families will become extinct and only families with the required altruism will remain. This explanation, of course, assumes that altruism is heritable.

Social altruism is explained in three ways. First, in the *Principles of Ethics*, Spencer employs a critical mass argument. If a society has too few altruists it will undergo decline as a society and all members will experience a decrease in the level of his or her personal satisfaction. These social structures will not survive due to the decreasing level of personal satisfaction. One assumes that, on some occasions, forces such as revolution, emigration, and so forth may play a role in weakening and destroying such societies. Second, in the *Principles of Psychology*, he employs a "reciprocal altruism" argument. He claims that reciprocally beneficial behavior would give rise to a disposition for altruistic behavior because such reciprocity would result in the immediate evolutionary reward of enhanced survival. Over time the struggle for survival would result in an increase in altruism because those who had acquired the habit would pass it on to their children and there would be ever new cases of the behavior yielding enhanced survival. This way of formulating the argument depends on an acceptance of the inheritance of acquired characteristics. With only slight modifications, however, Spencer's position could be recast to employ the current sociobiological conception of reciprocal altruism based on individual selection.

Third, in the *Principles of Ethics*, he seems to suggest that the very act of adapting to the conditions of the freedom-maximizing society will bring about altruism. The effect of the habitual adaptation to the society will produce a heritable disposition to behave altruistically.

Spencer defined *altruism* as truly nonselfish behavior. One behaved altruistically to benefit someone else, not to reap a benefit for oneself at the time or later. Of course, some benefit to oneself may occur but this is not the motivation for the behavior. This may seem at odds with the sociobiological concept of altruism according to which altruistic behavior persists only because it benefits the altruist by increasing the probability that his or her genes will be passed on to the next generation. Consequently, the basis for altruism is ultimately selfish. This difference between Spencer and sociobiologists, however, is more apparent than real. Spencer's arguments for the evolution of altruism clearly rest on selection and the benefit to the individual or society of altruistic behavior. He accounts for the origin of the behavior differently (acquired habits that are inherited) but not its spread through the population (selection because of its benefit in enhancing survival). What Spencer was focusing on in his definition of altruism was the psychological motivation. Spencer did not accept that humans calculate outcomes for most of their moral actions. They behave in certain ways because they have a disposition to do so. The disposition for altruistic behavior is in large part a function of a disposition of compassion that has evolved because of its individual or group benefit in the struggle for survival. Hence, individuals behave altruistically without a conscious motive for benefit but the disposition to do so has evolved because of its benefit to the individual or group. This is similar to the sociobiologist's epigenetic rules that govern behavior and have a genetic basis. The rules evolved because behaving in accordance with them enhanced reproduction. The conscious motivation of the individual for the behavior, however, is not necessarily aimed at benefit for that individual. One acts in accordance with one's "conscience" in ways one would describe as nonselfish.

I have indicated that the first two of Spencer's arguments for the evolution of altruism have counterparts in current sociobiology and that his definition of *altruism* is not inconsistent with sociobiological conceptions of altruism. There are, however, two notable differences. Spencer relied heavily on the inheritance of acquired characteristics. Modern evolutionary biology rejects this view of inheritance and works within a Mendelian framework within which genes are altered by forces such as mutation. In the modern framework selection works on the pool of genes available in a given generation. Population genetics was not developed in a form that integrated it with natural selection until the work of Fisher, Haldane, and Wright in the late 1920s and early 1930s. Hence, this theory was not available to Spencer (or for that matter to Darwin, who also employed the inheritance of acquired characteristics in his theory, although Spencer clearly made it do much more work within his theory).

Spencer also employs a group selection argument for altruism. Sociobiology, by contrast, is grounded in a mechanism of individual selection and, largely, rejects group selection (see Part II of this Introduction).

Neither of these differences should be elevated in importance. As I have indicated Darwin also accepted these mechanisms at points in his work. When crediting Darwin with establishing the foundations of modern evolutionary theory we do not concern ourselves with the fact that a number of his arguments relied on views we now reject (in the case of heredity, his view—pangenesis—is now regarded as entirely false). We simply "update" his views using current theories. If the same generosity is accorded to Spencer, many elements of his theory of the evolution of morality are compatible with, if not identical to, those of sociobiology. And, it is significant that a frequent, and for many decisive, charge against both Spencer and sociobiology is that they both commit the naturalistic fallacy. Whether this is so and, if it is, whether it is a logical problem are something that the articles in this collection explore.

A concluding point on the overall plan and motivation for Spencer's theory of the evolution of morality will aid in making sense of his writings. Robert Richards has convincingly argued that Spencer's moral theory drove his evolutionary theory, "I have argued that Spencer constructed his evolutionary theory to meet the demands of his moral theory, and not the reverse" (Richards 1987, p. 309). This conception of Spencer's strategy and motivation makes sense of many of his evolutionary arguments that diverge from those of Darwin in the emphasis he placed on certain mechanisms. It also makes sense of his commitment to evolutionary progress: his moral theory required it.

An excellent exposition and re-evaluation of Spencer's evolutionary ethics (as well as his related evolutionary epistemology) can be found in *Darwin and the Emergence of Evolutionary Theories of Mind and Behavior* by Robert J. Richards (Chapters 6 and 7).

3. Thomas Henry Huxley (1825–1895)

Thomas Huxley possessed an outstanding intellect. He was self-educated in his younger years. In 1842 he entered Charing Cross Hospital for education as a physician. While at the hospital he had a distinguished record, winning awards in chemistry, anatomy, and physiology. In 1846–1850 he traveled on *H.M.S. Rattlesnake* as assistant surgeon. Upon his return in 1851 he was elected a Fellow of the Royal Society. He was a strong defender of state-sponsored education for the lower classes.

In his early years, he championed Darwin's theory of evolution. His success in rebutting the anatomical views of Richard Owen and his victory over Samuel Wilberforce, bishop of Oxford, in a debate in 1860 played an extremely important role in boosting the credibility and acceptability of evolution. According to his son Leonard Huxley in his *Life and Letters of Thomas H. Huxley* (vol. 1, p. 391), Thomas Huxley once said "I am Darwin's bull-dog." This description has been widely used to describe Huxley's vigorous defenses of Darwin and Darwinism. He also was a good friend of Herbert Spencer.

In his later years his convictions about the extension of Darwin's theory to morality changed. At the time that *The Descent of Man* was published (1871), he defended Darwin's views on morality and evolution. For example, in a paper in *The Contemporary Review* in 1871 titled "Mr. Darwin's Critics" he responded, in typical "Darwin's bull-dog" fashion, to an anonymous review in the *Quarterly Review* (written by St. George Mivart). In it he vigorously demolished Mivart's views and objections. Mivart responded to Huxley in 1872 in a paper entitled "Evolution and Its Consequences: A Reply to Professor Huxley."

Huxley's Romanes Lecture (reprinted in this collection) expresses his later views which break with those of Darwin and, most dramatically, with those of Herbert Spencer. His friendship with Spencer had a hiatus beginning in February 1888 and lasting until 1894, the year before his death in the summer of 1895.

A central element in the Romanes Lecture is the divide between the process of evolution in nature and human activity. He was no longer convinced that Darwin or Spencer had bridged the divide. He allowed that natural selection gives rise to moral sentiments (propensities) but provides no basis for morality because it provides no basis for following the moral sentiments. Indeed, nature and morality are in opposition; for example, nature is indifferent to human suffering and although the propensity to be altruistic and cooperative have evolved by natural selection, they function only within groups and not among groups. In the printed version of the lecture he added a prolegomena that softens his claim, made in the lecture, that the divide cannot be bridged.

Part II. Some Central Contemporary Issues

1. The Naturalistic Fallacy

Probably the major philosophical criticism of evolutionary ethics has focused on the perceived naturalistic framework of the various theories. Ethical naturalism is the view that moral claims state facts about the natural world. The opposing, nonnaturalist, view holds that there is a fundamental difference between factual claims and moral claims: factual claims are descriptive; moral claims are prescriptive and evaluative. Consequently, empirical science and moral philosophy are two very distinct enterprises. For example, evolutionary biology may accurately describe the properties and behaviors of a group of organisms and how that kind of organism came to have those properties and behaviors, but it is outside its scope to determine whether those properties or behaviors are "good." That is, evolutionary biology can describe the way organisms *in fact* behave, but cannot determine whether that is how they *ought* to behave.

In an ethical nonnaturalist view, "evolutionary ethics" seems to be a simple contradiction in terms. At best, evolutionary theory may explain how we came to be ethical animals and why we have propensities to behave in certain ways. It, however, cannot morally justify such propensities. It is entirely reasonable to accept that as a result of our evolutionary development we have a propensity to behave in a particular way while maintaining that behaving in that way is immoral. That a behavior has a biological basis does not make it morally right.

In an ethical naturalist view, however, evolutionary ethics is not a contradiction in terms: moral claims state facts about the world and, therefore, are investigated and justified in the same way as other empirical claims about the nature and behavior of the world. One part of the investigation and justification might well be based on evolutionary theory. In this view, specific claims about the evolutionary basis of morality may be false but the enterprise is at least logically and conceptually coherent.

Ethical naturalism has faced two major challenges: Hume's challenge (Hume 1739, 1740, 1751) and Moore's challenge (Moore 1903). Hume's challenge can be summarized in the maxim that "ought" claims cannot be derived solely from "is" claims. Moore's challenge can be summarized in the maxim that "good" in the ethical sense is a nonnatural property. Although these challenges have much in common they are often discussed independently. Hence, I shall set out each challenge as though it were disconnected from the other. The label *naturalistic fallacy* has come to be used quite loosely to describe either Hume's or Moore's challenge. Its origin, however, is with Moore, and it is more appropriate to refer to Hume's position as *Hume's Law*. In the context of evolutionary ethics, it is Hume's Law that is most often cited as sounding the death knell.

Hume's claim is simple. Any argument employed to justify a moral claim must be such that a moral claim is used in the justification. In deductive logic, a *valid argument* is defined as one in which the conclusion necessarily is true if the premises are true (i.e., one cannot accept the premises as true and deny the truth of the conclusion). Arguments that purport to justify moral claims on the basis of factual claims alone are, according to Hume's Law, invalid. Such arguments can be made valid only by the explicit addition of one or more moral claims. In many cases these moral claims are implicit and undetected. Hence, it appears that the argument has only factual premises. Consider, for example, the claim, "War is morally wrong." To argue that this statement is justified by the factual statement, "War involves pain, suffering, bloodshed and the loss of loved ones," is, according to Hume's law, to argue fallaciously. It is fallacious because even if the factual statement is accepted as true, the moral statement simply cannot be deduced from it. That is, the truth of the conclusion (the moral claim) is not made necessary by the factual premise. One could accept the factual statement and, without contradiction, reject the moral statement. Indeed, many people do. An additional premise—a moral claim—is required; namely, "engaging in activities that bring about pain, suffering, bloodshed, and the loss of loved ones is morally wrong." This additional premise, however, is far from universally accepted. Most people will argue that "pain, suffering, bloodshed, and the loss of loved ones" are not desirable but sometimes they are morally necessary. For example, some "pain, suffering, and so on" may be necessary to avoid greater "pain, suffering, and so on" or to protect a more important moral principle. It is important to recognize that the moral controversy here is not over the facts (war does involve pain and so on) but over the moral claim (that engaging in activities that bring about pain and so on is morally wrong).

In the example just given, there is no shared view on the truth or falsity of the moral claim. Hence, there is moral disagreement. Often, however, there is widespread acceptance of a moral claim that is needed as a premise in an argument which has a moral claim as its conclusion. Because the moral claim is so widely shared it may not be stated in the argument, and a demand that it be stated may seem ridiculous. In informal conversation, the desire to leave commonly held assumptions unstated is reasonable. It allows one to focus on the points of disagreement without endless recitations of all the relevant points on which there is agreement. The danger, however, is that this reasonable strategy might lead one to ignore the necessity of the un-stated claims in a *formal* statement of an argument. The shared acceptance of a moral claim does not obviate the need for a reference to it in a complete moral argument. Without it, according to Hume's Law, the conclusion simply does not follow from the factual claim. That is, the argument is invalid.

As indicated, Moore's challenge is connected to Hume's. Moore argued that *good* used in a moral sense is a "nonnatural property." That is, in contrast to "red" or "fast" or "hard," which are natural properties of things (they are part of the nature of the thing to which they are ascribed), *good* is not a natural property. Moore also held that *good* is the fundamental entity of ethics and is unanalyzable into constituent elements—it has none—and is not definable in terms of any other natural or nonnatural properties. For Moore, any attempt to define *good* in terms of a natural property will commit the *naturalistic fallacy*: the fallacy of mistaking the *is* of predication for the *is* of identity. "The dog is large" is an example of the *is* of predication. The *is* attaches a property to the subject. "Lightning is an electrical discharge" is an example of the *is* of identity. The *is* asserts not a property of lightning but asserts that to which it is identical. The dog, on the other hand, is not identical to large or largeness. According to Moore, to claim that "achievement of one's aspirations is good" is to *predicate good* of the "achievement of one's aspirations." It is not to *identify good* with the achievement of one's aspirations. *Good* is not identical to any properties, rather *good* is a nonnatural, unanalyzable predicate.

Moore offers several arguments for this position, the most well known of which is his "open question" argument. The essence of this argument is that whatever natural property is used to define *good,* the question of whether the having of that property is *good* is left open. Suppose, for example, that *good* is defined in terms of happiness. And suppose that being happy is defined as some natural state of mind or psychological well-being. It will then be possible to assert of a person at a given time that she is happy. Of this assertion, it is normally believed that one can meaningfully ask, "is it good that she is happy?" However, if *good* by definition means "happy" the question is nonsensical. Of course, one could bite the bullet and just accept that it is nonsensical but the most reasonable position to take seems to be that defining *good* in this way renders a perfectly sensible question nonsensical and, hence, such a definition is suspect.

Moore's position is very similar to that expressed by Henry Sidgwick in his *Methods of Ethics* and his *Lectures on the Ethics of T. H. Green, Mr. Herbert Spencer, and J. Martineau*. Moore was a student of Sidgwick and attended his lectures. He seems to have taken this objection of Sidgwick to Spencer's ethical views and developed it into a general position against ethical naturalism.

Although Moore's view is embedded in a conception of *good* as a nonnatural, unanalyzable predicate, the upshot of his view for evolutionary ethics is that empirical facts alone cannot justify ethical claims—in essence, it is the same point as raised in Hume's Law.

This position is not without its critics, although its defenders are far more numerous. One important line of argument against Hume and Moore has been offered by John Searle. His argument captures the general character of the arguments offered by many others against Hume and Moore. The basis for his rejection of Hume's Law rests on an analysis of the justification of claims made from within an established institution. Consider, for example, a baseball game during which an angry spectator says, "The pitcher ought not to have moved to throw the ball to first base and then not done it. He had his foot on the rubber. It was a balk." To make this "ought" claim is to make a value claim about the pitcher's behavior. Clearly, the player can physically engage in the behavior but within the institutional structure of baseball it is wrong to do so. Within this institution the facts of the situation justify the claim "The pitcher ought not to have moved to throw the ball to the base and then not done it."

Searle provides the following example of a moral claim that he contends is justified by the facts of the case alone:

1. Jones uttered the words, "I hereby promise to pay you, Smith, five dollars."

2. Jones promised to pay Smith five dollars.

3. Jones placed himself under (undertook) an obligation to pay Smith five dollars.

4. Jones is under an obligation to pay Smith five dollars.

5. Jones ought to pay Smith five dollars.

Searle is aware that additional factual premises may be necessary to convince some that this argument is valid but, he contends, no moral premises are required to deduce the moral claim (5). The validity of this argument depends on the institution of promising. That is, within the institution of promising, the argument is valid. One could deny that making a promise entails an obligation but then one would be stepping outside the institution of promising.

Searle has met heavy opposition to this line of argument. J. L. Mackie in *Ethics: Inventing Right and Wrong* captures the essence of much of the opposition. He points out that either one analyzes the preceding argument from outside the institution or from within it. If it is analyzed from outside the institution then part of the description of the case is the rules of the institution. The argument is valid because one tacitly employs descriptive statements about the rules of the institution. For example, (2) follows from (1) because (1) is conjoined with the claim, "Within the institution of promising if someone utters a promise to do something, then one has committed oneself to do what one says one promises to do." This, from outside the institution of promising, is a purely descriptive claim, as will be the descriptions of all the other rules of the institution of promising. Hence, (5) can be deduced from (1) along with the factual statements describing the rules of the institution of promising. However, viewed from outside the institution, (5) will be a factual claim *describing* what is the case within the institution given (1). As such, only a factual claim has been deduced from a factual claim. Hume's Law is intact.

If one analyzes the argument from within the institution, then one has placed special constraints on the assessment of the argument. In effect, one has determined that the rules of the institution are rules of inference that, when used with the normal rules of inference, permit the deduction of (5) from (1). Mackie concedes that in this case (5) is a prescriptive and evaluative statement (an "ought" statement) but, he claims, "no-one who is concerned for the spirit rather than the letter of Hume's Law need be worried about a derivation of this sort." This is because the success of the derivation depends on accepting a "special logic" (one with special constraints or parochial additional rules of inference). Mackie contends that only by moving back and forth between the perspectives (within and without the institution) as the deduction proceeds can one give the appearance of real counterexample to Hume's Law. But moving back and forth between perspectives is clearly illegitimate.

Searle has responded to this objection. The essence of his response is to deny the distinction that Mackie has made regarding inside and outside the institution. Those interested in the further twists and turns of this debate should refer to Mackie's book and to Searle's *Speech Acts* (1969). The foregoing, I hope, will indicate the importance and unsettled character of Hume's and Moore's challenge to a naturalistic ethics and, insofar as it is naturalistic, evolutionary ethics.

2. Inclusive Fitness, Kin Selection and the Evolution of Altruism:

The ability to accommodate altruistic behavior is widely considered to be the litmus test for ethical theories. Insofar as a theory fails to account for altruism, it is taken to be deficient in a significant respect. This emphasis on altruism as a test of the viability of an ethical theory is not recent. For example, Spencer considered it an important element in an ethical theory and, hence, provided an account of it which is central in his moral theory (see Part I). For most ethical theorists, it is clear that the ability to account for altruism in humans is of crucial importance (a necessary, if not sufficient condition, of the viability of an ethical theory).

Modern attempts to ground morality in evolutionary theory have also taken altruism to be an important touchstone of success. Two broad approaches in accounting for altruism have dominated discussions: those based on mechanisms of group selection and those based on mechanisms of individual selection. Theories of group selection identify the group (usually a population of organisms) as the unit subject to selection. That is, several populations may have different organizational structures and intragroup behaviors. To the extent that the viability of a population is enhanced by such structures or behaviors, that population is fitter. Over time populations with those structures or behaviors will increase in number. Theories of individual selection identify the individual organism as the unit subject to selection.

During the 1960s, the most influential book to exploit group selection in explaining social behavior was *Animal Dispersion in Relation to Social Behaviour* by V. C. Wynne-Edwards. Group selection, however, has been out of favor since George C. Williams in *Adaptation and Natural Selection* (1966) provided a detailed analysis of the various extant versions of group selection and provided detailed objections to each of them. A more contemporary examination of group selection is found in "A Critical Review of the Models of Group Selection" by Michael Wade (1978). The best all-around examination of selection including the level at which selection occurs can be found in *The Nature of Selection* by Elliot Sober (1984).

Sociobiology follows Williams's view that selection works on the individual, not on the group. The most important justification for this is based on genetical theory. Genes are part of individual organisms not of groups of organisms. Genes reside within the cells that make up individuals, and individuals are the direct product of those genes. Furthermore individuals pass their genes to individuals in subsequent generations. Groups do not pass genes to subsequent generations except through individuals. It is the reproductive success of individuals that determines the genes that will be present in the individuals within a group in the next generation. Rarely, the survival of the individual can be determined by a second-order function at the group level (as the population geneticist Sewal Wright demonstrated), but this happens extremely rarely and is, nonetheless, a function of individual level selection. Within the context of individual selection, the two key mechanisms employed by sociobiologists, and to a discussion of which I shall now turn, are inclusive fitness and reciprocal altruism.

"Fitness" is a probabilistic measure of an organism's reproductive success. An organism's fitness is a function of its physical and behavioral traits (characteristics). Some sets of traits confer a higher probability of reproductive success on organisms than do other sets. Traditionally, the fitness of an organism with a certain set of traits has been calculated in terms of the average reproductive success of the organisms with those traits. Inclusive fitness expands the basis for calculating reproductive success by focusing on genes as the ultimate units of fitness. A physical or behavioral trait of the individual may provide the actual basis for selection to take place but it is only characteristics that have a genetic basis that can be passed on to the next generation. Hence, genes are the real hereditary-evolutionary bearers of the fitness derived from a trait. In terms of the prevalence and evolution of a trait in a population, the important measure is the prevalence of the genes for that trait. Hence, what is most important from an evolutionary point of view is the perpetuation or increase of particular genes. What inclusive fitness recognizes is that the gene(s) that code for a particular trait exist in a number of individuals in a population. The way for those genes to get passed to the next generation is by the reproduction of some of the individuals with those genes. From a genetic point of view it does not matter whether one individual with a particular gene has x offspring each bearing the gene or x individuals with that gene each has one offspring each bearing the gene. The result is the same.

Within this framework, an individual who has no offspring can contribute to the perpetuation or increase of the genes for a trait he or she possesses by increasing the reproductive success of another individual who also bears those genes. That is, instead of organism A and organism B each having one offspring with the genes for the trait, organism A has no offspring but assists organism B in having two or more offspring with the genes. From a genetic point of view, A's fitness is maintained (if B has two offspring) or increased (if B has three or more offspring) by this helping behavior even though A does not reproduce directly. In effect, A reproduces indirectly. Inclusive fitness takes into account this indirect contribution to the survival of A's genes when assessing A's fitness.

An important feature of inclusive fitness is that the particular trait must *selectively* increase the reproductive success of others. That is, it must be directed toward those who bear a reasonable proportion of the same genes as A bears. For this to occur there must be a genetically based method for directing the benefit of the trait to those who bear a reasonable proportion of the same genes as A bears. The mechanism by which this is believed to occur is a genetically based propensity to bestow the benefits of traits on those with a close kinship relation (siblings, for example). This mechanism is known as *kin selection*. The principle is that the closer the relationship of ancestral descent, the higher the fraction of shared genes will be. The relation of genetic descent is higher with parents and siblings, lower with cousins, lower still with other members of one's population, and lowest with those of another population. This propensity to bestow the benefits of the trait on those with a close relationship could be a function of genes linked to those producing the trait or could be part of the complex character of the trait.

If the trait itself is to become established in a population or maintained in a population, the probability must be high that those upon whom the reproductive benefit of the trait is bestowed bear the gene for the trait. Again, the closer the kinship relation the higher is the probability that the gene for the trait is shared.

Relating all this to altruism, it is claimed that altruism is a genetically based trait that, on average, increases the inclusive fitness of those who manifest it. Hence, although the altruist appears to behave in ways that can reduce his or her reproductive success, in fact, the altruist increases his or her inclusive fitness and, thereby, increases the representation of his or her genes (including those for altruism) in the population.

By way of illustration, consider the classic case of *Apis mellifera* (the honeybee) which belongs to the order Hymenoptera, an order of social insects that also includes ants. A honeybee hive consists of one queen bee, numerous worker bees (all female but sterile) and a small number of drones (male).

Drones are genetically unusual. Normally, the cells that make up an organism (all of which are genetically identical) contain, within their nuclei, chromosomes *in pairs*. Such cells are called *diploid*. During a process of cell reproduction, called *mitosis*, both pairs of chromosomes are reproduced and the nucleus of the original cell and the new cell contain both pairs of chromosomes. During a process called *meiosis*, which produces gametes (sperm and ovum), four cells are produced, each of which contains only one member (an original or a copy) from each pair present in the original cell. These cells are called *haploid*. When two haploid gametes unite to form a zygote (a fertilized ovum), the resulting cell has pairs of chromosomes again. In sexually reproducing organisms, the zygote has a new combination of chromosomes: each pair of chromosomes contains one member from each of the sperm and the ovum of the two mating organisms. This recombination of chromosomes partially preserves the genes of both the original cells but it also produces a new cell that is partially different from either of the original cells.

Drones are unusual because all their cells are *haploid*. Because all the cells are already *haploid,* when male gametes are produced, all the chromosomes in the original cell are present in the gametes. Hence, every gamete will be genetically identical. The queen (as well as all the workers) are *diploid*. Hence, the female gametes produced by the queen will contain different members of each original pair. The queen is fertilized once, in flight, by one drone. Hence all her ova are fertilized by genetically identical sperm. The queen produces drone eggs by withholding fertilization of an ovum. This produces the *haploid* state of the drone. In most organisms an unfertilized ovum will not develop. In the case of honeybees it develops into a drone (male).

As a result of this unusual genetic structure, worker bees are all highly related to each other genetically. Genes are constituents of chromosomes. Different locations (loci) on chromosomes consist of different genes. Hence, because each daughter of a particular queen (each worker) derives half of her chromosomes from a *haploid* drone, each worker shares exactly the same drone-contributed genes. The queen is *diploid* and her chromosomes are passed to her daughters in different assortments. On average, however, daughters will have 50 percent of the queen's chromosomes, and hence genes, in common. Therefore, daughters of a queen, on average, will share 75 percent of their genes in common:

Drone's contribution		Queen's contribution		Result
$^{1}/_{2} \times 1$	$+$	$^{1}/_{2} \times ^{1}/_{2}$	$=$	$^{3}/_{4}$

The *1* in the drone's contribution indicates that all the genes of the drone are contributed to each daughter. In the case of the queen, she contributes only half of her chromosomes to each daughter.

On the basis of this high genetic relationship the evolution of altruism in honeybees can be explained. Altruism in honeybees consists of workers giving up their lives to protect the hive. When a honeybee stings in defense of the hive, she has given up her life because the barbed stinger remains in the intruder with the result that the bee is either trapped or tears her abdomen off in attempting to escape. On the assumption that this behavior, like most behaviors of honeybees, is genetically based, the important evolutionary questions are, "how did this behavior increase in the population and how is it now sustained?" The answer can best be understood by comparing two colonies of bees. Colony A has no worker bees with genes for this behavior.

In Colony B all or almost all workers have the gene for this behavior.

If colony A, in which the workers are not genetically disposed to attack the aggressor, is attacked the colony will likely perish. If colony B, in which the workers are genetically disposed to attack the aggressor, is attacked the colony has a reasonable chance of survival. Hence, the behavior results in greater probability that colony B will survive than that colony A will. However, because almost all the members of colony B bear the gene for this behavior, the behavior results in the preservation of the gene for the behavior. This preservation of the gene for the behavior by the behavior itself is the basis for its increase in the species over time and its continuation.

The genetic mechanism by which the behavior is increased and then sustained is straightforward. Reproduction takes place through the queen. As long as a particular queen who bears the gene for altruistic behavior continues to produce workers for the hive, the gene will be passed to the next generation. New queens are created either to replace an existing queen in the hive or to create a queen for a new hive (a portion of the workers from the hive take flight with a queen to establish a new colony; a process called *swarming*). New queens are sisters of the existing workers (they are worker larvae that have been fed royal jelly), which means that they bear the gene for the altruistic behavior if the workers do . Hence, over time, hives with workers that have the gene for altruistic behavior will be more likely to survive than hives that do not, and they will be the basis for the subsequent generations through the current queen or through new queens in new hives created by swarming or in the existing hive.

Because of the high genetic relationship of sisters to each other, this behavior of honeybees provides an excellent illustration of the concepts of inclusive fitness and kin selection. The same concepts, however, apply in the case of other organisms. In the case of organisms in which males and females are *diploid*, offspring, on average, will have half of their genes in common.

Male's contribution		Female's contribution		Result
$1/2 \times 1/2$	+	$1/2 \times 1/2$	=	$1/2$

Hence, in terms of an organism A passing her genes to the next generation, this means that two offspring of a sibling of A equals one offspring of A. Consequently, any genetic-based trait of A that results in an increase of more than two offspring for A's siblings for every reduction of one offspring for A, increases A's inclusive fitness. And, just as in the honeybee case, such a trait, on average, will cause an increase in the gene for the trait in subsequent generations or will maintain it when it reaches maximum penetration in the population.

The second mechanism employed by sociobiologists to explain altruism is "reciprocal altruism." As the name indicates reciprocal altruism depends on a particular kind of cooperation between or among organisms. In essence, organisms with genes for cooperation will, on average, have a higher fitness than organisms who do not have such genes. If you are disposed genetically to help those who help you, you will increase your chances of survival because in times of difficulty you will be assisted. If you do not have this disposition others will soon cease to assist you because their disposition is to assist those who reciprocate. After an instance of nonreciprocation, assistance will no longer come your way. Without assistance the probability that you will leave offspring decreases. Hence, in each subsequent generation there will be fewer and fewer offspring without a disposition to assist others. Eventually, the population will consist largely, perhaps only, of those who have a disposition to assist others; that is, largely of altruists.

Inclusive fitness and reciprocal altruism are the two dominant sociobiological explanations of the existence of altruism. Both assume a high level of altruistic behavior in the population and both lead to the result that altruistic behavior, contrary to initial expectations, does not reduce the reproductive success of the altruistic individual—quite the contrary, it enhances it. In the final analysis, "altruism," in a sociobiological framework, is self-serving ("selfish") behavior. This feature has caused critics to argue that the concept of altruism employed by sociobiologists is not the same one used by ethicists and the general population. An excellent discussion of this issue is found in "What Is Evolutionary Altruism?" by Elliot Sober (1988).

3. Heterozygote Superiority

In the previous section, I indicated that chromosomes are paired in the nucleus of a *diploid* cell and that chromosomes are made up of genes. A gene is a segment of a chromosome that participates in coding for a trait of the organism. Genes, therefore, can be described as existing in a location on a chromosome. A location at which a gene exists is called a *locus*. Because chromosomes are paired, two genes (more accurately called *alleles*) will exist at the complementary locations of the two chromosomes. If the two alleles at a locus are identical, the organism is *homozygous* at that locus. If the two alleles are different, the organism is *heterozygous* at that locus.

If two organisms in a population mate, each organism will contribute one allele from each locus to their offspring. If the two mating organisms are homozygous for different alleles at a locus (e.g., one has two S alleles, the other has two W alleles), all the offspring will be heterozygous:

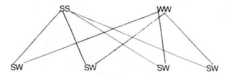

If both mating organisms are heterozygous (e.g., each has SW at that locus), then, on average, one-fourth of the offspring will be homozygous for S, one-fourth will be homozygous for W, and one-half will be heterozygous:

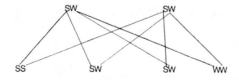

Sometimes, in heterzygotes, one of the alleles is dominant. That is, it will determine the trait that the organisms manifest. For example, if S were dominant, organisms that are heterozygous will have the trait of those that are homozygous for S. Only when an organism is homozygous for W will the trait for which W codes be apparent. Dominance, however, does not mean that the other allele is always completely overridden. Rather, its action often is muted by the dominant allele. Heterozygote superiority is a function of this combined action of different alleles. It occurs when the combination of two different alleles at a location affects the organism in ways that make it more likely to produce offspring than either of the homozygotes.

A classic example of heterozygote superiority is the sickle-cell allele. Sickle-cell anaemia is a disease in which the individual's red blood cells have a sickle shape and, as a result, a reduced oxygen-carrying capacity. The sickling is produced by the alleles controlling the formation of the protein *hemoglobin*. The sickle-cell allele (S) codes for a slightly different sequence of amino acids (the building blocks of proteins) than the normal hemoglobin allele (N). Although the difference is small the result is dramatic and fatal. Sickle-cell anaemia occurs only in homozygotes for the sickle-cell allele. That is, it only occurs in individuals with an SS combination. Given that the disease is fatal, one would expect that over time those with the sickle-cell allele would have diminished reproductive success, and the allele would disappear from the population. Hence, an explanation of its persistence is required.

The explanation is based on the reproductive superiority of the heterozygote in a particular environment. The environment is one in which malaria is prevalent. In this environment, those with the SS combination of alleles will still have low reproductive success (they will develop Sickle-cell anaemia) but so will those with the NN (normal allele) combination because they are susceptible to malaria. The SN (the heterozygote) individual, however, does not manifest Sickle-cell anaemia and is also resistant to malaria. This is one of those cases where there is a dominant allele (N). Hence, when N is present the effect of S is diminished and the disease is absent. The S allele, however, is not entirely overridden by the N allele. It affects the character of the hemoglobin but does not produce a fatal change. What it does is produce a change sufficient to inhibit the establishment in the blood stream of *Plasmodium falciparum* malaria. Hence, the S allele persists in malaria infested areas because it confers on the heterozygote protection against malaria while not causing Sickle-cell anaemia.

This model of heterozygote superiority is used by socio-biologists to explain the persistence of alleles that, in ho-mozygotes, code for traits that reduce reproductive success. The percentage of the population that displays these traits will be small (less than 25 percent) because, for the most part, they will arise from the mating of two heterozygotes. What the model of heterozygote superiority explains is why the traits continue to appear in every generation despite its deleterious effect on the organism's fitness.

This model has been used extensively by sociobiologists to explain animal behavior and it could be applied, as a hypothesis, to explain altruism. If, contrary to the assumption made when employing inclusive fitness and reciprocal altruism to explain altruism, altruism is deemed to diminish the reproductive success of the altruist and if there are very few true altruists in a population, one might hypothesize that it persists because of heterozygote superiority. Perhaps the heterozygote is not entirely selfish but also not entirely altruistic: kind and giving but with a strong sense of self-preservation. The homozygote for the altruism allele will be self-destructively altruistic. The homozygote for the nonaltruism allele will be self-destructively selfish. This is an interesting hypothesis but, as one can see, it involves numerous questionable assumptions that need to be established before it is reasonable to accept it.

4. Sociobiology and Biological Determinism

A foundational assumption of sociobiology is that most (some claim virtually all) animal behavior has a genetic basis and, consequently, can be explained using modern evolutionary theory. A major source of the controversy surrounding socio-biology is this assumption that most behavior has a genetic basis. To many critics, this assumption is nothing more than a crude statement of biological determinism (see Lewontin, Rose, and Kamin 1984; Gould 1976). That is, the behavior of animals is largely or entirely determined by biology. The strength of, and support for, this criticism of this assumption increases as the cognitive capacities of the animals under discussion increase. The claim that the behavior of earthworms or ants is largely biologically determined (a function of the genetic makeup of the organism) is less controversial than the claim that the behavior of primates—especially humans—is largely, or even significantly, genetically determined.

Sociobiological explanations of animal behavior, employ modern evolutionary theory. It is from this theory that the mechanisms are drawn. The most compact description of the theory is that a sufficient condition for evolution is (1) that there exists, in a randomly mating population of organisms, a variation in traits (physical or behavioral features); (2) that the traits are heritable (i.e., that they have a genetic basis); (3) that the traits are subject to selective pressure (i.e., that some varieties of the traits have a higher probability of promoting—or of being less detrimental to—the reproduction of an organism than some other varieties). A simple formula captures this structure: variation + selection + heredity = evolution. Hence, contemporary evolutionary theory embodies mechanisms of variation (their origin and maintenance in a population), mechanisms of selection, and mechanisms of heredity. It is the latter mechanisms that are provided by modern population genetics and molecular genetics.

Given the requirements of evolutionary theory, an evolutionary explanation of animal behavior has to establish that the behavior varies (or has in the past varied) among the members of the population; it has a genetic basis (is heritable); and it is advantageous (in a certain environment that is likely to exist or has existed during a relevant period) to the reproductive success of those that engage in it. This is a demanding set of conditions. To the extent that it is reasonable to accept that, for a specific behavior, the conditions are true, it is reasonable to accept a sociobiological (evolutionary) account of that behavior.

In the case of insect behavior it seems reasonable to accept that the conditions are true for a wide range of behaviors. In the case of humans, views differ radically about the reasonableness of accepting that the conditions are true for all but a narrow range of behaviors. The thrust of the sociobiological position with respect to humans is that a significant amount of human behavior is a function of physiology and neurophysiology. That is, a significant amount of behavior is hormonally controlled or determined by our neurological structures. These physiological and neurophysiological structures and processes are genetically based and are the result of evolution. Edward O. Wilson in *On Human Nature* states forcefully the position that a significant amount of human behavior is genetically based: "The question of interest is no longer whether human social behavior is genetically determined; it is to what extent. The accumulated evidence for a large hereditary component is more detailed and compelling than most persons, including geneticists, realize. I will go further: it is already decisive." (p. 19).

Many biologists disagree. They claim that many of the sociobiological explanations of human behavior are "just so stories" (see Gould 1978). The stories are interesting and have a superficial plausibility but the evidence for a genetic basis for the behaviors being explained is weak or nonexistent. In addition, critics have challenged the strong adaptationist assumption of sociobiology and, more generally, of many versions of evolution theory (see Gould and Lewontin 1978; Lewontin 1978). That is, they challenge the assumption that almost all traits are the result of selection and are, hence, an evolutionary adaptation to an environment.

Sociobiology is relevant to evolutionary ethics because behavior, including behavior that is considered to be morally right or wrong, is claimed to be genetically based and the result of evolution. Morally pertinent behavior is claimed to enhance reproductive success and, therefore, the type of human that engages in such patterns of behavior has increased during the course of evolution. The link between genes and ethical behavior is mediated by epigenetic rules. Epigenetic rules are genetically based controls on embryological development. They channel "the development of an anatomical, physiological, cognitive, or behavior trait in a particular direction." (Lumsden and Wilson, 1983 p. 370). The rules lead to the development in the organism of physiological (including neurological) structures that determine the patterns and processes of thought, learning, behavior, and so forth. The upshot is that, among other things, our propensity to behave in ways we describe as ethical and our propensity to construct an ethical basis for behavior are largely functions of our genes.

In addition to those who criticize the conceptual and theoretical basis of sociobiology are those who argue that, even if sociobiology is a well-grounded science that can explain the evolution of a propensity to behave in ways described as ethically (morally) correct, it cannot establish that it is in fact, the ethically correct way to behave. It only describes things as they are. It does not prescribe the way things ought to be. To claim that it does prescribe is, these critics maintain, to commit the naturalistic fallacy.

PART I

IN THE WAKE OF THE *ORIGIN*

Charles Darwin

Moral Sense

I fully subscribe to the judgment of those writers[1] who maintain that of all the differences between man and the lower animals, the moral sense or conscience is by far the most important. This sense, as Mackintosh[2] remarks, "has a rightful supremacy over every other principle of human action"; it is summed up in that short but imperious word *ought*, so full of high significance. It is the most noble of all the attributes of man, leading him without a moment's hesitation to risk his life for that of a fellow-creature; or after due deliberation, impelled simply by the deep feeling of right or duty, to sacrifice it in some great cause. Immanuel Kant exclaims, "Duty! Wondrous thought, that workest neither by fond insinuation, flattery, nor by any threat, but merely by holding up thy naked law in the soul, and so extorting for thyself always reverence, if not always obedience; before whom all appetites are dumb, however secretly they rebel; whence thy original?"[3]

This great question has been discussed by many writers[4] of consummate ability; and my sole excuse for touching on it, is the impossibility of here passing it over; and because, as far as I know, no one has approached it exclusively from the side of natural history. The investigation possesses, also, some independent interest, as an attempt to see how far the study of the lower animals throws light on one of the highest psychical faculties of man.

The following proposition seems to me in a high degree probable—namely, that any animal whatever, endowed with wellmarked social instincts,[5] the parental and filial affections being here included, would inevitably acquire a moral

From: *The Descent of Man and Selection in Relation to Race* 2d ed. (London: John Murray, 1874), pp. 148–194.

sense or conscience, as soon as its intellectual powers had become as well, or nearly as well developed, as in man. For, *firstly*, the social instincts lead an animal to take pleasure in the society of its fellows, to feel a certain amount of sympathy with them, and to perform various services for them. The services may be of a definite and evidently instinctive nature; or there may be only a wish and readiness, as with most of the higher social animals, to aid their fellows in certain general ways. But these feelings and services are by no means extended to all the individuals of the same species, only to those of the same association. *Secondly*, as soon as the mental faculties had become highly developed, images of all past actions and motives would be incessantly passing through the brain of each individual; and that feeling of dissatisfaction, or even misery, which invariably results, as we shall hereafter see, from any unsatisfied instinct, would arise, as often as it was perceived that the enduring and always present social instinct had yielded to some other instinct, at the time stronger, but neither enduring in its nature, nor leaving behind it a very vivid impression. It is clear that many instinctive desires, such as that of hunger, are in their nature of short duration; and after being satisfied, are not readily or vividly recalled. *Thirdly,* after the power of language had been acquired, and the wishes of the community could be expressed, the common opinion how each member ought to act for the public good, would naturally become in a paramount degree the guide to notion. But it should be borne in mind that however great weight we may attribute to public opinion, our regard for the approbation and disapprobation of our fellows depends on sympathy, which, as we shall see, forms an essential part of the social instinct, and is indeed its foundation-stone. *Lastly,* habit in the individual would ultimately play a very important part in guiding the conduct of each member; for the social instinct, together with sympathy, is, like any other instinct, greatly strengthened by habit, and so consequently would be obedience to the wishes and judgment of the community. These several subordinate propositions must now be discussed, and some of them at considerable length.

It may be well first to premise that I do not wish to maintain that any strictly social animal, if its intellectual faculties were to become as active and as highly developed as in man, would acquire exactly the same moral sense as ours. In the same manner as various animals have some sense of beauty, though they admire widely different objects, so they might have a sense of right and wrong, though led by it to follow widely different lines of conduct. If, for instance, to take an extreme case, men were reared under precisely the same conditions as hive-bees, there can hardly be any doubt that our unmarried females would, like the worker bees, think it a sacred duty to kill their brothers, and mothers would strike to kill their fertile daughters; and no one would think of interfering.[6] Nevertheless, the bee, or any other Social animal, would gain in our supposed case, as it appears to me, some feeling of right or wrong, or conscience. For each individual would have an inward sense of possessing certain stronger or more enduring instincts, and others less strong or enduring; so that there would often be a struggle as to which impulse would be followed; and satisfaction, dissatisfaction, or even misery would be felt, as past impressions were compared during their incessant passage through the mind. In this case an inward monitor would tell the animal that it would have been better to have followed the one impulse rather than the other. The one course ought to have been followed, and the other ought not; the one would have been right and the other wrong; but to these terms I shall recur.

Sociability

Animals of many kinds are social; we find even distinct species living together; for example, some American monkeys; and united flocks of rooks, jackdaws, and starlings. Man shews the same feeling in his strong love for the dog, which the dog returns with interest. Every one must have noticed how miserable horses, dogs, sheep, &c., are when separated from their companions, and what strong mutual

affection the two former kinds, at least, shew on their re-
union. It is curious to speculate on the feelings of a dog,
who will rest peacefully for hours in a room with his master
or any of the family, without the least notice being taken of
him; but if left for a short time by himself, barks or howls
dismally. We will confine our attention to the higher Social
animals; and pass over insects, although some of these are
social, and aid one another in many important ways. The
most common mutual service in the higher animals is to
warn one another of danger by means of the united senses
of all. Every sportsman knows, as Dr. Jaeger remarks,[7] how
difficult it is to approach animals in a herd or troop. Wild
horses and cattle do not, I believe, make any danger-signal;
but the attitude of any one of them who first discovers an
enemy, warns the others. Rabbits stamp loudly on the ground
with their hind-feet as a signal: sheep and chamois do the
same with their forefeet, uttering likewise a whistle. Many
birds, and some mammals, post sentinels, which in the case
of seals are said[8] generally to be the females. The leader of
a troop of monkeys acts as the sentinel, and utters cries
expressive both of danger and of safety.[9] Social animals
perform many little services for each other: horses nibble,
and cows lick each other, on any spot which itches: monkeys search each other for external parasites; and Brehm
states that after a troop of the *Cercopithecus griseo-viridis* has
rushed through a thorny brake, each monkey stretches itself
on a branch, and another monkey sitting by, "conscientiously" examines its fur, and extracts every thorn or burr.

Animals also render more important services to one
another: thus wolves and some other beasts of prey hunt in
packs, and aid one another in attacking their victims. Peli-
cans fish in concert. The Hamadryas baboons turn over stones
to find insects, &c.; and when they come to a large one, as
many as can stand round, turn it over together and share
the booty. Social animals mutually defend each other Bull
bisons in N. America, when there is danger, drive the cows
and calves into the middle of the herd, whilst they defend
the outside. I shall also in a future chapter give an account
of two young wild bulls at Chillingham attacking an old
one in concert, and of two stallions together trying to drive

away a third stallion from a troop of mares. In Abyssinia, Brehm encountered a great troop of baboons who were crossing a valley: some had already ascended the opposite mountain, and some were still in the valley: the latter were attacked by the dogs, but the old males immediately hurried down from the rocks, and with mouths widely opened, roared so fearfully, that the dogs quickly drew back. They were again encouraged to the attack; but by this time all the baboons had reascended the heights, excepting a young one, about six months old, who, loudly calling for aid, climbed on a block of rook, and was surrounded. Now one of the largest males, a true hero, came down again from the mountain, slowly went to the young one, coaxed him, and triumphantly led him away—the dogs being too much astonished to make an attack. I cannot resist giving another scene which was witnessed by this same naturalist; an eagle seized a young Cercopithecus, which, by clinging to a branch, was not at once carried off; it cried loudly for assistance, upon which the other members of the troop, with much uproar, rushed to the rescue, surrounded the eagle, and pulled out so many feathers, that he no longer thought of his prey, but only how to escape. This eagle, as Brehm remarks, assuredly would never again attack a single monkey of a troop.[10]

It is certain that associated animals have a feeling of love for each other, which is not felt by non-social adult animals. How far in most cases they actually sympathise in the pains and pleasures of others, is more doubtful, especially with respect to pleasures. Mr. Buxton, however, who had excellent means of observation,[11] states that his macaws, which lived free in Norfolk, took "an extravagant interest" in a pair with a nest; and whenever the female left it, she was surrounded by a troop "screaming horrible acclamations in her honour." It is often difficult to judge whether animals have any feeling for the sufferings of others of their kind. Who can say what cows feel, when they surround and stare intently on a dying or dead companion; apparently, however, as Houzeau remarks, they feel no pity. That animals sometimes are far from feeling any sympathy is too certain; for they will expel a wounded animal from the herd, or gore or worry it to death. This is almost the blackest fact in natural history, unless, indeed, the explanation which has been suggested is true, that their instinct or reason leads them to expel an injured companion, lest beasts of prey, including man, should be tempted to follow the troop. In this case their conduct is not much worse than that of the North American Indians, who leave their feeble comrades to perish on the plains; or the Fijians, who, when their parents get old, or fall ill, bury them alive.[12]

Many animals, however, certainly sympathise with each other's distress or danger. This is the case even with birds. Captain Stansbury[13] found on a salt lake in Utah an old and completely blind pelican, which was very fat, and must have been well fed for a long time by his companions. Mr. Blyth, as he informs me, saw Indian crows feeding two or three of their companions which were blind; and I have heard of an analogous case with the domestic cock. We may, if we choose, call these actions instinctive; but such cases are much too rare for the development of any special instinct.[14] I have myself seen a dog, who never passed a cat who lay sick in a basket, and was a great friend of his, without giving her a few licks with his tongue, the surest sign of kind feeling in a dog.

It must be called sympathy that leads a courageous dog to fly at any one who strikes his master, as he certainly will. I saw a person pretending to beat a lady, who had a very timid little dog on her lap, and the trial had never been made before; the little creature instantly jumped away, but after the pretended beating was over, it was really pathetic to see how perseveringly he tried to lick his mistress's face, and comfort her. Brehm[15] states that when a baboon in confinement was pursued to be punished, the others tried to protect him. It must have been sympathy in the cases above given which led the baboons and Cercopitheci to defend their young comrades from the dogs and the eagle. I will give only one other instance of sympathetic and heroic conduct, in the case of a little American monkey. Several years ago a keeper at the Zoological gardens showed me some deep and scarcely healed wounds on the nape of his own neck, inflicted on him, whilst kneeling on the floor, by a fierce baboon. The little American monkey, who was a warm friend of this keeper, lived in the same large compartment, and was dreadfully afraid of the great baboon. Nevertheless, as soon as he saw his friend in peril, he rushed to the rescue, and by screams and bites so distracted the baboon that the man was able to escape, after, as the surgeon thought, running great risk of his life.

Besides lore and sympathy, animals exhibit other qualities connected with the social instincts, which in us would be called moral; and I agree with Agassiz[16] that dogs possess something very like a conscience.

Dogs possess some power of self-command, and this does not appear to be wholly the result of fear. As Braubach[17] remarks, they will refrain from stealing food in the absence of their master. They have long been accepted as the very type of fidelity and obedience. But the elephant is likewise very faithful to his driver or keeper, and probably considers him as the leader of the herd. Dr. Hooker informs me that an elephant, which he was riding in India, became so deeply bogged that he remained stuck fast until the next day, when he was extricated by men with ropes. under such circumstances elephants will seize with their trunks any object, dead or alive, to place under their knees, to prevent their sinking deeper in the mud; and the driver was dreadfully afraid lest the animal should have seized Dr. Hooker and crushed him to death. But the driver himself, as Dr. Hooker was assured, ran no risk. This forbearance under an emergency so dreadful for a heavy animal, is a wonderful proof of noble fidelity.[18]

All animals living in a body, which defend themselves or attack their enemies in concert, must indeed be in some degree faithful to one another; and those that follow a leader must be in some degree obedient. When the baboons in Abyssinia[19] plunder a garden, they silently follow their leader; and if an imprudent young animal makes a noise, he receives a slap from the others to teach him silence and obedience. Mr. Galton, who has had excellent opportunities for observing the half wild cattle in S. Africa, says,[20] that they cannot endure even a momentary separation from the herd. They are essentially slavish, and accept the common determination, seeking no better lot than to be led by any one ox who has enough self-reliance to accept the position. The men who break in these animals for harness, watch assiduously for those who, by grazing apart, shew a self-reliant disposition, and these they train as fore-oxen. Mr. Dalton adds that such animals are rare and valuable; and if many were born they would soon be eliminated, as lions are always on the look-out for the individuals which wander from the herd.

With respect to the impulse which leads certain animals to associate together, and to aid one another in many ways, we may infer that in most cases they are impelled by the same sense of satisfaction or pleasure which they experience in performing other instinctive actions; or by the same sense of dissatisfaction as when other instinctive actions are checked. We see this in innumerable instances, and it is illustrated in a striking manner by the acquired instincts of our domesticated animals; thus a young shepherd-dog delights in driving and running round a flock of sheep, but not in worrying them; a young fox-hound delights in hunting a fox, whilst some other kinds of dogs, as I have witnessed, utterly disregard foxes. What a strong feeling of inward satisfaction must impel a bird, so full of activity, to brood day after day over her egg. Migratory birds are quite miserable if stopped from migrating; perhaps they enjoy starting on their long flight; but it is hard to believe that the poor pinioned goose, described by Audubon, which started on foot at the proper time for its journey of probably more than a thousand miles, could have felt any joy in doing so. Some instincts are determined solely by painful feelings, as by fear, which leads to self-preservation, and is in some cases directed towards special enemies. No one, I presume, can analyze the sensations of pleasure or pain. In many instances, however, it is probable that instincts are persistently followed from the mere force of inheritance, without the stimulus of either pleasure or pain. A young pointer, when it first scents game, apparently cannot help pointing. A squirrel in a cage who pats the nuts which it cannot eat, as if to bury them in the ground, can hardly be thought to act thus, either from pleasure or pain. Hence the common assumption that men must be impelled to every action by experiencing some pleasure or pain may be erroneous. Although a habit may be blindly and implicitly followed, independently of any pleasure or pain felt at the moment, yet if it be forcibly and abruptly checked, a vague sense of dissatisfaction is generally experienced.

It has often been assumed that animals were in the first place rendered social, and that they feel as a consequence uncomfortable when separated from each other, and comfortable whilst together; but it is a more probable view that these sensations were first developed, in order that those animals which would profit by living in society, should be induced to live together, in the same manner as the sense of hunger and the pleasure of eating were, no doubt, first acquired in order to induce animals to eat. The feeling of pleasure from society is probably an extension of the parental or filial affections, since the social instinct seems to be developed be the young remaining for a long time with their parents; and this extension may be attributed in part to habit, but chiefly to natural selection. With those animals which were benefited by living in close association, the individuals which took the greatest pleasure in society would best escape various dangers, whilst those that cared least for their comrades, and lived solitary, would perish in greater numbers. With respect to the origin of the parental and filial affections, which apparently lie at the base of the social instincts, we know not the steps by which they have been gained; but we may infer that it has been to a large extent through natural selection. So it has almost certainly been with the unusual and opposite feeling of hatred between the nearest relations, as with the worker-bees which kill their brother-drones, and with the queen-bees which kill their daughter- queens; the desire to destroy their nearest relations having been in this case of service to the community. Parental affection, or some feeling which replaces it, has been developed in certain animals extremely low in the scale, for example, in star-fishes and spiders. It is also occasionally present in a few members alone in a whole group of animals, as in the genus Forficula, or earwigs.

The all-important emotion of sympathy is distinct from that of love. A mother may passionately love her sleeping and passive infant, but she can hardly at such times be said to feel sympathy for it. The love of a man for his dog is distinct from sympathy and so is that of a dog for his master. Adam Smith formerly argued, as has Mr. Bain recently, that the basis of sympathy lies in our strong retentiveness of former states of pain or pleasure. Hence, "the sight of another person enduring hunger, cold, fatigue, revives in us some recollection of these states, which are painful even in idea." We are thus impelled to relieve the sufferings of another, in order that our own painful feelings may be at the same time relieved. In like manner we are led to participate in the pleasures of others.[21] But I cannot see how this view explains the fact that sympathy is excited, in an immeasurably stronger degree, by a beloved, than by an indifferent person. The mere sight of Suffering, independently of love, would suffice to call up in us vivid recollections and associations. The explanation may lie in the fact that, with all animals, sympathy is directed solely towards the members of the same community, and therefore towards known, and more or less beloved members, but not to all the individuals of the same species. This fact is not more surprising than that the fears of many animals should be directed against special enemies. Species which are not social, such as lions and tigers, no doubt feel sympathy for the suffering of their own young, but not for that of any other animal. With mankind, selfishness, experience, and imitation, probably add, as Mr. Bain has shown, to the power of sympathy; for we are led by the hope of receiving good in return to perform acts of sympathetic kindness to others; and sympathy is much strengthened by habit. In however complex a manner this feeling may have originate, as it is one of high importance to all those. animals which aid and defend one another, it will have been increased through natural selection; for those communities, which included the greatest number of the most sympathetic members, would flourish best, and rear the greatest number of offspring.

It is, however, impossible to decide in many cases whether certain social instincts have been acquired through natural selection, or are the indirect result of other instincts and faculties, such as sympathy, reason, experience, and a tendency to imitation; or again, whether they are simply the result of long-continued habit. So remarkable an instinct as the placing sentinels to warn the community of danger can hardly have been the indirect result of any of these faculties; it must, therefore, have been directly acquired. On the other hand, the habit followed by the males of some social animals of defending the community, and of attacking their enemies or their prey in concert, may perhaps have originated from mutual sympathy; but courage, and in most cases strength, must have been previously acquired, probably through natural selection.

Of the various instincts and habits, some are much stronger than others; that is, some either give more pleasure in their performance, and more distress in their prevention, than others; or, which is probably quite as important, they are, through inheritance, more persistently followed, without exciting any special feeling of pleasure or pain. We are ourselves conscious that some habits are much more difficult to cure or change than others. Hence a struggle may often be observed in animals between different instincts, or between an instinct and some habitual disposition; as when a dog rushes after a hare, is rebuked, pauses, hesitates, pursues again, or returns ashamed to his master; or as between the love of a female dog for her young puppies and for her master,—for she may be seen to slink away to them, as if half ashamed of not accompanying her master. But the most curious instance known to me of one instinct getting the better of another, is the migratory instinct conquering the maternal instinct. The former is wonderfully strong; a confined bird will at the proper season beat her breast against the wires of her cage, until it is bare and bloody. It causes young salmon to leap out of the fresh water, in which they could continue to exist, and thus unintentionally to commit suicide. Every one knows how strong the maternal instinct is, leading even timid birds to face great danger, though with hesitation, and in opposition to the instinct of selfpreservation. Nevertheless, the migratory instinct is so powerful, that late in the autumn swallows, housemartins, and swifts frequently desert their tender young, leaving them to perish miserably in their nests.[22]

We can perceive that an instinctive impulse, if it be in any way more beneficial to a species than some other or opposed instinct, would be rendered the more potent of the two through natural selection; for the individual which had it most strongly developed would survive in larger numbers. Whether this is the case with the migratory in comparison with the maternal instinct, may be doubted. The great persistence, or steady action of the former at certain seasons of the year during the whole day, may give it for a time paramount force.

Man a Social Animal

Every one will admit that man is a social being. We see this in his dislike of solitude, and in his wish for society beyond that of his own family. Solitary confinement is one of the severest punishments which can be inflicted. Some authors suppose that man primevally lived in single families; but at the present day, though single families, or only two or three together, roam the solitudes of some savage land, they always, as far as I can discover, hold friendly relations with other families inhabiting the same district. Such families occasionally meet in council, and unite for their common defence. It is no argument against savage man being a social animal, that the tribes inhabiting adjacent districts are almost always at war with each other; for the social instincts never extend to all the individuals of the same species. Judging from the analogy of the majority of the Quadrumana, it is probable that the early ape-like progenitors of man were likewise social; but this is not of much importance for us. Although man, as he now exists, has few special instincts, having lost any which his early progenitors may have possessed, this is no reason why he should not have retained from an extremely remote period some degree of instinctive love and sympathy for his fellows. We are indeed all conscious that we do possess such sympathetic feelings;[23] but our consciousness does not tell us whether they are instinctive, having originated long ago in the same manner as with the lower animals, or whether they have been acquired by each of us during our early years. As man is a social animal, it is almost certain that he would inherit a tendency to be faithful to his comrades, and obedient to the leader of his tribe; for these qualities are common to most social animals. He would consequently possess some capacity for self-command. He would from an inherited tendency be willing to defend, in concert with others, his fellow-men; and would be ready to aid them in any way, which did not too greatly interfere with his own welfare or his own strong desires.

The social animals which stand at the bottom of the scale are guided almost exclusively, and those which stand higher in the scale are largely guided, by special instincts in the aid which they give to the members of the same community; but they are likewise in part impelled by mutual love and sympathy, assisted apparently by some amount of reason. Although man, as just remarked, has no special instincts to tell him how to aid his fellow-men, he still has the impulse, and with his improved intellectual faculties would naturally be much guided in this respect by reason and experience. Instinctive sympathy would also cause him to value highly the approbation of his fellows; for, as Mr. Bain has clearly shewn,[24] the love of praise and the strong feeling of glory, and the still stronger horror of scorn and infamy, "are due to the workings of sympathy." Consequently man would be influenced in the highest degree by the wishes, approbation, and blame of his fellow-men, as expressed by their gestures and language. Thus the social instincts which must have been acquired by man in a very rude state, and probably even by his early ape-like progenitors, still give the impulse to some of his best actions; but his actions are in a higher degree determined by the expressed wishes and judgment of his fellow-men, and unfortunately very often by his own strong selfish desires. But as love, sympathy and self-command become strengthened by habit, and as the power of reasoning becomes clearer, so that man can value justly the judgments of his fellows, he will feel himself impelled, apart from any transitory pleasure or pain, to certain lines of conduct. He might then declare—not that any barbarian or uncultivated man could thus think—I am the supreme judge of my own conduct, and in the words of Kant, I will not in my own person violate the dignity of humanity.

The More Enduring Social Instinct Conquer the Less Persistent Instincts

We have not, however, as yet considered the main point, on which, from our present point of view, the whole question of the moral sense turns. Why should a man feel that he ought to obey one instinctive desire rather than another? Why is he bitterly regretful, if he has yielded to a strong sense of self-preservation, and has not risked his life to save that of a fellow-creature? or why does he regret having stolen food from hunger?

It is evident in the first place, that with mankind the instinctive impulse have different degrees of strength; a savage will risk his own life to save that of a member of the same community, but will be wholly indifferent about a stranger: a young and timid mother urged by the maternal instinct will, without a moment's hesitation, run the greatest danger for her own infant, but not for a mere fellow-creature. Nevertheless many a civilized man, or even boy, who never before risked his life for another, but full of courage and empathy, has disregarded the instinct of self-preservation, and plunged at once into a torrent to save a drowning man, though a stranger. In this case man is impelled by the same instinctive motive, which made the heroic little American monkey, formerly described, save his keeper, by attacking the great and dreaded baboon. Such actions as the above appear to be the simple result of the greater strength of the social or maternal instincts than that of any other instinct or motive; for they are performed too instantaneously for reflection, or for pleasure or pain to be felt at the time; though, if prevented by any cause, distress or even misery might be felt. In a timid man, on the other hand, the instinct of self-preservation might be so strong, that he would be unable to force himself to run any such risk, perhaps not even for his own child.

I am aware that some persons maintain that actions performed impulsively, as in the above cases, do not come under the dominion of the moral sense, and cannot be called moral. They confine this term to actions done deliberately after a victory over opposing desires, or when prompted by some exalted motive. but it appears scarcely possible to draw any clear line of distinction of this kind.[25] As far as exalted motive are concerned, many instances have been recorded of savages, destitute of any feeling of general benevolence toward mankind, and not guided by any religious motive, who have deliberately sacrificed their lives as prisoners,[26] rather than betray their comrades; and surely their conduct ought to be considered as moral. As far as deliberation, and the victory over opposing motives are concerned, animals may be seen doubting between opposed instincts, in rescuing their offspring or comrades from danger; yet their actions, though done for the good of others, are not called moral. Moreover, anything performed very often by us, will at last be done without deliberation or hesitation, and can then hardly be distinguished from an instinct; yet surely no one will pretend that such an action ceases to be moral. On the contrary, we all feel that an act cannot be considered as perfect, or as performed in the most noble manner, unless it be done impulsively, without deliberation or effort, in the same manner as by a man in whom the requisite qualities are innate. He who is forced to overcome his fear or want of sympathy before he acts, deserves, however, in one way higher credit than the man whose innate disposition leads him to a good act without effort. As we cannot distinguish between motives, we rank all actions of a certain class as moral, if performed by a moral being. A moral being is one who is capable of comparing his past and future actions or motives, and of approving or disapproving of them. We have no reason to suppose that any of the lower animals have this capacity; therefore, when a Newfoundland dog drags a child out of the water, or a monkey faces danger to rescue its comrade, or takes charge of an orphan monkey, we do not call its conduct moral. But in the case of man, who alone can with certainty be ranked as a moral being, actions of a certain class are called moral, whether performed deliberately, after a struggle with opposing motives, or impulsively through instinct, or from the effect of slowly-gained habit.

But to return to our more immediate subject. although some instincts are more powerful than others, and thus lead to corresponding actions, yet it is untenable, that in man the social instinct (including the love of praise and fear of blame) possess greater strength, or have, through long habit, acquired greater strength than the instincts of self-preservation, hunger, lust, vengeance, &c. Why then does man regret, even though trying to banish such regret, that he has followed the one natural impulse rather than the other; and why does he further feel that he ought to regret his conduct? Man in this respect differs profoundly from the lower animals. Nevertheless we can, I think, see with some degree of clearness the reason of this difference.

Man, from the activity of his mental faculties, cannot avoid reflection: past impression and images are incessantly and clearly passing through his mind. Now with those animals which live permanently in a body, the social instincts are ever present and persistent. Such animals are always ready to utter the danger-signal, to defend the community, and to give aid to their fellows in accordance with their habits; they feel at all times, without the stimulus of any special passion or desire, some degree of love and sympathy for them; they are unhappy if long separate from them, and always happy to be again in their company. So it is with ourselves. Even when we are quite alone, how often do we think with pleasure or pain of what others think of us,—of their imagined approbation or disapprobation; and this all follows from sympathy, a fundamental element of the social instinct. A man who possessed no trace of such instincts would be an unnatural monster. On the other hand, the desire to satisfy hunger, or any passion such as vengeance, is in its nature temporary, and can for a time be fully satisfied. Nor is it easy, perhaps hardly possible, to call up with complete vividness the feeling, for instance, of hunger; nor indeed, as has often been remarked, of any suffering. The instinct of self-preservation is not felt except in the presence of danger; and many a coward has thought himself brave until he has met his enemy face to face. The wish for another man's property is perhaps as persistent a desire as any that can be named; but even in this case the satisfaction of actual possession is generally a weaker feeling than the desire: many a thief, if not a habitual one, after success has wondered why he stole some article.[27]

A man cannot prevent past impressions often repassing through his mind; he will thus be driven to make a comparison between the impressions of past hunger, vengeance satisfied, or danger shunned at other men's cost, with the almost ever-present instinct of sympathy, and with his early knowledge of what others consider as praiseworthy or blamable. This knowledge cannot be banished from his mind, and from instinctive sympathy is esteemed of great moment. He will then feel as if he had been baulked in following a present instinct or habit, and this with all animals cause dissatisfaction, or even misery.

The above case of the swallow affords an illustration, though of a reversed nature, of a temporary though for the time strongly persistent instinct conquering another instinct, which is usually dominant over all others. At the proper season these birds seem all day long to be impressed with the desire to migrate; their habits change; they become restless, are noisy and congregate in flock. Whilst the mother-bird is feeding, or brooding over her nestlings, the maternal instinct is probably stronger than the migratory; but the instinct which is the more persistent gains the victory, and at last, at a moment when her young ones are not in sight, she takes flight and deserts them. When arrived at the end of her long journey, and the migratory instinct has ceased to act, what an agony of remorse the bird would feel, if, from being endowed with great mental activity, she could not prevent the image constantly passing through her mind, of her young ones perishing in the bleak north from cold and hunger.

At the moment of action, man will no doubt be apt to follow the stronger impulse; and though this may occasionally prompt him to the noblest deeds, it will more commonly lead him to gratify his own desires at the expense of other men. But after their gratification when past and weaker impressions are judged by the ever-enduring social instinct, and by his deep regard for the good opinion of his fellows, retribution will surely come. He will then feel remorse, repentance, regret, or shame; this latter feeling, however, relates almost exclusively to the judgment of others. He will consequently resolve more or less firmly to act differently for the future; and this is conscience; for conscience looks backwards, and serves as a guide for the future.

The nature and strength of the feelings which we call regret, shame, repentance or remorse, depend apparently not only on the strength of the violated instinct, but partly on the strength of the temptation, and often still more on the judgment of our fellows. How far each man values the appreciation of others, depends on the strength of his innate or acquired feeling of sympathy; and on his own capacity for reasoning out the remote consequences of his acts. Another element is most important, although not necessary, the reverence or fear of the gods, or Spirits believed in by each man: and this applies especially in cases of remorse. Several critics have objected that though some slight regret or repentance may be explained by the view advocated in this chapter, it is impossible thus to account for the soul-shaking feeling of remorse. But I can see little force in this objection. My critics do not define what they mean by remorse, and I can find no definition implying more than an overwhelming sense of repentance. Remorse seems to bear the same relation to repentance, as rage does to anger, or agony to pain. It is far from strange that an instinct so strong and so generally admired, as maternal love, should, if disobeyed, lead to the deepest misery, as soon as the impression of the past cause of disobedience is weakened. Even when an action is opposed to no special instinct, merely to know that our friends and equals despise us for it is enough to cause great misery. Who can doubt that the refusal to fight a duel through fear has caused many men an agony of shame? Many a Hindoo, it is said, has been stirred to the bottom of his soul by having partaken of unclean food. Here is another case of what must, I think, be called remorse. Dr. Landor acted as a magistrate in West Australia, and relates,[28] that a native on his farm, after losing one of his wives from disease, came and said that "he was going to a distant tribe to spear a woman, to satisfy his sense of duty to his wife. I told him that if he did so, I would send him to prison for life. He remained about the farm for some months, but got exceedingly thin, and complained that he could not rest or eat, that his wife's spirit was haunting him, because he had not taken a life for hers. I was inexorable, and assured him that nothing should save him if he did." Nevertheless the man disappeared for more than a year, and then returned in high condition; and his other wife told Dr. Landor that her husband had taken the life of a woman belonging to a distant tribe; but it was impossible to obtain legal evidence of the act. The breach of a rule held sacred by the tribe, will thus, as it seems, give rise to the deepest feelings,—and this quite apart from the social instincts, excepting insofar as the rule is grounded on the judgment of the community. How so many strange superstitions have arisen throughout the world we know not; nor can we tell how some real and great crimes, such as incest, have come to be held in an abhorrence (which is not however quite universal) by the lowest savages. It is even doubtful whether in some tribes incest would be looked on with greater horror, than would the marriage of a man with a woman bearing the same name, though not a relation. "To violate this law is a crime which the Australians hold in the greatest abhorrence, in this agreeing exactly with certain tribes of North America. When the question is put in either district, is it worse to kill a girl of a foreign tribe, or to marry a girl of one's own, an answer just opposite to ours would be given without hesitation."[29] We may, therefore, reject the belief, lately insisted on by some writers, that the abhorrence of incest is due to our possessing a special God-implanted conscience. On the whole it is intelligible, that a man urged by so powerful a sentiment as remorse, though arising as above explained, should be led to act in a manner, which he has been taught to believe serves as an expiation, such as delivering himself up to justice.

Man prompted by his concience, will through long habit acquire such perfect self-command, that his desires and passions will at last yield instantly and without a struggle to his social sympathies and instincts, including his feeling for the judgment of his fellows. The still hungry, or the still revengeful man will not think of stealing food, or of wreaking his vengeance. It is possible, or as we shall hereafter see, even probable, that the habit of self-command may, like other habits, be inherited. Thus at last man comes to feel, through acquired and perhaps inherited habit, that it is best for him to obey his more persistent impulses. The imperious word ought seems merely to imply the consciousness of the existence of a rule of conduct, however it may have originated. Formerly it must have been often vehemently urged that an insulted gentleman ought to fight a duel. We even say that a pointer ought to point, and a retriever to retrieve game. If they fail to do so, they fail in their duty and act wrongly.

If any desire or instinct leading to an action opposed to the good of others still appears, when recalled to mind, as strong as, or stronger than, the social instinct, a man will feel no keen regret at having followed it; but he will be conscious that if his conduct were known to his fellows, it would meet with their disapprobation; and few are so destitute of sympathy as not to feel discomfort when this is realized. If he has no such sympathy, and if his desires leading to bad actions are at the time strong, and when recalled are not over-mastered by the persistent social instincts, and the judgment of others, then he is essentially a bad man;[30] and the sole restraining motive left is the fear of punishment, and the conviction that in the long run it would be best for his own selfish interests to regard the good of others rather than his own.

It is obvious that everyone may with an easy conscience gratify his own desires, if they do not interfere with his social instincts, that is with the good of others; but in order to be quite free from self-reproach, or at least of anxiety, it is almost necessary for him to avoid the disapprobation, whether reasonable or not, of his fellow-men. Nor must he break through the fixed habits of his life, especially if these are supported by reason; for if he does, he will assuredly feel dissatisfaction. He must likewise avoid the reprobation of the one God or gods in whom, according to his knowledge or superstition, he may believe; but in this case the additional fear of divine punishment often supervenes.

The Strictly Social Virtues at First Alone Regarded

The above view of the origin and nature of the moral Sense, which tells us what we ought to do, and of the conscience which reproves us if we disobey it, accords well with what we see of the early and undeveloped condition of this faculty in mankind. The virtues which must be practiced, at least generally, by rude men, so that they may associate in a body, are those which are still recognized as the most important. But they are practised almost exclusively in relation to the men of the same tribe; and their opposites are not regarded as crimes in relation to the men of other tribes. No tribe could hold together if murder, robbery, treachery, &c., were common; consequently such crimes within the limits of the same tribe "are branded with everlasting infamy";[31] but excite no such sentiment beyond these limits. A North-American Indian is well pleased with himself, and is honoured by others, when he scalps a man of another tribe; and a Dyak cuts off the head of an unoffending person, and dries it as a trophy. The murder of infants has prevailed on the largest scale throughout the world,[32] and has met with no reproach; but infanticide, especially of females, has been thought to be good for the tribe, or at least not injurious. Suicide during former times was not generally considered as a crime,[33] as but rather, from the courage displayed, as an honourable act; and it is still practiced by some semi-civilised and savage nations without reproach, for it does not obviously concern others of the tribe. It has been recorded that an Indian Thug conscientiously regretted that he had not robbed and strangled as many travellers as did his father before him. In a rude state of civilisation the robbery of strangers is, indeed, generally considered as honourable.

Slavery, although in some ways beneficial during ancient times,[34] is a great crime; yet it was not so regarded until quite recently, even by the most civilized nations. And this was especially the case, because the slaves belonged in general to a race different from that of their masters. As barbarians do not regard the opinion of their women, wives are commonly treated like slaves. Most savages are utterly indifferent to the sufferings of strangers, or even delight in witnessing them. It is well known that the women and children of the North-American Indians aided in torturing their enemies. Some savages take a horrid pleasure in cruelty to animals,[35] and humanity is an unknown virtue. Nevertheless, besides the family affections, kindness is common, especially during sickness, between the members of the same tribe, and is sometimes extended beyond these limits. Mungo Park's touching account of the kindness of the negro women of the interior to him is well known. Many instances could be given of the noble fidelity of savages towards each other, but not to strangers; common experience justifies the maxim of the Spaniard, "Never, never trust an Indian." There cannot be fidelity without truth; and this fundamental virtue is not rare between the members of the same tribe: thus Mungo Park heard the negro women teaching their young children to love the truth. This, again, is one of the virtues which becomes so deeply rooted in the mind, that it is sometime practiced by savages, even at a high cost, towards strangers; but to lie to your enemy has rarely been thought a sin, as the history of modern diplomacy too plainly shews. As soon as a tribe has a recognized leader, disobedience becomes a crime, and even abject submission is looked at as a sacred virtue.

As during rude times no man can be useful or faithful to his tribe without courage, this quality has universally been placed in the highest rank; and although in civilised countries a good yet timid man may be far more useful to the community than a brave one, we cannot help instinctively honouring the latter above a coward, however benevolent. Prudence, on the other hand, which does not concern the welfare of others, though a very useful virtue, has never been highly esteemed. As no man can practice the virtues necessary for the welfare of his tribe without self-sacrifice, self-command, and the power of endurance, these

qualities have been at all times highly and most justly valued. The American savage voluntarily submits to the most
horrid tortures without a groan, to prove and strengthen his
fortitude and courage; and we cannot help admiring him,
or even an Indian Fakir, who, from a foolish religious motive, swings suspended by a hook buried in his flesh.

The other so-called self-regarding virtues, which do not
obviously, though they may really, affect the welfare of the
tribe, have never been esteemed by savages, though now
highly appreciated by civilised nations. The greatest intem-
perance is no reproach with savages. Utter licentiousness,
and unnatural crime, prevail to an astounding extent.[36] As
soon, however, as marriage, whether polygamous, or monogamous, becomes common, jealousy will lead to the inculcation of female virtue; and this, being honoured, will
tend to spread to the unmarried females. How slowly it
spreads to the male sex, we see at the present day. Chastity
eminently requires self-command; therefore it has been
honoured from a very early period in the moral history of
civilized man. As a consequence of this, the senseless practice of celibacy has been ranked from a remote period as a
virtue.[37] The hatred of indecency, which appears to us so
natural as to be thought innate, and which is so valuable
an aid to chastity, is a modern virtue, appertaining exclusively, as Sir G. Staunton remarks,[38] to civilised life. This is
shewn by the ancient religious rites of various nations, by
the drawings on the walls of Pompeii, and by the practices
of many savages.

We have now seen that actions are regarded by savages, and were probably so regarded by primeval man, as
good or bad, solely as they obviously affect the welfare of
the tribe,—not that of the species, nor that of an individual
member of the tribe. This conclusion agrees well with the
belief that the so-called moral sense is aboriginally derived
from the social instincts, for both relate at first exclusively
to the community.

The chief causes of the low morality of savages, as judged
by our standard, are, firstly, the confinement of sympathy to
the same tribe. Secondly, powers of reasoning insufficient
to recognize the bearing of many virtues, especially of the

self-regarding virtues, on the general welfare of the tribe. Savages, for instance, fail to trace the multiplied evils consequent on a want of temperance, chastity, &c. And, thirdly, weak power of self-command; for this power has not been strengthened through long-continued, perhaps inherited, habit, instruction and religion.

I have entered into the above detail on the immorality of savages,[39] because some authors have recently taken a high view of their moral nature, or have attributed most of their crimes to mistaken benevolence.[40] These authors appear to rest their conclusion on savages possessing those virtues which are serviceable, or even necessary, for the existence of the family and of the tribe,—qualities which they undoubtedly do possess, and often in a high degree.

Concluding Remarks

It was assumed formerly by philosophers of the derivative[41] school of morals that the foundation of morality lay in a form of selfishness; but more recently the "Greatest happiness principle" has been brought prominently forward. It is, however, more correct to speak of the latter principle as the standard, and not as the motive of conduct. Nevertheless, all the authors whose works l have consulted, with a few exceptions,[42] write as if there must be a distinct motive for every action, and that this must be associated with some pleasure or displeasure. But man seems often to act impulsively, that is from instinct or long habit, without any consciousness of pleasure, in the same manner as does probably a bee or ant, when it blindly follows its instincts. Under circumstances of extreme peril, as during a fire, when a man endeavors to save a fellow-creature without a moment's hesitation, he can hardly feel pleasure; and still less has he time to reflect on the dissatisfaction which he might subsequently experience if he did not make the attempt. Should he afterwards reflect over his own conduct, he would feel that there lies within him an impulsive power widely different from a search after pleasure or happiness; and this seem to be the deeply planted social instinct.

In the case of the lower animals it seems much more appropriate to speak of their social instincts, as having been developed for the general good rather than for the general happiness of the Species. The term, general good, may be defined as the rearing of the greatest number of individuals in full vigour and health, with all their faculties perfect, under the condition to which they are subjected. As the social instincts both of man and the lower animals have no doubt been developed by nearly the same steps, it would be advisable, if found practicable, to use the same definition in both cases, and to take as the standard of morality, the general good or welfare of the community, rather than the general happiness; but this definition would perhaps require some limitation on account of political ethics.

When a man risks his life to save that of a fellow-creature, it seems also more correct to say that he acts for the general good, rather than for the general happiness of mankind. No doubt the welfare and the happiness of the individual usually coincide; and a contented, happy tribe will flourish better than one that is discontented and unhappy. We have seen that even by an early period in the history of man, the expressed wishes of the community will have naturally influenced to a large extent the conduct of each member; and as all wish for happiness, the "greatest happiness principle" will have become a most important secondary guide and object; the social instinct, however, together with sympathy (which leads to our regarding the approbation and disapprobation of others), having served as the primary impulse and guide. Thus the reproach is removed of laying the foundation of the noblest part of our nature in the base principle of selfishness; unless, indeed, the satisfaction which every animal feels, when it follows its proper instincts, and the dissatisfaction felt when prevented, be called selfish.

The wishes and opinions of the members of the same community, expressed at first orally, but later by writing also, either form the sole guides of our conduct, or greatly reinforce the social instincts; such opinions, however, have sometimes a tendency directly opposed to these instincts. This latter fact is well exemplified by the Law of Honour, that is, the law of the opinion of our equals, and not of all our countrymen. The breach of this law, even when the breach is known to be strictly accordant with true morality, has caused many a man more agony than a real crime. We recognize the same influence in the burning sense of shame which most of us have felt, even after the interval of years, when calling to mind some accidental breach of a trifling, though fixed, rule of etiquette. The judgment of the community will generally be guided by some rude experience of what is best in the long run for all the members; but this judgment will not rarely err from ignorance and weak powers of reasoning. Hence the strangest customs and superstitions, in complete opposition to the true welfare and happiness of mankind, have become all-powerful throughout the world. We see this in the horror felt by a Hindoo who breaks his caste, and in many other such cases. It would be difficult to distinguish between the remorse felt by a Hindoo who has yielded to the temptation of eating unclean food, from that felt after committing a theft; but the former would probably be the more severe.

How so many absurd rules of conduct, as well as so many absurd religious beliefs, have originated, we do not know; nor how it is that they have become, in all quarters of the world, so deeply impressed on the mind of men; but it is worthy of remark that a belief constantly inculcated during the early years of life, whilst the brain is impressible, appears to acquire almost the nature of an instinct; and the very essence of an instinct is that it is followed independently of reason. Neither can we say why certain admirable virtues, such as the love of truth, are much more highly appreciated by some savage tribes than by others;[43] nor, again, why similar differences prevail even amongst highly civilized nations. Knowing how firmly fixed many strange customs and superstitions have become, we need feel no surprise that the self regarding, virtues, supported as they are by reason, should now appear to us so natural as to be thought innate, although they were not valued by man in his early condition.

Notwithstanding many sources of doubt, man can generally and readily distinguish between the higher and lower moral rules. The higher are founded on the social instincts, and relate to the welfare of others. They are supported by the approbation of our fellowmen and by reason. The lower rules, though some of them when implying self-sacrifice hardly deserve to be called lower, relate chiefly to self, and arise from public opinion, matured by experience and cultivation; for they are not practised by rude tribes.

As man advances in civilisation, and small tribes are united into larger communities, the simplest reason would tell each individual that he ought to extend his social instincts and sympathies to all the members of the same nation, though personally unknown to him. This point being once reached, there is only an artificial barrier to prevent his sympathies extending to the men of all nations and races. If, indeed, such men are separated from him by great differences in appearance or habits, experience unfortunately shews us how long it is, before we look at them as our fellow-creatures. Sympathy beyond the confines of man, that is, humanity to the lower animals, seems to be one of the latest moral acquisitions. It is apparently unfelt by savages, except towards their pets. How little the old Romans knew of it is shewn by their abhorrent gladiatorial exhibition. The very idea of humanity, as far as I could observe, was new to most of the Gauchos of the Pampas. This virtue, one of the noblest with which man is endowed, seems to arise incidentally from our sympathies becoming more tender and more widely diffused, until they are extended to all sentient beings. As soon as this virtue is honoured and practiced by some few men, it spreads through instruction and example to the young, and eventually becomes incorporated in public opinion.

The highest possible stage in moral culture is when we recognise that we ought to control our thoughts, and "not even in inmost thought to think again the sins that made the past so pleasant to us."[44] Whatever makes any bad action familiar to the mind, renders its performance by so much the easier. As "habitual thoughts, such also will be the character of thy mind; for the soul is dyed by the thoughts."[45]

Our great philosopher, Herbert Spencer, has recently explained his views on the moral sense. He says[46] "I believe that the experience of utility organised and consolidated through all past generations of the human race, have been producing corresponding modifications, which, by continued transmission and accumulation, have become in us certain faculties of moral intuition—certain emotions responding to right and wrong conduct, which have no apparent basis in the individual experiences of utility." There is not the least inherent improbability, as it seems to me, in virtuous tendencies being more or less strongly inherited; for, not to mention the various dispositions and habits transmitted by many of our domestic animals to their offspring, I have heard of authentic cases in which a desire to steal and a tendency to lie appeared to run in families of the upper ranks; and as stealing is a rare crime in the wealthy classes, we can hardly account by accidental coincidence for the tendency occurring in two or three members of the same family. If bad tendencies are transmitted, it is probable that good ones are likewise transmitted. That the state of the body by affecting the brain, has great influence on the moral tendencies is known to most of those who have suffered from chronic derangements of the digestion or liver. The same fact is likewise shewn by the "perversion or destruction of the moral sense being often one of the earliest symptoms of mental derangement";[47] and insanity is notoriously often inherited. Except through the principle of the transmission of moral tendencies, we cannot understand the differences believed to exist in this respect between the various races of mankind. Even the partial transmission of virtuous tendencies would be an immense assistance to the primary impulse derived directly and indirectly from the social instincts. Admitting for a moment that virtuous tendencies are inherited, it appears probable, at least in such cases as chastity, temperance, humanity to animals, &c., that they become first impressed on the mental organization through habit, instruction and example, continued during several generations in the same family, and in a quite subordinate degree, or not at all, by the individuals possessing such virtues having succeeded best in the struggle for life. My chief source of doubt with respect to any such inheritance, is that senseless customs, superstitions, and tastes, such as the horror of a Hindoo for unclean food, ought on the same principle to be transmitted. I have not met with any evidence in support of the transmission of superstitious customs or senseless habits, although in itself it is perhaps not less probable than that animals should acquire inherited taste for certain kinds of food or fear of certain foes.

Finally the social instincts, which no doubt were acquired by man as by the lower animal for the good of the community, will from the first have given to him some wish to aid his fellows, some feeling of sympathy, and have compelled him to regard their approbation and disapprobation. Such impulses will have served him at a very early period as a rude rule of right and wrong. But as man gradually advanced in intellectual power, and was enabled to trace the more remote consequences of his actions; as he acquired sufficient knowledge to reject baneful customs and superstitions; as he regarded more and more, not only the welfare, but the happiness of his fellow-men; as from habit, following on beneficial experience, instruction and example, his sympathies became more tender and widely diffused, extending to men of all races, to the imbecile, maimed, and other useless members of society, and finally to the lower animals,—so would the standard of his morality rise higher and higher. And it is admitted by moralists of the derivative school and by some intuitionists, that the standard of morality has risen since an early period in the history of man.[48]

As a struggle may sometimes be seen going on between the various instincts of the lower animals, it is not surprising that there should be a struggle in man between his social instincts, with their derived virtues, and his lower, though momentarily stronger impulses or desires. This, as Mr. Galton[49] has remarked, is all the less surprising, as man has emerged from a state of barbarism within a comparatively recent period. After having yielded to some temptation we feel a sense of dissatisfaction, shame, repentance, or remorse, analogous to the feelings caused by other powerful instincts or desires, when left unsatisfied or baulked. We compare the weakened impression of a past temptation with the ever present social instincts, or with habits, gained in early youth and strengthened during our whole lives, until they have become almost as strong as instincts. If with the temptation still before us we do not yield, it is because either the social instinct or some custom is at the moment predominant, or because we have learnt that it will appear to us hereafter the stronger, when compared with the weakened impression of the temptation, and we realise that its violation would cause us suffering. Looking to future generations, there is no cause to fear that the social instincts will grow weaker, and we may expect that virtuous habit will grow stronger, becoming perhaps fixed by inheritance. In this case the struggle between our higher and lower impulses will be less severe, and virtue will be triumphant.

Summary of the Last Two Chapters

There can be no doubt that the difference between the mind of the lowest man and that of the highest animal is immense. An anthropomorphous ape, if he could take a dispassionate view of his own case, would admit that though he could form an artful plan to plunder a garden—though he could use stones for fighting or for breaking open nuts, yet that the thought of fashioning a stone into a tool was quite beyond his scope. Still less, as he would admit, could he follow out a train of metaphysical reasoning, or solve a mathematical problem, or reflect on God, or admire a grand natural scene. Some apes, however, would probably declare that they could and did admire the beauty of the coloured skin and fur of their partners in marriage. They would admit, that though they could make other apes understand by cries some of their perceptions and simpler wants, the notion of expressing definite ideas by definite sounds had never crossed their minds. They might insist that they were ready to aid their fellow-apes of the same troop in many ways, to risk their lives for them, and to take charge of their orphans; but they would be forced to acknowledge that disinterested love for all living creatures, the most noble attribute of man, was quite beyond their comprehension.

Nevertheless the difference in mind between man and the higher animals, great as it is, certainly is one of degree and not of kind. We have seen that the senses and intuitions, the various emotions and faculties, such as love, memory, attention, curiosity, imitation, reason, &c., of which man boasts, may be found in an incipient, or even sometimes in a well-developed condition, in the lower animals. They are also capable of some inherited improvement, as we see in the domestic dog compared with the wolf or jackal. If it could be proved that certain high mental powers, such as the formation of general concepts, self-consciousness, &c., were absolutely peculiar to man, which seems extremely doubtful, it is not improbable that these qualities are merely the incidental results of other highly-advanced intellectual faculties; and these again mainly the result of the continued use of a perfect language. At what age does the new-born infant possess the power of abstraction, or become self-conscious, and reflect on its own existence? We cannot answer; nor can we answer in regard to the ascending organic scale. The half-art, half-instinct of language still bears the stamp of its gradual evolution. The ennobling belief in God is not universal with man; and the belief in spiritual agencies naturally follows from other mental powers. The moral sense perhaps affords the best and highest distinction between man and the lower animals; but I need say nothing on this head, as I have so lately endeavored to shew that the social instincts,—the prime principle of man's moral constitution[50]— with the aid of active intellectual powers and the effects of habit, naturally lead to the golden rule, "As ye would that men should do to you, do ye to them likewise"; and this lies at the foundation of morality.

In the next chapter I shall make some few remarks on the probable steps and means by which the several mental and moral faculties of man have been gradually evolved. That such evolution is at least possible ought not to be denied, for we daily see these faculties developing in every infant; and we may trace a perfect gradation from the mind of an utter idiot, lower than that of an animal low in the scale, to the mind of a Newton.

Notes

1. See, for Instance, on this subject, Quatrefages, 'Unité de l'Espèce Humaine,' 1861, p. 21, &c.

2. 'Dissertation on Ethical Philosophy,' 1837, p. 231, &c.

3. 'Metaphysics of Ethics,' translated by J. W. Semple, Edinburgh, 1836, p. 136.

4. Mr. Bain gives a list ('Mental and Moral Science.' 1868, pp. 543–725) of twenty-six British authors who have written on this subject, and whose names are familiar to every reader; to these Mr. Bain's own name, and those of Mr. Lecky, Mr. Shadworth Hodgson, Sir J. Lubbock, and others, might be•added.

5. Sir B. Brodie, after observing that man is a social animal ('Psychological Enquiries,' 1854, p. 192), asks the pregnant question, "ought not this to settle the disputed question as to the existence of a moral sense?" Similar ideas probably occurred to many persons, as they did long ago to Marcus Aurelius. Mr. J. S. Mill speaks, in his celebrated work, 'Utilitarianism,' (1864, pp. 45, 46), of the social feeling as a "powerful natural sentiment," and as "the natural basis of sentiment for utilitarian morality." Again he says, "Like the other aquired capacities above referred to, the moral faculty, if not a part of our nature, is a natural outgrowth from it; capable, like them, in a certain small degree of springing up spontaneously." But in opposition to all this, he also remarks, "if, as is my own belief, the moral feelings are not innate, but aquired, they are not for that reason less natural." It is with hesitation that I venture to differ at all from so profound a thinker, but it can hardly be disputed that the social feeling are instinctive or innate in the lower animals; and why should they not be so in man? Mr. Bain (see, for instance, 'The Emotions and the Will,' 1865, p. 481) and others believe that the moral sense is acquired by each individual during his lifetime. On the general theory of evolution this is at least extremely improbable. The ignoring of all transmitted mental qualities will, as it seems to me, be hereafter judged as a most serious blemish in the works of Mr. Mill.

6. Mr. H. Sidgwick remarks, in an able discussion on this subject (the 'Academy,' June 15th, 1872, p. 231), "a superior bee, we may feel sure, would aspire to a milder solution of the population question." Judging, however, from the habits of many or most savages, man solves the problem by female infanticide, polyandry and promiscuous intercourse; therefore it may well be doubted whether it would be by a milder method. Miss Cobbe, in commenting ('Darwinism in Morals,' 'Theological Review,' April, 1872, pp. 188–191) on the same illustration, says, the *principles* of social duty would be thus reversed; and by this, I presume, she means that the fulfilment of a social duty would tend to the injury of individu-

als; but she overlooks the fact, which she would doubtless admit, that the inctincts of the bee have been acquired for the good of the community. She goes so far as to say that if the theory of ethics advocated in this chapter were ever generally accepted, "I cannot but believe that in the hour of their triumph would be sounded the knell of the virtue of mankind!" It is to be hoped that the belief In the permanence of virtue on this earth is not held by many persons on so weak a tenure.

7. 'Die Darwin'sche Theorie,'s. 101.

8. Mr. R. Brown in 'Proc. Zoolog. Soc.' 1868, p. 409.

9. Brehm, 'Thierleben,' B. i. 1864, s. 52, 79. For the case of the monkeys extracting thorns from each other, see e. 54. With respect to the Hamadryas turning over stones, the fact is given (s. 76) on the evidence of Alvarez, whose observations Brehm thinks quite trustworthy. For the cases of the old male baboons attacking the dogs, see s. 79; and with respect to the eagle, s. 56.

10. Mr. Belt gives the case of a spider-monkey (Ateles) in Nicaragua, which was heard screaming for nearly two hours in the forest, and was found with an eagle perched close by it. The bird apparently feared to attack as long as it remained face to face; and Mr. Belt believes, from what he has seen of the habits of these monkeys, that they protect themselves from eagles by keeping two or three together. 'The Naturalist in Nicaragua,' 1874, p.118.

11. 'Annals of Mag. of Nat. Hist.,' November 1868, p. 382.

12. Sir J. Lubbock, 'Prehistoric Times,' 2nd edit. p. 446.

13. As quoted by Mr. L. H. Morgan, 'The American Beaver,' 1868, p. 272. Capt. Stansbury also gives an interesting account of the manner in which a very young pelican, carried away by a strong stream, was guided and encouraged in its attempts to reach the shore by half a dozen old birds.

14. As Mr. Bain states, 'effective aid to a sufferer springs from sympathy proper:" 'Mental and Moral Science, 1868, p. 245.

15. 'Thierleben,' B. i. s. 85.

16. 'De l'Espèce et de la Classe,' 1869, p. 97.

17. 'Die Darwin'sche Artlehre,' 1869, s. 54.

18. See also Hooker's 'Himalayan Journals,' vol. ii., 1854, p. 333.

19. Brehm, 'Thierleben,' B. i. s. 76.

20. See his extremely interesting paper on 'Gregariousness in Cattle, and in Man,' 'Macmillan's Mag.' Feb. 1871, p. 353.

21. See the first and striking chapter in Adam Smith's 'Theory of Moral Sentiments.' Also Mr. Bains 'Mental and Moral Science,' 1868, pp. 244 and 275–282. Mr. Bain states, that, "sympathy is, indirectly, a source of pleasure to the sympathizer;" and he accounts for this through reciprocity. He remarks that "the person benefited, or others in his stead, may make up, by sympathy and good offices returned, for all the sacrifice." But if, as appears to be the case, sympathy is strictly an instinct, its exercise would give direct pleasure, in the same manner as the exercise, as before remarked, of almost every other instinct.

22. This fact, the Rev. L. Jenyns states (see his edition of 'White's Nat. Hist. of Selborne,' 1863, p. 204) was first recorded by the illustrious Jenner, in 'Phil. Transact,' 1824, and has since been confirmed by several observers, especially by Mr. Blackwall. This latter careful observer examined, late in the autumn, during two years, thirty-six nests; he found that twelve contained young dead birds, five contained eggs on the point of being hatched, and three, eggs not nearly hatched. Many birds, not yet old enough for a prolonged flight, are likewise deserted and left behind. See Blackwall, 'Researches in Zoology,' 1834, pp. 108, 118. For some additional evidence, although this is not wanted, see Leroy, 'Lettres Phil.' 1802, p. 217. For swifts, Gould's 'Introduction to the Birds of Great Britain,' 1823, p. 5. Similar cases have been observed in Canada by Mr. Adams; 'Pop. Science Review,' July, 1873, p. 283.

23. Hume remarks ('An Enquiry Concerning the Principles of Morals,' edit. of 1751, p. 132), "There seems a necessity for confessing that the happiness and misery of others are not spectacles altogether indifferent to us, but that the view of the former . . . communicates a secret joy; the appearance of the latter . . . throws a melancholy damp over the imagination."

24. 'Mental and Moral Science,' 1868, p. 254.

25. I refer here to the distinction between what has been called *material* and *formal* morality. I am glad to find that Professor Huxley ('Critiques and Addresses,' 1873, p. 287) takes the same view on this subject as I do. Mr. Leslie Stephen remarks ('Essays on Freethinking and Plain Speaking,' 1873, p. 83), "the metaphysical distinction between material and formal morality is as irrelevant as other such distinctions."

26. I have given one such case, namely of three Patagonian Indians who preferred being shot, one after the other, to betraying the plans of their companions in war ('Journal of Researches,' 1845, p. 103.

27. Enmity or hatred seems also to be a highly persistent feeling, perhaps more so than any other that can be named. Envy is defined as hatred of another for some excellence or success; and Bacon insists (Essay ix) "of all other affections envy is the most importune and continual." Dogs are very apt to hate both strange men and strange dogs, especially

if they live near at hand, but do not belong to the same family, tribe, or clan; this feeling would thus seem to be innate, and is certainly a most persistent one. It seems to be the complement and converse of the true social instinct. From what we hear of savages, it would appear that something of the same kind holds good with them. If this be so, it would be a small step in any one to transfer such feelings to any member of the same tribe if he had done him an injury and had become his enemy. Nor is it probable that the primitive conscience would reproach a man for injuring his enemy: rather it would reproach him, if he had not revenged himself, To do good in return for evil, to love your enemy, is a height of morality to which it may be doubted whether the social instincts would, by themselves, have ever led us. It is necessary that these instincts, together with sympathy, should have been highly cultivated and extended by the aid of reason, instruction, and the love or fear of God, before any such golden rule would ever be thought of and obeyed.

28. 'Insanity in Relation to Law'; Ontario, United States, 1871, p. 1.

29. E. B. Tylor in 'Contemporary Review,' April, 1873, p. 707.

30. Dr. Prosper Despine in his 'Pychologie Naturelle,' 1868 (tom. i. p. 243; tom. ii. p. 169) gives many curious cases of the worst criminals, who apparently have been entirely destitute of conscience.

31. See an able article in the 'North British Review,' 1867, p. 395. See also Mr. W. Bagehot's articles on the Importance of Obedience and Coherence to Primitive Man, in the 'Fortnightly Review,' 1867, p.529, and 1868, p. 457, &c.

32. The fullest account which I have met with is by Dr. Gerland, in his 'Ueber dan Aussterben der Naturvölker,' 1868; but I shall have to recur to the subject of infanticide in a future chapter.

33. See the very interesting discussion on Suicide in Lecky's 'History of European Morals,' vol. i, 1869, p. 223. With respect to savages, Mr. Winwood Reade informs me that the negros of West Africa often commit suicide. It is well known how common it was amongst the miserable aborigines of South America after the Spanish conquest. For New Zealand, see the voyage of the "Novara," and for the Aleutian Islands, Müller, as quoted by Houzeau, 'Les Facultés Mentales,' &c., tom. ii. p. 136.

34. See Mr. Bagehot, 'Physics and Politics,' 1872, p. 72.

35. See, for instance, Mr. Hamilton's account of the Kaffirs, 'Anthropological Review,' 1870, p. xv.

36. Mr. M'Lennan has given ('Primitive Marriage,' 1865, p. 176) a good collection of facts on this head.

37. Lecky, 'History of European Morals,' vol. i. 1869, p. 109.

38. 'Embassy in China,' vol. ii. p. 348.

39. See on this subject copious evidence in Chap. vii. of Sir J. Lubbock, 'Origin of Civilization,' 1870.

40. For instance Lecky, 'Hist. European Morals,' vol. i. p. 124.

41. This term is used in an able article in the 'Westminister Review,' Oct. 1869, p. 498. For the "Greatest happiness principle," see J. S. Mill, 'Utilitarianism,' p. 17.

42. Mill recognises (A System of Logic,' vol. ii. p. 422) in the clearest manner, that actions may be performed through habit without the anticipation of pleasure. Mr. H. Sidgwick also, in his Essay on Pleasure and Desire ('The Contemporary Review,' April 1872, p. 671), remarks "To sum up, in contravention of the doctrine that our conscious active impulses are always directed towards the production of agreeable sensations in ourselves, would maintain that we find everywhere in consciousness extra-regarding impulse, directed towards something that is not pleasure; that in many cases the impulse is so far incompatible with the self-regarding that the two do not easily co-exist in the same moment of consciousness." A dim feeling that our impulses do not by any means always arise from any contemporaneous or anticipated pleasure, has, I cannot but think, been one chief cause of the acceptance of the intuitive theory of morality, and of the rejection of the utilitarian or "Greatest happiness" theory. With respect to the latter theory the standard and the motive of conduct have no doubt often been confused but they are really in some degree blended.

43. Good instances are given by Mr. Wallace in 'Scientific Opinion,' Sept. 15, 1869; and more fully in his 'Contibutions to the Theory of Natural Selection,' 1870, p. 353.

44. Tennyson, 'Idylls of the King,' p. 244.

45. 'The Thoughts of the Emperor M. Aurelius Antoninus,' Eng. Translat., 2nd. edit., 1869, p. 112. Marcus Aurelius was born A.D. 121.

46. Letter to Mr. Mill in Bain's 'Mental and Moral Science,' 1868, p. 722.

47. Maudsley, 'Body and Mind,' 1870, p. 60.

48. A writer in the 'North British Review' (July 1869, p. 531), well capable of forming a sound judgment, expresses himself strongly in favour of this conclusion. Mr. Lecky ('Hist. of Morals,' vol. i. p. 143) seems to a certain extent to coincide therein.

49. See his remarkable work on 'Hereditary Genius,' 1869, p. 349. The Duke of Argyll ('Primitive Man,' 1869, p. 188) has some good remarks on the contest in man's nature between right and wrong.

50. 'The Thoughts of Marcus Aurelius,' &c., p. 139.

Herbert Spencer

Ways of Judging Conduct

§17. Intellectual progress is by no one trait so adequately characterized, as by development of the idea of causation; since development of this idea involves development of so many other ideas. Before any way can be made, thought and language must have advanced far enough to render properties or attributes thinkable as such, apart from objects; which, in low stages of human intelligence, they are not. Again, even the simplest notion of cause, as we understand it, can be reached only after many like instances have been grouped into a simple generalization; and through all ascending steps, higher notions of causation imply wider notions of generality. Further, as there must be clustered in the mind, concrete cause of many kinds before there can emerge the conception of cause, apart from particular cause; it follows that progress in abstractness of thought is implied. Concomitantly, there is implied the recognition of constant relations among phenomena, generating ideas of uniformity of sequence and of co-existence—the idea of natural law. These advances can go on only as fast as perceptions and resulting thoughts, are made definite by the use of measures; serving to familiarize the mind with exact correspondence, truth, certainty. And only when growing science accumulates examples of quantitative relations, foreseen and verified, throughout a widening range of phenomena, does causation come to be conceived as necessary and universal. So that though all these cardinal conceptions aid one another in developing, we may properly say that the conception of causation especially depends for its development on the developments

From: *The Principles of Ethics*, vol. 1 (1893), pp. 47–83. (The first volume of *The Principles of Ethics* is a reprint of *The Data of Ethics*.)

of the rest; and therefore is the best measure of intellectual development at large.

How slowly, as a consequence of its dependence, the conception of causation evolves, a glance at the evidence shows. We hear with surprise of the savage who, falling down a precipice, ascribes the failure of his foothold to a malicious demon; and we smile at the kindred notion of the ancient Greek, that his death was prevented by a goddess who unfastened for him the thong of the helmet by which his enemy was dragging him. But daily, without surprise, we hear men who describe themselves as saved from ship-wreck by "divine interposition," who speak of having "providentially" missed a train which met with a fatal disaster, and who call it a "mercy" to have escaped injury from a falling chimney-pot—men who, in such cases, recognize physical causation no more than do the uncivilized or semicivilized. The Veddah who thinks that failure to hit an animal with his arrow, resulted from inadequate invocation of an ancestral spirit, and the Christian priest who says prayers over a sick man in the expectation that the course of his disease will so be stayed, differ only in respect of the agent from whom they expect supernatural aid and the phenomena to be altered by him: the necessary relations among causes and effects are tacitly ignored by the last as much as by the first. Deficient belief in causation is, indeed, exemplified even in those whose discipline has been specially fitted to generate this belief—even in men of science. For a generation after geologists had become uniformitarians in geology, they remained catastrophists in Biology: while recognizing none but natural agencies in the genesis of the Earth's crust, they ascribed to supernatural agency the genesis of the organisms on its surface. Nay more—among those who are convinced that living things in general have been evolved by the continued inter-action of forces everywhere operating, there are some who make an exception of man; or who, if they admit that his body has been evolved in the same manner as the bodies of other creatures, allege that his mind has been not evolved but specially created. If, then, universal and necessary causation is only now approaching full recognition, even by those whose investigations are daily re-illustrating it, we may expect to find it very little recognized among men at large, whose culture has not been calculated to impress them with it; and we may expect to find it least recognized by them in respect of those classes of phenomena amid which, in consequence of their complexity, causation is most difficult to trace—the psychical, the social, the moral.

Why do I here make these reflections on what seems an irrelevant subject? I do it because on studying the various ethical theories, I am struck with the fact that they are all characterized either by entire absence of the idea of causation, or by inadequate presence of it. Whether theological, political, intuitional, or utilitarian, they all display, if not in the same degree, still, each in a large degree, the defects which result from this lack. We will consider them in the order named.

§18. The school of morals properly to be considered as the still-extant representative of the most ancient school, is that which recognizes no other rule of conduct than the alleged will of God. It originates with the savage whose only restraint beyond fear of his fellow man, is fear of an ancestral spirit; and whose notion of moral duty as distinguished from his notion of social prudence, arises from this fear. Here the ethical doctrine and the religious doctrine are identical—have in no degree differentiated.

This primitive form of ethical doctrine, changed only by the gradual dying out multitudinous minor supernatural. Agents and accompanying development of one universal supernatural agent, survives in great strength down to our own day. Religious creeds, established and dissenting, all embody the belief that right and wrong are right and wrong simply in virtue of divine enactment. And this tacit assumption has passed from system of theology into system of morality; or rather, let us say that moral systems in early stages of development, little differentiated from the accompanying theological systems, have participated in this assumption. We see this in the works of the Stoics, as well as in the works of certain Christian moralists. Among recent ones I may instance the *Essays on the Principles of Morality*, by Jonathan Dymond, a Quaker, which makes "the authority of the Deity the sole ground of duty, and His communicated will the only ultimate standard of right and wrong." Nor is it by writers belonging to so relatively unphilosophical a sect only, that this view is held; it is held with a difference by writers belonging to sects contrariwise distinguished. For these assert that in the absence of belief in a deity, there would be no moral guidance; and this amounts to asserting that moral truths have no other origin than the will of God, which, if not considered as revealed in sacred writings, must be considered as revealed in conscience.

This assumption when examined, proves to be suicidal. If there are no other origins for right and wrong than this enunciated or intuited divine will, then, as alleged, were there no knowledge of the divine will, the acts now known as wrong would not be known as wrong. But if men did not know such acts to be wrong because contrary to the divine will, and so, in committing them, did not offend by disobedience; and if they could not otherwise know them to be wrong; then they might commit them indifferently with the acts now classed as right: the results, practically considered, would be the same. In so far as secular matters are concerned, there would be no difference between the two; for to say that in the affairs of life, any evils would arise from continuing to do the acts called wrong and ceasing to do the acts called right, is to say that these produce in themselves certain mischievous consequences and certain beneficial consequences; which is to say there is another source for moral rules than the revealed or inferred divine will: they may be established by induction from these observed consequence.

From this implication I see no escape. It must be either admitted or denied that the acts called good and the acts called bad, naturally conduce, the one to human well-being and the other to human ill-being. Is it admitted? Then the admission amounts to an assertion that the conduciveness is shown by experience; and this involves abandonment of the doctrine that there is no origin for morals apart from divine injunctions. Is it denied, that acts classed as good and bad differ in their effects? Then it is tacitly affirmed that human affairs would go on just as well in ignorance of the distinction; and the alleged need for commandments from God disappears.

And here we see how entirely wanting is the conception of cause. This notion that such and such actions are made respectively good and bad simply by divine injunction, is tantamount to the notion that such and such actions have not in the nature of things such and such kinds of effects. If there is not an unconsciousness of causation there is an ignoring of it.

§19. Following Plato and Aristotle, who make State-enactments the sources of right and wrong; and following Hobbes, who holds that there can be neither justice nor injustice till a regularly-constitute coercive power exists to issue and enforce commands; not a few modern thinkers hold that there is no other origin for good and bad in conduct than law. And this implies the belief that moral obligation originates with Acts of Parliament, and can be changed this way or that way by majorities. They ridicule the idea that men have any natural rights, and allege that rights are wholly results of convention: the necessary implication being that duties are so too. Before considering whether this theory coheres with outside truths, let us observe how far it is coherent within itself.

In pursuance of his argument that rights and duties originate with established social arrangements, Hobbes says—

> Where no covenant hath preceded, there hath no right been transferred, and every man has right to every thing; and consequently, no action can be unjust. But when a covenant is made, then to break it is *unjust*; and the definition of INJUSTICE, is no other than *the not performance of covenant*. And whatsoever is not unjust, is *just*. . . . Therefore before the names of just and unjust can have place, there must be some coercive power, to compel men equally to the performance of their covenants, by the terror of some punishment, greater than the benefit they expect by the breach of their covenant.[*]

---

[*] *Leviathan*, ch. xv.

In this paragraph the essential propositions are:—justice is fulfillment of covenant; fulfillment of covenant implies a power enforcing it: "just and unjust *can* have no place" unless men are compelled to perform their covenants. But this is to say that men *cannot* perform their covenants without compulsion. Grant that justice is performance of covenant. Now suppose it to be performed voluntarily: there is justice. In such case, however, there is justice in the absence of coercion; which is contrary to the hypothesis. The only conceivable rejoinder is an absurd one:—voluntary performance of covenant is impossible. Assert this, and the doctrine that right and wrong come into existence with the establishment of sovereignty is defensible. Decline to assert it, and the doctrine vanishes.

From inner incongruities pass now to outer ones. The justification for his doctrine of absolute civil authority as the source of rules of conduct, Hobbes seeks in the miseries entailed by the chronic war between man and man which must exist in the absence of society; holding that under any kind of government a better life is possible than in the state of nature. Now whether we accept the gratuitous and baseless theory that men surrendered their liberties to a sovereign power of some kind, with a view to the promised increase of satisfactions; or whether we accept the rational theory, inductively based, that a state of political subordination gradually became established through experience of the increased satisfactions derived under it; it equally remains obvious that the acts of the sovereign power have no other warrant than their subservience to the purpose for which it came into existence. The necessities which initiate government, themselves prescribe the actions of government. If its actions do not respond to the necessities, they are unwarranted. The authority of law is, then, by the hypothesis, derived; and can never transcend the authority of that from which it is derived. If general good, or welfare, or utility, is the supreme end; and if State-enactments are justified as means to this supreme end; then, State-enactments have such authority only as arises from conduciveness to this supreme end. When they are right, it is only because the original authority endorses them; and they are wrong if they do not bear its endorsement. That is to say, conduct cannot be made good or bad by law; but its goodness or badness is to the last determined by its effects as naturally furthering, or not furthering, the lives of citizens.

Still more when considered in the concrete, than when considered in the abstract, do the views of Hobbes and his disciples prove to be inconsistent. Joining in the general belief that without such security for life as enables men to go fearlessly about their business, there can be neither happiness nor prosperity, individual or general, they agree that measures for preventing murder, manslaughter, assault, &c., are requisite; and they advocate this or that penal system as furnishing the best deterrents: so arguing, both in respect of the evils and the remedies, that such and such causes will, by the nature of things, produce such and such effects. They recognize as inferable *à priori*, the truth that men will not lay by property unless they can count with great probability on reaping advantages from it; that consequently where robbery is unchecked, or where a rapacious ruler appropriates whatever earnings his subjects do not effectually hide, production will scarcely exceed immediate consumption; and that necessarily there will be none of that accumulation of capital required for social development, with all its aids to welfare. In neither case, however, do they perceive that they are tacitly asserting the need of certain restraints on conduct as deducible from the necessary conditions to complete life in the social state; and are so making the authority of law derivative and not original.

If it be said by any belonging to this school, that certain moral obligations to be distinguished as cardinal, must be admitted to have a basis deeper than legislation, and that it is for legislation not to create but merely to enforce them—if, I say, admitting this, they go on to allege a legislative origin for minor claims and duties; then we have the implication that whereas some kinds of conduct do, in the nature of things, tend to work out certain kinds of results, other kinds of conduct do not, in the nature of things, tend to work out certain kinds of results. While of these acts the natural good or bad consequences must be allowed, it may be denied of those acts that they have naturally good or bad consequences. Only after asserting this can it be consistently asserted that acts of the last class are made right or wrong by law. For if such acts have any intrinsic tendencies to produce beneficial or mischievous effects, then these intrinsic tendencies furnish the warrant for legislative requirements or interdicts; and to say that the requirements or interdicts make them right or wrong, is to say that they have no intrinsic tendencies to produce beneficial or mischievous effects.

Here, then, we have another theory betraying deficient consciousness of causation. An adequate consciousness of causation yields the irresistible belief that from the most serious to the most trivial actions of men in society, there must flow consequences which, quite apart from legal agency, conduce to well-being or ill-being in greater or smaller degrees. If murders are socially injurious whether forbidden by law or not—if one man's appropriation of another's gains by force, brings special and general evils, whether it is or is not contrary to a ruler's edicts—if non-fulfillment of contract, if cheating, if adulteration, work Mischief on a community in proportion as they are common, quite irrespective of prohibitions; then, is it not manifest that the like holds throughout all the details of men's behaviour? Is it not clear that when legislation insists on certain acts which have naturally beneficial effects, and forbids others that have naturally injurious effects, the acts are not made good or bad by legislation; but the legislation derived its authority from the natural effects of the acts? Non-recognition of this implies non-recognition of natural causation.

§20. Nor is it otherwise with the pure intuitionists, who hold that moral perceptions are innate in the original sense thinkers whose view is that men have been divinely endowed with moral faculties; not that these have resulted from inherited modifications caused by accumulated experiences.

To affirm that we know some things to be right and other things to be wrong, by virtue of a supernaturally-given conscience; and thus tacitly to affirm that we do not otherwise know right from wrong; is tacitly to deny any natural relations between acts and results. For if there exists any such relations, then we may ascertain by induction, or deduction, or both, what these are. And if it be admitted that because of such natural relations, happiness is produced by this kind of conduct, which is therefore to be approved, while misery is produced by that kind of conduct, which is therefore to be condemned; then it is admitted that the rightness or wrongness of actions are determinable, and must finally be determined, by the goodness or badness of the effects that flow from them; which is contrary to the hypothesis.

It may, indeed, be rejoined that effects are deliberately ignored by this school; which teaches that courses recognized by moral intuition as right, must be pursued without regard to consequence. But on inquiry it turns out that the consequences to be disregarded are particular consequences and not general consequences. When, for example, it is said that property lost by another ought to be restored irrespective of evil to the finder, who possibly may, by restoring it, lose that which would have preserved him from starvation; it is meant that in pursuance of the principle, the immediate and special consequences must be disregarded, not the diffused and remote consequences. By which we are shown that though theory forbids overt recognition of causation, there is an unavowed recognition of it.

And this implies the trait to which I am drawing attention. The conception of natural causation is so imperfectly developed, that there is only an indistinct consciousness that throughout the whole of human conduct, necessary relations of causes and effects prevail; and that from them are ultimately derived all moral rules, however much these may be proximately derived from moral intuitions.

§21. Strange to say even the utilitarian school, which, at first sight, appears to be distinguished from the rest by recognizing natural causation, is, if not so far from complete recognition of it, yet very far.

Conduct, according to its theory, is to be estimated by observation of results. When, in sufficiently numerous cases, it has been found that behaviour of this kind works evil while behaviour of that kind works good, these kinds of behaviour are to be judged as wrong and right respectively. Now though it seems that the origin of moral rules in natural causes, is thus asserted by implication, it is but partially asserted. The implication is simply that we are to ascertain by induction that such and such mischiefs or benefits *do go* along with such and such acts; and are then to infer that the like relations will hold in future. But acceptance of these generalizations and the inferences from them, does not amount to recognition of causation in the full sense of the word. So long as only *some* relation between cause and effect in conduct is recognized, and not *the* relation, a completely-scientific form of knowledge has not been reached. At present, utilitarians pay no attention to this distinction. Even when it is pointed out, they disregard the fact that empirical utilitarianism is but a transitional form to be passed through on the way to rational utilitarianism. In a letter to Mr. Mill, written some sixteen years ago, repudiating the title anti-utilitarian which he had applied to me (a letter subsequently published in Mr. Bain's work on *Mental and Moral Science*), I endeavored to make clear the difference above indicated; and I must here quote certain passages from that letter.

> The view for which I contend is, that Morality properly so-called—the science of right conduct—has for its object to determine *how* and *why* certain modes of conduct are detrimental, and certain other modes beneficial. These good and bad results cannot be accidental but must be necessary consequences of the constitution of things; and I conceive it to be the business of Moral Science to deduce, from the laws of life and the conditions of existence, what kinds of action necessarily tend to produce happiness, and what kinds to produce unhappiness. Having done this, its deductions are to be recognized as laws of conduct; and are to be conformed to irrespective of a direct estimation of happiness of misery. Perhaps an analogy will most clearly show my meaning. During its early stages, planetary Astronomy consisted of nothing more than accumulated observations respecting the positions and motions of the sun and planets; from which accumulated observations it came by and by to be empirically predicted, with an approach to truth, that certain of the heavenly bodies would have certain positions at certain times. But the modern science of planetary Astronomy consists

of deductions from the law of gravitation—deductions showing why the celestial bodies *necessarily* occupy certain places at certain times. Now, the kind of relation which thus exists between ancient and modern Astronomy, is analogous to the kind of relation which, I conceive, exists between the Expediency-Morality and Moral Science properly so called. And the objections which I have to the current Utilitarianism is, that it recognizes no more developed form of Morality—does not see that it has reached but the initial stage of Moral Science.

Doubtless if utilitarians are asked whether it can be by mere chance that this kind of action works evil and that works good, they will answer—No: they will admit that such sequences are parts of a necessary order among phenomena. But though this truth is beyond question; and though if there are causal relations between acts and their results, rules of conduct can become scientific only when they are deduced from these causal relations; there continues to be entire satisfaction with that form of utilitarianism in which these causal relations are practically ignored. It is supposed that in future, as now, utility is to be determined only by observation of result; and that there is no possibility of knowing by deduction from fundamental principles, what conduct *must* be detrimental and what conduct *must* be beneficial.

§22. To make more specific that conception of ethical science here indicated, let me present it under a concrete aspect; beginning with a simple illustration and complicating this illustration by successive steps.

If, by tying its main artery, we stop most of the blood going to a limb, then, for as long as the limb performs its function, those parts which are called into play must be wasted faster than they are repaired: whence eventually disablement. The relation between due receipt of nutritive matters through its arteries, and due discharge of its duties by the limb, is a part of the physical order. If, instead of cutting off the supply to a particular limb, we bleed the patient largely, so drafting away the materials needed for repairing not one limb but all limbs, and not limbs only but viscera, there results both a muscular debility and an enfeeblement of the vital functions. Here, again, cause and effect are necessarily related. The mischief that results from great depletion, result apart from any divine command, or political enactment, or moral intuition. Now advance a step. Suppose the man to be prevented from taking in enough of the solid and liquid food containing those substances continually abstracted from his blood in repairing his tissue: suppose he has cancer of the esophagus and cannot swallow—what happens? By this indirect depletion, as by direct depletion, he is inevitably made incapable of performing the actions of one in health. In this case, as in the other cases, the connection between cause and effect is one that cannot be established, or altered, by any authority external to the phenomena themselves. Again, let us say that instead of being stopped after passing his mouth, that which he would swallow is stopped before reaching his mouth; so that day after day the man is required to waste his tissues in getting food, and day after day the food he has got to meet this waste, he is forcibly prevented from eating. As before, the progress towards death by starvation is inevitable—the connection between acts and effects is independent of any alleged theological or political authority. And similarly if, being forced by the whip to labour, no adequate return in food is supplied to him, there are equally certain evils, equally independent of sacred or secular enactment. Pass now to those actions more commonly thought of as the occasion for rules of conduct. Let us assume the man to be continually robbed of that which was given him in exchange for his labour, and by which he was to make up for nervomuscular expenditure and renew his powers. No less than before is the connexion between conduct and consequence rooted in the constitution of things; unchangeable by State-made law, and not needing establishment by empirical generalization. If the action by which the man is affected is a stage further away from the results, or produces result of a less decisive kind, still we see the same basis for morality in the physical order. Imagine that payment for his services is made partly in bad coin; or that it is delayed beyond the date agreed upon; or that what he buys to eat is adulterated with innutritive matter. Manifestly, by any of these deeds which we condemn as unjust, and which are punished by law, there is, as before, an interference with the normal adjustment of physiological repair to physiological waste. Nor is it otherwise when we pass to kinds of conduct still more remotely operative. If he is hindered from enforcing his claim— if class-predominance prevents him from proceeding, or if a bribed judge gives a verdict contrary evidence, or if a witness swears falsely; have not these deeds, though they affect him more indirectly, the same original cause for their wrongness? Even with actions which work diffused and indefinite mischiefs it is the same. Suppose that the man, instead of being dealt with fraudulently, is calumniated. There is, as before, a hindrance to the carrying on of life-sustaining activities; for the loss of character detrimentally affects his business. Nor is this all. The mental depression caused partially incapacitates him for energetic activity, and perhaps brings on ill-health. So that maliciously or carelessly propagating false statements, tends both to diminish his life and to diminish his ability to maintain life. Hence its flagitousness. Moreover, if we trace to their ultimate ramifications the effects wrought by any of these acts which morality called intuitive reprobates—if we ask what results not to the individual himself only, but also to his belongings—if we observe how impoverishment hinders the rearing of his children, by entailing under-feeding or inadequate clothing, resulting perhaps in the death of some and the constitutional injury of others; we see that by the necessary connexions of things these acts, besides tending primarily to lower the life of the individual aggressed upon, tend, secondarily, to lower the lives of all his family, and, thirdly, to lower the life of society at large; which is damaged by whatever damages its units.

A more distinct meaning will now be seen in the statement that the utilitarianism which recognizes only the principles of conduct reached by induction, is but preparatory to the utilitarianism which deduces these principles from the processes of life as carried on under established conditions of existence.

§22a. Thus, then, is justified the allegation made at the outset, that, irrespective of their distinctive characters and their special tendencies, all the current methods of ethics have one general defect—they neglect ultimate causal connexions. Of course I do not mean that they wholly ignore the natural consequences of actions; but I mean that they recognize them only incidentally. They do not erect into a method the ascertaining of necessary relations between causes and effects, and deducing rules of conduct from formulated statements of them.

Every science begins by accumulating observations, and presently generalizes these empirically; but only when it reaches the stage at which its empirical generalizations are included in a rational generalization, does it become developed science. Astronomy has already passed through its successive stages: first collections of facts; then inductions from them; and lastly deductive interpretations of these,—as corollaries from a universal principle of action among masses in space. Accounts of structures and tabulations of strata, grouped and compared, have led gradually to the assigning of various classes of geological changes to igneous and aqueous actions; and it is now tacitly admitted that Geology becomes a science proper, only as fast as such changes are explained in terms of those natural processes which have arisen in the cooling and solidifying Earth, exposed to the Sun's heat and the action of the moon upon its ocean. The science of life has been, and is still, exhibiting a like series of steps: the evolution of organic forms at large, is being affiliated on physical actions in operation from the beginning; and the vital phenomena each organism presents, are coming to be understood as connected sets of changes, in parts formed of matters that are affected by certain forces and disengage other forces. So is it with mind. Early ideas concerning thought and feeling ignored everything like cause, save in recognizing those effects of habit which were forced on men's attention and expressed in proverbs; but there are growing up interpretations of thought and feeling as correlates of the actions and reactions of a nervous structure, that is influenced by outer changes and works in the body adapted changes: the implication being that Psychology becomes a science, as fast as these relations of phenomena are explained as consequences of ultimate principles. Sociology, too, represented down to recent times only by stray idea about social organization, scattered through the masse of worthless gossip furnished us by historians, is coming to be recognized by some as also a science; and such adumbrations of it as have from time to time appeared in the shape of empirical generalizations, are now beginning to assume the character of generalizations made coherent by derivation from cause lying in human nature placed under given conditions. Clearly, then, Ethics, which is a science dealing with the conduct of associated human beings, regarded under one of its aspects, has to undergo a like transformation; and, at present undeveloped, can be considered a developed science only when it has undergone this transformation.

A preparation in the simpler sciences is pre-supposed. Ethics has a physical aspect; since it treats of human activities which, in common with all expenditures of energy, conform to the law of the persistence of energy: moral principles must conform to physical necessities. It has a biological aspect; since it concerns certain effects, inner and outer, individual and social, of the vital changes going on in the highest type of animal. It has a psychological aspect; for its subject-matter is an aggregate of actions that are prompted by feelings and guided by intelligence. And it has a sociological aspect; for these actions, some of them directly and all of them indirectly, affect associated beings.

What is the implication? Belonging under one aspect to each of these sciences—physical, biological, psychological, sociological,—it can find its ultimate interpretations only in those fundamental truths which are common to all of them. Already we have concluded in a general way that conduct at large, including the conduct Ethics deals with, is to be fully understood only as an aspect of evolving life; and now we are brought to this conclusion in a more special way.

§23. Here, then, we have to enter on the consideration of moral phenomena as phenomena of evolution; being forced to do this by finding that they form a part of the aggregate of phenomena which evolution has wrought out.

If the entire visible universe has been evolved—if the solar system as a whole, the earth as a part of it, the life in general which the earth bears, as well as that of each individual organism—if the mental phenomena displayed by all creatures, up to the highest, in common with the phenomena presented by aggregates of these highest—if one and all conform to the laws of evolution; then the necessary implication is that those phenomena of conduct in these highest creatures with which morality is concerned, also conform. The preceding volumes have prepared the way for dealing with morals as thus conceived. Utilizing the conclusions they contain, let us now observe what data are furnished by these. We will take in succession—the physical view, the biological view, the psychological view, and the sociological view.

Chapter V.
The Physical View

§24. Every moment we pass instantly from men's perceived actions to the motives implied by them; and so are led to formulate these actions in mental terms rather than in bodily terms. Thoughts and feelings are referred to when we speak of any one's deed with praise or blame; not those outer manifestation which reveal the thoughts and feelings. Hence we become oblivious of the truth that conduct as actually experienced, consist of changes recognized by touch, sight and healing.

This habit of contemplating only the psychical face of conduct, is so confirmed that an effort is required to contemplate only the physical face. Undeniable as it is that another's behaviour to us is made up of movements of his body and limbs, of his facial muscles, and of his vocal apparatus; it yet seems paradoxical to say that these are the only elements of conduct really known by us, while the elements of conduct which we exclusively think of as constituting it, are not known but inferred.

Here, however, ignoring for the time being the inferred elements in conduct, we have to deal with the perceived elements—we have to observe its traits considered as a set of combined motions. Taking the evolution point of view, and remembering that while an aggregate evolves, not only the matter composing it, but also the motion of that matter, passes from an indefinite incoherent homogeneity to a definite coherent heterogeneity, we have now to ask whether conduct as it rises to its higher forms, displays in increasing degrees these characters; and whether it does not display them in the greatest degree when it reaches that highest form which we call moral.

§25. It will be convenient to deal first with the trait of increasing coherence. The conduct of lowly-organized creatures is broadly contrasted with the conduct of highly-organized creatures, in having its successive portions feebly connected. The random movements which an animalcule makes, have severally no reference to movements made a moment before; nor do they affect in specific ways the movements made immediately after. To-day's wanderings of a fish in search of food, though perhaps showing by their adjustments to catching different kinds of prey at different hours, a slightly-determined order, are unrelated to the wanderings of yesterday and to-morrow. But such more developed creatures as birds, show us in the building of nests, the sitting on eggs, the rearing of chicks, and the aiding of them after they fly, sets of motions which form a dependent series, extending over a considerable period. And on observing the complexity of the acts performed in fetching and fixing the fibers of the nest or in catching and bringing to the young each portion of food, we discover in the combined motions, lateral cohesion as well as longitudinal cohesion.

Man, even in his lowest state, displays in his conduct far more coherent combinations of motions. By the elaborate manipulations gone through in making weapons that are to serve for the chase next year, or in building canoes and wigwams for permanent uses—by acts of aggression and defense which are connected with injuries long since received or committed, the savage exhibits an aggregate of motions which, in some of its parts, holds together over great periods. Moreover, if we consider the many movements implied by the transactions of each day, in the wood, on the water, in the camp, in the family; we see that this coherent aggregate of movements is composed of many minor aggregates, that are severally coherent within themselves and with one another. In civilized man this trait of developed conduct becomes more conspicuous still. Be his business what it may, its processes involve relatively-numerous dependent motions; and day by day it is so carried on as to show connexions between present motions and motions long gone by, as well as motions anticipated in the distant future. Besides the many doings, related to one another, which the farmer goes through in looking after his cattle, directing his labourers, keeping an eye on his dairy, buying his implements, selling his produce, &c.; the business of getting his lease involves numerous combined movements on which the movements of subsequent years depend; and in manuring his fields with a view to larger returns, or putting down drains with the like motive, he is performing acts which are parts of a coherent combination relatively extensive. That the like holds of the shopkeeper, manufacturer, banker, is manifest; and this increased coherence of conduct among the civilized, will strike us even more when we remember how its parts are often continued in a connected arrangement through life, for the purpose of making a fortune, founding a family, gaining a seat in parliament.

Now mark that a greater coherence among its component motions, broadly distinguishes the conduct we call moral from the conduct we call immoral. The application of the word dissolute to the last, and of the word self-restrained to the first, implies this—implies that conduct of the lower kind, constituted of disorderly acts, has its parts relatively loose in their relations with one another; while conduct of the higher kind, habitually following a fixed order, so gains a characteristic unity and coherence. In proportion as the conduct is what we call moral, it exhibits comparatively settled connexions between antecedents and consequents; for the doing right implies that under given conditions the combined motions constituting conduct will follow in a way that can be specified. Contrariwise, in the conduct of one whose principles are not high, the sequences of motions are doubt-ful. He may pay the money or he may not; he may keep his appointment or he may fail; he may tell the truth or he may lie. The words trustworthiness and untrustworthiness, as used to characterize the two respectively, sufficiently imply that the actions of the one can be foreknown while those of the other cannot; and this implies that the successive move-ments composing the one bear more constant relations to one another than do those composing the other—are more coherent.

§26. Indefiniteness accompanies incoherence in conduct that is little evolved; and throughout the ascending stages of evolving conduct, there is an increasingly-definite co-ordination of the motions constituting it.

Such changes of form as the rudest protozoa show us, are utterly vague—admit of no precise description; and though in higher kinds the movements of the parts are more definable, yet the movement of the whole in respect of direc-tion is indeterminate: there is no adjustment of it to this or the other point in space. In such coelenterate animals as polypes, we see the parts moving in ways which lack preci-sion; and in one of the locomotive forms, as a medusa, the course taken, otherwise at random, can be described only as one which carries it towards the light, where degrees of light and darkness are present. Among annulose creatures the contrast between the track of a worm, turning this way or that at hazard, and the definite course taken by a bee in its flight from flower to flower or back to the hive, shows us the same thing: the bee's acts in building cells and feeding lar-vae further exhibiting precision in the simultaneous move-ments as well as in the successive movements. Though the motions made by a fish in pursuing its prey have consider-able definiteness, yet they are of a simple kind, and are in this respect contrasted with the many definite motions of body, head, and limbs gone through by a carnivorous mammal in the course of waylaying, running down, and seizing a herbivore; and further, the fish shows us none of those definitely-adjusted sets of motions which in the mam-mal subserve the rearing of young.

Much greater definiteness, if not in the combined movements forming single acts, still in the adjustments of many combined acts to various purposes, characterizes human conduct, even in its lowest stages. In making and using weapons and in the maneuverings of savage warfare, numerous movements all precise in their adaptations to proximate ends, are arranged for the achievement of remote ends, with a precision not paralleled among lower creatures. The lives of civilized men exhibit this trait far more conspicuously. Each industrial art exemplifies the effects of movements which are severally definite; and which are definitely arranged in simultaneous and successive order. Business transactions of every kind are characterized by exact relations between the sets of motions constituting acts, and the purposes fulfilled, in time, place, and quantity. Further, the daily routine of each person shows us in its periods and amounts of activity, of rest, of relaxation, a measured arrangement which is not shown us by the doings of the wandering savage; who has no fixed times for hunting, sleeping, feeding, or any one kind of action.

Moral conduct differs from immoral conduct in the same manner and in a like degree. The conscientious man is exact in all his transactions. He supplies a precise weight for a specified sum; he gives a definite quality in fulfillment of understanding; he pays the full amount he bargained to do. In times as well as in quantities, his acts answer completely to anticipations. If he has made a business contract he is to the day; if an appointment he is to the minute. Similarly in respect to truth: his statements correspond accurately with the facts. It is thus too in his family life. He maintains marital relations that are definite in contrast with the relations that result from breach of the marriage contract; and as a father, fitting his behaviour with care to the nature of each child and to the occasion, he avoids the too much and the too little of praise or blame, reward or penalty. Nor is it otherwise in his miscellaneous acts. To say that he deals equitably with those he employs, whether they behave well or ill, is to say that he adjusts his acts to their deserts; and to say that he is judicious in his charities, is to say that he portions out his aid with discrimination instead of distributing it indiscriminately to good and bad, as do those who have no adequate sense of their social responsibilities.

That progress towards rectitude of conduct is progress towards duly-proportioned conduct, and that duly-proportioned conduct is relatively definite, we may see from another point of view. One of the traits of conduct we call immoral, is excess; while moderation habitually characterizes moral conduct. Now excesses imply extreme divergences of actions from some medium, while maintenance of the medium is implied by moderation; whence it follows that actions of the last kind can be defined more nearly than those of the first. Clearly conduct which, being unrestrained, runs into great and incalculable oscillations, therein differs from restrained conduct of which, by implication, the oscillations fall within narrower limits. And falling within narrower limits necessitates relative definiteness of movements.

§27. That throughout the ascending forms of life, along with increasing heterogeneity of structure and function, there goes increasing heterogeneity of conduct—increasing diversity in the sets of external motions and combined sets of such motions—need not be shown in detail. Nor need it be shown that becoming relatively great in the motions constituting the conduct of the uncivilized man, this heterogeneity has become still greater in those which the civilized man goes through. We may pass at once to that further degree of the like contrast which we see on ascending from the conduct of the immoral to that of the moral.

Instead of recognizing this contrast, most readers will be inclined to identify a moral life with a life little varied in its activities. But here we come upon a defect in the current conception of morality. This comparative uniformity in the aggregate of motions, which goes along with morality as commonly conceived, is not only not moral but is the reverse of moral. The better a man fulfils every requirement of life, alike as regards his own body and mind, as regards the bodies and minds of those dependent on him, and as regards the bodies and minds of his fellow-citizens, the more varied do his activities become. The more fully he does all these things, the more heterogeneous must be his movements.

One who satisfies personal needs only, goes through, other things equal, less multiform processes than one who also administers to the needs of wife and children. Supposing there are no other differences, the addition of family relations necessarily renders the actions of the man who fulfils the duties of husband and parent, more heterogeneous than those of the man who has no such duties to fulfil, or, having them, does not fulfil them; and to say that his actions are more heterogeneous is to say that there is a greater heterogeneity in the combined motions he goes through. The like holds of social obligations. These, in proportion as a citizen duly performs them, complicate his movements considerably. If he is helpful to inferiors dependent on him, if he takes a part in political agitation, if he aids in diffusing knowledge, he, in each of these ways, adds to his kinds of activity—makes his set of movements more multiform; so different from the man who is the slave of one desire or group of desires.

Though it is unusual to consider as having a moral aspect, those activities which culture involves, yet to the few who hold that due exercise of all the higher faculties, intellectual and aesthetic, must be included in the conception of complete life, here identified with the ideally moral life, it will be manifest that a further heterogeneity is implied by them. For each of such activities, constituted by that play of these faculties which is eventually added to their life-subserving uses, adds to the multiformity of the aggregated motions.

Briefly, then, if the conduct is the best possible on every occasion, it follows that as the occasions are endlessly varied the acts will be endlessly varied to suit—the heterogeneity in the combinations of motions will be extreme.

§28. Evolution in conduct considered under its moral aspect; is, like all other evolution, towards equilibrium. I do not mean that it is towards the equilibrium reached at death, though this is, of course, the final state which the evolution of the highest man has in common with all lower evolution; but I mean that it is towards a moving equilibrium.

We have seen that maintaining life, expressed in physical terms, is maintaining a balanced combination of internal actions in face of external forces tending to overthrow it; and we have seen that advance towards a higher life, has been an acquirement of ability to maintain the balance for a longer period, by the successive additions of organic appliance which by their actions counteract, more and more fully, the disturbing forces. Here, then, we are led to the conclusion that the life called moral is one in which this maintenance of the moving equilibrium reaches completeness, or approaches most nearly to completeness.

This truth is clearly disclosed on observing how those physiological rhythms which vaguely show themselves when organization begins, become more regular as well as more various in their kinds, as organization advances. Periodicity is but feebly marked in the actions, inner and outer, of the rudest types. Where life is low there is passive dependence on the accidents of the environment; and this entails great irregularities in the vital processes. The taking in of food by a polype is at intervals now short now very long, as circumstances determine; and the utilization of it is by a slow dispersion of the absorbed part through the tissues, aided only by the irregular movements of the creature's body; while such aeration as is effected is similarly without a trace of rhythm. Much higher up we still find very imperfect periodicities; as in the inferior molluscs which, though possessed of vascular systems, have no proper circulation, but merely a slow movement of the crude blood, now in one direction through the vessels and then, after a pause, in the opposite direction. Only with well-developed structures do there come a rhythmical pulse and a rhythm of the respiratory action. And then in birds and mammals, along with great rapidity and regularity in these essential rhythms, and along with a consequently great vital activity and therefore great expenditure, comparative regularity in the rhythm of the alimentary actions is established, as well as in the rhythm of activity and rest; since the rapid waste to which rapid pulsation and respiration are instrumental, necessitates tolerably regular supplies of nutriment, as well as recurring intervals of sleep during which repair may overtake waste. And from these stages the moving equilibrium characterized by such inter-dependent rhythms, is continually made better by the counteracting of more and more of those actions which tend to perturb it. So it is as we ascend from savage to civilized and from the lowest among the civilized to the highest. The rhythm of external actions required to maintain the rhythm of internal actions, becomes at once more complicated and more complete; making them into a better moving equilibrium. The irregularities which their conditions of existence entail on primitive men, continually cause wide deviations from the mean state of the moving equilibrium—wide oscillations; which imply imperfection of it for the time being, and bring about its premature overthrow. In such civilized men as we call ill-conducted, frequent perturbations of the moving equilibrium are caused by those excesses characterizing a career in which the periodicities are much broken; and a common result is that the rhythm of the internal actions being often deranged, the moving equilibrium, rendered by so much imperfect, is generally shortened in duration. While one in whom the internal rhythms are best maintained is one by whom the external actions required to fulfil all needs and duties, severally performed on the recurring occasions, conduce to a moving equilibrium that is at once involved and prolonged.

Of course the implication is that the man who thus reaches the limit of evolution, exists in a society congruous with his nature—is a man among men similarly constituted, who are severally in harmony with that social environment which they have formed. This is, indeed, the only possibility. For the production of the highest type of man, can go on only *pari passu* with the production of the highest type of society. The implied conditions are those before described as accompanying the most evolved conduct—conditions under which each can fulfil all his needs and rear the due number of progeny, not only without hindering others from doing the like, but while aiding them in doing the like. And evidently, considered under its physical aspect, the conduct of the individual so constituted, and associated with like individuals, is one in which all the actions, that is the combined motions of all kinds, have become such as duly to meet every daily process, every ordinary occurrence, and every contingency in his environment. Complete life in a complete society is but another name for complete equilibrium between the co-ordinated activities of each social unit and those of the aggregate of units.

§29. Even to readers of preceding volumes, and still more to other readers, there will seem a strangeness, or even an absurdity, in this presentation of moral conduct in physical terms. It has been needful to make it however. If that re-distribution of matter and motion constituting evolution goes on in all aggregates, its laws must be fulfilled in the most developed being as in every other thing; and his actions, when decomposed into motions, must exemplify its laws. This we find that they do. There is an entire correspondence between moral evolution and evolution as physically defined.

Conduct as actually known to us in perception and not as interpreted into the accompanying feelings and ideas, consists of combined motions. On ascending through the various grades of animate creatures, we find these combined motions characterized by increasing coherence, increasing definiteness considered singly and in their co-ordinated groups, and increasing heterogeneity; and in advancing from lower to higher types of man, as well as in advancing from the less moral to the more moral type of man, these traits of evolving conduct become more marked still. Further, we see that the increasing coherence, definiteness, and heterogeneity, of the combined motions, are instrumental to the better maintenance of a moving equilibrium. Where the evolution is small this is very imperfect and soon cut short; with advancing evolution, bringing greater power and intelligence, it becomes more steady and longer continued in face of adverse actions; in the human race at large it is comparatively regular and enduring; and its regularity and enduringness are greatest in the highest.

Chapter VI.
The Biological View

§30. The truth that the ideally moral man is one in whom the moving equilibrium is perfect, or approaches nearest to perfection, becomes, when translated into physiological language, the truth that he is one in whom the functions of all kinds are duly fulfilled. Each function has some relation, direct or indirect, to the needs of life: the fact of its existence as a result of evolution, being itself a proof that it has been entailed, immediately or remotely, by the adjustment of inner actions to outer actions. Consequently, non-fulfillment of it in normal proportion is nonfulfilment of a requisite to complete life. If there is defective discharge of the function, the organism experiences some detrimental result caused by the inadequacy. If the discharge is in excess, there is entailed a reaction upon the other functions, which in some way diminishes their efficiencies.

It is true that during full vigour, while the momentum of the organic actions is great, the disorder caused by moderate excess or defect of any one function, soon disappears—the balance is re-established. But it is none the less true that always some disorder results from excess or defect, that it influences every function bodily and mental, and that it constitutes a lowering of the life for the time being.

Beyond the temporary falling short of complete life implied by undue or inadequate discharge of a function, there is entailed, as an ultimate result, decreased length of life. If some function is habitually performed in excess of the requirement, or in defect of the requirement; and if, as a consequence, there is an often-repeated perturbation of the functions at large; there results some chronic derangement in the balance of the functions. Necessarily reacting on the structures, and registering in them its accumulated effects, this derangement works a general deterioration; and when the vital energies begin to decline, the moving equilibrium, further from perfection than it would else have been, is sooner overthrown: death is more or less premature.

Hence the moral man is one whose functions—many and varied in their kinds as we have seen—are all discharged in degrees duly adjusted to the conditions of existence.

§31. Strange as the conclusion looks, it is nevertheless a conclusion to be here drawn, that the performance of every function is, in a sense, a moral obligation. It is usually thought that morality requires us only to restrain such vital activities as, in our present state, are often pushed to excess, or such as conflict with average welfare, special or general; but it also requires us to carry on these vital activities up to their normal limits. All the animal functions, in common with all the higher functions, have, as thus understood, their imperativeness. While recognizing the fact that in our state of transition, characterized by very imperfect adaptation of constitution to conditions, moral obligations of supreme kinds often necessitate conduct which is physically injurious; we must also recognize the fact that, considered apart from other effects, it is immoral so to treat the body as in any way to diminish the fullness or vigour of its vitality. Hence results one test of actions. There may in every case be put the questions—Does the action tend to maintenance of complete life for the time being? and does it tend to prolongation of life to its full extent? To answer yes or no to either of these questions, is implicitly to class the action as right or wrong in respect of its immediate bearings, whatever it may be in respect of its remote bearings.

The seeming paradoxicalness of this statement results from the tendency, so difficult of avoidance, to judge a conclusion which pre-supposes an ideal humanity, by its applicability to humanity as now existing. The foregoing conclusion refers to that highest conduct in which, as we have seen, the evolution of conduct terminates—that conduct in which the making of all adjustments of acts to ends subserving complete individual life, together with all those subserving maintenance of offspring and preparation of them for maturity, not only consist with the making of like adjustments by others, but furthers it. And this conception of conduct in its ultimate form, implies the conception of a nature having such conduct for its spontaneous outcome—the product of its normal activities. So understanding the matter, it becomes manifest that under such conditions, any falling short of function, as well as any excess of function, implies deviation from the best conduct or from perfectly moral conduct.

§32. Thus far in treating of conduct from the biological point of view, we have considered its constituent actions under their physiological aspects only; leaving out of sight their psychological aspects. We have recognized the bodily changes and have ignored the accompanying mental changes. And at first sight it seems needful for us here to do this; since taking account of states of consciousness, apparently implies an inclusion of the psychological view in the biological view.

This is not so however. As we pointed out in the *Principles of Psychology* (§§52, 53) we enter upon psychology proper, only when we begin to treat of mental states and their relations, considered as referring to external agents and their relations. While we concern ourselves exclusively with modes of mind as correlatives of nervous changes, we are treating of what was there distinguished as aestho-physiology. We pass to psychology only when we consider the correspondence between the connexions among subjective state and the connexions among objective actions. Here, then, without transgressing the limits of our immediate topic, we may deal with feelings and functions in their mutual dependencies.

We cannot omit doing this; because the psychical changes which accompany many of the physical changes in the organism, are biological factors in two ways. Those feelings, classed as sensations, which, directly initiated in the bodily framework, go along with certain states of the vital organs and more conspicuously with certain states of the external organs, now serve mainly as guides to the performance of functions but partly as stimuli, and now serve mainly as stimuli but in a smaller degree as guides. Visual sensations which, as co-ordinated, enable us to direct our movements, also, if vivid, raise the rate of respiration; while sensations of cold and heat, greatly depressing or raising the vital actions, serve also for purposes of discrimination. So, too, the feelings classed as emotions, which are not localizable in the bodily framework, act in more general ways, alike as guides and stimuli—having influences over the performance of functions more potent even than have most sensations. Fear, at the same time that it urges flight and evolves the forces spent in it, also affects the heart and the alimentary canal; while joy prompting persistence in the actions bringing it, simultaneously exalts the visceral processes.

Hence in treating of conduct under its biological aspect, we are compelled to consider that inter-action of feelings and functions, which is essential to animal life in all its more developed forms.

§33. In the *Principles of Psychology*, §124, it was shown that necessarily, throughout the animate world at large, "pains are the correlatives of actions injurious to the organism, while pleasures are the correlatives of actions conducive to its welfare"; since "it is an inevitable deduction from the hypothesis of Evolution, that races of sentient creatures could have come into existence under no other conditions." The argument was as follows:—

> If we substitute for the word Pleasure the equivalent phrase—a feeling which we seek to bring into consciousness and retain there, and if we substitute for the word Pain the equivalent phrase—a feeling which we seek to get out of consciousness and to keep out; we see at once that, if the states of consciousness which a creature endeavours to maintain are the correlatives of injurious action, and if the state of consciousness which it endeavours to expel are the correlatives of beneficial actions, it must quickly disappear through persistence in the injurious and avoidance of the beneficial. In other words, those races of beings only can have survived in which, on the average, agreeable or desired feelings went along with activities conducive to the maintenance of life, while disagreeable and habitually-avoided feelings went along with activities directly or indirectly destructive of life; and there must ever have been, other things equal, the most numerous and long continued survival among races in which these adjustments of feelings to actions were the best, tending ever to bring about perfect adjustment

Fit connexions between acts and results must establish themselves in living things, even before consciousness arises;

and after the rise of consciousness these connexions can change in so other way than to become better established. At the very outset, life is maintained by persistence in acts which conduce to it, and desistance from acts which impede it; and whenever sentiency makes its appearance as an accompaniment, its forms must be such that in the one case the produced feeling is of a kind that will be sought—pleasure, and in the other case is of a kind that will be shunned—pain. Observe the necessity of these relations as exhibited in the concrete.

A plant which envelops a buried bone with a plexus of rootlets, or a potato which directs its blanched shoots towards a grating through which light comes into the cellar, shows us that the changes which outer agents themselves set up in its tissues are changes which aid the utilization of these agents. If we ask what would happen if a plant's roots grew not towards the place where there was moisture but away from it, or if its leaves, enabled by light to assimilate, nevertheless bent themselves toward the darkness; we see that death would result in the absence of the existing adjustments. This general relation is still better shown in an insectivorous plant, such as the *Dionoea muscipula,* which keeps its trap closed round animal matter but not round other matter. Here it is manifest that the stimulus arising from the first part of the absorbed substance, itself sets up those actions by which the mass of the substance is utilized for the plant's benefit. When we pass from vegetal organisms to unconscious animal organisms, we see a like connexion between proclivity and advantage. On observing how the tentacles of a polype attach themselves to, and begin to close round, a living creature, or some animal substance, while they are indifferent to the touch of other substance; we are similarly shown that diffusion of some of the nutritive juices into the tentacles, which is an incipient assimilation, causes the motions effecting prehension. And it is obvious that life would cease were these relations reversed. Nor is it otherwise with this fundamental connexion between contact with food and taking in of food, among conscious creatures, up to the very highest. Tasting a substance implies the passage of its molecules through the mucous membrane of the tongue and palate; and this absorption, when it occurs with a substance serving for food, is but a commencement of the absorption carried on throughout the alimentary canal. Moreover, the sensation accompanying this absorption, when it is of the kind produced by food, initiates at the place where it is strongest, in front of the pharynx, an automatic act of swallowing, in a manner rudely analogous to that in which the stimulus of absorption in a polype's tentacles initiates prehension.

If from these processes and relations that imply contact between a creature's surface and the substance it takes in, we turn to those set up by diffused particles of the substance, constituting to conscious creatures its odour, we meet a kindred general truth. Just as, after contact, some molecules of a mass of food are absorbed by the part touched, and excite the act of prehension; so are absorbed such of its molecules as, spreading through the water, reach the organism; and, being absorbed by it, excite those actions by which contact with the mass is effected. If the physical stimulation caused by the dispersed particles is not accompanied by consciousness, still the motor changes set up must conduce to survival of the organism if they are such as end in contact; and there must be relative in nutrition and mortality of organisms in which the produced contractions do not bring about this result. Nor can it be questioned that whenever and wherever the physical stimulation has a concomitant sentiency, this must be such as consists with, and conduces to, movement towards the nutritive matter: it must be not a repulsive but an attractive sentiency. And this which holds with the lowest consciousness, must hold throughout; as we see it do in all such superior creatures as are drawn to their food by odour.

Besides those movements which cause locomotion, those which effect seizure must no less certainly become thus adjusted. The molecular changes caused by absorption of nutritive matter from organic substance in contact, or from adjacent organic substance, initiate motions which are indefinite where the organization is low, and which become more definite with the advance of organization. At the outset, while the undifferentiated protoplasm is everywhere absorbent and everywhere contractile, the changes of form initiated by the physical stimulation of adjacent nutritive matter are vague, and ineffectually adapted to utilization of it; but gradually, along with the specialization into parts that are contractile and parts that are absorbent, these motions become better adapted; for necessarily individuals in which they are least adapted disappear faster than those in which they are most adapted. Recognizing this necessity we have here especially to recognize a further necessity. The relation between these stimulation and adjusted contractions must be such that increase of the one causes increase of the other; since the directions of the discharges being once established, greater stimulation cause greater contraction, and the greater contraction causing closer contact with the stimulating agent, causes increase of stimulus and is thereby itself further increased. And now we reach the corollary which more particularly concerns us. Clearly as fast as an accompanying sentiency arises, this cannot be one that is disagreeable, prompting desistance, but must be one that is agreeable, prompting persistence. The pleasurable sensation must be itself the stimulus to the contraction by which the pleasurable sensation is maintained and increased; or must be so bound up with the stimulus that the two increase together. And this relation which we see is directly established in the case of a fundamental function, must be indirectly established with all other functions; since nonestablishment of it in any particular case implies, in so far, unfitness to the conditions of existence.

In two ways then, it is demonstrable that there exists a primordial connexion between pleasure-giving acts and continuance or increase of life, and, by implication, between pain-giving acts and decrease or loss of life. On the one hand, setting out with the lowest living things, we see that the beneficial act and the act which there is a tendency to perform, are originally two sides of the same; and cannot be disconnected without fatal results. On the other hand, if we contemplate developed creatures as now existing, we see that each individual and species is from day to day kept alive by pursuit of the agreeable and avoidance of the disagreeable.

Thus approaching the facts from a different side, analysis brings us down to another face of that ultimate truth disclosed by analysis in a preceding chapter. We found it was no more possible to frame ethical conceptions from which the consciousness of pleasure, of some kind, at some time, to some being, is absent, than it is possible to frame the conception of an object from which the consciousness of space is absent. and now we see that this necessity of thought originates in the very nature of sentient existence. Sentient existence can evolve only on condition that pleasure-giving acts are life-sustaining acts.

Thomas H. Huxley

Evolution and Ethics

Soleo enim et in aliena castra transire, non tanqnam transfuga sed tanquam explorator.

(L. Annaei Senecae Epist. II. 4.)

There is a delightful child's story, known by the title of "Jack and the Bean-stalk," with which my contemporaries who are present will be familiar. But so many of our grave and reverend juniors have been brought up on severer intellectual diet, and, perhaps, have become acquainted with fairyland only through primers of comparative mythology, that it may be needful to give an outline of the tale. It is a legend of a bean-plant, which grows and grows until it reaches the high heavens and there spreads out into a vast canopy of foliage. The hero, being moved to climb the stalk, discovers that the leafy expanse supports a world composed of the same elements as that below, but yet strangely new; and his adventures there, on which I may not dwell, must have completely changed his views of the nature of things; though the story, not having been composed by, or for, philosophers, has nothing to say about views.

My present enterprise has a certain analogy to that of the daring adventurer. I beg you to accompany me in an attempt to reach a world which, to many, is probably strange, by the help of a bean. It is, as you know, a simple, inert looking thing. Yet, if planted under proper conditions, of which sufficient warmth is one of the most important, it manifests active powers of a very remarkable kind. A small

From: *Evolution and Ethics* (London: MacMillan and Co., 1894), pp. 46–86 [published version of his 1893 *The Romanes Lecture*].

green seedling emerges, rises to the surface of the soil, rapidly increases in size and, at the same time, undergoes a series of metamorphoses which do not excite our wonder as much as those which meet us in legendary history, merely because they are to be seen every day and all day long.

By insensible steps, the plant builds itself up into a large and various fabric of root, stem, leaves, flowers, and fruit, every one moulded within and without in accordance with an extremely complex but, at the same time, minutely defined pattern. In each of these complicated structures, as in their smallest constituents, there is an immanent energy which, in harmony with that resident in all the others, incessantly works towards the maintenance of the whole and the efficient performance of the part which it has to play in the economy of nature. But no sooner has the edifice, reared with such exact elaboration, attained completeness, than it begins to crumble. By degrees, the plant withers and disappears from view, leaving behind more or fewer apparently inert and simple bodies, just like the bean from which it sprang; and, like it, endowed with the potentiality of giving rise to a similar cycle of manifestations.

Neither the poetic nor the scientific imagination is put to much strain in the search after analogies with this process of going forth and, as it were, returning to the starting-point. It may be likened to the ascent and descent of a slung stone, or the course of an arrow along its trajectory. Or we may say that the living energy takes first an upward and then a downward road. Or it may seem preferable to compare the expansion of the germ into the full-grown plant, to the unfolding of a fan, or to the rolling forth and widening of a stream; and thus to arrive at the conception of 'development,' or 'evolution.' Here as elsewhere, names are 'noise and smoke'; the important point is to have a clear and adequate conception of the fact signified by a name. And, in this case, the fact is the Sisyphaean process, in the course of which, the living and growing plant passes from the relative simplicity and latent potentiality of the seed to the full epiphany of a highly differentiated type, thence to fall back to simplicity and potentiality.

The value of a strong intellectual grasp of the nature of this process lies in the circumstance that what is true of the bean is true of living things in general. From very low forms up to the highest—in the animal no less than in the vegetable kingdom—the process of life presents the same appearance[1] of cyclical evolution. Nay, we have but to cast our eyes over the rest of the world and cyclical change presents itself on all sides. It meets us in the water that flows to the sea and returns to the springs; in the heavenly bodies that wax and wane, go and return to their places; in the inexorable sequence of the ages of man's life; in that successive rise, apogee, and fall of dynasties and of states which is the most prominent topic of civil history.

As no man fording a swift stream can dip his foot twice into the same water, so no man can, with exactness, affirm of anything in the sensible world that it is.[2] As he utters the words, nay, as he thinks them, the predicate ceases to be applicable; the present has become the past; the 'is' should be 'was.' And the more we learn of the nature of things, the more evident is it that what we call rest is only unperceived activity; that seeming peace is silent but strenuous battle. In every part, at every moment, the state of the cosmos is the expression of a transitory adjustment of contending forces; a scene of strife, in which all the combatants fall in turn. What is true of each part, is true of the whole. Natural knowledge tends more and more to the conclusion that "all the choir of heaven and furniture of the earth" are the transitory forms of parcels of cosmic substance wending along the road of evolution, from nebulous potentiality, through endless growths of sun and planet and satellite; through all varieties of matter; through infinite diversities of life and thought; possibly, through modes of being of which we neither have a conception, nor are competent to form any, back to the indefinable latency from which they arose. Thus the most obvious attribute of the cosmos is its impermanence. It assumes the aspect not so much of a permanent entity as of a changeful process, in which naught endures save the flow of energy and the rational order which pervades it.

We have climbed our bean-stalk and have reached a wonderland in which the common and the familiar become things new and strange. In the exploration of the cosmic process thus typified, the highest intelligence of man finds inexhaustible employment; giants are subdued to our service; and the spiritual affections of the contemplative philosopher are engaged by beauties worthy of eternal constancy.

But there is another aspect of the cosmic process, so perfect as a mechanism, so beautiful as a work of art. Where the cosmopoietic energy works through sentient beings, there arises, among its other manifestations, that which we call pain or suffering. This baleful product of evolution increases in quantity and in intensity, with advancing grades of animal organization, until it attains its highest level in man. Further, the consummation is not reached in man, the mere animal; nor in man, the whole or half savage; but only in man, the member of an organized polity. And it is a necessary consequence of his attempt to live in this way; that is, under those conditions which are essential to the full development of his noblest powers.

Man, the animal, in fact, has worked his way to the headship of the sentient world, and has become the superb animal which he is, in virtue of his success in the struggle for existence. The conditions having been of a certain order, man's organization has adjusted itself to them better than that of his competitors in the cosmic strife. In the case of mankind, the self-assertion, the unscrupulous seizing upon all that can be grasped, the tenacious holding of all that can be kept, which constitute the essence of the struggle for existence, have answered. For his successful progress, throughout the savage state, man has been largely indebted to those qualities which he shares with the ape and the tiger; his exceptional physical organization; his cunning, his sociability, his curiosity, and his imitativeness; his ruthless and ferocious destructiveness when his anger is roused by opposition.

But, in proportion as men have passed from anarchy to social organization, and in proportion as civilization has grown in worth, these deeply ingrained serviceable qualities have become defects. After the manner of successful persons, civilized man would gladly kick down the ladder by which he has climbed. He would be only too pleased to see 'the ape and tiger die.' But they decline to suit his convenience; and the unwelcome intrusion of these boon companions of his hot youth into the ranged existence of civil life adds pains and griefs, innumerable and immeasurably great, to those which the cosmic process necessarily brings on the mere animal. In fact, civilized man brands all these ape and tiger promptings with the name of sins; he punishes many of the acts which flow from them as crimes; and, in extreme cases, he does his best to put an end to the survival of the fittest of former days by axe and rope.

I have said that civilized man has reached this point; the assertion is perhaps too broad and general; I had better put it that ethical man has attained thereto. The science of ethics professes to furnish us with a reasoned rule of life; to tell us what is right action and why it is so. Whatever differences of opinion may exist among experts, there is a general consensus that the ape and tiger methods of the struggle for existence are not reconcilable with sound ethical principles.

The hero of our story descended the bean-stalk, and came back to the common world, where fare and work were alike hard; where ugly competitors were much commoner than beautiful princesses; and where the everlasting battle with self was much less sure to be crowned with victory than a turn-to with a giant. We have done the like. Thousands upon thousands of our fellows, thousands of years ago, have preceded us in finding themselves face to face with the same dread problem of evil. They also have seen that the cosmic process is evolution; that it is full of wonder, full of beauty, and, at the same time, full of pain. They have sought to discover the bearing of these great facts on ethics; to find out whether there is, or is not, a sanction for morality in the ways of the cosmos.

Theories of the universe, in which the conception of evolution plays a leading part, were extant at least six centuries before our era. Certain knowledge of them, in the fifth century, reaches us from localities as distant as the valley of the Ganges and the Asiatic coasts of the Aegean. To the early philosophers of Hindostan, no less than to those of Ionia, the salient and characteristic feature of the phenomenal world was its changefulness; the unresting flow of all things, through birth to visible being and thence to not being, in which they could discern no sign of a beginning and for which they saw no prospect of an ending. It was no less plain to some of these antique forerunners of modern philosophy that suffering is the badge of all the tribe of sentient things; that it is no accidental accompaniment, but an essential constituent of the cosmic process. The energetic Greek might find fierce joys in a world in which 'strife is father and king'; but the old Aryan spirit was subdued to quietism in the Indian sage; the mist of suffering which spread over humanity hid everything else from his view; to him life was one with suffering and suffering with life.

In Hindostan, as in Ionia, a period of relatively high and tolerably stable civilization had succeeded long ages of semi-barbarism and struggle. Out of wealth and security had come leisure and refinement, and, close at their heels, had followed the malady of thought. To the struggle for bare existence, which never ends, though it may be alleviated and partially disguised for a fortunate few, succeeded the struggle to make existence intelligible and to bring the order of things into harmony with the moral sense of man, which also never ends, but, for the thinking few, becomes keener with every increase of knowledge and with every step towards the realization of a worthy ideal of life.

Two thousand five hundred years ago, the value of civilization was as apparent as it is now; then, as now, it was obvious that only in the garden of an orderly polity can the finest fruits humanity is capable of bearing be produced. But it had also become evident that the blessings of culture were not unmixed. The garden was apt to turn into a hothouse. The stimulation of the senses, the pampering of the emotions, endlessly multiplied the sources of pleasure. The constant widening of the intellectual field indefinitely extended the range of that especially human faculty of looking before and after, which adds to the fleeting present those old and new worlds of the past and the future, wherein men dwell the more the higher their culture. But that very sharpening of the sense and that subtle refinement of emotion, which brought such a wealth of pleasures, were fatally attended by a proportional enlargement of the capacity for suffering; and the divine faculty of imagination, while it created new heavens and new earths, provided them with the corresponding hells of futile regret for the past and morbid anxiety for the future.[3] Finally, the inevitable penalty of over-stimulation, exhaustion, opened the gates of civilization to its great enemy, ennui; the stale and flat weariness when man delights not, nor woman neither; when all things are vanity and vexation; and life seems not worth living except to escape the bore of dying.

Even purely intellectual progress brings about its revenges. Problems settled in a rough and ready way by rude men, absorbed in action, demand renewed attention and show themselves to be still unread riddles when men have time to think. The beneficent demon, doubt, whose name is Legion and who dwells amongst the tombs of old faiths, enters into mankind and thenceforth refuses to be cast out. Sacred customs, venerable dooms of ancestral wisdom, hallowed by tradition and professing to hold good for all time, are put to the question. Cultured reflection asks for their credentials; judges them by its own standards; finally, gathers those of which it approves into ethical systems, in which the reasoning is rarely much more than a decent pretext for the adoption of foregone conclusions.

One of the oldest and most important elements in such systems is the conception of justice. Society is impossible unless those who are associated agree to observe certain rules of conduct towards one another; its stability depends on the steadiness with which they abide by that agreement; and, so far as they waver, that mutual trust which is the bond of society is weakened or destroyed. Wolves could not hunt in packs except for the real, though unexpressed, understanding that they should not attack one another during the chase. The most rudimentary polity is a pack of men living under the like tacit, or expressed, understanding; and having made the very important advance upon wolf society, that they agree to use the force of the whole body against individuals who violate it and in favour of those who observe it. This observance of a common understanding, with the consequent distribution of punishments and rewards according to accepted rules, received the name of justice, while the contrary was called injustice. Early ethics did not take much note of the animus of the violator of the rules. But civilization could not advance far, without the establishment of a capital distinction between the case of involuntary and that of wilful misdeed; between a merely wrong action and a guilty one. And, with increasing refinement of moral appreciation, the problem of desert, which arises out of this distinction, acquired more and more theoretical and practical importance. If life must be given for life, yet it was recognized that the unintentional slayer did not altogether deserve death; and, by a sort of compromise between the public and the private conception of justice, a sanctuary was provided in which he might take refuge from the avenger of blood.

The idea of justice thus underwent a gradual sublimation from punishment and reward according to acts, to punishment and reward according to desert; or, in other words, according to motive. Righteousness, that is, action from right motive, not only became synonymous with justice, but the positive constituent of innocence and the very heart of goodness.

Now when the ancient sage, whether Indian or Greek, who had attained to this conception of goodness, looked the world, and especially human life, in the face, he found it as hard as we do to bring the course of evolution into harmony with even the elementary requirements of the ethical ideal of the just and the good.

If there is one thing plainer than another, it is that neither the pleasures nor the pains of life, in the merely animal world, are distributed according to desert; for it is admittedly impossible for the lower orders of sentient beings to deserve either the one or the other. If there is a generalization from the facts of human life which has the assent of thoughtful men in every age and country, it is that the violator of ethical rules constantly escapes the punishment which he deserves; that the wicked flourishes like a green bay tree, while the righteous begs his bread; that the sins of the fathers are visited upon the children; that, in the realm of nature, ignorance is punished just as severely as wilful wrong; and that thousands upon thousands of innocent beings suffer for the crime, or the unintentional trespass, of one.

Greek and Semite and Indian are agreed upon this subject. The book of Job is at one with the "Works and Days" and the Buddhist Sutras; the Psalmist and the Preacher of Israel, with the Tragic Poets of Greece. What is a more common motive of the ancient tragedy in fact, than the unfathomable injustice of the nature of things; what is more deeply felt to be true than its presentation of the destruction of the blameless by the work of his own hands, or by the fatal operation of the sins of others? Surely Oedipus was pure of heart; it was the natural sequence of events—the cosmic process—which drove him, in all innocence, to slay his father and become the husband of his mother, to the desolation of his people and his own headlong ruin. Or to step, for a moment, beyond the chronological limits I have set myself, what constitutes the sempiternal attraction of Hamlet but the appeal to deepest experience of that history of a no less blameless dreamer, dragged, in spite of himself, into a world out of joint; involved in a tangle of crime and misery, created by one of the prime agents of the cosmic process as it works in and through man?

Thus, brought before the tribunal of ethics, the cosmos might well seem to stand condemned. The conscience of man revolted against the moral indifference of nature, and the microcosmic atom should have found the illimitable macrocosm guilty. But few, or none, ventured to record that verdict.

In the great Semitic trial of this issue, Job takes refuge in silence and submission; the Indian and the Greek, less wise perhaps, attempt to reconcile the irreconcilable and plead for the defendant. To this end, the Greeks invented Theodicies; while the Indians devised what, in its ultimate form, must rather be termed a Cosmodicy. For, though

Buddhism recognizes gods many and lords many, they are products of the cosmic process; and transitory, however long enduring, manifestations of its eternal activity. In the doctrine of transmigration, whatever its origin, Brahminical and Buddhist speculation found, ready to hand,[4] the means of constructing a plausible vindication of the ways of the cosmos to man. If this world is full of pain and sorrow; if grief and evil fall, like the rain, upon both the just and the unjust; it is because, like the rain, they are links in the endless chain of natural causation by which past, present, and future are indissolubly connected; and there is no more injustice in the one case than in the other. Every sentient being is reaping as it has sown; if not in this life, then in one or other of the infinite series of antecedent existences of which it is the latest term. The present distribution of good and evil is, therefore, the algebraical sum of accumulated positive and negative deserts; or, rather, it depends on the floating balance of the account. For it was not thought necessary that a complete settlement should ever take place. Arrears might stand over as a sort of 'hanging gale'; a period of celestial happiness just earned might be succeeded by ages of torment in a hideous nether world, the balance still overdue for some remote ancestral error.[5]

Whether the cosmic process looks any more moral than at first, after such a vindication, may perhaps be questioned. Yet this plea of justification is not less plausible than others; and none but very hasty thinkers will reject it on the ground of inherent absurdity. Like the doctrine of evolution itself, that of transmigration has its roots in the world of reality; and it may claim such support as the great argument from analogy is capable of supplying.

Everyday experience familiarizes us with the facts which are grouped under the name of heredity. Every one of us bears upon him obvious marks of his parentage, perhaps of remoter relationships. More particularly, the sum of tendencies to act in a certain way, which we call "character," is often to be traced through a long series of progenitors and collaterals. So we may justly say that this 'character'—this moral and intellectual essence of a man—does veritably pass over from one fleshly tabernacle to another, and does really transmigrate from generation to generation. In the new-born infant, the character of the stock lies latent, and the Ego is little more than a bundle of potentialities. But, very early, these become actualities; from childhood to age they manifest themselves in dullness or brightness, weakness or strength, viciousness or uprightness; and with each feature modified by confluence with another character, if by nothing else, the character passes on to its incarnation in new bodies.

The Indian philosophers called character, as thus defined, 'karma.'[6] It is this karma which passed from life to life and linked them in the chain of transmigrations; and they held that it is modified in each life, not merely by confluence of parentage, but by its own acts. They were, in fact, strong believers in the theory, so much disputed just at present, of the hereditary transmission of acquired characters. That the manifestation of the tendencies of a character may be greatly facilitated, or impeded, by conditions, of which self-discipline, or the absence of it, are among the most important, is indubitable; but that the character itself is modified in this way is by no means so certain; it is not so sure that the transmitted character of an evil liver is worse, or that of a righteous man better, than that which he received. Indian philosophy, however, did not admit of any doubt on this subject; the belief in the influence of conditions, notably of self-discipline, on the karma was not merely a necessary postulate of its theory of retribution, but it presented the only way of escape from the endless round of transmigrations.

The earlier forms of Indian philosophy agreed with those prevalent in our own times, in supposing the existence of a permanent reality, or 'substance,' beneath the shifting series of phenomena, whether of matter or of mind. The substance of the cosmos was 'Brahma,' that of the individual man 'Atman'; and the latter was separated from the former only, if I may so speak, by its phenomenal envelope, by the casing of sensations, thoughts and desires, pleasures and pains, which make up the illusive phantasmagoria of life. This the ignorant take for reality; their 'Atman' therefore remains eternally imprisoned in delusions, bound by the fetters of desire and scourged by the whip of misery. But the man who has attained enlightenment sees that the apparent reality is mere illusion, or, as was said a couple of thousand years later, that there is nothing good nor bad but thinking makes it so. If the cosmos "is just and of our pleasant vices makes instruments to scourge us," it would seem that the only way to escape from our heritage of evil is to destroy that fountain of desire whence our vices flow; to refuse any longer to be the instruments of the evolutionary process, and withdraw from the struggle for existence. If the karma is modifiable by self-discipline, if its coarser desires, one after another, can be extinguished, the ultimate fundamental desire of self-assertion, or the desire to be, may also be destroyed.[7] Then the bubble of illusion will burst, and the freed individual 'Atman' will lose itself in the universal 'Brahma.'

Such seems to have been the pre-Buddhistic conception of salvation, and of the way to be followed by those who would attain thereto. No more thorough mortification of the flesh has ever been attempted than that achieved by the Indian ascetic anchorite; no later monachism has so nearly succeeded in reducing the human mind to that condition of impassive quasi-somnambulism, which, but for its acknowledged holiness, might run the risk of being confounded with idiocy.

And this salvation, it will be observed, was to be attained through knowledge, and by action based on that knowledge; just as the experimenter, who would obtain a certain physical or chemical result, must have a knowledge of the natural laws involved and the persistent disciplined will adequate to carry out all the various operations required. The supernatural, in our sense of the term, was entirely excluded. There was no external power which could affect the sequence of cause and effect which gives rise to karma; none but the will of the subject of the karma which could put an end to it. Only one rule of conduct could be based upon the remarkable theory of which I have endeavoured to give a reasoned outline. It was folly to continue to exist when an overplus of pain was certain; and the probabilities in favour of the increase of misery with the prolongation of existence, were so overwhelming. Slaying the body only made matters worse; there was nothing for it but to slay the soul by the voluntary arrest of all its activities. Property, social ties, family affections, common companionship, must be abandoned; the most natural appetites, even that for food, must be suppressed, or at least minimized; until all that remained of a man was the impassive, extenuated, mendicant monk, self-hypnotised into cataleptic trances, which the deluded mystic took for foretastes of the final union with Brahma.

The founder of Buddhism accepted the chief postulates demanded by his predecessors. But he was not satisfied with the practical annihilation involved in merging the individual existence in the unconditioned—the Atman in Brahma. It would seem that the admission of the existence of any substance whatever—even of the tenuity of that which has neither quality nor energy and of which no predicate whatever can be asserted—appeared to him to be a danger and a snare. Though reduced to a hypostatized negation, Brahma was not to be trusted; so long as entity was there, it might conceivably resume the weary round of evolution, with all its train of immeasurable miseries. Gautama got rid of even that shade of a shadow of permanent existence by a metaphysical *tour de force* of great interest to the student of philosophy, seeing that it supplies the wanting half of Bishop Berkeley's well-known idealistic argument.

Granting the premises, I am not aware of any escape from Berkeley's conclusion, that the 'substance' of matter is a metaphysical unknown quantity, of the existence of which there is no proof. What Berkeley does not seem to have so clearly perceived is that the non-existence of a substance of mind is equally arguable; and that the result of the impartial applications of his reasonings is the reduction of the All to co-existences and sequences of phenomena, beneath and beyond which there is nothing cognoscible. It is a remarkable indication of the subtlety of Indian speculation that Gautama should have seen deeper than the greatest of modern idealists; though it must be admitted that, if some of Berkeley's reasonings respecting the nature of spirit are pushed home, they reach pretty much the same conclusion.[8]

Accepting the prevalent Brahminical doctrine that the whole cosmos, celestial, terrestrial, and infernal, with its population of gods and other celestial beings, of sentient animals, of Mara and his devils, is incessantly shifting through recurring cycles of production and destruction, in each of which every human being has his transmigratory representative, Gautama proceeded to eliminate substance altogether; and to reduce the cosmos to a mere flow of sensations, emotions, volitions, and thoughts, devoid of any substratum. As, on the surface of a stream of water, we see ripples and whirlpools, which last for a while and then vanish with the causes that gave rise to them, so what seem individual existences are mere temporary associations of phenomena circling round a centre, "like a dog tied to a post." In the whole universe there is nothing permanent, no eternal substance either of mind or of matter. Personality is a metaphysical fancy; and in very truth, not only we, but all things, in the worlds without end of the cosmic phantasmagoria, are such stuff as dreams are made of.

What then becomes of karma? Karma remains untouched. As the peculiar form of energy we call magnetism may be transmitted from a loadstone to a piece of steel, from the steel to a piece of nickel, as it may be strengthened or weakened by the conditions to which it is subjected while resident in each piece, so it seems to have been conceived that karma might be transmitted from one phenomenal association to another by a sort of induction. However this may be, Gautama doubtless had a better guarantee for the abolition of transmigration, when no wrack of substance, either of Atman or of Brahma, was left behind when, in short, a man had but to dream that he willed not to dream, to put an end to all dreaming.

This end of life's dream is Nirvana. What Nirvana is the learned do not agree. But, since the best original authorities tell us there is neither desire nor activity, nor any possibility of phenomenal reappearance for the sage who has entered Nirvana, it may be safely said of this acme of Buddhistic philosophy—"the rest is silence."[9]

Thus there is no very great practical disagreement between Gautama and his predecessors with respect to the end of action; but it is otherwise as regards the means to that end. With just insight into human nature, Gautama declared extreme ascetic practices to be useless and indeed harmful. The appetites and the passions are not to be abolished by mere mortification of the body; they must, in addition, be attacked on their own ground and conquered by steady cultivation of the mental habits which oppose them; by universal benevolence; by the return of good for evil; by humility; by abstinence from evil thought; in short, by total renunciation of that self-assertion which is the essence of the cosmic process.

Doubtless, it is to these ethical qualities that Buddhism owes its marvellous success.[10] A system which knows no God in the western sense; which denies a soul to man; which counts the belief in immortality a blunder and the hope of it a sin; which refuses any efficacy to prayer and sacrifice; which bids men look to nothing but their own efforts for salvation; which, in its original purity, knew nothing of vows of obedience, abhorred intolerance, and never sought the aid of the secular arm; yet spread over a considerable moiety of the Old World with marvellous rapidity, and is still, with whatever base admixture of foreign superstitions, the dominant creed of a large fraction of mankind.

Let us now set our faces westwards, towards Asia Minor and Greece and Italy, to view the rise and progress of another philosophy, apparently independent, but no less pervaded by the conception of evolution.[11]

The sages of Miletus were pronounced evolutionists; and, however dark may be some of the sayings of Heracleitus of Ephesus, who was probably a contemporary of Gautama, no better expressions of the essence of the modern doctrine of evolution can be found than are presented by some of his pithy aphorisms and striking metaphors.[12] Indeed, many of my present auditors must have observed that, more than once, I have borrowed from him in the brief exposition of the theory of evolution with which this discourse commenced.

But when the focus of Greek intellectual activity shifted to Athens, the leading minds concentrated their attention upon ethical problems. Forsaking the study of the macrocosm for that of the microcosm, they lost the key to the thought of the great Ephesian, which, I imagine, is more intelligible to us than it was to Socrates, or to Plato. Socrates, more especially, set the fashion of a kind of inverse agnosticism, by teaching that the problems of physics lie beyond the reach of the human intellect; that the attempt to solve them is essentially vain; that the one worthy object of investigation is the problem of ethical life; and his example was followed by the Cynics and the later Stoics. Even the comprehensive knowledge and the penetrating intellect of Aristotle failed to suggest to him that in holding the eternity of the world, within its present range of mutation, he was making a retrogressive step. The scientific heritage of Heracleitus passed into the hands neither of Plato nor of Aristotle, but into those of Democritus. But the world was not yet ready to receive the great conceptions of the philosopher of Abdera. It was reserved for the Stoics to return to the track marked out by the earlier philosophers; and, professing themselves disciples of Heracleitus, to develop the idea of evolution systematically. In doing this, they not only omitted some characteristic features of their master's teaching, but they made additions altogether foreign to it. One of the most influential of these importations was the transcendental theism which had come into vogue. The restless, fiery energy, operating according to law, out of which all things emerge and into which they return, in the endless successive cycles of the great year; which creates and destroys worlds as a wanton child builds up, and anon levels, sand castles on the seashore; was metamorphosed into a material world-soul and decked out with all the attributes of ideal Divinity; not merely with infinite power and transcendent wisdom, but with absolute goodness.

The consequences of this step were momentous. For if the cosmos is the effect of an immanent, omnipotent, and infinitely beneficent cause, the existence in it of real evil, still less of necessarily inherent evil, is plainly inadmissible.[13] Yet the universal experience of mankind testified then, as now, that, whether we look within us or without us, evil stares us in the face on all sides; that if anything is real, pain and sorrow and wrong are realities.

It would be a new thing in history if *a priori* philosophers were daunted by the factious opposition of experience; and the Stoics were the last men to allow themselves to be beaten by mere facts. 'Give me a doctrine and I will find the reasons for it,' said Chrysippus. So they perfected, if they did not invent, that ingenious and plausible form of pleading, the Theodicy; for the purpose of showing firstly, that there is no such thing as evil; secondly, that if there is, it is the necessary correlate of good; and, moreover, that it is either due to our own fault, or inflicted for our benefit. Theodicies have been very popular in their time, and I believe that a numerous, though somewhat dwarfed, progeny of them still survives. So far as I know, they are all variations of the theme set forth in those famous six lines of the "Essay on Man," in which Pope sums up Bolingbroke's reminiscences of stoical and other speculations of this kind—

> "All nature is but art, unknown to thee;
> All chance, direction which thou canst not see;
> All discord, harmony not understood;
> All partial evil, universal good;
> And spite of pride, in erring reason's spite
> One truth is clear: whatever is is right."

Yet, surely, if there are few more important truths than those enunciated in the first triad, the second is open to very grave objections. That there is a 'soul of good in things evil' is unquestionable; nor will any wise man deny the disciplinary value of pain and sorrow. But these considerations do not help us to see why the immense multitude of irresponsible sentient beings, which cannot profit by such discipline, should suffer; nor why, among the endless possibilities open to omnipotence—that of sinless, happy existence among the rest—the actuality in which sin and misery abound should be that selected. Surely it is mere cheap rhetoric to call arguments which have never yet been answered by even the meekest and the least rational of Optimists, suggestions of the pride of reason. As to the concluding aphorism, its fittest place would be as an inscription in letters of mud over the portal of some 'stye of Epicurus';[14] for that is where the logical application of it to practice would land men, with every aspiration stifled and every effort paralyzed. Why try to set right what is right already? Why strive to improve the best of all possible worlds? Let us eat and drink, for as today all is right, so to-morrow all will be. But the attempt of the Stoics to blind themselves to the reality of evil, as a necessary concomitant of the cosmic process, had less success than that of the Indian philosophers to exclude the reality of good from their purview. Unfortunately, it is much easier to shut one's eyes to good than to evil. Pain and sorrow knock at our doors more loudly than pleasure and happiness; and the prints of their heavy footsteps are less easily effaced. Before the grim realities of practical life the pleasant fictions of optimism vanished. If this were the best of all possible worlds, it nevertheless proved itself a very inconvenient habitation for the ideal sage.

The stoical summary of the whole duty of man, 'Live according to nature,' would seem to imply that the cosmic process is an exemplar for human conduct. Ethics would thus become applied Natural History. In fact, a confused employment of the maxim, in this sense, has done immeasurable mischief in later times. It has furnished an axiomatic foundation for the philosophy of philosophasters and for the moralizing of sentimentalists. But the Stoics were, at bottom, not merely noble, but sane, men; and if we look closely into what they really meant by this ill-used phrase, it will be found to present no justification for the mischievous conclusions that have been deduced from it.

In the language of the Stoa, 'Nature' was a word of many meanings. There was the 'Nature' of the cosmos and the 'Nature' of man. In the latter, the animal 'nature,' which man shares with a moiety of the living part of the cosmos, was distinguished from a higher 'nature.' Even in this higher nature there were grades of rank. The logical faculty is an instrument which may be turned to account for any purpose. The passions and the emotions are so closely tied to the lower nature that they may be considered to be pathological, rather than normal, phenomena. The one supreme, hegemonic, faculty, which constitutes the essential 'nature' of man, is most nearly represented by that which, in the language of a later philosophy, has been called the pure reason. It is this 'nature' which holds up the ideal of the supreme good and demands absolute submission of the will to its behests. It is this which commands all men to love one another, to return good for evil, to regard one another as fellow-citizens of one great state. Indeed, seeing that the progress towards perfection of a civilized state, or polity, depends on the obedience of its members to these commands, the Stoics sometimes termed the pure reason the 'political' nature. Unfortunately, the sense of the adjective has undergone so much modification, that the application of it to that which commands the sacrifice of self to the common good would now sound almost grotesque.[15]

But what part is played by the theory of evolution in this view of ethics? So far as I can discern, the ethical system of the Stoics, which is essentially intuitive, and reverences the categorical imperative as strongly as that of any later moralists, might have been just what it was if they had held any other theory; whether that of special creation, on the one side, or that of the eternal existence of the present order, on the other.[16] To the Stoic, the cosmos had no importance for the conscience, except insofar as he chose to think it a pedagogue to virtue. The pertinacious optimism of our philosophers hid from them the actual state of the case. It prevented them from seeing that cosmic nature is no school of virtue, but the headquarters of the enemy of ethical nature. The logic of facts was necessary to convince them that the cosmos works through the lower nature of man, not for righteousness, but against it. And it finally drove them to confess that the existence of their ideal "wise man" was incompatible with the nature of things; that even a passable approximation to that ideal was to be attained only at the cost of renunciation of the world and mortification, not merely of the flesh, but of all human affections. The state of perfection was that 'apatheia'[17] in which desire, though it may still be felt, is powerless to move the will, reduced to the sole function of executing the commands of pure reason.

Even this residuum of activity was to be regarded as a temporary loan, as an efflux of the divine world-pervading spirit, chafing at its imprisonment in the flesh, until such time as death enabled it to return to its source in the all-pervading logos.

I find it difficult to discover any very great difference between Apatheia and Nirvana, except that stoical speculation agrees with pre-Buddhistic philosophy, rather than with the teachings of Gautama, insofar as it postulates a permanent substance equivalent to 'Brahma' and 'Atman'; and that, in stoical practice, the adoption of the life of the mendicant cynic was held to be more a counsel of perfection than an indispensable condition of the higher life.

Thus the extremes touch. Greek thought and Indian thought set out from ground common to both, diverge widely, develop under very different physical and moral conditions, and finally converge to practically the same end.

The Vedas and the Homeric epos set before us a world of rich and vigorous life, full of joyous fighting men

> That ever with a frolic welcome took
> The thunder and the sunshine. . . .

and who were ready to brave the very Gods themselves when their blood was up. A few centuries pass away, and under the influence of civilization the descendants of these men are 'sicklied o'er with the pale cast of thought'—frank pessimists, or, at best, make-believe optimists. The courage of the warlike stock may be as hardly tried as before, perhaps more hardly, but the enemy is self. The hero has become a monk. The man of action is replaced by the quietist, whose highest aspiration is to be the passive instrument of the divine Reason. By the Tiber, as by the Ganges, ethical man admits that the cosmos is too strong for him; and, destroying every bond which ties him to it by ascetic discipline, he seeks salvation in absolute renunciation.[18]

Modern thought is making a fresh start from the base whence Indian and Greek philosophy set out; and, the human mind being very much what it was six-and-twenty centuries ago, there is no ground for wonder if it presents indications of a tendency to move along the old lines to the same results.

We are more than sufficiently familiar with modern pessimism, at least as a speculation; for I cannot call to mind that any of its present votaries have sealed their faith by assuming the rags and the bowl of the mendicant Bhikku, or the cloak and the wallet of the Cynic. The obstacles placed in the way of sturdy vagrancy by an unphilosophical police have, perhaps, proved too formidable for philosophical consistency. We also know modern speculative optimism, with its perfectibility of the species, reign of peace, and lion and lamb transformation scenes; but one does not hear so much of it as one did forty years ago; indeed, I imagine it is to be met with more commonly at the tables of the healthy and wealthy, than in the congregations of the wise. The majority of us, I apprehend, profess neither pessimism nor optimism. We hold that the world is neither so good, nor so bad, as it conceivably might be; and, as most of us have reason, now and again, to discover that it can be. Those who have failed to experience the joys that make life worth living are, probably, in as small a minority as those who have never known the griefs that rob existence of its savour and turn its richest fruits into mere dust and ashes.

Further, I think I do not err in assuming that, however diverse their views on philosophical and religious matters, most men are agreed that the proportion of good and evil in life may be very sensibly affected by human action. I never heard anybody doubt that the evil may be thus increased, or diminished; and it would seem to follow that good must be similarly susceptible of addition or subtraction. Finally, to my knowledge, nobody professes to doubt that, so far forth as we possess a power of bettering things, it is our paramount duty to use it and to train all our intellect and energy to this supreme service of our kind.

Hence the pressing interest of the question, to what extent modern progress in natural knowledge, and, more especially, the general outcome of that progress in the doctrine of evolution, is competent to help us in the great work of helping one another? The propounders of what are called the "ethics of evolution," when the 'evolution of ethics' would usually better express the object of their speculations, adduce a number of more or less interesting facts and more or less sound arguments in favour of the origin of the moral sentiments, in the same way as other natural phenomena, by a process of evolution. I have little doubt, for my own part, that they are on the right track; but as the immoral sentiments have no less been evolved, there is, so far, as much natural sanction for the one as the other. The thief and the murderer follow nature just as much as the philanthropist. Cosmic evolution may teach us how the good and the evil tendencies of man may have come about; but, in itself, it is incompetent to furnish any better reason why what we call good is preferable to what we call evil than we had before. Some day, I doubt not, we shall arrive at an understanding of the evolution of the aesthetic faculty; but all the understanding in the world will neither increase nor diminish the force of the intuition that this is beautiful and that is ugly.

There is another fallacy which appears to me to pervade the so-called "ethics of evolution." It is the notion that because, on the whole, animals and plants have advanced in perfection of organization by means of the struggle for existence and the consequent 'survival of the fittest'; therefore men in society, men as ethical beings, must look to the same process to help them towards perfection. I suspect that this fallacy has arisen out of the unfortunate ambiguity of the phrase 'survival of the fittest.' 'Fittest' has a connotation of 'best'; and about 'best' there hangs a moral flavour. In cosmic nature, however, what is 'fittest' depends upon the conditions. Long since,[19] I ventured to point out that if our hemisphere were to cool again, the survival of the fittest might bring about, in the vegetable kingdom, a population of more and more stunted and humbler and humbler organisms, until the 'fittest' that survived might be nothing but lichens, diatoms, and such microscopic organisms as those which give red snow its colour; while, if it became hotter, the pleasant valleys of the Thames and Isis might be uninhabitable by any animated beings save those that flourish in a tropical jungle. They, as the fittest, the best adapted to the changed conditions, would survive.

Men in society are undoubtedly subject to the cosmic process. Asamong other animals, multiplication goes on without cessation, and involves severe competition for the means of support. The struggle for existence tends to eliminate those less fitted to adapt themselves to the circumstances of their existence. The strongest, the most self-assertive, tend to tread down the weaker. But the influence of the cosmic process on the evolution of society is the greater the more rudimentary its civilization. Social progress means a checking of the cosmic process at every step and the sub-stitution for it of another, which may be called the ethical process; the end of which is not the survival of those who may happen to be the fittest, in respect of the whole of the conditions which obtain, but of those who are ethically the best.[20]

As I have already urged, the practice of that which is ethically best—what we call goodness or virtue—involves a course of conduct which, in all respects, is opposed to that which leads to success in the cosmic struggle for existence. In place of ruthless self-assertion it demands self-restraint; in place of thrusting aside, or treading down, all competitors, it requires that the individual shall not merely respect, but shall help his fellows; its influence is directed, not so much to the survival of the fittest, as to the fitting of as many as possible to survive. It repudiates the gladiatorial theory of existence. It demands that each man who enters into the enjoyment of the advantages of a polity shall be mindful of his debt to those who have laboriously constructed it; and shall take heed that no act of his weakens the fabric in which he has been permitted to live. Laws and moral pre-cepts are directed to the end of curbing the cosmic process and reminding the individual of his duty to the community, to the protection and influence of which he owes, if not existence itself, at least the life of something better than a brutal savage.

It is from neglect of these plain considerations that the fanatical individualism[21] of our time attempts to apply the analogy of cosmic nature to society. Once more we have a misapplication of the stoical injunction to follow nature; the duties of the individual to the state are forgotten, and his tendencies to self-assertion are dignified by the name of rights. It is seriously debated whether the members of a community are justified in using their combined strength to constrain one of their number to contribute his share to the mainte- nance of it; or even to prevent him from doing his best to destroy it. The struggle for existence, which has done such admirable work in cosmic nature, must, it appears, be equally beneficent in the ethical sphere. Yet if that which I have insisted upon is true; if the cosmic process has no sort of relation to moral ends; if the imitation of it by man is in- consistent with the first principles of ethics; what becomes of this surprising theory?

Let us understand, once for all, that the ethical progress of society depends, not on imitating the cosmic process, still less in running away from it, but in combating it. It may seem an audacious proposal thus to pit the microcosm against the macrocosm and to set man to subdue nature to his higher ends; but I venture to think that the great intel- lectual difference between the ancient times with which we have been occupied and our day, lies in the solid founda- tion we have acquired for the hope that such an enterprise may meet with a certain measure of success.

The history of civilization details the steps by which men have succeeded in building up an artificial world within the cosmos. Fragile reed as he may be, man, as Pascal says, is a thinking reed:[22] there lies within him a fund of energy, operating intelligently and so far akin to that which per- vades the universe, that it is competent to influence and modify the cosmic process. In virtue of his intelligence, the dwarf bends the Titan to his will. In every family, in every polity that has been established, the cosmic process in man has been restrained and otherwise modified by law and custom; in surrounding nature, it has been similarly influ- enced by the art of the shepherd, the agriculturist, the arti- san. As civilization has advanced, so has the extent of this interference increased; until the organized and highly devel- oped sciences and arts of the present day have endowed man with a command over the course of non-human nature greater than that once attributed to the magicians. The most impressive, I might say startling, of these changes have been brought about in the course of the last two centuries; while a right comprehension of the process of life and of the means of influencing its manifestations is only just dawning upon us. We do not yet see our way beyond generalities; and we are befogged by the obtrusion of false analogies and crude anticipations. But Astronomy, Physics, Chemistry, have all had to pass through similar phases, before they reached the stage at which their influence became an important factor in human affairs. Physiology, Psychology, Ethics, Political Science, must submit to the same ordeal. Yet it seems to me irrational to doubt that, at no distant period, they will work as great a revolution in the sphere of practice.

The theory of evolution encourages no millennial anticipations. If, for millions of years, our globe has taken the upward road, yet, some time, the summit will be reached and the downward route will be commenced. The most daring imagination will hardly venture upon the suggestion that the power and the intelligence of man can ever arrest the procession of the great year.

Moreover, the cosmic nature born with us and, to a large extent, necessary for our maintenance, is the outcome of millions of years of severe training, and it would be folly to imagine that a few centuries will suffice to subdue its masterfulness to purely ethical ends. Ethical nature may count upon having to reckon with a tenacious and powerful enemy as long as the world lasts. But, on the other hand, I see no limit to the extent to which intelligence and will, guided by sound principles of investigation, and organized in common effort, may modify the conditions of existence, for a period longer than that now covered by history. And much may be done to change the nature of man himself.[23] The intelligence which has converted the brother of the wolf into the faithful guardian of the flock ought to be able to do something towards curbing the instincts of savagery in civilized men.

But if we may permit ourselves a larger hope of abatement of the essential evil of the world than was possible to those who, in the infancy of exact knowledge, faced the problem of existence more than a score of centuries ago, I deem it an essential condition of the realization of that hope that we should cast aside the notion that the escape from pain and sorrow is the proper object of life.

We have long since emerged from the heroic childhood of our race, when good and evil could be met with the same 'frolic welcome'; the attempts to escape from evil, whether Indian or Greek, have ended in flight from the battle-field; it remains to us to throw aside the youthful overconfidence and the no less youthful discouragement of nonage. We are grown men, and must play the man

strong in will
To strive, to seek, to find, and not to yield,

cherishing the good that falls in our way, and bearing the evil, in and around us, with stout hearts set on diminishing it. So far, we all may strive in one faith towards one hope:

It may be that the gulfs will wash us down,
It may be we shall touch the Happy Isles,

. . . but something ere the end,
Some work of noble note may yet be done. [24]

Notes

1. I have been careful to speak of the "appearance" of cyclical evolution presented by living things; for on critical examination, it will be found that the course of vegetable and of animal life is not exactly represented by the figure of a cycle which returns into itself. What actually happens, in all but the lowest organisms, is that one part of the growing germ (A) gives rise to tissues and organs; while another part (B) remains in its primitive condition, or is but slightly modified. The moiety A becomes the body of the adult and, sooner or later, perishes, while portions of the moiety B are detached and, as offspring, continue the life of the species. Thus, if we trace back an organism along the direct line of descent from its remotest ancestor, B, as a whole, has never suffered

death; portions of it, only, have been cast off and died in each individual offspring.

Everybody is familiar with the way in which the "suckers" of a strawberry plant behave. A thin cylinder of living tissue keeps on growing at its free end, until it attains a considerable length. At successive intervals, it develops buds which grow into strawberry plants; and these become independent by the death of the parts of the sucker which connect them. The rest of the sucker, however, may go on living and growing indefinitely, and, circumstances remaining favourable, there is no obvious reason why it should ever die. The living substance B, in a manner, answers to the sucker. If we could restore the continuity which was once possessed by the portions of B, contained in all the individuals of a direct line of descent, they would form a sucker, or *stolon*, on which these individuals would be strung, and which would never have wholly died.

A species remains unchanged so long as the potentiality of development resident in B remains unaltered; so long, *e.g.*, as the buds of the strawberry sucker tend to become typical strawberry plants. In the case of the progressive evolution of a species, the developmental potentiality of B becomes of a higher and higher order. In retrogressive evolution, the contrary would be the case. The phenomena of atavism seem to show that retrogressive evolution, that is, the return of a species to one or other of its earlier forms, is a possibility to be reckoned with. The simplification of structure, which is so common in the parasitic members of a group, however, does not properly come under this head. The worm-like, limbless *Lernoea* has no resemblance to any of the stages of development of the many-limbed active animals of the group to which it belongs.

2. Heracleitus says, Ποταμω γαρ ουκ εστι δις εμβηναι τω αυτω; but, to be strictly accurate, the river remains, though the water of which it is composed changes—just as a man retains his identity though the whole substance of his body is constantly shifting.

This is put very well by Seneca (Ep. lvii. i. *20*, Ed. Ruhkopf): "Corpora nostra rapiuntur fluminum more, quidquid vides currit cum tempore; nihil ex his quce videmus manet. Ego ipse dum loquor mutari ista, mutatus sum. Hoc est quod ait Heraclitus 'In idem flumen bis non descendimus.' Manet idem fluminis nomen, aqua transmissa est. Hoc in amne manifestius est quam in homine, sed nos quoque non minus velox cursus praetervehit."

3. "Multa bona nostra nobis nocent, timoris enim tormentum memoria reducit, providentia anticipat. Nemo tantum praesentibus miser est." (Seneca, Ed. v. 7.)

Among the many wise and weighty aphorisms of the Roman Bacon, few sound the realities of life more deeply than "Multa bona nostra nobis nocent." If there is a soul of good in things evil, it is at least equally true that there is a soul of evil in things good: for things, like men, have "les defauts de leurs qualites." It is one of the last lessons one learns from experience, but not the least important, that a heavy tax is levied upon all forms of success; and that failure is one of the commonest disguises assumed by blessings.

4. "There is within the body of every man a soul which, at the death of the body, flies away from it like a bird out of a cage, and enters upon a new life ... either in one of the heavens or one of the hells or on this earth. The only exception is the rare case of a man having in this life acquired a true knowledge of God. According to the pre-Buddhistic theory, the soul of such a man goes along the path of the Gods to God, and, being united with Him, enters upon an immortal life in which his individuality is not extinguished. In the latter theory, his soul is directly absorbed into the Great Soul, is lost in it, and has no longer any independent existence. The souls of all other men enter, after the death of the body, upon a new existence in one or other of the many different modes of being. If in heaven or hell, the soul itself becomes a god or demon without entering a body; all superhuman beings, save the great gods, being looked upon as not eternal, but merely temporary creatures. If the soul returns to earth it may or may not enter a new body; and this either of a human being, an animal, a plant, or even a material object. For all these are possessed of souls, and there is no essential difference between these souls and the souls of men—all being alike mere sparks of the Great Spirit, who is the only real existence." (Rhys Davids, *Hibbert Lectures,* 1881, p. 83.)

For what I have said about Indian Philosophy, I am particularly indebted to the luminous exposition of primitive Buddhism and its relations to earlier Hindu thought, which is given by Prof. Rhys Davids in his remarkable *Hibbert Lectures* for 1881, and *Buddhism* (1890). The only apology I can offer for the freedom with which I have borrowed from him in these notes, is my desire to leave no doubt as to my indebtedness. I have also found Dr. Oldenberg's *Buddha* (Ed. 2, 1890) very helpful. The origin of the theory of transmigration stated in the above extract is an unsolved problem. That it differs widely from the Egyptian metempsychosis is clear. In fact, since men usually people the other world with phantoms of this, the Egyptian doctrine would seem to presuppose the Indian as a more archaic belief.

Prof. Rhys Davids has fully insisted upon the ethical importance of the transmigration theory. "One of the latest speculations now being put forward among ourselves would seek to explain each man's character, and even his outward condition in life, by the character he inherited from his ancestors, a character gradually formed during a practically endless series of past existences, modified only by the conditions into which he was born, those very conditions being also, in like manner, the last result of a practically endless series of past causes. Gotama's speculation might be stated in the same words. But it attempted also to explain, in a way different from that which would be adopted by the exponents of the modern theory, that strange problem which it is also the motive of the wonderful drama of the book of Job to explain—the fact that the actual distribution here of good fortune, or misery, is entirely independent of the moral qualities which men call good or bad. We cannot wonder that a teacher, whose whole system was so essentially an ethical reformation, should have felt it incumbent upon him to seek an explanation of this apparent injustice. And all the more so, since the belief he had inherited, the theory of the transmigration of souls, had provided a solution perfectly sufficient to any one who could accept that belief." *(Hibbert Lectures,* p. 93.) I should venture to suggest the substitution of 'largely' for 'entirely' in the foregoing passage. Whether a ship makes a good or a bad voyage is largely independent of the conduct of the captain, but it is largely affected by that conduct. Though powerless before a hurricane he may weather many a bad gale.

5. The outward condition of the soul is, in each new birth, determined by its actions in a previous birth; but by each action in succession, and not by the balance struck after the evil has been reckoned off against the good. A good man who has once uttered a slander may spend a hundred thousand years as a god, in consequence of his goodness, and when the power of his good actions is exhausted, may be born as a dumb man on account of his transgression; and a robber who has once done an act of mercy, may come to life in a king's body as the result of his virtue, and then suffer torments for ages in hell or as a ghost without a body, or be re-born many times as a slave or an outcast, in consequence of his evil life.

"There is no escape, according to this theory, from the result of any act; though it is only the consequences of its own acts that each soul has to endure. The force has been set in motion by itself and can never stop; and its effect can never be foretold. If evil, it can never be modified or prevented, for it depends on a cause already completed, that is now for ever beyond the soul's control. There is even no continuing consciousness, no memory of the past that could guide the soul to any knowledge of its fate. The only advantage open to it is to add in this life to the sum of its good actions, that it may bear fruit with the rest. And even this can only happen in some future life under essentially the same conditions as the present one: subject, like the present one, to old age, decay, and death; and affording opportunity, like the present one, for the commission of errors, ignorances, or sins, which in their turn must inevitably produce their due effect of sickness, disability, or woe. Thus is the soul tossed about from life to life, from billow to billow in the great ocean of transmigration. And there is no escape save for the very few, who, during their birth as men, attain to a right knowledge of the Great Spirit: and thus enter into immortality, or, as the later philosophers taught, are absorbed into the Divine Essence." (Rhys Davids, *Hibbert Lectures,* pp. 85, 86.)

The state after death thus imagined by the Hindu philosophers has a certain analogy to the purgatory of the Roman Church; except that escape from it is dependent, not on a divine decree modified, it may be, by sacerdotal or saintly intercession, but by the acts of the individual himself; and that while ultimate emergence into heavenly bliss of the good, or well-prayed for, Catholic is professedly assured, the chances in favour of the attainment of absorption, or of Nirvana, by any individual Hindu are extremely small.

6. "That part of the then prevalent transmigration theory which could not be proved false seemed to meet a deeply felt necessity, seemed to supply a moral cause which would explain the unequal distribution here of happiness or woe, so utterly inconsistent with the present characters of men." Gautama "still therefore talked of men's previous existence, but by no means in the way that he is generally represented to have done." What he taught was "the transmigration of character." He held that after the death of any being, whether human or not, there survived nothing at all but that being's 'Karma,' the result, that is, of its mental and bodily actions. Every individual, whether human or divine, was the last inheritor and the last result of the Karma of a long series of past individuals—a series so long that its beginning is beyond the reach of calculation, and its end will be coincident with the destruction of the world." (Rhys Davids, *Hibbert Lectures*, p. 92.)

In the theory of evolution, the tendency of a germ to develop according to a certain specific type, *e.g.* of the kidney bean seed to grow into a plant having all the characters of *Phaseous vulgaris*, is its 'Karma.' It is the "last inheritor and the last result" of all the conditions that have affected a line of ancestry which goes back for many millions of years to the time when life first appeared on the earth. The moiety B of the substance of the bean plant (see *Note* l) is the last link in a once continuous chain extending from the primitive living substance: and the characters of the successive species to which it has given rise are the manifestations of its gradually modified Karma. As Prof Rhys Davids aptly says, the snowdrop "is a snowdrop and not an oak, and just that kind of snowdrop, because it is the outcome of the Karma of an endless series of past existences." (*Hibbert Lectures*, p. 114.)

7. "It is interesting to notice that the very point which is the weakness of the theory—the supposed concentration of the effect of the Karma in one new being—presented itself to the early Buddhists themselves as a difficulty. They avoided it, partly by explaining that it was a particular thirst in the creature dying (a craving, Tanha, which plays otherwise a great part in the Buddhist theory) which actually caused the birth of the new individual who was to inherit the Karma of the former one. But, how this took place, how the craving desire produced this effect, was acknowledged to be a mystery patent only to a Buddha." (Rhys Davids, *Hibbert Lectures*, p. 95.)

Among the many parallelisms of Stoicism and Buddhism, it is curious to find one for this Tanha, 'thirst,' or 'craving desire' for life. Seneca writes (Epist. lxxvi. 18): "Si enim ullum aliud est bonum quam honestum, sequetur nos *aviditas vitae* aviditas rerum vitam instruentium: quod est intolerabile infinitum, vagum."

8. "The distinguishing characteristic of Buddhism was that it started a new line, that it looked upon the deepest questions men have to solve from an entirely different standpoint. It swept away from the field of its vision the whole of the great soul-theory which had hitherto so completely filled and dominated the minds of the superstitious and the thoughtful alike. For the first time in the history of the world, it proclaimed a salvation which each man could gain for himself and by himself, in this world, during this life, without any the least reference to God, or to Gods, either great or small. Like the Upanishads, it placed the first importance on knowledge but it was no longer a knowledge of God, it was a clear perception of the real nature, as they supposed it to be, of men and things. And it added to the necessity of knowledge, the necessity of purity, of courtesy, of uprightness, of peace and of a universal love far reaching, grown great and beyond measure." (Rhys Davids, *Hibbert Lectures*, p. 29.)

The contemporary Greek philosophy takes an analogous direction. According to Heracleitus, the universe was made neither by Gods nor men; but, from all eternity, has been, and to all eternity, will be, immortal fire, glowing and fading in due measure. (Mullach, *Heracliti Fragmenta*, 27.) And the part assigned by his successors, the Stoics, to the knowledge and the volition of the 'wise man' made their Divinity (for logical thinkers) a subject for compliments, rather than a power to be reckoned with. In Hindu speculation the 'Arahat,' still more the 'Buddha,' becomes the superior of Brahma; the stoical 'wise man' is, at least, the equal of Zeus.

Berkeley affirms over and over again that no idea can be formed of a soul or spirit—"If any man shall doubt of the truth of what is here delivered, let him but reflect and try if he can form any idea of power or active being; and whether he hath ideas of two principal powers marked by the names of *will* and *understanding* distinct from each other, as well as from a third idea of substance or being in general, with a relative notion of its supporting or being the subject of the aforesaid power, which is signified by the name *soul* or *spirit*. This is what some hold: but, so far as I can see, the words *will, soul, spirit,* do not stand for different ideas or, in truth, for any idea at all, but for something which is very different from ideas, and which, being an agent, cannot be like unto or represented by any idea whatever [though it must be owned at the same time, that we have some notion of soul, spirit, and the operations of the mind, such as willing, loving, hating, inasmuch as we know or understand the meaning of these words]." (*The Principles of Human Knowledge, lxxvi.* See also §§ lxxxix., cxxxv., cxlv.)

It is open to discussion, I think, whether it is possible to have 'some notion' of that of which we can form no 'idea.'

Berkeley attaches several predicates to the "perceiving active being mind, spirit, soul or myself" (Parts 1. II.) It is said, for example, to be "indivisible, incorporeal, unextended, and incorruptible." The predicate indivisible, though negative in form, has highly positive consequences. For, if 'perceiving active being' is strictly indivisible, man's soul must be one with the Divine spirit: which is good Hindu or Stoical doctrine, but hardly orthodox Christian philosophy. If, on the other hand, the 'substance' of active perceiving 'being' is actually divided into the one Divine and innumerable human entities, how can the predicate 'indivisible' be rigorously applicable to it?

Taking the words cited, as they stand, they amount to the denial of the possibility of any knowledge of substance. 'Matter' having been resolved into mere affections of 'spirit,' 'spirit' melts away into an admittedly inconceivable and unknowable hypostasis of thought and power—consequently the existence of anything in the universe beyond a flow of phenomena is a purely hypothetical assumption. Indeed a pyrrhonist might raise the objection that if 'esse' is 'percipi' spirit itself can have no existence except as a perception, hypostatized into a 'self,' or as a perception of some other spirit. In the former case, objective reality vanishes; in the latter, there would seem to be the need of an infinite series of spirits each perceiving the others.

It is curious to observe how very closely the phraseology of Berkeley sometimes approaches that of the Stoics: thus (cxlviii.) "It seems to be a *general pretence of the unthinking* herd that *they cannot see God.* But, alas, we need only open our eyes to see the Sovereign Lord of all things with a more full and clear view, than we do any of our fellow-creatures we do at all times and in all places perceive manifest tokens of the Divinity: everything we see, hear, feel, or any wise perceived by sense, being a sign or effect of the power of God " . . . exlix. "It is therefore plain, that *nothing can be more evident* to anyone that is capable of the least reflection, *than the existence of God,* or a spirit who is intimately present to our minds, producing in them all that variety of ideas or sensations which continually affect us, on whom we have an absolute and entire dependence, in short, *in whom we live and move and have our being."* cl. [But you will say hath Nature no share in the production of natural things, and must they be all ascribed to the immediate and sole operation of God? . . . if by *Nature* is meant some being distinct from God, as well as from the laws of nature and things perceived by sense, I must confess that word is to me an empty sound, without any intelligible meaning annexed to it.] Nature in this acceptation is a vain *Chimoera* introduced by those heathens, who had not just notions of the omnipresence and infinite perfection of God."

Compare Seneca *(De Beneficii~, iv. 7):*

"Natura, inquit, haec mihi praestat. Non intelligis te, quum hoc dicis, mutare Nomen Deo? Quid enim est aliud Natura quam Deus, et divina ratio, toti mundo et partibus ejus inserta? Quoties voles tibi licet aliter hunc auctorem rerum nostrarum compellare, et Jovem illum optimum et maximum rite dices, et tonantem, et statorem: qui non, ut historici tradiderunt, ex eo quod post votum susceptum acies Romanorum fugientum stetit, sed quod stant beneficio ejus omnia, stator, stabilitorque est: hunc eundem et fatum si dixeris, non mentieris, nam quum fatum nihil aliud est, quam series implexa causarum, ille est prima omnium causa, ea qua caeterae pendent." It would appear, therefore, that the good Bishop is somewhat hard upon the 'heathen,' of whose words his own might be a paraphrase.

There is yet another direction in which Berkeley's philosophy, I will not say agrees with Gautama's, but at any rate helps to make a fundamental dogma of Buddhism intelligible.

"I find I can excite ideas in my mind at pleasure, and vary and shift the scene as often as I think fit. It is no more than willing, and straightway this or that idea arises in my fancy: and by the same power, it is obliterated, and makes way for another. This making and unmaking of ideas doth very properly denominate the mind active. This much is certain and grounded on experience. . . ." *(Principles,* xxviii.)

A good many of us, I fancy, have reason to think that experience tells them very much the contrary; and are painfully familiar with the obsession of the mind by ideas which cannot be obliterated by any effort of the will and steadily refuse to make way for others. But what I desire to point out is that if Gautama was equally confident that he could 'make and unmake' ideas—then, since he had resolved self into a group of ideal phantoms—the possibility of abolishing self by volition naturally followed.

9. According to Buddhism, the relation of one life to the next is merely that borne by the flame of one lamp to the flame of another lamp which is set alight by it. To the 'Arahat' or adept "no outward form, no compound thing, no creature, no creator, no existence of any kind, must appear to be other than a temporary collocation of its component parts, fated inevitably to be dissolved."—(Rhys Davids, *Hibbert Lectures,* p. 211.)

The self is nothing but a group of phenomena held together by the desire of life; when that desire shall have ceased, "the karma of that particular chain of lives will cease to influence any longer any distinct individual, and there will be no more birth; for birth, decay, and death, grief, lamentation, and despair will have come, so far as regards that chain of lives, for ever to an end."

The state of mind of the Arahat in which the desire of life has ceased is Nirvana. Dr. Oldenberg has very acutely and patiently considered the various interpretations which have been attached to 'Nirvana' in the work to which I have referred (pp. 285 *et seq.*). The result of his and other discussions of the question may I think be briefly stated thus:

1. Logical deduction from the predicates attached to the term 'Nirvana' strips it of all reality, conceivability, or perceivability, whether by Gods or men. For all practical purposes, therefore, it comes to exactly the same thing as annihilation.
2. But it is not annihilation in the ordinary sense, inasmuch as it could take place in the living Arahat or Buddha.
3. And, since, for the faithful Buddhist, that which was abolished in the Arahat was the possibility of further pain, sorrow, or sin; and that which was attained was perfect peace; his mind directed itself exclusively to this joyful consummation, and personified the negation of all conceivable existence and of all pain into a

positive bliss. This was all the more easy, as Gautama refused to give any dogmatic definition of Nirvana. There is something analogous in the way in which people commonly talk of the 'happy release' of a man who has been long suffering from mortal disease. According to their own views, it must always be extremely doubtful whether the man will be any happier after the 'release' than before. But they do not choose to look at the matter in this light.

The popular notion that, with practical, if not metaphysical, annihilation in view, Buddhism must needs be a sad and gloomy faith seems to be inconsistent with fact; on the contrary, the prospect of Nirvana fills the true believer, not merely with cheerfulness, but with an ecstatic desire to reach it.

10. The influence of the picture of the personal qualities of Gautama, afforded by the legendary anecdotes which rapidly grew into a biography of the Buddha; and by the birth stories, which coalesced with the current folk-lore, and were intelligible to all the world, doubtless played a great part. Further, although Gautama appears not to have meddled with the caste system, he refused to recognize any distinction, save that of perfection in the way of salvation, among his followers; and by such teaching, no less than by the inculcation of love and benevolence to all sentient beings, he practically levelled every social, political, and racial barrier. A third important condition was the organization of the Buddhists into monastic communities for the stricter professors, while the laity were permitted a wide indulgence in practice and were allowed to hope for accommodation in some of the temporary abodes of bliss. With a few hundred thousand years of immediate paradise in sight, the average man could be content to shut his eyes to what might follow.

11. In ancient times it was the fashion, even among the Greeks themselves, to derive all Greek wisdom from Eastern sources; not long ago it was as generally denied that Greek philosophy had any connection with Oriental speculation; it seems probable, however, that the truth lies between these extremes.

The Ionian intellectual movement does not stand alone. It is only one of several sporadic indications of the working of some powerful mental ferment over the whole of the area comprised between the Aegean and Northern Hindostan during the eighth, seventh, and sixth centuries before our era. In these three hundred years, prophetism attained its apogee among the Semites of Palestine; Zoroasterism grew and became the creed of a conquering race, the Iranic Aryans; Buddhism rose and spread with marvellous rapidity among the Aryans of Hindostan; while scientific naturalism took its rise among the Aryans of Ionia. It would be difficult to find another three centuries which have given birth to four events of equal importance. All the principal existing religions of mankind have grown out of the first three: while the fourth is the little spring, now

swollen into the great stream of positive science. So far as physical possibilities go, the prophet Jeremiah and the oldest Ionian philosopher might
have met and conversed. If they had done so, they would probably have
disagreed a good deal; and it is interesting to reflect that their discussions
might have embraced questions which, at the present day, are still hotly
controverted.

The old Ionian philosophy, then, seems to be only one of many
results of a stirring of the moral and intellectual life of the Aryan and the
Semitic populations of Western Asia. The conditions of this general awak-
ening were doubtless manifold; but there is one which modern research
has brought into great prominence. This is the existence of extremely
ancient and highly advanced societies in the valleys of the Euphrates and
of the Nile.

It is now known that, more than a thousand—perhaps more than
two thousand—years before the sixth century B.C., civilization had attained a relatively high pitch among the Babylonians and the Egyptians.
Not only had painting, sculpture, architecture, and the industrial arts
reached a remarkable development; but in Chaldaea, at any rate, a vast
amount of knowledge had been accumulated and methodized, in the
departments of grammar, mathematics, astronomy, and natural history.
Where such traces of the scientific spirit are visible, naturalistic speculation is rarely far off, though, so far as I know, no remains of an Accadian,
or Egyptian, philosophy, properly so called, have yet been recovered.

Geographically, Chaldaea occupied a central position among the
oldest seats of civilization. Commerce, largely aided by the intervention
of those colossal peddlars, the Phoenicians, had brought Chaldaea into
connection with all of them, for a thousand years before the epoch at
present under consideration. And in the ninth, eighth, and seventh centuries, the Assyrian, the depositary of Chaldaean civilization, as the
Macedonian and the Roman, at a later date, were the depositaries of
Greek culture, had added irresistible force to the other agencies for the
wide distribution of Chaldaean literature, art, and science.

I confess that I find it difficult to imagine that the Greek immi-
grants—who stood in somewhat the same relation to the Babylonians
and the Egyptians as the later Germanic barbarians to the Romans of the
Empire—should not have been immensely influenced by the new life with
which they became acquainted. But there is abundant direct evidence of
the magnitude of this influence in certain spheres. I suppose it is not
doubted that the Greek went to school with the Oriental for his primary
instruction in reading, writing, and arithmetic; and that Semitic theology
supplied him with some of his mythological lore. Nor does there now
seem to be any question about the large indebtedness of Greek art to that
of Chaldaea and that of Egypt.

But the manner of that indebtedness is very instructive. The obligation is clear, but its limits are no less definite. Nothing better exemplifies
the indomitable originality of the Greeks than the relations of their art to
that of the Orientals. Far from being subdued into mere imitators by the

technical excellence of their teachers, they lost no time in bettering the instruction they received, using their models as mere stepping stones on the way to those unsurpassed and unsurpassable achievements which are all their own. The shibboleth of Art is the human figure. The ancient Chaldaeans and Egyptians, like the modern Japanese, did wonders in the representation of birds and quadrupeds; they even attained to something more than respectability in human portraiture. But their utmost efforts never brought them within range of the best Greek embodiments of the grace of womanhood, or of the severer beauty of manhood.

It is worth while to consider the probable effect upon the acute and critical Greek mind of the conflict of ideas, social, political, and theological, which arose out of the conditions of life in the Asiatic colonies. The Ionian polities had passed through the whole gamut of social and political changes, from patriarchal and occasionally oppressive kingship to rowdy and still more burdensome mobship—no doubt with infinitely eloquent and copious argumentation, on both sides, at every stage of their progress towards that arbitrament of force which settles most political questions. The marvellous speculative faculty, latent in the Ionian, had come in contact with Mesopotamian, Egyptian, Phoenician theologies and cosmogonies; with the illuminati of Orphism and the fanatics and dreamers of the Mysteries; possibly with Buddhism and Zoroasterism; possibly even with Judaism. And it has been observed that the mutual contradictions of antagonistic supernaturalisms are apt to play a large part among the generative agencies of naturalism.

Thus, various external influences may have contributed to the rise of philosophy among the Ionian Greeks of the sixth century. But the assimilative capacity of the Greek mind—its power of Hellenizing whatever it touched—has here worked so effectually, that, so far as I can learn, no indubitable traces of such extraneous contributions are now allowed to exist by the most authoritative historians of Philosophy. Nevertheless, I think it must be admitted that the coincidences between the Heracleito-stoical doctrines and those of the older Hindu philosophy are extremely remarkable. In both, the cosmos pursues an eternal succession of cyclical changes. The great year, answering to the Kalpa, covers an entire cycle from the origin of the universe as a fluid to its dissolution in fire—"Humor initium, ignis exitus mundi," as Seneca has it. In both systems, there is immanent in the cosmos a source of energy, Brahma, or the Logos, which works according to fixed laws. The individual soul is an efflux of this world-spirit, and returns to it. Perfection is attainable only by individual effort, through ascetic discipline, and is rather a state of painlessness than of happiness; if indeed it can be said to be a state of anything, save the negation of perturbing emotion. The hatchment motto "In Caelo Quies" would serve both Hindu and Stoic; and absolute quiet is not easily distinguishable from annihilation.

Zoroasterism, which, geographically, occupies a position intermediate between Hellenism and Hinduism, agrees with the latter in recognizing the essential evil of the cosmos; but differs from both in its intensely anthropomorphic personification of the two antagonistic principles, to the one of which it ascribes all the good; and, to the other, all the evil.

In fact, it assumes the existence of two worlds, one good and one bad; the latter created by the evil power for the purpose of damaging the former. The existing cosmos is a mere mixture of the two, and the 'last judgment' is a root-and-branch extirpation of the work of Ahriman.

12 There is no snare in which the feet of a modern student of ancient lore are more easily entangled, than that which is spread by the similarity of the language of antiquity to modern modes of expression. I do not presume to interpret the obscurest of Greek philosophers; all I wish is to point out, that his words, in the sense accepted by competent interpreters, fit modern ideas singularly well.

So far as the general theory of evolution goes there is no difficulty. The aphorism about the river; the figure of the child playing on the shore; the kingship and fatherhood of strife, seem decisive. The οδος ανω κατω μιη expresses, with singular aptness, the cyclical aspect of the one process of organic evolution in individual plants and animals: yet it may be a question whether the Heracleitean strife included any distinct conception of the struggle for existence. Again, it is tempting to compare the part played by the Heracleitean 'fire' with that ascribed by the moderns to heat, or rather to that cause of motion of which heat is one expression; and a little ingenuity might find a foreshadowing of the doctrine of the conservation of energy, in the saying that all the things are changed into fire and fire into all things, as gold into goods and goods into gold.

13. Pope's lines in the *Essay on Man* (Ep. i. 267–8)

> "All are but parts of one stupendous whole,
> Whose body Nature is, and God the soul,"

simply paraphrase Seneca's "quem in hoc mundo locum deus obtinet, hunc in homine animus: quod est illic materia, id nobis corpus est."—(Ep. 1xv. 24); which again is a Latin version of the old Stoical doctrine, ειζ απαν του κοσμου μεροζ διηκει ο νουζ καθαπερ αφ ημων η ψυχη.

So far as the testimony for the universality of what ordinary people call 'evil' goes, there is nothing better than the writings of the Stoics themselves. They might serve as a storehouse for the epigrams of the ultra-pessimists. Heracleitus *(Circa* 500 B.C.) says just as hard things about ordinary humanity as his disciples centuries later; and there really seems no need to seek for the causes of this dark view of life in the circumstances of the time of Alexander's successors or of the early Emperors of Rome. To the man with an ethical ideal, the world, including himself, will always seem full of evil.

14. I use the well-known phrase, but decline responsibility for the libel upon Epicurus, whose doctrines were far less compatible with existence

in a stye than those of the Cynics. If it were steadily borne in mind that the conception of the 'flesh' as the source of evil, and the great saying 'Initium est salutis notitia peccati,' are the property of Epicurus, fewer illusions about Epicureanism would pass muster for accepted truth.

15. The Stoics said that man was a ζωον λογικον πολιτικον φιλαλληλον or a rational, a political, and an altruistic or philanthropic animal. In their view, his higher nature tended to develop in these three directions, as a plant tends to grow up into its typical form. Since, without the introduction of any consideration of pleasure or pain, whatever thwarted the realization of its type by the plant might be said to be bad, and whatever helped it good; so virtue, in the Stoical sense, as the conduct which tended to the attainment of the rational, political, and philanthropic ideal, was good in itself, and irrespectively of its emotional concomitants.

Man is an "animal sociale communi bono genitum." The safety of society depends upon practical recognition of the fact. "Salva autem esse societas nisi custodia et amore partium non possit," says Seneca. *(De. Ira,* ii. 31.)

16. The importance of the physical doctrine of the Stoics lies in its clear recognition of the universality of the law of causation, with its corollary, the order of nature: the exact form of that order is an altogether secondary consideration.

Many ingenious persons now appear to consider that the incompatibility of pantheism, of materialism, and of any doubt about the immortality of the soul, with religion and morality, is to be held as an axiomatic truth. I confess that I have a certain difficulty in accepting this dogma. For the Stoics were notoriously materialists and pantheists of the most extreme character; and while no strict Stoic believed in the eternal duration of the individual soul, some even denied its persistence after death. Yet it is equally certain that of all gentile philosophies, Stoicism exhibits the highest ethical development, is animated by the most religious spirit, and has exerted the profoundest influence upon the moral and religious development not merely of the best men among the Romans, but among the moderns down to our own day.

Seneca was claimed as a Christian and placed among the saints by the fathers of the early Christian Church; and the genuineness of a correspondence between him and the apostle Paul has been hotly maintained in our own time, by orthodox writers. That the letters, as we possess them, are worthless forgeries is obvious; and writers as wide apart as Baur and Lightfoot agree that the whole story is devoid of foundation.

The dissertation of the late Bishop of Durham *(Epistle to the Philippians)* is particularly worthy of study, apart from this question, on account of the evidence which it supplies of the numerous similarities of thought between Seneca and the writer of the Pauline epistles. When it is remembered that the writer of the Acts puts a quotation from Aratus, or Cleanthes, into the mouth of the apostle; and that Tarsus was a great seat of philosophical and especially stoical learning (Chrysippus himself was a native of the adjacent town of Soi), there is no difficulty in understanding the origin of these resemblances. See, on this subject, Sir Alexander Grant's dissertation in his edition of *The Ethics of Aristotle* (where there is an interesting reference to the stoical character of Bishop Butler's ethics), the concluding pages of Dr. Weygoldt's instructive little work *Die Philosophie der Stoa,* and Aubertin's *Seneque et Saint Paul.*

It is surprising that a writer of Dr. Lightfoot's stamp should speak of Stoicism as a philosophy of 'despair.' Surely, rather, it was a philosophy of men who, having cast off all illusions, and the childishness of despair among them, were minded to endure in patience whatever conditions the cosmic process might create, so long as those conditions were compatible with the progress towards virtue, which alone, for them, conferred a worthy object on existence. There is no note of despair in the stoical declaration that the perfected 'wise man' is the equal of Zeus in everything but the duration of his existence. And, in my judgment, there is as little pride about it, often as it serves for the text of discourses on stoical arrogance. Grant the stoical postulate that there is no good except virtue; grant that the perfected wise man is altogether virtuous, in consequence of being guided in all things by the reason, which is an effluence of Zeus, and there seems no escape from the stoical conclusion.

17. Our "Apathy" carries such a different set of connotations from its Greek original that I have ventured on using the latter as a technical term.

18. Many of the stoical philosophers recommended their disciples to take an active share in public affairs; and in the Roman world, for several centuries, the best public men were strongly inclined to Stoicism. Nevertheless, the logical tendency of Stoicism seems to me to be fulfilled only in such men as Diogenes and Epictetus.

19. "Criticisms on the Origin of Species," 1864. *Collected Essays,* vol. ii. p. 91. [1894.]

20. Of course, strictly speaking, social life, and the ethical process in virtue of which it advances towards perfection, are part and parcel of the general process evolution, just as the gregarious habit of innumerable plants and animals, which has been of immense advantage to them, is so. A hive of bees is an organic polity, a society in which the part played by each member is determined by organic necessities. Queens, workers, and drones are, so to speak, castes, divided from one another by marked physical barriers. Among birds and mammals, societies are formed, of which the bond in many cases seems to be purely psychological; that is to say, it appears to depend upon the liking of the individuals for one another's company. The tendency of individuals to over self-assertion is kept down by fighting. Even in these rudimentary forms of society, love and fear come into play, and enforce a greater or less renunciation of self-will. To this extent the general cosmic process begins to be checked

by a rudimentary ethical process, which is, strictly speaking, part of the former, just as the 'governor' in a steam-engine is part of the mechanism of the engine.

21. See "Government: A Anarchy or Regimentation," *Collected Essays,* vol. i. pp. 413–418. It is this form of political philosophy to which I conceive the epithet of 'reasoned savagery' to be strictly applicable. [1894.]

22. "L'homme n'est qu'un roseau, le plus faible de la nature, mais c'est un roseau pensant. il ne faut pas que l'univers entier s'arme pour l'ecraser. Une vapeur, une goutte d'eau, suffit pour le tuer. Mais quand l'univers l'ecraserait, l'homme serait encore plus noble que ce qui le tue, parce qu'il sait qu'il meurt; et l'avantage que l'univers a sur lui, l'univers n'en sait rien."—*Pensees de Pascal.*

23. The use of the word "Nature" here may be criticised. Yet the manifestation of the natural tendencies of men is so profoundly modified by training that it is hardly too strong. Consider the suppression of the sexual instinct between near relations.

24. A great proportion of poetry is addressed by the young to the young; only the great masters of the art are capable of divining, or think it worthwhile to enter into, the feelings of retrospective age. The two great poets whom we have so lately lost, Tennyson and Browning, have done this, each in his own inimitable way; the one in the *Ulysses,* from which I have borrowed; the other in that wonderful fragment 'Childe Roland to the dark Tower came.'

PART II

IN THE WAKE OF *SOCIOBIOLOGY*

Edward O. Wilson

The Morality of the Gene

Camus said that the only serious philosophical question is suicide. That is wrong even in the strict sense intended. The biologist, whose concerned with questions of physiology and evolutionary history, realizes that self-knowledge is constrained and shaped by the emotional control centers in the hypothalamus and limbic system of the brain. These centers flood our consciousness with all the emotions—hate, love, guilt, fear, and others—that are consulted by ethical philosophers who wish to intuit the standards of good and evil. What, we are then compelled to ask, made the hypothalamus and limbic system? They evolved by natural selection. That simple biological statement must be pursued to explain ethics and ethical philosophers, if not epistemology and epistemologists, at all depths. Self-existence, or the suicide that terminates it, is not the central question of philosophy. The hypothalamic-limbic complex automatically denies such logical reduction by countering it with feelings of guilt and altruism. In this one way the philosopher's own emotional control centers are wiser than his solipsist consciousness, "knowing" that in evolutionary time the individual organism counts for almost nothing. In a Darwinist sense the organism does not live for itself. Its primary function is not even to reproduce other organisms; it reproduces genes, and it serves as their temporary carrier. Each organism generated by sexual reproduction is a unique, accidental subset of all the genes constituting the species. Natural selection is the process whereby certain genes gain representation in the following generations superior to that of other genes located at the same chromosome positions. When new sex cells are manufactured in each generation, the winning genes are pulled apart and reassembled to manufacture new organisms that, on the average, contain a higher proportion of the same genes. But the individual organism is only their vehicle, part of an elaborate device to preserve and spread them with the least possible biochemical perturbation. Samuel Butler's famous aphorism, that the chicken is only an egg's way of making another egg, has been modernized: the organism is only DNA's way of making more DNA. More to the point, the hypothalamus and limbic system are engineered to perpetuate DNA.

In the process of natural selection, then, any device that can insert a higher proportion of certain genes into subsequent generations will come to characterize the species. One class of such devices promotes prolonged individual survival. Another promotes superior mating performance and care of the resulting offspring. As more complex social behavior by the organism is added to the genes' techniques for replicating themselves, altruism becomes increasingly prevalent and eventually appears in exaggerated forms. This brings us to the central theoretical problem of sociobiology: how can altruism, which by definition reduces personal fitness, possibly evolve by natural selection? The answer is kinship: if the genes causing the altruism are shared by two organisms because of common descent, and if the altruistic act by one organism increases the joint contribution of these genes to the next generation, the propensity to altruism will spread through the gene pool. This occurs even though the altruist make less of a solitary contribution to the gene pool as the price of its altruistic act.

To his own question, "Does the Absurd dictate death?" Camus replied that the struggle toward the heights is itself enough to fill a man's heart. This arid judgment is probably correct, but it makes little sense except when closely examined in the light of evolutionary theory. The hypothalamic-limbic complex of a highly social species, such as man, "knows," or more precisely it has been programmed to perform as if it knows, that its underlying genes will be proliferated maximally only if it orchestrates behavioral responses that bring into play an efficient mixture of personal survival, reproduction, and altruism. Consequently, the centers of the complex tax the conscious mind with ambivalences whenever the organisms encounter stressful situations. Love joins hate; aggression, fear; expansiveness, withdrawal; and so on; in blends designed not to promote the happiness and survival of the individual, but to favor the maximum transmission of the controlling genes.

The ambivalences stem from counteracting pressures on the units of natural selection. Their genetic consequences will be explored formally later in this book. For the moment suffice it to note that what is good for the individual can be destructive to the family; what preserves the family can be harsh on both the individual and the tribe to which its family belongs; what promotes the tribe can weaken the family and destroy the individual; and so on upward through the permutations of levels of organization. Counteracting selection on these different units will result in certain genes being multiplied and fixed, others lost, and combinations of still others held in static proportions. According to the present theory, some of the genes will produce emotional states that reflect the balance of counteracting selection forces at the different levels.

I have raised a problem in ethical philosophy in order to characterize the essence of sociobiology. Sociobiology is defined as the systematic study of the biological basis of all social behavior. For the present it focuses on animal societies, their population structure, castes, and communication, together with all of the physiology underlying the social adaptations. But the discipline is also concerned with the social behavior of early man and the adaptive features of organization in the more primitive contemporary human societies. Sociology *sensu stricto*, the study of human societies at all levels of complexity, still stands apart from sociobiology because of its largely structuralist and nongenetic approach. It attempts to explain human behavior primarily by empirical description of the outermost phenotypes and by unaided intuition, without reference to evolutionary explanations in the true genetic sense. It is most successful, in the way descriptive taxonomy and ecology have been most successful, when it provides a detailed description of particular phenomena and demonstrates first-order correlations with features of the environment. Taxonomy and ecology, however, have been reshaped entirely during the past forty years by integration into neo-Darwinist evolutionary theory—the "Modern Synthesis," as it is often called—in which each phenomenon is weighed for its adaptive significance and then related to the basic principles of population genetics. It may not be too much to say that sociology and the other social sciences, as well as the humanities, are the last branches of biology waiting to be included in the Modern Synthesis. One of the functions of sociobiology, then, is to reformulate the foundations of the social science in a way that draws these subjects into the Modern Synthesis. Whether the social sciences can be truly biologicized in this fashion remains to be seen.

This book makes an attempt to codify sociobiology into a branch of evolutionary biology and particularly of modern population biology. I believe that the subject has an adequate richness of detail and aggregate of self-sufficient concepts to be ranked as coordinate with such disciplines as molecular biology and developmental biology. In the past its development has been slowed by too close an identification with ethology and behavioral physiology. In the view presented here, the new sociobiology should be compounded of roughly equal parts of invertebrate zoology, vertebrate zoology, and population biology. Figure 1 shows the schema with which I closed *The Insect Societies,* suggesting how the amalgam can be achieved. Biologists have always been intrigued by comparisons between societies of invertebrates, especially insect societies, and those of vertebrates. They have dreamed of identifying the common properties of such disparate units in a way that would provide insight into all aspects of social evolution, including that of man. The goal can be expressed in modern terms as follows: when the same parameters and quantitative theory are used to analyze both termite colonies and troops of rhesus macaques, we will have a unified science of sociobiology. This may seem an impossibly difficult task. But as my own studies have advanced, I have been increasingly impressed with the functional simi-

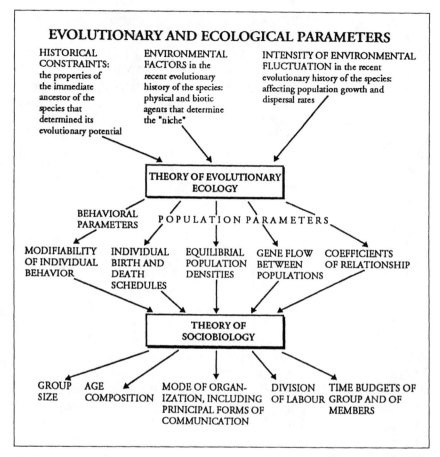

Figure 1. The connections that can be made between phylogenetic studies, ecology, and sociobiology.

larities between invertebrate and vertebrate societies and less
so with the structural differences that seem, at first glance,
to constitute such an immense gulf between them. Consider
for a moment termites and monkeys. Both are formed into
cooperative groups that occupy territories. The group members communicate hunger, alarm, hostility, caste status or
rank, and reproductive status among themselves by means
of something on the order of 10 to 100 nonsyntactical signals. Individuals are intensely aware of the distinction between group mates and nonmembers. Kinship plays an

important role in group structure and probably served as a chief generative force of sociality in the first place. In both kinds of society there is a well-marked division of labor, although in the insect society there is a much stronger reproductive component. The details of organization have been evolved by an evolutionary optimization process of unknown precision, during which some measure of added fitness was given to individuals with cooperative tendencies—at least toward relatives. The fruits of cooperativeness depend upon the particular conditions of the environment and are available to only a minority of animal species during the course of their evolution.

This comparison may seem facile, but it is out of such deliberate oversimplification that the beginnings of a general theory are made. The formulation of a theory of sociobiology constitutes, in my opinion, one of the great manageable problems of biology for the next twenty or thirty years. The prolegomenon of Figure 1 guesses part of its future outline and some of the directions in which it is most likely to lead animal behavior research. Its central precept is that the evolution of social behavior can be fully comprehended only through an understanding, first, of demography, which yields the vital information concerning population growth and age structure, and, second, of the genetic structure of the populations, which tells us what we need to know about effective population size in the genetic sense, the coefficients of relationship within the societies, and the amounts of gene flow between them. The principal goal of a general theory of sociobiology should be an ability to predict features of social organization from a knowledge of these population parameters combined with information on the behavioral constraints imposed by the genetic constitution of the species. It will be a chief task of evolutionary ecology, in turn, to derive the population parameters from a knowledge of the evolutionary history of the species and of the environment in which the most recent segment of that history unfolded. The most important feature of the prolegomenon, then, is the sequential relation between evolutionary studies, ecology, population biology, and sociobiology.

In stressing the tightness of this sequence, however, I do not wish to underrate the filial relationship that sociobiology has had in the past with the remainder of behavioral biology. Although behavioral biology is traditionally spoken of as if it were a unified subject, it is now emerging as two distinct disciplines centered on neurophysiology and on sociobiology, respectively. The conventional wisdom also speaks of ethology, which is the naturalistic study of whole patterns of animal behavior, and its companion enterprise, comparative psychology, as the central, unifying fields of behavioral biology. They are not; both are destined to be cannibalized by neurophysiology and sensory physiology from one end and sociobiology and behavioral ecology from the other (see Figure 2).

I hope not too many scholars in ethology and psychology will be offended by this vision of the future of behavioral biology. It seems to be indicated both by the extrapolation of current events and by consideration of the logical relationship behavioral biology holds with the remainder of science. The future, it seems clear, cannot be with the ad hoc terminology, crude models, and curve fitting that characterize most of contemporary ethology and comparative psychology. Whole patterns of animal behavior will inevitably be explained within the framework, first, of integrative neurophysiology, which classifies neurons and reconstructs their circuitry, and, second, of sensory physiology, which seeks to characterize the cellular transducers at the molecular level. Endocrinology will continue to play a peripheral role, since it is concerned with the cruder tuning devices of nervous activity. To pass from this level and reach the next really distinct discipline, we must travel all the way up to the society and the population. Not only are the phenomena best described by families of models different from those of cellular and molecular biology, but the explanations become largely evolutionary. There should be nothing surprising in this distinction. It is only a reflection of the larger division that separates the two greater domains of evolutionary biology and functional biology. As Lewontin (1972a) has truly said: "Natural selection of the character states themselves is the essence of Darwinism. All else is molecular biology."

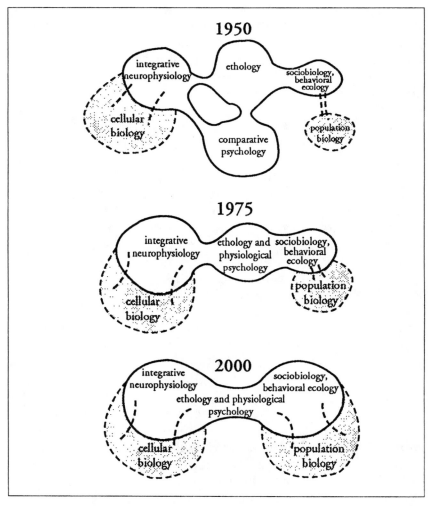

Figure 2. A subjective conception of the relative number of ideas in various disciplines in and adjacent to behavioral biology to the present time and as it might be in the future.

* * *

Scientists and humanists should consider together the possibility that the time has come for ethics to be removed temporarily from the hands of the philosophers and biologicized. The subject at present consists of several oddly disjunct conceptualizations. The first is *ethical intuitionism*, the belief that the mind has a direct awareness of true right and wrong that it can formalize by logic and translate into rules of social action. The purest guiding precept of secular Western thought has been the theory of the social contract as formulated by Locke, Rousseau, and Kant. In our time the precept has been rewoven into a solid philosophical system by John Rawls (1971). His imperative is that justice should be not merely integral to a system of government but rather the object of the original contract. The principles called by Rawls "justice as fairness" are those which free and rational persons would choose if they were beginning an association from a position of equal advantage and wished to define the fundamental rules of the association. In judging the appropriateness of subsequent laws and behavior, it would be necessary to test their conformity to the unchallengeable starting position.

The Achilles heel of the intuitionist position is that it relies on the emotive judgment of the brain as though that organ must be treated as a black box. While few will disagree that justice as fairness is an ideal state for disembodied spirits, the conception is in no way explanatory or predictive with reference to human beings. Consequently, it does not consider the ultimate ecological or genetic consequences of the rigorous prosecution of its conclusions. Perhaps explanation and prediction will not be needed for the millennium. But this is unlikely—the human genotype and the ecosystem in which it evolved were fashioned out of extreme unfairness. In either case the full exploration of the neural machinery of ethical judgment is desirable and already in progress. One such effort, constituting the second mode of conceptualization, can be called *ethical behaviorism*. Its basic proposition, which has been expanded most fully by J. F. Scott (1971), holds that moral commitment is entirely learned, with operant conditioning being the dominant mechanism. In other words, children simply internalize the behavioral norms of the society. Opposing this theory is the *developmental-genetic conception* of ethical behavior. The best-documented version has been provided by Lawrence Kohlberg (1969). Kohlberg's viewpoint is structuralist and specifically Piagetian, and therefore not yet related to the remainder of biology. Piaget has used the expression "genetic epistemology" and Kohlberg "cognitive-developmental" to label the general concept. However, the results will eventually become incorporated into a broadened developmental biology and genetics. Kohlberg's method is to record and classify the verbal responses of children to moral problems. He has delineated six sequential stages of ethical reasoning through which an individual may progress as part of his mental maturation. The child moves from a primary dependence on external controls and sanctions to an increasingly sophisticated set of internalized standards (see Table 1). The analysis has not yet been directed to the question of plasticity in the basic rules. Intracultural variance has not been measured, and heritability therefore not assessed. The difference between ethical behaviorism and the current version of developmental-genetic analysis is that the former postulates a mechanism (operant conditioning) without evidence and the latter presents evidence without postulating a mechanism. No great conceptual difficulty underlies this disparity. The study of moral development is only a more complicated and less tractable version of the genetic variance problem (see Chapters 2 and 7). With the accretion of data the two approaches can be expected to merge to form a recognizable exercise in behavioral genetics.

Even if the problem were solved tomorrow, however, an important piece would still be missing. This is the *genetic evolution of ethics.* In the first chapter of this book I argued that ethical philosophers intuit the deontological canons of morality by consulting the emotive centers of their own hypothalamic-limbic system. This is also true of the developmentalists, even when they are being their most severely objective. Only by interpreting the activity of the emotive center as a biological adaptation can the meaning of the canons be deciphered. Some of the activity is likely to be outdated, a relic of adjustment to the most primitive form of tribal organization. Some of it may prove to be *in statu nascendi,* constituting new and quickly changing adaptations to agrarian and urban life. The resulting confusion will be reinforced by other factors. To the extent that unilaterally altruistic genes have been established in the popula-

Table 1 The classification of moral judgment into levels and stages of development. (Based on Kohlberg, 1969.)

Level	Basis of moral judgment	Stage of development
I	Moral value is defined by punishment and reward	1. Obedience to rules and authority to avoid punishment 2. Conformity to obtain rewards and to exchange favors
II	Moral value resides in filling the correct roles, in maintaining order and meeting the expectations of others	3. Good-boy orientation: conformity to avoid dislike and rejection by others 4. Duty orientation: conformity to avoid censure by authority, disruption of order and resulting guilt
III	Moral value resides in conformity to shared standards, rights, and duties	5. Legalistic orientation: recognition of the value of contracts, some arbitrariness in rule formation to maintain the common good 6. Conscience or principle orientation: primary allegiance to principles of choice, which can overrule law in cases where the law is judged to do more harm than good

tion by group selection, they will be opposed by allelomorphs favored by individual selection. The conflict of impulses under their various controls is likely to be widespread in the population, since current theory predicts that the genes will be at best maintained in a state of balanced polymorphism (Chapter 5). Moral ambivalency will be further intensified by the circumstance that a schedule of sex- and age-dependent ethics can impart higher genetic fitness than a single moral code which is applied uniformly to all sex-age groups. The argument for this statement is the special case of the Gadgil-Bossert distribution in which the contributions of social interactions to survivorship and fertility schedules are specified (see Chapter 4). Some of the differences in the Kohlberg stages could be explained in this manner. For example, it should be of selective advantage for young children to be self-centered and relatively disinclined to perform altruistic acts based on personal principle. Similarly, adolescents should be more tightly bound by age-peer bonds within their own sex and hence unusually sensitive to peer approval. The reason is that at this time greater advantage accrues to the formation of alliances and rise in status than later, when sexual and parental morality become the paramount determinants of fitness. Genetically programmed sexual and parent-offspring conflict of the kind predicted by the Trivers models (Chapters 15 and 16) are also likely to promote age differences in the kinds and degrees of moral commitment. Finally, the moral standards of individuals during early phases of colony growth should differ in many details from those of individuals at demographic equilibrium or during episodes of overpopulation. Metapopulations subject to high levels of r extinction will tend to diverge genetically from other kinds of populations in ethical behavior (Chapter 5).

If there is any truth to this theory of innate moral pluralism, the requirement for an evolutionary approach to ethics is self-evident. It should also be clear that no single set of moral standards can be applied to all human populations, let alone all sex-age classes within each population. To impose a uniform code is therefore to create complex, intractable moral dilemmas—these, of course, are the current condition of mankind.

J. L. Mackie

The Law of the Jungle: Moral Alternatives and Principles of Evolution

When people speak of 'the law of the jungle', they usually mean unrestrained and ruthless competition, with everyone out solely for his own advantage. But the phrase was coined by Rudyard Kipling, in *The Second Jungle Book,* and he meant something very different. His law of the jungle is a law that wolves in a pack are supposed to obey. His poem says that 'the strength of the Pack is the Wolf, and the strength of the Wolf is the Pack', and it states the basic principles of social co-operation. Its provisions are a judicious mixture of individualism and collectivism, prescribing graduated and qualified rights for fathers of families, mothers with cubs, and young wolves, which constitute an elementary system of welfare services. Of course, Kipling meant his poem to give moral instruction to human children, but he probably thought it was at least roughly correct as a description of the social behaviour of wolves and other wild animals. Was he right, or is the natural world the scene of unrestrained competition, of an individualistic struggle for existence?

Views not unlike those of Kipling have been presented by some recent writers on ethology, notably Robert Ardrey and Konrad Lorenz. These writers connect their accounts with a view about the process of evolution that has brought this behaviour, as well as the animals themselves, into existence. They hold that the important thing in evolution is the good of the species, or the group, rather than the good of the individual. Natural selection favours those groups and species whose members tend, no doubt through some instinctive programming, to co-operate for a common good;

Reprinted with the permission of Cambridge University Press, "The Law of the Jungle: Moral Alternatives and Principles of Evolution," *Philosophy* (1978): 455–464. © 1978 Cambridge University Press.

this would, of course, explain why wolves, for example, behave cooperatively and generously towards members of their own pack, if indeed they do.

However, this recently popular view has been keenly attacked by Richard Dawkins in his admirable and fascinating book, *The Selfish Gene*.[1] He defends an up-to-date version of the orthodox Darwinian theory of evolution, with special reference to 'the biology of selfishness and altruism'. One of his main theses is that there is no such thing as group selection, and that Lorenz and others who have used this as an explanation are simply wrong. This is a question of some interest to moral philosophers, particularly those who have been inclined to see human morality itself as the product of some kind of natural evolution.[2]

It is well, however, to be clear about the issue. It is not whether animals ever behave for the good of the group in the sense that this is their conscious subjective goal, that they aim at the well-being or survival of the whole tribe or pack: the question of motives in this conscious sense does not arise. Nor is the issue whether animals ever behave in ways which do in fact promote the well-being of the group to which they belong, or which help the species of which they are members to survive: of course they do. The controversial issue is different from both of these: it is whether the good of the group or the species would ever figure in a correct evolutionary account. That is, would any correct evolutionary account take either of the following forms?

1. The members of this species tend to do these things which assist the survival of this species because their ancestors were members of a sub-species whose members had an inheritable tendency to do these things, and as a result that sub-species survived, whereas other sub-species of the ancestral species at that time had members who tended not to do these things and as a result their sub-species did not survive.

2. The members of this species tend to do these things which help the group of which they are members to flourish because some ancestral groups happened to have members who tended to do these things and these groups, as a result, survived better than related groups of the ancestral species whose members tended not to do these things.

In other words, the issue is this: is there natural selection by and for group survival or species survival as opposed to selection by and for individual survival (or, as we shall see, gene survival)? Is behaviour that helps the group or the species, rather than the individual animal, rewarded by the natural selection which determines the course of evolution?

However, when Dawkins denies that there is selection by and for group or species survival, it is not selection by and for individual survival that he puts in its place. Rather it is selection by and for the survival of each single gene— the genes being the unit factors of inheritance, the portions of chromosomes which replicate themselves, copy themselves as cells divide and multiply. Genes, he argues, came into existence right back at the beginning of life on earth, and all more complex organisms are to be seen as their products. We are, as he picturesquely puts it, gene-machines: our biological function is just to protect our genes, carry them around, and enable them to reproduce themselves. Hence the title of his book, *The Selfish Gene*. Of course what survives is not a token gene: each of these perishes with the cell of which it is a part. What survives is a gene-type, or rather what we might call a gene-clone, the members of a family of token genes related to one another by simple direct descent, by replication. The popularity of the notions of species selection and group selection may be due partly to confusion on this point. Since clearly it is only types united by descent, not individual organisms, that survive long enough to be of biological interest, it is easy to think that selection must be by and for species survival. But this is a mistake: genes, not species, are the types which primarily replicate themselves and are selected. Since Dawkins roughly defines the gene as 'a genetic unit which is small enough to last for a number of generations and to be distributed around in the form of many copies', it is (as he admits) practically a tautology that the gene is the basic unit of natural selection and therefore, as he puts it, 'the fundamental unit of self-interest', or, as we might put it less picturesquely, the primary beneficiary of natural selection. But behind this near-tautology is a synthetic truth, that this basic unit, this primary beneficiary, is a small bit of a chromosome. The reason

why this is so, why what is differentially effective and therefore subject to selection is a small bit of a chromosome, lies
in the mechanism of sexual reproduction by way of meiosis,
with crossing over between chromosomes. When male and
female cells each divide before uniting at fertilization, it is
not chromosomes as a whole that are randomly distributed
between the parts, but sections of chromosomes. So sections
of chromosomes can be separately inherited, and therefore
can be differentially selected by natural selection.

The issue between gene selection, individual selection,
group selection, and species selection might seem to raise
some stock questions in the philosophy of science. Many
thinkers have favoured reductionism of several sorts, including methodological individualism. Wholes are made up of
parts, and therefore in principle whatever happens in any
larger thing depends upon and is explainable in terms of
what happens in and between its smaller components. But
though this metaphysical individualism is correct, methodological individualism does not follow from it. It does not
follow that we must always conduct our investigations and
construct our explanations in terms of component parts,
such as the individual members of a group or society. Scientific accounts need not be indefinitely reductive. Some wholes
are obviously more accessible to us than their components.
We can understand what a human being does without
analysing this in terms of how each single cell in his body
or his brain behaves. Equally we can often understand what
a human society does without analysing this in terms of the
behaviour of each of its individual members. And the same
holds quite generally: we can often understand complex
wholes as units, without analysing them into their parts. So
if, in the account of evolution, Dawkins's concentration upon
genes were just a piece of methodological individualism or
reductionism, it would be inadequately motivated. But it is
not: there is a special reason for it. Dawkins's key argument
is that species, populations, and groups, and individual
organisms too, are as genetic units too temporary to qualify
for natural selection. 'They are not stable through evolutionary time. Populations are constantly blending with other
populations and so losing their identity', and, what is vitally

important, 'are also subject to evolutionary change from within' (p. 36).

This abstract general proposition may seem obscure. But it is illustrated by a simple example which Dawkins gives (pp. 197–201).

A species of birds is parasitized by dangerous ticks. A bird can remove the ticks from most parts of its own body, but, having only a beak and no hands, it cannot get them out of the top of its own head. But one bird can remove ticks from another bird's head: there can be mutual grooming. Clearly if there were an inherited tendency for each bird to take the ticks out of any other bird's head, this would help the survival of any group in which that tendency happened to arise for the ticks are dangerous: they can cause death. Someone who believed in group selection would, therefore, expect this tendency to be favoured and to evolve and spread for this reason. But Dawkins shows that it would not. He gives appropriate names to the different 'strategies', that is, the different inheritable behavioural tendencies. The strategy of grooming anyone who needs it he labels 'Sucker'. The strategy of accepting grooming from anyone, but never grooming anyone else, even someone who has previously groomed you, is called 'Cheat'. Now if in some population both these tendencies or strategies, and only these two, happen to arise, it is easy to see that the cheats will always do better than the suckers. They will be groomed when they need it, and since they will not waste their time pecking out other birds' ticks, they will have more time and energy to spare for finding food, attracting mates, building nests, and so on. Consequently the gene for the Sucker strategy will gradually die out. So the population will come to consist wholly of cheats, despite the fact that this is likely to lead to the population itself becoming extinct, if the parasites are common enough and dangerous enough, whereas a population consisting wholly of suckers would have survived. The fact that the group is open to evolutionary change from within, because of the way the internal competition between Cheat and Sucker genes works out, prevents the group from developing or even retaining a feature which would have helped the group as a whole.

This is just one illustration among many, and Dawkins's arguments on this point seem pretty conclusive. We need, as he shows, the concept of an *evolutionarily stable strategy* or ESS (p. 74 *et passim*). A strategy is evolutionarily stable, in relation to some alternative strategy or strategies, if it will survive indefinitely in a group in competition with those alternatives. We have just seen that where Cheat and Sucker alone are in competition, Cheat is an ESS but Sucker is not. We have also seen, from this example, that an ESS may not help a group, or the whole species, to survive and multiply. Of course we must not leap to the conclusion that an ESS never helps a group or a species: if that were so we could not explain much of the behaviour that actually occurs. Parents sacrifice themselves for their children, occasionally siblings for their siblings, and with the social insects, bees and ants and termites, their whole life is a system of communal service. But the point is that these results are not to be explained in terms of group selection. They can and must be explained as consequences of the selfishness of genes, that is, of the fact that gene-clones are selected for whatever helps each gene-clone itself to survive and multiply.

But now we come to another remarkable fact. Although the gene is the hero of Dawkins's book, it is not unique either in principle or in fact. It is not the only possible subject of evolutionary natural selection, nor is it the only actual one. What is important about the gene is just that it has a certain combination of logical features. It is a replicator: in the right environment it is capable of producing multiple copies of itself; but in this process of copying some mistakes occur; and these mistaken copies—mutations—will also produce copies of themselves; and, finally, the copies produced may either survive or fail to survive. Anything that has these formal, logical, features is a possible subject of evolution by natural selection. As we have seen, individual organisms, groups, and species do not have the required formal features, though many thinkers have supposed that they do. They cannot reproduce themselves with sufficient constancy of characteristics. But Dawkins, in his last chapter, introduces another sort of replicators. These are what are often called cultural items or traits; Dawkins christens them *memes*—to make a term a bit like 'genes'—because they replicate by memory and imitation (mimesis). Memes include tunes, ideas, fashions, and techniques. They require, as the environment in which they can replicate, a collection of minds, that is, brains that have the powers of imitation and memory. These brains (particularly though not exclusively human ones) are themselves the products of evolution by gene selection. But once the brains are there gene selection has done its work: given that environment, memes can themselves evolve and multiply in much the same way as genes do, in accordance with logically similar laws. But they can do so more quickly. Cultural evolution may be much faster than biological evolution. But the basic laws are the same. Memes are selfish in the same sense as genes. The explanation of the widespread flourishing of a certain meme, such as the idea of a god or the belief in hell fire, may be simply that it is an efficiently selfish meme. Something about it makes it well able to infect human minds, to take root and spread in and among them, in the same way that something about the smallpox virus makes it well able to take root and spread in human bodies. There is no need to explain the success of a meme in terms of any benefit it confers on individuals or groups; it is a replicator in its own right. Contrary to the optimistic view often taken of cultural evolution, this analogy shows that a cultural trait can evolve, not because it is advantageous to society, but simply because it is advantageous to itself. It is ironical that Kipling's phrase 'the law of the jungle' has proved itself a more efficient meme than the doctrine he tried to use it to propagate.

So far I have been merely summarizing Dawkins's argument. We can now use it to answer the question from which I started. Who is right about the law of the jungle? Kipling, or those who have twisted his phrase to mean almost the opposite of what he intended? The answer is that neither party is right. The law by which nature works is not unrestrained and ruthless competition between individual organisms. But neither does it turn upon the advantages to a group, and its members, of group solidarity, mutual care and respect, and co-operation. It turns upon the self-preservation of gene-clones. This has a strong tendency to express itself in individually selfish behaviour, simply because each agent's genes are more certainly located in him than in anyone else. But it can and does express itself also in certain forms of what Broad called self-referential altruism, including special care for one's own children and perhaps one's siblings, and, as we shall see, reciprocal altruism, helping those (and only those) who help you.

But now I come to what seems to be an exception to Dawkins's main thesis, though it is generated by his own argument and illustrated by one of his own examples. We saw how, in the example of mutual grooming, if there are only suckers and cheats around, the strategy Cheat is evolutionarily stable, while the strategy Sucker is not. But Dawkins introduces a third strategy, Grudger. A grudger is rather like you and me. A grudger grooms anyone who has previously groomed him, and any stranger, but he remembers and bears a grudge against anyone who cheats him— who refuses to groom him in return for having been groomed—and the grudger refuses to groom the cheat ever again. Now when all three strategies are in play, both Cheat and Grudger are evolutionarily stable. In a population consisting largely of cheats, the cheats will do better than the others, and both suckers and grudgers will die out. But in a population that starts off with more than a certain critical proportion of grudgers, the cheats will first wipe out the suckers, but will then themselves become rare and eventually extinct: cheats can flourish only while they have suckers to take advantage of, and yet by doing so they tend to eliminate those suckers.

It is obvious, by the way, that a population containing only suckers and grudgers, in any proportions, but no cheats, would simply continue as it was. Suckers and grudgers behave exactly like one another as long as there are no cheats around, so there would be no tendency for either the Sucker of the Grudger gene to do better than the other. But if there is any risk of an invasion of Cheat genes, either through mutation or through immigration, such a pattern is not evolutionarily stable, and the higher the proportion of suckers, the more rapidly the cheats would multiply.

So we have two ESSs, Cheat and Grudger. But there is a difference between these two stable strategies. If the parasites are common enough and dangerous enough, the population of cheats will itself die out, having no defence against ticks in their heads; whereas a separate population of grudgers will flourish indefinitely. Dawkins says, 'If a population arrives at an ESS which drives it extinct, then it goes extinct, and that is just too bad' (p. 200). True: *but is this not group selection after all?* Of course, this will operate only if the populations are somehow isolated. But if the birds in question were distributed in geographically isolated regions, and Sucker, Cheat and Grudger tendencies appeared (after the parasites became plentiful) in randomly different proportions in these different regions, then some populations would become pure grudger populations, and others would become pure cheat populations, but then the pure cheat populations would die out, so that eventually all surviving birds would be grudgers. And they would be able to re-colonize the areas where cheat populations had perished.

Another name for grudgers is 'reciprocal altruists'. They act as if on the maxim 'Be done by as you did'. One implication of this story is that this strategy is not only evolutionarily stable within a population, it is also viable for a population as a whole. The explanation of the final situation, where all birds of this species are grudgers, lies partly in the non-viability of a population of pure cheats. So this is, as I said, a bit of group selection after all.

It is worth noting how and why this case escapes Dawkins's key argument that a population is 'not a discrete enough entity to be a unit of natural selection, not stable and unitary enough to be "selected" in preference to another population' (p. 36). Populations can be made discrete by geographical (or other) isolation, and can be made stable and unitary precisely by the emergence of an ESS in each, but perhaps different ESSs in the different regional populations of the same species. This case of group selection is necessarily a second order phenomenon: it arises where gene selection has produced the ESSs which are then persisting selectable features of groups. In other words, an ESS may be a third variety of replicator, along with genes and memes; it is a self-reproducing feature *of groups.*

Someone might reply that this is not really group selection because it all rests ultimately on gene selection, and a full explanation can be given in terms of the long-run self-extinction of the Cheat gene, despite the fact that within a population it is evolutionarily stable in competition with the two rival genes. But this would be a weak reply. The monopoly of cheating *over a population* is an essential part of the causal story that explains the extinction. Also, an account at the group level, though admittedly incomplete, is here correct as far as it goes. The reason why all ultimately surviving birds of this species are grudgers is partly that *populations* of grudgers can survive whereas *populations* of cheats cannot, though it is also partly that although a population of suckers could survive—it would be favoured by group selection, if this possibility arose, just as much as a population of grudgers—internal changes due to gene selection after an invasion of Cheat genes would prevent there being a population of suckers. In special circumstances group selection (or population selection) can occur and could be observed and explained as such, without going down to the gene selection level. It would be unwarranted methodological individualism or reductionism to insist that we not merely can but must go down to the gene selection level here. We must not fall back on this weak general argument when Dawkins's key argument against group selection fails.

I conclude, then, that there can be genuine cases of group selection. But I admit that they are exceptional. They require rather special conditions, in particular geographical isolation, or some other kind of isolation, to keep the populations that are being differentially selected apart. For if genes from one could infiltrate another, the selection of populations might be interfered with. (Though in fact in our example *complete* isolation is not required: since what matters is whether there is more or less than a certain critical proportion of grudgers, small-scale infiltrations would only delay, not prevent, the establishing of pure populations.) And since special conditions are required, there is no valid general principle that features which would enable a group to flourish will be selected. And even these exceptional cases conform thoroughly to the general logic of Dawkins's doctrine. Sometimes, but only sometimes, group characteristics have the formal features of replicators that are open to natural selection.

Commenting on an earlier version of this paper, Dawkins agreed that there could be group selection in the sort of case I suggested, but stressed the importance of the condition of geographical (or other) isolation. He also mentioned a possible example, that the prevalence of sexual reproduction itself may be a result of group selection. For if there were a mutation by which asexual females, producing offspring by parthenogenesis, occurred in a species, this clone of asexual females would be at once genetically isolated from the rest of the species, though still geographically mixed with them. Also, in most species males contribute little to the nourishment or care of their offspring; so from a genetic point of view males are wasters: resources would be more economically used if devoted only to females. So the genetically isolated population of asexual females would out-compete the normal sexually reproducing population with roughly equal numbers of males and females. So the species would in time consist only of asexual females. But then, precisely because all its members were genetically identical, it would not have the capacity for rapid adaptation by selection to changing conditions that an ordinary sexual population has. So when conditions changed, it would be unable to adapt, and would die out. Thus there would in time be species selection against any species that produced an asexual female mutation. Which would explain why nearly all existing species go in for what, in the short run, is the economically wasteful business of sexual reproduction.[3]

What implications for human morality have such biological facts about selfishness and altruism? One is that the possibility that morality is itself a product of natural selection is not ruled out, but care would be needed in formulating a plausible speculative account of how it might have been favoured. Another is that the notion of an ESS may be a useful one for discussing questions of practical morality. Moral philosophers have already found illumination in such simple items of game theory as the Prisoners' Dilemma; perhaps these rather more complicated evolutionary 'games' will prove equally instructive. Of course there is no simple transition from 'is' to 'ought', no direct argument from what goes on in the natural world and among non-human animals to what human beings ought to do. Dawkins himself explicitly warns against any simple transfer of conclusions. At the very end of the book he suggests that conscious foresight may enable us to develop radically new kinds of behaviour. 'We are built as gene machines and cultured as meme machines, but we have the power to turn against our creators. We, alone on earth, can rebel against the tyranny of the selfish replicators' (p. 215). This optimistic suggestion needs fuller investigation. It must be remembered that the human race as a whole cannot act as a unit with conscious foresight. Arrow's Theorem shows that even quite small groups of rational individuals may be unable to form coherent rational preferences, let alone to act rationally. Internal competition, which in general prevents a group from being a possible subject of natural selection, is even more of an obstacle to its being a rational agent. And while we can turn against some memes, it will be only with the help and under the guidance of other memes.

This is an enormous problematic area. For the moment I turn to a smaller point. In the mutual grooming model, we saw that the Grudger strategy was, of the three strategies considered, the only one that was healthy in the long run. Now something closely resembling this strategy, reciprocal altruism, is a well known and long established tendency in human life. It is expressed in such formulae as that justice consists in giving everyone his due, interpreted, as Polemarchus interprets it in the first book of Plato's *Republic*, as doing good to one's friends and harm to one's enemies, or repaying good with good and evil with evil. Morality itself has been seen, for example by Edward Westermarck, as an outgrowth from the retributive emotions. But some moralists, including Socrates and Jesus, have recommended something very different from this, turning the other cheek and repaying evil with good. They have tried to substitute 'Do as you would be done by' for 'Be done by as you did'.

Now this, which in human life we characterize as a Christian spirit or perhaps as saintliness, is roughly equivalent to the strategy Dawkins has unkindly labelled 'Sucker'. Suckers are saints, just as grudgers are reciprocal altruists, while cheats are a hundred per cent selfish. And as Dawkins points out, the presence of suckers endangers the healthy Grudger strategy. It allows cheats to prosper, and could make them multiply to the point where they would wipe out the grudgers, and ultimately bring about the extinction of the whole population. This seems to provide fresh support for Nietzsche's view of the deplorable influence of moralities of the Christian type. But in practice there may be little danger. After two thousand years of contrary moral teaching, reciprocal altruism is still dominant in all human societies; thoroughgoing cheats and thoroughgoing saints (or suckers) are distinctly rare. The sucker slogan is an efficient meme, but the sucker behaviour pattern far less so. Saintliness is an attractive topic for preaching, but with little practical persuasive force. Whether in the long run this is to be deplored or welcomed, and whether it is alterable or not, is a larger question. To answer it we should have carefully to examine our specifically human capacities and the structure of human societies, and also many further alternative strategies. We cannot simply apply to the human situation conclusions drawn from biological models. Nevertheless they are significant and challenging as models; it will need to be shown how and where human life diverges from them.

Notes

1. R. Dawkins, *The Selfish Gene* (Oxford, 1976).

2. I am among these: see p. 113 of my *Ethics: Inventing Right and Wrong* (Penguin, Harmondsworth, 1977).

3. This suggestion is made in a section entitled 'The paradox of sex and the cost of paternal neglect' of the following article: R. Dawkins, 'The value judgements of evolution', in M. A. H. Dempster and D. J. McFarland (eds.) *Animal Economics* (Academic Press, London and New York, forthcoming).

R. D. Alexander

A Biological Interpretation of Moral Systems

ABSTRACT. Moral systems are described as systems of indirect reciprocity, existing because of histories of conflicts of interest and arising as outcomes of the complexity of social interactions in groups of long-lived individuals with varying conflicts and confluences of interest and indefinitely iterated social interactions. Although morality is commonly defined as involving justice for all people, or consistency in the social treatment of all humans, it may have arisen for immoral reasons, as a force leading to cohesiveness within human groups but specifically excluding and directed against other human groups with different interests.

A moral system is essentially a society with rules. Rules are agreements about what is permitted and what is not, about what rewards and punishments are likely for specific acts, about what is right and wrong. The definition of rules can be variously expanded or restricted. If it is used so as to include only consciously understood, deliberately applied rules, then moral systems may be uniquely human. This may also be the case—if certain kinds of unconscious or nonconscious elements are allowed into the definition. I will leave this problem for now, only noting that it is my intent here to concentrate on moral systems as they are known or discussed with respect to humans.

Aside from its reference to values, the concept of morality implies altruism or self-sacrifice. Not all moral acts call for self-sacrifice, however, and not all self-serving acts, by any means, would be termed immoral. On the other hand, I suspect most would agree that a moral life will inevitably

Reprinted with permission of the publisher, "A Biological Interpretation of Moral Systems," *Zygon* 20 (1985): 3–20.

call for *some* acts with net cost to the actor. Similarly, many acts with a net value to the actor would be judged immoral because alternative courses of action of value to others are available at the time but are not taken. Generally speaking, then, *immoral* is a label we apply to certain kinds of acts by which we help ourselves or hurt others, while acts that hurt ourselves or help others are more likely to be judged moral than immoral. As virtually endless arguments in the philosophical literature attest, it is not easy to be more precise in defining morality *per se.*

Agreement seems to be universal (and consistent with the above remarks) that moral (and ethical) questions and problems arise because of conflicts of interest; I have never found an author who disagrees. If there were no conflicts of interest among people and societies it is difficult to see how concepts of right and wrong, ethics and morality, and selfishness and altruism could ever have arisen. Probably, society would have remained simple in structure, and nothing like humans would ever have evolved.

Few people would deny that most or all humans tend to behave selfishly on occasion—indeed, in ways that would almost universally be termed immoral. This being true, it is difficult to apply the adjectives *moral* and *immoral* to human individuals let alone whole societies (hence, the moral philosophers' problem of "duality" in human nature); rather, these terms seem most appropriately applied to individual acts. Moreover, there is the complication that morality within groups (patriotism, loyalty, group effort) often, at least, correlates with opposite kinds of behavior to members of other groups, thus raising the question whether cooperation-to-compete has been the historical function of group unity. If it has, then we are faced with the possibility that morality was invented or instituted (and maintained and elaborated) for reasons that in a modern or intellectually consistent discussion would necessarily be seen as immoral. This is true unless the members of other groups can successfully be judged subhuman or nonhuman—a telling point in view of depictions of enemies during wartime and the widespread tendency of peoples to call themselves by names meaning *human* or *the people.*

The general idea of morality as serving others, or at least taking account of their interests rather than concentrating wholly on one's own, seems to be responsible for the generation of models of idealized moral conditions, or societies within which all people treat the interests of all people as equal in importance. These models, which prevail in the modern literature of moral philosophy, represent hypothetical societies in which conflicts of interest have been erased or supplanted by a concern for the welfare of all people in the society or for (in the utilitarian concept) the "greatest good to the greatest number." Presumably, the culmination of putting such a model into practice—or the true ideal of morality—would be a *world* in which *all people everywhere* viewed as equally important the interests of *all people everywhere.*

Probably, nearly everyone would accept the improbability of achieving an idealized morality involving universal indiscriminate altruism. On the other hand, many people might support the idea of striving to realize an idealized morality while accepting its improbability. Many would regard it as immoral deliberately to abandon such a goal.

The paradoxes inherent in these propositions have preoccupied philosophers and, indeed, people in all walks of life throughout history. In some sense they are the most important questions humans can ponder, if for no other reason than that we tend to draw into the moral and ethical realm every social problem that assumes increasing significance—notably the international arms race, exploitation and pollution of environments, medical uses of technology, population growth, racism, sexism, pornography, drug use, and many others. All together such issues account for virtually all major news stories, attesting to the centrality of conflicts of interest in our lives.

The difficulties in understanding the network of paradoxes that seems to make up the structure of moral and ethical propositions and practices, and the apparent incompatibility of morality as self-sacrifice with a history of evolution by natural selection, have caused even biologist-philosophers to base their conclusions, or appeal to readers, on grounds other than biological information and arguments, or to declare that trends toward morality are contrary to evolution and that biological knowledge cannot explain moral behavior (e.g., Huxley 1898; Lack 1954; Dobzhansky 1967).

I think that evolutionary subtheories in biology developed in the past twenty-six years (Fisher 1958; Williams 1957,1966a, 1966b; Hamilton 1964; Trivers 1971, 1974; Alexander 1979) place us in a new situation, in which we can start to resolve the age-old paradoxes surrounding the concepts of morality and ethics and in which modern views of idealized moralities can be accounted for. What follows here is an effort to show that *morality need not be contrary to natural selection or inconsistent with it but that, at least as practiced and perhaps also as imagined by most, it may instead be a logical outgrowth or extension of the practice of social reciprocity by a complexly social organism which changes as a result of both genetic evolution and cumulative social learning.*[1]

Interests

Leaving aside the question of conscious belief or personal opinion about one's goals or intentions, there is every reason to accept that humans like other organism are so evolved that their "interests" are reproductive. Said differently, the interests of an individual human (i.e., the directions of its striving) are expected to be toward ensuring the indefinite survival of its genes and their copies, whether these are resident in the individual, its descendants, or its collateral relatives.

In today's novelty-filled environments, human activities may often be directed in ways that do not in fact lead to increased success in reproduction or the perpetuation of one's own genes. Moreover, people aware of their background in evolution may be able to use conscious reflection and deliberate decisions to live their lives contrary to, or irrespective of, whatever their evolutionary background has prepared them to be. Neither of these possibilities, however, affects the essential certainty that humans have evolved to maximize survival of their genes through reproduction.

We need not be concerned with the possible argument that interests are only definable in terms of what people consciously believe are their interests or intentions. Biologists continually investigate the life interests of nonhuman organisms while lacking knowledge on this point and nonhuman organisms live out their lives serving their interest without knowing in the human sense what those interests are. Moreover, it is axiomatic that we are not consciously aware of all that motivates us, and that consciousness (hence, at least to some extent which parts of our knowledge and attitudes are conscious and which parts are not) could not have evolved if it did not serve reproductive interests.

Conflicts of Interests

Recognizing that interests are reproductive provides us with the mean for understanding and quantifying their conflicts. The first step is realizing that, for several well-described and documented reasons, selection is usually most effective at low levels in the hierarchy of organization of life (Fisher 1958; Williams 1966a; Lewontin 1970; Dawkins 1976, 1982; Alexander and Borgia 1978; Alexander 1979; Leigh 1983). One consequence is that individuals may be expected to behave so as to serve their own (genetic, reproductive) interests rather than the interests of others or of the whole group whenever the interests of others or the group conflict with those of the individual.

The second step, in recognizing and quantifying conflicts of interest is to realize that an evolutionary history of genetic individuality, which is a consequence of sexual reproduction, ought to yield individuals evolved to judge partial overlaps of interest with other individuals through, first, proximate mechanisms that correlate with numbers and kinds of genealogical links and, second, opportunities to achieve goals or deflect threats by cooperative efforts with others.

Several facts support the hypothesis that conflicts of interests arise out of a history of genetic individuality. First, there are evidently no reports of conflict among genetically identical individuals within clones among species that have for a long time reproduced asexually; and evidence of extraordinary cooperativeness in such cases abounds (cf. Alexander, in prep.). Second, altruism appears generally to diminish with decreasing degrees of relatedness in sexual species wherever it is studied, in humans as well as nonhuman species. Third, in cases in which identity or near-identity of genetic interests is achieved in sexual species (without genetic identity *per se)* cooperation is also dramatic. Examples are the two partners in lifetime monogamy and the members of the large social insect colonies that are actually nuclear families of enormous size (e.g., honeybees, ants, termites). In each case the cooperating parties (spouses, or workers and queens) reproduce via the same third parties (offspring, or siblings and offspring) to which they are more or less equally related genetically and which are usually the closest (needy) relatives available to each of them (Hamilton 1964; West Eberhard 1975; Alexander in prep.).

Life Effort and Social Interactions

The recent development of evolutionary subtheories about senescence, life patterns, reproductive value, and the costs and benefits of different kinds of social interactions enables us to begin constructing a general theory or picture of the components of human social life, the reproductive significance of these components, and how they interrelate.

Figure 1 describes a hypothetical human lifetime in terms of some ideas from modern evolutionary biology. The lifetime is postulated to be made up of *effort,* defined as expenditure of calories and taking of risks in the interests of reproducing (actually, in the interests of carrying out the best effort to cause one's genes to be immortal) (Williams 1966a).[2]

Lifetimes can be divided into somatic effort and reproductive effort. *Somatic effort* is designed (by evolution) to lead to growth, development, and maintenance of the soma, always, presumably, in such ways as to maximize effectiveness of later reproductive effort. Somatic effort, then, amounts

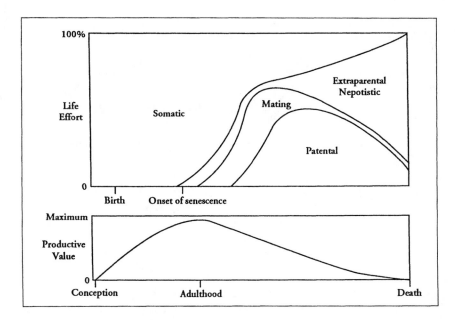

Figure 1. A hypothetical human lifetime, showing a plausible distribution of different kinds of effort and changes in reproductive value. All early effort is somatic, and somatic effort continues until death. Reproductive effort onsets before adulthood, here postulated in the form of extraparental nepotistic effort (e.g., help, or yielding of resources to siblings). Senescence onsets shortly afterward, when the effect of reproductive effort becomes sufficient to reduce residual reproductive value. Mating and parental effort onset later, and each of the three forms of reproductive effort are postulated to maximize at different times during adult life.

to the accumulation and conversion of resources in the interests of reproduction. Somatic effort typifies what is commonly termed the juvenile stages, although as maintenance it obviously has to occur in adults expecting to reproduce repeatedly or across a long period. Juvenile stages evidently evolve solely because, as amassers of resources, they raise the peak of reproductive value (achieved at about the usual age of first reproduction—see Fig. l) sufficiently to more than offset the expenses of mortality and lengthened generation time that are inevitably associated with the juvenile stage (cf. Low and Alexander, in prep.).

Reproductive effort, unlike somatic effort, lowers residual reproductive value, and for this reason its usual age of onset is predicted to correspond to the usual age of onset of senescence (defined as increasing susceptibility to environmental insults) (Williams 1957,1966a). Reproductive effort includes *mating effort* (on behalf of gametes), *parental effort* (on behalf of offspring), and *extraparental nepotistic effort* (on behalf of collateral relatives and descendants other than offspring) (Low 1978; Alexander and Borgia 1978). Theoretically, senescence can be caused to onset from any of these kinds of effort.

Because of male-female differences in early investment in the zygote, leading in turn to differences in investment in gametes before zygote formation, some acts by one sex (e.g., males) may represent mating effort for them (and be judged selfish) while the consequences of the acts (e.g., gifts or other resources) may represent (or be converted to) parental effort by the other sex (the female, in this case). The use of such resources by females to contribute to the reproductive value of prezygotic eggs, moreover, may be regarded as altruistic, because of the eventual usefulness of the resources to the zygote, which of course contains genetic materials from the male (Alexander and Borgia 1979). In all these cases the involved effort is reproductively (or genetically) selfish even if phenotypically costly or altruistic (Hamilton 1964; Alexander 1974).

Somatic effort can be further analyzed by dividing it into direct and indirect forms (see Fig. 2). *Direct somatic effort* is that engaged in by an individual with direct effects upon its own survival or well-being—for example, eating, drinking, fleeing a predator, or taking shelter from a storm—without help from anyone. *Indirect somatic effort* is that involving assistance from others (efforts to secure resources for relatives through such interaction would be termed *indirect nepotistic effort).* Indirect somatic effort thus always involves investments in reciprocity, although the nature of such investments may vary considerably, as between, say, a nursing infant and its

	Effects	
Kind of Effort	Phenotypically	Genetically
Somatic Effort		
Direct	selfish	selfish
Immediate		
Delayed		
Indirect (involves	selfish	selfish
reciprocity, *s. lat.*)		
Direct Reciprocity		
Immediate		
Delayed		
Indirect Reciprocity		
Immediate		
Delayed		
Reproductive Effort (= nepotism, *s. lat.*)		
Mating Effort	altruistic	selfish
Parental Effort	altruistic	selfish
Extraparental	altruistic	selfish
Nepotistic effort		

Figure 2. Kinds of effort and their outcomes. Direct somatic effort refers to self-help that involves no other persons. Indirect somatic effort involves reciprocity, which may be direct or indirect. Returns from direct or indirect reciprocity may be immediate or delayed. Reciprocity can be indirect for two different reasons, or in two different ways. First, returns (payment) for a social investment (positive or negative) can come from someone other than the recipient of the investment, and second, returns can go either to the original investor or to a relative or friend of the original investor.

mother as compared to two partners in a business venture. It is contended here that investments in social reciprocity evolve (or the proximate mechanisms by which they are effected evolve) so as to yield returns greater than their expenses, that is, they always represent indirect somatic or indirect nepotistic effort. Such acts would therefore be judged not altruistic but (when indirect somatic effort) both phenotypically and genetically selfish or (when indirect nepotistic effort) phenotypically altruistic but genetically selfish.

Reciprocity can be direct or indirect, and immediate or delayed. *Direct reciprocity* occurs when an individual's social contribution or investment (positive or negative) is returned (not necessarily in the same currency) by the same individual in which the original actor invested. *Indirect reciprocity* I have defined as those cases in which the dividends from social investments are likely to come from individuals other than those helped (or hurt) by the original actor (Alexander 1977, 1979).[3]

I think these considerations bring us closer to taking the vagueness out of the concept of morality and tend to reinforce the theory that, in biological terms, the social life of humans is composed of nepotism—one-way flows of benefits to relatives in which the return is genetic (Hamilton 1964) and reciprocity—two-way or still more complex flows of benefits involving both relatives and nonrelatives (Trivers 1971; Axelrod and Hamilton 1981).

The essence of moral systems seems to lie in patterns of indirect reciprocity (Alexander 1977, 1979, in prep.), and so I will now concentrate on describing such patterns and their results, while acknowledging and attempting to explain how nepotism and direct reciprocity may influence the development and maintenance of indirect reciprocity.

Indirect reciprocity is what happens when direct reciprocity occurs in the presence of an interested audience. Some of its consequences are described in Figures 3, 4, and 5. These consequences include the concomitant spread of altruism (as genetically valuable social investment), rules, and cheating. I am not contending that cost-benefit analyses of the kind depicted in Figures 3, 4, and 5 are always carried out deliberately or consciously but only that they do occur, sometimes consciously sometimes not, and that we are evolved to be exceedingly accurate and quick at making such analyses.

Indirect Reciprocity

Rewards (why altruism spreads):

---

1. A helps B	*or* 1. A helps B
2. B helps (or overhelps) A	2. B does not help A
3. C, observing, helps B, expecting that	3. C, observing, does not help B expecting that, if he does
4. B will also help (or overhelp) C (etc.)	4. B will not return the help (etc.)

Figure 3. Indirect reciprocity: why altruism spreads.

Indirect Reciprocity

Punishment (why rules spread):

---

1. A hurts B	3. A will also hurt C
2. C, observing, punishes A expecting that, if he does not,	*or that*
	4. someone else, also observing, will hurt C, expecting no cost (etc.)

Figure 4. Indirect reciprocity: why cheating spreads.

Indirect Reciprocity

Deception (why cheating spreads):

---

1. A1 makes it look as though he helps B	4. A2, better at cheating, fools C2
2. C1 helps A1, expecting that A1 will also help him	5. C3 detects A2's cheating (etc.)
3. C2 observes more keenly and detects A1's cheating and does not help him (avoids or punishes him)	C1 $\rightarrow$ C2 $\rightarrow$ C3 \ either learning or evolution (or both) A1 $\rightarrow$ A2 $\rightarrow$ A3/

Figure 5. Indirect reciprocity: why punishment spreads.

The long-term existence of complex patterns of indirect reciprocity may be seen as favoring the evolution of
keen abilities, first, to make one's self seem more altruistic
than is the case and, second, to influence others to be
altruistic in such fashions as to be deleterious to themselves and beneficial to the moralizer, for example, to lead
others to invest too much, invest wrongly in the moralizer
or his relatives and friends, or invest indiscriminately on a
larger scale than would otherwise be the case. Thus, individuals are expected to parade the ideas of much altruism
and of indiscriminate altruism as beneficial, so as to encourage people in general to engage in increasing amounts
of social investment whether or not it is beneficial to their
interests. They may be expected to locate and exploit av-
enues of genetic relatedness leading to nepotistic flows of
benefits (e.g., to insinuate themselves deceptively into the
role of relative or reciprocator so as to receive the benefits
therefrom). They may also be expected to depress the fitness
of competitors by identifying them, deceptively or not, as
reciprocity cheaters; to internalize rules or evolve the ability to acquire a conscience, which I have interpreted as the
ability to use our own judgment to serve our own interests;
and to self-deceive and display false sincerity as defenses
against detection of cheating and attributions of deliber-
ateness in cheating (Trivers 1971; Campbell 1975; Alexander
1974, 1977, 1979, 1982, in prep.).

Moral Behavior as Self-Beneficial

If current views of evolutionary processes are correct, reciprocity will flourish when the benefits donated by each
partner are relatively inexpensive compared to the returns
(Trivers 1971, West Eberhard 1975). This kind of asymmetry
is prevalent under two circumstances: the first is when threats
or promises extrinsic to the interactants cause joint similar
efforts to be worth more than the sum of their separate
contributions, leading to more or less symmetrical cooperation. The second is when the contributions of partners in
reciprocity are different, leading to division of labor. The

second situation can arise out of different abilities or training in different contributors, or from differences in their accumulated resources.

Indirect reciprocity must have arisen out of the search for interactants and situations by which to maximize returns from asymmetrical, hence highly profitable social reciprocity. One consequence of large, complex societies in which reciprocity is the principal social cement and indirect reciprocity is prevalent is that opportunities for such mutually profitable asymmetrical reciprocal interactions are vastly multiplied. This situation in turn fosters the appearance of tendencies to engage in *indiscriminate social investment* (or indiscriminate altruism)—willingness to risk relatively small expenses in certain kinds of social donations to whomever may be needy—because of the prevalence and keenness of observation and the use of such acts by others to identify individuals appropriate for later reciprocal interactions.[4] In complex social systems with much reciprocity, being judged as attractive for such possibilities may become an essential ingredient for success. Similarly, to be judged harshly because of failure to deliver small social benefits indiscriminately in appropriate situations may lead to formidable disadvantages because of either direct penalties or lost opportunities in subsequent reciprocal interactions.

Figure 6 describes hypothetical social stages through which the evolving human species might have passed (many times). These seem to lead toward a utilitarian or idealized model of morality in which all social investment becomes indiscriminate altruism (but, as argued here, have so far invariably fallen short).

Direct reciprocity must have occurred early in the human line as a part of the male-female interaction. Initially it may have functioned as mating effort, subsequently as indirect nepotism through effects on offspring produced jointly by the pair. Alternatively, direct reciprocity may have arisen as a modification of nepotistic altruism. I suggest that indirect reciprocity followed quickly from one (or all) of these beginnings, leading to the evolution of ever keener abilities to observe and interpret situations with moral overtones. In such a milieu, I would argue, a modicum of

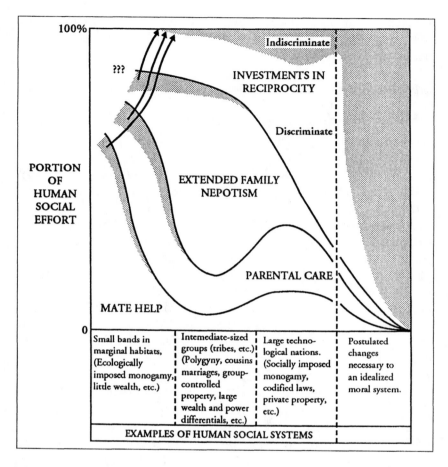

Figure 6. A speculation about the relative importance of different kinds of social interactions in some different kinds of societies. The principal purpose is to show the probable origins of indiscriminate altruism, its probable significance in different societies, and the changes from existing societies that would be necessary to realize an idealized model of morality in which everyone was indiscriminately altruistic.

indiscriminate altruism would arise as social investments because of benefits to individuals of being viewed as altruists.

General encouragement of indiscriminate altruism and general acceptance of its beneficial effects result in a society with high social unity. This encouragement and acceptance is expected to occur partly because of the likelihood, much of the time, that nearly everyone benefits from living in a unified society and partly because individuals gain from inducing indiscriminate altruism in others (and from inducing degrees of it that are deleterious to those others). I would postulate that self-serving indiscriminate social investment—because it was seen as net-cost altruism and was interpreted wrongly as part of a real trend toward universal indiscriminate (net-cost) altruism—provided the impetus for the idealized modern model of morality portrayed in Figure 6.

It is a crucial part of the argument that indiscriminate altruism seems to have been viewed widely not as a beneficial social investment to the altruist but as self-sacrificial or net-cost altruism (i.e., as both phenotypically and genetically altruistic). In turn, morality in general was viewed as self-sacrificing, and it seemed logical to project the expansion of indiscriminate, self-sacrificial altruism to include most or all social interactions—thus providing, perhaps, part of the reason for the idealized moral models of many modern thinkers which call for utilitarianism based on a self-sacrificing kind of indiscriminate altruism (cf. Alexander in prep.).

The concepts of justice as fairness, or equal opportunities for all, and of justice and equality as moral must have gained currency during human history in relation, first, to the suppression of widespread nepotistic favoritism and, second, to the expansion of a base of indiscriminate altruism; both changes seem to have occurred as reciprocity, rather than nepotism, became the principal social cement of increasingly large and complex human societies (cf., Alexander 1979). These trends must have contributed to the rise of universal indiscriminate altruism as an ideal of morality and a rational social objective. I find it an easy speculation that the concept of a *single just* God for *all people* bears a close relationship to the same trend. If followed to its logical consequences (a goal evidently not yet achieved), this concept disallows ethnocentrism, political and national chauvinism, and other forms of cooperation-to-compete that may have characterized the course of human history, even

perhaps providing its central driving force, and that sometimes also characterize the practice of religion.

It would seem that societies become more close-knit and
congenial environments as the base of self-serving indiscriminate social investment expands to include a higher
proportion and a broader diversity of social activities. Within
small bands of close relatives such investment will necessarily be largely nepotistic in its effects. In large technological
societies this cannot be true; there expansion of indiscriminate social investment must be fueled by the complexity
and effectiveness of indirect reciprocity. Such expansion seems
obviously more likely to occur when the nature and imme-
diacy of external threats favor high levels of cooperativeness, when within-group opportunities are expanding so
as to yield a broadening base of profitable opportunities
from both cooperation and division of labor, and when accountability for one's acts (including rewards for evidence of
altruistic tendencies) is high. By the same argument, indiscriminate social investment is expected to diminish in urban
or other situations involving high geographic mobility, low
likelihood of repetitive interactions, and other circumstances
that, in effect, create societies of strangers within which
individuals are neither stigmatized for failures to invest socially nor rewarded for providing such investments readily.
Indiscriminate social investment also seems less likely to
expand in societies with contracting economies (as opposed
to expanding economies in which everyone seems to be
gaining, even if some gain more than others), societies in
which social mobility is excessively restricted (new coalitions
will not be sought if they have no function), and societies
that lack external threats.

It is a novel aspect of the view of society presented here
that it can explain in evolutionary terms, first, human
morality as practiced, second, society's view of itself and of
morality as seemingly contrary to evolutionary history, and,
third, the existence of idealized moral models that are clearly
unlikely in evolutionary or any other terms. It also justifies
indiscriminate altruism as a model worth pursuing, but
without necessarily calling for the regular existence or practice of genetically deleterious forms of altruism (or, in mod-

ern environments, altruism based on proximate responses appropriate to such effects). In other words, morality and moral systems, moralizing, self-deceit, conscience, and a host of other human traits and tendencies do appear explainable *only* in light of our history of evolution by natural selection, rather than being paradoxical both in evolutionary terms and to those not concerned with biological arguments. The key lies in the argument that systems of indirect reciprocity cause some (indeterminate and adjustable) amounts of indiscriminate altruism to be reproductively favorable to the altruist or to relate to peoples' proximate feelings and attitudes as if this were the case, and that misinterpretation of this indiscriminate altruism as costly, rather than as social investment likely to be profitable to the investor, has been responsible for a widespread if not universal misinterpretation of what it means to be moral.[5]

World Peace?

The most serious moral or conflict-of-interest problem in the world today is surely the international arms race. Efforts to resolve it seem to reduce to two diametrically opposed alternatives. The first is a kind of nasty, unfettered mutual deterrence about which one can scarcely be optimistic over the long run (perhaps even the short run, e.g., Rothschild 1983). The second is one or another brand of what I call universal brotherhood, which scarcely any thoughtful person can see as realistic because the models involved call for an uninhibited willingness to self-sacrifice. The prevalence of this second approach, in connection with this most serious of all world problems, seems to me sufficient to demonstrate that the idealized indiscriminate altruism I have been discussing here is by no means a straw man (e.g. Schell 1982; Singer 1981).[6]

We have not so far been presented with a social model that moves us toward a kind of universal brotherhood that is explicitly based on individually self-serving behavior or that caters to the usual proximate mechanisms of such behavior. The view of moral systems given here suggests that, perhaps with a considerable amount of creative imagination, such models may be developed.

I am hypothesizing, then, that part of the key to approaching the increasingly urgent human goal of world peace and world harmony (conditions heretofore unrealized in the living world, human or otherwise) lies in the kind of self-understanding, discussed here, that comes from biological knowledge. In 1971 I suggested that arguments of facts appealing to selfish motivations, rather than exhortations to serve humanity, are most likely to solve the problem of rising population levels. This prediction has probably been borne out (Ehrlich and Ehrlich 1979; Alexander in prep.); lowered rates of population growth seem to have come about because of such factors as declining economies, rigid and sometimes extreme governmental penalties for large families, the pill as a route to the good life, and the social stigmatizing of large families.[7]

In lieu of universal deep understanding of evolution and its cumulative effects on human nature (such deep understanding being evidently a condition not likely to be realized in the foreseeable future), the goal of world peace, unfortunately, may also be achievable only—or most likely—through routes that also appeal widely to the traits and tendencies elaborated through the human history of evolution by natural selection.

References

Alexander, R. D. 1971. "The Search for an Evolutionary Philosophy of Man." *Proceedings of the Royal Society of Victoria, Melbourne* 84: 99–120.

———. 1974. "The Evolution of Social Behavior." *Annual Review of Ecology and Systematics* 5: 325–383.

———.1977. "Natural Selection and the Analysis of Human Sociality." In *Changing Scenes in the Natural Sciences, 1776–1976*, ed. C. E. Coulden, pp. 283–337. Special Publication 12, Philadelphia Academy of Natural Sciences.

———. 1979. *Darwinism and Human Affairs*. Seattle: University of Washington Press.

————. 1982. "Biology and the Moral Paradoxes." *Journal of Social and Biological Structures* 5: 389–395.

————. (in prep.). "The Biology of Moral Systems."

————. and Gerald Borgia. 1978. "Group Selection. Altruism, and the Levels of Organization of Life." *Annual Review of Ecology and Systematics* 9: 449–474.

———— and Gerald Borgia, 1979. "On the Origin and Basis of the Male-Female Phenomenon." In *Sexual Selection and Reproduction Competition in Insects,* ed. M. F. and N. Blum, pp. 417–440. New York: Academic Press.

Axelrod, R., and W. D. Hamilton. 1981. "The Evolution of Cooperation." *Science* 21: 1390–1396.

Campbell, D. T. 1975. "On the Conflicts Between Biological and Social Evolution and Between Psychology and Moral Tradition." *American Psychologist* 206: 139–148.

Darwin, Charles. 1871. *The Descent of Man and Selection in Relation to Sex.* New York: Appleton.

Dawkins, R. 1976. *The Selfish Gene.* New York: Oxford University Press.

————. 1982. *The Extended Phenotype.* Oxford and San Francisco: W. H. Freeman.

Dobzhansky, T. 1967. *The Biology of Ultimate Concern.* New York: New American Library.

Ehrlich, P. R., and A. H. Ehrlich. 1979. "What Happened to the Population Bomb?" *Human Nature* 2: 88–92.

Fisher, R. A. [1930] 1958. *The Genetical Theory of Natural Selection,* 2d ed. New York: Dover.

Hamilton, W. D. 1964. "The Genetical Evolution of Social Behaviour, I, II." *Journal of Theoretical Biology* 7: 1–52.

Huxley, T. H. 1898. *Evolution and Ethics and Other Essays.* New York: Appleton.

Lack, D. 1954. *The Natural Regulation of Animal Numbers.* New York: Oxford University Press.

————. 1957. *Evolutionary Theory and Christian Belief.* London: Methuen.

Leigh, E. G. 1983. "When Does the Good of the Group Override the Advantage of the Individual?" *Proceedings of the National Academy of Science* 80: 2985–2589.

Lewontin, R. C. 1970. "The Units of Selection." *Annual Review of Ecology and Systematics* 1: 1–18.

Low, B. S. 1978. "Environmental Uncertainty and the Parental Strategies of Marsupials and Placentals." *American Naturalist* 112: 197–213.

────── and R. D. Alexander. (in prep.). "Evolutionary Theory and Studies of Child Development."

Rothschild, E. 1983. "Review of Defense Department Annual Report to Congress Fiscal Year 1984." *New York Review of Books,* 30 (April 14): 40–50.

Sahlins, M. D. 1965. "On the Sociology of Primitive Exchange." In *The Relevance of Models for Social Anthropology,* ed. M. Banton, pp. 139–236. London: Tavistock.

Schell, J. 1982. "Reflections (Nuclear Arms, Part III): The Fate of the Earth." *New Yorker* (February 15): 45–107.

Singer, P. 1981. *The Expanding Circle.* New York: Farrar, Straus and Giroux.

Trivers, R. L. 1971. "The Evolution of Reciprocal Altruism," *Quarterly Review of Biology* 46: 35–57.

──────. 1974. "Parent-Offspring Conflict." *American Zoologist* 14:249–264.

West Eberhard, M. J. 1975. "The Evolution of Social Behavior by Kin Selection." *Quarterly Review of Biology* 50: 1–33.

Williams, C. C. 1957. "Pleiotropy, Natural Selection, and the Evolution of Senescence." *Evolution* 11: 398–411.

────── . 1966a. "Natural Selection, the Costs of Reproduction, and a Refinement of Lack's Principle." *American Naturalist* 100: 687–690.

──────. 1966b. *Adaptation and Natural Selection.* Princeton, N.J.: Princeton University Press.

Notes

1. I do not use the adjective *biological* in the title of this essay to mean *genetic, physiological,* or *hard-wired* as it is used almost universally by human-oriented scholars outside biology. Biology is the science of life, and I deplore the misleading and erroneous dichotomy that opposes "biological" to "cultural" or "learned." Because of it, every time a biologist stands up to speak on human behavior, he is saddled with the accusation of genetic determinism and expected to speak only about

some kind of at least extremely rare behavior that cannot be modified adaptively by the varying and somewhat predictable circumstances of life. No evolutionary theory or subtheory worthy of consideration excludes environmentally adjustable behaviors. It is a fiction to suppose that evolution by natural selection does not produce traits that change predictably and adaptively to meet changing circumstances. Epigenesis is universal, phenotypes are universal, and the function of epigenesis and of phenotypes is to allow adjustment to local and temporary conditions. As one example, the differences among the worker, soldier, and queen castes of termites and ants (involving morphology, physiology, behavior, life length, senescence pattern, etc.) are determined solely by environmental variations. No one supposes for a moment that this means that the potential and tendency for these variations to occur when they do did not evolve.

2. Theoretically, effort can be defined entirely in terms of calories. This would require measuring wasted calories, which is probably most difficult in cases of premature death as a result of risk-taking. One would have to calculate lifetime availabilities of calories and the amount of reproduction per lifetime, then subtract the proportion of calories already used by the deceased individual to reproduce effectively. To my knowledge no one has yet incorporated such difficult calculations into a specific use of the concept of effort, but the concept of risk must still be taken into account.

3. Trivers (1971) referred to this aspect of sociality as "generalized reciprocity." For reasons unknown to me I missed this designation when I initiated the phrase "indirect reciprocity." I do recall that I avoided the term "generalized reciprocity" explicitly because of the way Sahlins (1965) had used it (cf. Alexander 1979). Sahlins typified generalized reciprocity as involving one-way flows of benefits in which the expectation of return is vague or nonexistent. He included nepotism, citing the case of a mother nursing her child, and with respect to nonrelatives seemed to be referring to what we would now call genetic or reproductive altruism. Perhaps both terms will survive: indirect reciprocity for cases in which the return explicitly comes from someone other than the recipient of the original beneficence and generalized reciprocity for social systems in which indirect reciprocity has become complex and general.

4. I do not mean to imply that aid will be given regardless of the likely net cost or benefit; indeed, my arguments indicate that this is not likely to happen. The implication of "indiscriminate" is rather that the aid will be given, regardless of the identity of the individual to whom it is given. Even this is obviously an oversimplification, since it is likely that some kinds of aid will be given only to close relatives, some only to relatives and friends, some to strangers only if there is evidence of reciprocating ability, some to strangers only when friends or associates will know, etc. Nevertheless, I think that we all regard it as important to be

convinced that there are some kinds of aid-giving that our associates will give to any person, regardless of identity or other variables. Many contributions to charity are of just this sort.

5. Charles Darwin developed an evolutionary theory of morality different from that presented here (and highly sexist!), which is summarized in the following words: "Ultimately our moral sense or conscience becomes a highly complex sentiment—originating in the social instincts, largely guided by the approbation of our fellow-men, ruled by self-reason, and confirmed by instruction and habit. It must not be forgotten that although a high standard of morality gives but a slight or no advantage to each individual . . . man and his children over the other men of the same tribe, yet that an increase in the number of well-endowed men and advancement in the standard of morality will certainly give an immense advantage to one tribe over another. A tribe including many members who, from possessing in a high degree the spirit of patriotism, fidelity, obedience, courage, and sympathy, were always ready to aid one another, and to sacrifice themselves for the common good, would be victorious over most other tribes; and this would be natural selection. At all times throughout the world tribes have supplanted other tribes; and as morality is one important element in their success, the standard of morality and the number of well-endowed men will thus everywhere tend to rise and increase" (Darwin 1871, p. 500).

This is a group selection model, and not an unreasonable one. Darwin is not entirely clear in his arguments, however, as is suggested by his phrases (above) "slight or no advantage" and "largely guided by approbation of our fellow-men [and] . . . self-interest . . . " He notes that "It is obvious, that the members of the same tribe would approve of conduct which appeared to them to be for the general good, and would reprobate that which appeared evil. To do good unto others—to do unto others as ye would they should do unto you—is the foundation-stone of morality. It is, therefore, hardly possible to exaggerate the importance during rude times of the love of praise and the dread of blame. A man who was not impelled by any deep, instinctive feeling, to sacrifice his life for the good of others, yet was roused to such actions by a sense of glory, would by his example excite the same wish for glory in other men, and would strengthen by exercise the noble feeling of admiration. He might thus do far more good to his tribe than by begetting offspring with a tendency to inherit his own high character" (Darwin 1871, p. 500).

Darwin sometimes gives the impression that he sees the "approbation and disapprobatlon" of "fellow-men" as a manipulative device that turns what would otherwise be selfish acts into expensive ones or altruistic acts into self-interested ones. But he does not ever clarify this point and frequently says something that indicates the opposite: "Finally the social instincts, which no doubt were acquired by man as by the lower animals for the good of the community, will from the first have given to him some wish to aid his fellows, some feeling of sympathy, and have compelled him to regard their approbation and disapprobation" (Darwin 1871, p. 493). Accordingly I think we must give authorship of the idea that "heroism" is reproductive to Fisher: "The mere fact that the prosperity of the group is at stake makes the sacrifice of individual lives occasionally advantageous, though this, I believe, is a minor consideration compared with the enormous advantage conferred by the prestige of the hero upon all his kinsmen" (Fisher [1930] 1958, p. 265). Fisher at once shows that the group and individual level selection arguments are not entirely incompatible (both may be operative), while supporting the latter as of greater importance. His theory is, in general, the same as that I am presenting here.

Huxley states similarly: "So far as it [the ethical process] tends to make any human society more efficient. In the struggle for existence with the state of nature, or with other societies, it works in harmonious contrast with the cosmic process [natural selection]. But it is none the less true that, since law and morals are restraints upon the struggle for existence between men in society, the ethical process is in opposition to the principle of the cosmic process, and tends to the suppression of the qualities best fitted for success in that struggle" (Huxley 1898, p. 31). Here and elsewhere Huxley does not make it clear that showing moral tendencies is in fact a quality essential for reproductive success when one's environment is a closely knit society of humans.

Huxley's understanding, however, is more complete than many who quote him imply. Thus he says that "the practice of that which is ethically best—what we call goodness or virtue—involves a course of conduct which, in all respects is opposed to that which leads to success in the cosmic struggle for existence" (Huxley 1898, pp. 81–82). "Let us understand once for all, that the ethical progress of society depends, not on imitating the cosmic process, still less in running away from it, but in combating it" (Huxley 1898, p. 83). But he footnotes the first of these quotes as follows: "Of course, strictly speaking, social life, and the ethical process in virtue of which it advances toward perfection, are part and parcel of the general process of evolution, just as the gregarious habit of innumerable plants and animals, which has been of immense advantage to them, is so. A hive of bees is an organic polity, a society in which the part played by each member is determined by organic necessities. . . . Even in these rudimentary forms of society, love and fear come into play, and enforce a greater or less renunciation of self-will. To this extent the general cosmic process begins to be checked by a rudimentary ethical process, which is, strictly speaking, part of the former, just as the 'governor' in a steam-engine is part of the mechanism of the engine."

6. It seems possible to me that social changes in some technological societies during the past few centuries, in the direction of egalitarianism with respect to opportunity (e.g. universal suffrage, civil rights, affirmative action, and similar phenomena have actually influenced moral philosophy significantly, causing much more attention to what I am here calling the idealized model of indiscriminate altruism.

7. One caveat: It is a virtue of the deliberate pursuit of an idealized model of Indiscriminate altruism that no one can afford to lag too far behind the behavior of the most altruistic or of the majority when most are altruistic. But this virtue as I am seeing it disappear when such pursuits become mired in *we-they* exclusions contradictory to the model.

The Hypothalamic Imperative

We come to the most ambitious of pop sociobiological adventures in philosophy. The opening lines of Wilson's *Sociobiology* announce a program. Given that "self-knowledge is constrained and shaped by the emotional control centers in the hypothalamus and limbic system of the brain" and that these systems evolved by natural selection, evolutionary biology must undertake "to explain ethics and ethical philosophers, if not epistemology and epistemologists, at all depths" (1975, p. 3). At the end of the same volume Wilson returns to the theme, inviting his readers to consider "the possibility that the time has come for ethics to be removed temporarily from the hands of the philosophers and biologicized" (p. 562). For, according to Wilson, "In the first chapter of this book I argued that ethical philosophers intuit the deontological canons of morality by consulting the emotive centers of their own hypothalamic-limbic system" (p. 563). Wilson's self-knowledge seems constrained by his own optimism. Despite the frequency of assertion, there is no vestige of *argument* for any such conclusion.

The idea recurs with monotonous regularity (see, for example, Wilson 1978, pp. 5–7, 196; Lumsden and Wilson 1983, p. 175). Like many intellectual hobbyhorses, however, Wilson's *idée fixe is* not entirely easy to grasp. In what exactly does the biologicization of ethics consist? We can imagine four possibilities:

A. Evolutionary biology has the task of explaining how people come to acquire ethical concepts, to make ethical judgments about themselves and others, and to formulate systems of ethical principles.

Reprinted by permission of the publisher from *Vaulting Ambition* by Philip Kitcher, Cambridge, Mass.: The MIT Press, Copyright © 1985, pp. 417–434.

B. Evolutionary biology can teach us facts about human beings that, in conjunction with moral principles that we already accept, can be used to derive normative principles that we had not yet appreciated.

C. Evolutionary biology can explain what ethics is all about and can settle traditional questions about the objectivity of ethics. In short, evolutionary theory is the key to meta-ethics.

D. Evolutionary theory can lead us to revise our system of ethical principles, not simply by leading us to accept new derivative statements—as in (B)—but by teaching us new fundamental normative principles. In short, evolutionary biology is not just a source of facts but a source of norms.

Wilson appears to accept all four projects, (A) through (D). I shall argue that (A) and (B) are legitimate tasks—although this is hardly news—and that Wilson's attempts to articulate (C) and (D) are thoroughly confused.

Since our ethical behavior has a history, it is perfectly appropriate to ask for the details of that history. Presumably, if we could trace the history sufficiently far back into the past, we would discern the co-evolution of genes and culture, the framing of social institutions, and the introduction of norms. It is quite possible, however, that evolutionary biology would play a very minor role in the story. All that selection may have done for us is to equip us with the capacity for various social arrangements and the capacity to understand and to formulate ethical rules. Recognizing that not every trait we care to focus on need have been the target of natural selection, we shall no longer be tempted to argue that any respectable history of our ethical behavior must identify some selective advantage for those beings who first adopted a system of ethical precepts. It is entirely possible that evolution fashioned the basic cognitive capacities—*alles ubriges ist Menschenwerk.*

So (A) is sanctioned as long as we do not overinterpret it. There is a legitimate enterprise of trying to reconstruct the history of our ethical behavior—although it must inevitably be fraught with speculation. Evolutionary biology will play some role at some level in whatever history we achieve. But we must allow for the possibility that that role is very indirect. The ethical attributes of formulating and obeying normative principles may have very little to do with the operations of selection.

Nor should we believe that to reconstruct the history of ethics, say by showing how ethical principles originated in myths used to buttress social arrangements (for example, the myth of a deity who would punish those who violated the precepts), is to cast doubt on the objectivity or the correctness of the principles we espouse. Just as a detailed history of arithmetical concepts and counting practices might show us a succession of myths and errors, yet would not lead us to question the objectivity of the arithmetical statements we now accept, so too reconstructions of the historical development of ethical ideas and practices do not preclude the possibility that we have now achieved a justified system of moral precepts. Wilson is far too hasty in assuming that the evolutionary scenario he gives for the emergence of religious ideas—a scenario that stresses the adaptive advantages of religious beliefs and practices—undercuts the doctrine that religious statements are true. Even if Wilson's scenario were correct, the devout could reasonably reply that, like our arithmetical ideas and practices, our religious claims have become more accurate as we have learned more about the world.

Lumsden and Wilson offer a cryptic rejoinder: "But the philosophers and theologians have not yet shown us how the final ethical truths will be recognized as things apart from the idiosyncratic development of the human mind" (1983, pp. 182–183). This is effectively to introduce a different type of argument. Independent of the question of our ability to trace the history of ethical (or religious) behavior, the task required of the philosopher who believes in the objectivity of ethics (or the believer who claims that certain religious doctrines are true) is to provide a convincing account of how the relevant claims are justified. As we shall see when we look at project (C), there is an important challenge here. (We shall also discover that the analogy with arithmetic proves helpful in responding to it.) The existence of this *separate* challenge does not entitle us to infer that a natural history of ethical behavior (or of religious practices) will automatically show that our ethical beliefs (religious beliefs) are not objectively justifiable. Conclusions reached through the acceptance of myths or dubious analogies may later obtain rigorous justification. Kekule is supposed to have thought of the structure of the benzene molecule by staring into a fire. Kepler's discovery of the laws that bear his name was achieved partly through his acceptance of dubious ideas about the souls of planets and the music of the heavens.

So, while (A) is a reasonable enterprise, it hardly amounts to a dramatic removal of ethics from the hands of the philosophers. (B) is similarly innocuous. Ethicists have long appreciated the idea that facts about human beings, or about other parts of nature, might lead us to elaborate our fundamental ethical principles in previously unanticipated ways. Card-carrying Utilitarians who defend the view that morally correct actions are those that promote the greatest happiness of the greatest number, and who suppose that those to be numbered are presently existing human beings and that happiness consists in certain states of physical and psychological well-being, will derive concrete ethical precepts by learning how the maximization of happiness can actually be achieved. Analogous points apply to rival systems of ethical principles.

Sometimes biologists restrict themselves to helping in this legitimate and uncontroversial enterprise. Alexander writes, "I will argue, and I hope show, that evolutionary analysis can tell us much about our history and the existing systems of laws and norms, and also about how to achieve any goals deemed desirable; but that it has essentially nothing to say about what goals are desirable, or the directions in which laws and norms should be modified in the future" (1979, p. 220). As I understand him, Alexander—quite correctly restricts himself to (A) and (B). These are projects that genuinely fall within the scope of the natural sciences— although, as we have seen (Chapter 9), there is no reason to think that Alexander brings them to successful completion. Wilson, however, has his mind set on higher things.

There is an apparent tension in the pop sociobiological pursuit of (C) and (D). The central theme of Wilson's ideas in meta-ethics is that ethical statements are not objective;

they simply record the emotional reactions of people. However, evolutionary theory is to allow us to *improve* ethics. The subject can no longer "be left in the hands of the merely wise" (1978, p. 7). Knowledge of human nature is needed if we are to make "optimum choices." Wilson appeals to biology to formulate a new system of principles. But if ethics stems from our emotions, what is the source of the imperative to alter it? In what sense can ethics be improved? What makes the optimal choices optimal? It is hard to wear the hats of skeptic and reformer at the same time.

For the moment I shall ignore the tension and concentrate on the two separate parts of the "biologicization" of ethics. Wilson's meta-ethics is prompted by impatience at the inability of philosophers to reach agreement about the systematization of ethical principles. It receives additional support from his conception of the possible theories of objectivity in ethics. The conclusion to which he is led is formulated in the following passage:

> Like everyone else, philosophers measure their personal emotional responses to various alternatives as though consulting a hidden oracle. That oracle resides in the deep emotional centers of the brain, most probably within the limbic system, a complex array of neurons and hormone-secreting cells located just beneath the "thinking" portion of the cerebral cortex. Human emotional responses and the more general ethical practices based on them have been programmed to a substantial degree by natural selection over thousands of generations. (1978, p. 6)

Stripped of references to the neural machinery, the account Wilson adopts is a very simple one. The content of ethical statements is exhausted by reformulating them in terms of our emotional reactions. Those who assent to "Killing innocent children is morally wrong" are doing no more than report on a feeling of repugnance. Ethical statements turn out to be on a par with statements we make when moved by our gastronomic preferences. Just as there is no objective standard against which those who like lutefisk are to be judged, so too there is no objective appraisal of those who disagree with us about the propriety of killing innocent children. Their hypothalamic-limbic complexes incline them to different emotional responses. That is all.

Wilson explicitly acknowledges his commitment to different sets of "moral standards" for different populations and different groups within the same population (1975, p. 564). But I doubt that he appreciates the full character of the position to which his subjectivist meta-ethics leads him. Perhaps Wilson believes that the emotional responses of the deviant can somehow be discounted. How? One suggestion might be that they are to be dismissed because they disagree with the attitudes of the majority. To embrace this proposal not only embodies the dubious idea that majority responses are somehow correct or justified. It also reintroduces the very notion of objectivity that Wilson finds so mysterious. A different suggestion, perhaps more in the spirit of pop sociobiology, might be that emotional responses that maximize fitness are to be preferred to those that detract from fitness. If this is to succeed, however, it must be possible to defend both the thesis that the attitudes of the deviant detract from their fitness (in what environment?) and the claim that fitness maximizing reactions are objectively preferable to other emotional responses. The notion of ethical objectivity, ostentatiously expelled through the front door, sneaks back through the rear.

Wilson is driven to a position that is very difficult to sustain. Faced with the deviants who respond to the "limbic oracle" by willfully torturing children, our reaction is strictly analogous to that evoked by people who consume food we find disgusting. We are revolted. Our revulsion may even lead us to interfere. Yet if we are pressed to defend ourselves, we shall have to concede that there is no standpoint from which our actions can be judged as objectively more worthy than the actions of those whom we try to restrain. They follow their hypothalamic imperative, we follow ours.

Given that the conclusions are unpalatable, we do well to look at the line of reasoning that leads to them. Should we be discomfited by the fact that there are rival systems of ethical principles? Should this lead us to conclude that there is no objective standard against which the rival systems can be judged, so that it is "every man his own emoter"? I think not. There are numerous areas of human inquiry in which theoretical disputes persist unresolved, and in which we do not abandon the idea that there is an ultimate possibility of objective solution.

Just as the fact that there have been, and continue to be, large theoretical disputes in evolutionary biology does not tell against the existence of a consensus on all kinds of important claims about the history of life, so too the presence of rival philosophical theories of the foundations of ethics should not blind us to the substantial areas in which reflective people agree in their moral appraisals. Philosophers who practice normative ethics rightly attempt to decide the *unclear* cases, for these are where philosophical advice is most needed. On the other hand, those who attempt to systematize our ethical judgments face all the problems inherent in any effort at theoretical systematization. Disagreement about difficult cases and foundational concepts can persist in the presence of agreement about easier cases and even when there is unanimity about generalizations.

Wilson's second line of argument is more persuasive, and does succeed in raising a serious philosophical question. The challenge for those who advocate the objectivity of ethics is to explain in what this objectivity consists. Skeptics can reason as follows: If ethical maxims are to be objective, then they must be objectively true or objectively false. If they are objectively true or false, then they must be true or false in virtue of their correspondence with (or failure to correspond with) the moral order, a realm of abstract objects (values) that persists apart from the natural order. Not only is it highly doubtful that there is any such order, but, even if there were, it is utterly mysterious how we might ever come to recognize it. Apparently, we would be forced to posit some ethical intuition, by means of which we become aware of the fundamental moral facts. Not only would it be necessary to explain just how this intuition works, but we would also be pressed to understand the refinement of our ethical views in the course of history. If we are able to apprehend the moral order, how is it that our ancestors so conspicuously failed to do so? And how is it that disagreements in ethics continue to this day?

Thus the skeptic. Before we abandon ethical objectivity in dismay, however, we should remind ourselves that a parallel argument goes through for mathematics. If mathematical truths are to be objective, then they must be objectively true or false. If they are objectively true or false, then they must be true or false in virtue of their correspondence with (or failure to correspond with) a realm of abstract objects (sets, numbers, and so forth). Even if we concede the existence of these objects, it is mysterious how we might ever come to interact with them and to appreciate their properties. Apparently, we are forced to postulate some mathematical intuition by means of which we become aware of the fundamental mathematical facts. Not only are we required to explain how this intuition works, but we are also pressed to understand the refinement of our mathematical views in the course of history. If we are able to apprehend the mathematical heaven, how is it that our predecessors failed to do so (how did they land themselves in muddles about infinite sets and infinitesimals, complex numbers, and so forth)? And how is it that disagreements in certain parts of mathematics (for example, in the foundations of set theory) continue to this day?

Few will sacrifice the objectivity of mathematics without a struggle. Philosophers disagree about exactly how to reply to the skeptic. Few advocate the view that the objectivity of arithmetic (and many other parts of mathematics) is thereby impugned. There are too many alternatives to be explored. Extreme Platonists will accept the position that the skeptic reconstructs and will try to answer the questions directly. Others will protest that there are important errors at early stages of the skeptic's argument. Some may wish to assert the objectivity of mathematics without claiming that mathematical statements are objectively true or false. Others may develop an account of the truth or falsity of mathematics that does not assume the existence of abstract objects. Still others may allow abstract objects but try to dispense with mathematical intuition.

Parallel moves are available in the ethical case. One possibility is to give up the idea of objective truth or falsehood for ethical statements in favor of the notion that some statements are objectively *justified* while others are not. Thus we may try to work out the view that, strictly speaking, "Killing innocent children is morally wrong" is neither true nor false, but that we are objectively justified in accepting this statement. (As Norman Dahl pointed out to me, we count a judge's verdict as correct or incorrect and we admit objectivity in the law, even though we do not think of verdicts as being true or false.) A variant on the same theme is to suppose that what truth and falsehood amount to in the case of ethics is not some correspondence (failure to correspond) with some independent moral order; instead, we may propose that an ethical statement is true if it would be accepted by a rational being who proceeded in a particular way. A distinct position is to declare that ethical statements correspond (or fail to correspond) to the moral order, but to attempt to understand the moral order in natural terms. For example, one may suppose that moral goodness is to be equated with the maximization of human happiness, and view morally right acts as those that promote moral goodness (or those that accord with procedures that can be expected to promote moral goodness). Yet another option is to claim that there are indeed non-natural values but that these are accessible to us in a thoroughly familiar way—for example, through our perception of people and their actions. Finally, as I have already noted, the defender of ethical objectivity may accept all the baggage that the skeptic assembles and try to explain the phenomena that the skeptic takes to be incomprehensible.

Wilson's rush to emotivism depends on slashing the number of alternatives. Only two possible accounts of ethical objectivity figure in Wilson's many pages on the topic. One of these, the attempt to give a religious foundation for ethics, does not occur in my list of options. Wilson mentions religious systems of morality only to dismiss them; his reason is spurious: "If religion . . . can be systematically analyzed and explained as a product of the brain's evolution, its power as an external source of morality will be gone forever" (1978, p. 201). The argument turns on a crucial ambiguity. If religious concepts are nothing but products of our brains, then, of course, religion is just a story. If, however, the history of religious belief shows human beings gaining knowledge of entities that actually exist, then there are no grounds for Wilson's conclusion. As we saw in discussing (A), there is no quick argument for debunking religion (or mathematics) on the grounds that it has a checkered history.

There are far better reasons for neglecting religious foundations for ethics. They have been familiar to philosophy ever since Plato. Suppose that we take actions to be good because they are prescribed in divine commands. Then either the character and prescriptions of the divinity are themselves objectively good, or they are not. If they are, then the fundamental notion of goodness is not fixed by the commands of the deity but is independent of them. If they are not, then it is appropriate to ask why people should obey the prescriptions. Either way, it appears that divine commands are incapable of grounding the moral order. (I should note that some philosophers have attempted to rebut Plato's argument and to refurbish divine command theories. See, for example, Quinn 1981.)

The other alternative that Wilson considers is the possibility that ethical principles should be known by some mysterious intuition. In his most explicit account Wilson defines *ethical intuitionism* as "the belief that the mind has a direct awareness of true right and wrong that it can formalize by logic and translate into rules of social action" (1975, p. 562). Having encumbered the defenders of ethical objectivity with all the problematic notions assembled in the skeptical argument, he can then announce that the philosophers have really been deceiving themselves. They have thought that they were intuiting mind-independent values. They were really consulting their own hypothalamic-limbic systems. If only we could replace their muddled emotings with some scientific system of ethics!

> For now, though, the scientists can offer no guidance on whether we are really correct in making certain decisions, because no way is known to define what is *correct* without total reference to the moral feelings under scrutiny. Perhaps this is the ultimate burden of the free will bequeathed to us by our genes: in the final analysis, even when we know what we are

likely to do and why, each of us must still choose. (Lumsden and Wilson 1983, p. 183)

We shall see later that Lumsden and Wilson are sometimes prepared to be more optimistic about the future of scientific ethics. Here, however, they toy with the possibility that there may be no objective standard for moral choice. The argument that inclines them to this possibility is based on skepticism about the prospects for giving an account of ethical objectivity.

Wilson (and, I assume, Lumsden with him) hurtles down the road to emotivism by ignoring the two dominant positions in the last two centuries of reflecting about ethics. Utilitarians attempt to explain what goodness is (and derivatively what the moral rightness of an action is) through the idea that goodness consists in the maximization of human welfare. Immanuel Kant and his philosophical descendants conceive of the problem of moral objectivity as one of showing that fundamental moral principles would be those adopted by rational beings, placed in a certain ideal situation. Their proposal can be elaborated in two slightly different ways. They may suggest that there is a moral order that is independent of our beliefs and feelings and that this moral order is determined by the judgments of rational beings who follow a certain kind of procedure. (On this construal, ethical statements are objectively true or false, and what makes them true or false is coincidence—or failure to coincide—with the outcome of a certain procedure.) Or they may give up the notion of ethical truth while emphasizing the concept of ethical justification. Some principles are objectively justified, and they have this status because they would be reached by beings who followed the special procedure.

In recent years the first type of Kantian view has received a detailed and profound elaboration by John Rawls, who states the central idea as follows:

Apart from the procedure of constructing the principles of justice, there are no moral facts. Whether certain facts are to be recognized as reasons of right and justice, or how much they are to count, can be ascertained only from within the constructive procedure, that is, from the undertakings of rational agents of construction when suitably represented as free and equal moral persons. (1980, p. 519)

Both the Utilitarian approach to the question of ethical objectivity and the "Kantian constructivism" defended by Rawls are prefigured in my list of options for replying to the skeptic. At best, Wilson's argument for his emotivism is the line of reasoning I attributed to the skeptic. Why then are the genuine options, the ones philosophers have labored to find and to explore, absent from Wilson's discussions?

The answer is evident when we read Wilson's explicit comments on Rawls's views. Because he does not formulate the skeptical argument carefully, and because he does not attend to the formulations and arguments of the ethicists whom he dismisses as "blind emoters," Wilson fails to see any possibility for ethical objectivism except the most extreme form of intuitionism. All philosophers who believe in the objectivity of ethics turn out to be extreme intuitionists. Indeed, in his initial critique of theories that rely on ethical intuition of "true right and wrong," Wilson's prime target is Rawls! (If Rawls is an intuitionist in *any* sense, he certainly does not adopt the simple picture of the untutored intellect apprehending abstract values, the picture that Wilson attributes to him.) There is no subtle new argument for debunking ethical objectivity. Wilson reaches his conclusion by ignoring the serious alternatives. He ignores them because, apparently, he does not understand them.

Nevertheless, there is a genuine challenge here. Philosophers do owe a cogent response to the skeptical attack on ethical objectivity, and the lack of a broadly accessible discussion of the problem has probably encouraged many scientists (and other nonphilosophers) to think of Wilson's crude incursions as welcome relief from the unrigorous musings of philosophy. I hope that the analysis already given undercuts any such reaction. I shall return to the issue of ethical objectivity at the end of the chapter, after we have looked at the final phase of Wilson's project.

In the search for new normative principles it is not clear whether pop sociobiology is to offer promise or performance. The most recent expression of (D) supposes only that greater self-knowledge will be the key to an improved system of ethics: "Only by penetrating to the physical basis of moral thought and considering its evolutionary meaning will people have the power to control their own lives. They will then be in a better position to choose ethical precepts and the forms of social regulation needed to maintain the precepts" (Lumsden and Wilson 1983, p. 183). Having examined the emotivist meta-ethics defended by Wilson (and, apparently, by Lumsden), we are now able to appreciate just how curious this idea is. If there is no sense to moral correctness, then what exactly is meant by the claim that greater self-knowledge might place us in a better position to choose ethical precepts? The obvious way to answer the question is to say that greater awareness of our hypothalamic-limbic systems might put us in a better position to satisfy our desires over the course of our lives. So indeed it might. But given that ethical statements simply record our emotional responses, why is one set of responses—even an "informed" set—any better than another? Is emotivism giving way to the position that ethical precepts are those that, if followed, would maximize long-term happiness? And whose happiness is to be relevant?

Such questions are academic. Wilson has some general project of "biologicizing ethics" and there is no serious attempt to distinguish separate enterprises such as (A) through (D). Hence it is hardly surprising that when routine philosophical distinctions are introduced, contradictions quickly emerge. It is still possible, though, that in his uncharted wanderings across the ethical map Wilson might stumble upon an important insight.

So let us consider the character of the intended advance. Our biological knowledge is not simply to be used to obtain derivative moral principles from more abstract normative premises, as in (B). It is also supposed to affect our most fundamental values. In his earlier writings Wilson was prepared to sketch the improved morality that would emerge from biological analysis. After one of his advertisements for the power of neurophysiology and phylogenetic reconstruction to fashion "a biology of ethics, which will make possible the selection of a more deeply understood and enduring code of moral values," Wilson allows us to sample his wares:

> In the beginning the new ethicists will want to ponder the cardinal value of the survival of human genes in the form of a common pool over generations. Few persons realize the true consequences of the dissolving action of sexual reproduction and the corresponding unimportance of "lines" of descent. The DNA of an individual is made up of about equal contributions of all the ancestors in any given generation, and it will be divided about equally among all descendants at any future moment. . . . The individual is an evanescent combination of genes drawn from this pool, one whose hereditary material will soon be dissolved back into it. (1978, pp. 196–197)

As I understand him, Wilson claims that there is a fundamental ethical principle, which we can formulate as follows:

> W. Human beings should do whatever may be required to ensure the survival of a common gene pool for *Homo sapiens.*

He also maintains that this principle is ethically fundamental in the sense that it is not derived from any higher-level ethical statement but is entirely justified by certain facts about sexual reproduction. (Wilson is going for bigger game than the uncontroversial (B), which allows for the use of biological premises in conjunction with ethical premises to yield new ethical consequences.) Hence there is supposed to be a good argument to (W) from a premise about the facts of sex:

> S. The DNA of any individual human being is derived from many people in earlier generations and—if the person reproduces—will be distributed among many people in later generations.

Two questions arise from these Wilsonian claims. Is the argument from (S) to (W) a good one? Is (W) an objectively correct moral principle?

The first question leads into one of the most famous passages in the history of ethics, Hume's identification of the "naturalistic fallacy." According to Hume, normative conclusions are not deducible from factual premises. The point is not difficult to appreciate. Normative statements provide guidelines for action; factual statements apparently do not. (See Singer 1981, pp. 74ff., for a good explanation of the point in the context of Wilson's example.) It is easy to add ethical premises to (S) that will enable us to deduce (W), but this is to give up the ambitious enterprise (D). Nor can we suppose that there is some other type of argument, nondeductive but nonetheless good, that enables us to infer (W) from (S) alone. The common types of reasoning that occur in arguments that we approve seem to be of no avail. No familiar form of inductive or statistical argument will lead from (S) to (W). Nor can we claim that (W) is somehow acceptable because it provides an explanation for the truth of (S). The explanation of (S) is provided by genetics, not by ethical theory. There may be a momentary charm in the idea that our DNA dissolves back into a common gene pool because it is a cardinal moral principle that we ought to ensure the survival of that gene pool, but it is the charm born of appreciation of absurdity.

Wilson is aware that a famous fallacy threatens his enterprise. He consoles himself with the idea that criticism on this basis "has lost a great deal of its force in the last few years" (1980a, p. 431) and with the claim that "the naturalistic fallacy is much less a fallacy than previously supposed" (1980b, p. 68). He amplifies his remarks by proposing that a system of ethics that had nothing to do with genetic fitness, and therefore (?) ran counter to the commands of the limbic system, would produce "an ultimate dissatisfaction of the spirit and eventually social instability and massive losses in genetic fitness" (1980b, p. 69). Do these dire possibilities hint at a possible bridge from biological facts to moral principles?

The most obvious ways to reconstruct a Wilsonian argument from (S) to (W) introduce further ethical claims. Perhaps Wilson intends to claim that acting against (W)—

allowing the common human gene pool to cease to be—
would inevitably cause "dissatisfaction of the spirit" or "social instability" or "massive losses in genetic fitness" or
possibly all three. To parlay these claims into an argument
for (W) apparently presupposes that we should not do those
things that lead to dissatisfaction of the spirit or to social
instability or to massive losses in genetic fitness. Whichever
option (or options) we choose, the argument is not promising. Wilson has no reason to assert any of the factual premises: there is no evidence that people are unable to face
the idea that a common human gene pool should no longer
exist. Moreover, in each case the ethical work would be
done by some background ethical theory to the effect that
dissatisfaction of the spirit, social instability, and loss of
fitness are always to be avoided (presumably at any cost).
Since this ethical theory does not appear on stage, we have
no idea about how Wilson would try to support it. Furthermore, if the construal that I have offered is correct, then the
enterprise of biologicizing ethics seems to reduce to the entirely uncontroversial project (B), pursued in a muddled and
ineffective way because crucial ethical assumptions are not
stated clearly or developed in detail.

Scattered hints do not encourage the confidence of interpreters. It is possible that Wilson has something entirely
different in mind. One thing, however, is plain. Pop sociobiology makes no serious attempt to face up to the naturalistic fallacy—to pinpoint the conditions under which normative assertions can be garnered from biological premises
and to show that the moral principles of the new scientific
ethics really do stand in the proper relation to the biological
findings. (If the naturalistic fallacy is not a fallacy, then
there will be *some* good arguments from factual premises to
normative conclusions. That does not mean that *every* argument from fact to value compels our assent.) All we have
been offered is a stark juxtaposition of a biological com-
monplace, (S), with a statement allegedly encapsulating a
"cardinal value," (W). The connection is left as an exercise
for the reader. After studying the exercise, it is not surprising
that critics are tempted to exclaim "Fallacy!"

So far we have considered only the possibility of justifying an ethical principle on the basis of a biological premise. Let us now ask if the ethical principle itself is correct. There are grounds for doubt. Under most circumstances the exhortation to preserve the human gene pool requires very little of us. It is quite compatible with our allowing millions of people to die—or even with our hastening their ends. (Mass murder would even be compatible with Wilson's second principle, which enjoins us to favor genetic diversity. We just have to be careful to ensure that those we kill carry duplicates of genes already present.) When life gets tough, however, the principle implies some controversial recommendations.

Imagine the stereotypic situation after a holocaust. There are five survivors: four women, all between menarche and menopause, and one man. Assume that they know themselves to be the only survivors and that they recognize that the future of the species depends on their decisions and actions. After lengthy reflections and discussions each of the four women decides that she is not prepared to bear a child. All are sickened by the recent history of their planet, and, though all are aware of the biology of sexual reproduction, they resolutely oppose the idea of transmitting their genes. The man has the power to force at least one of them to copulate with him, to impregnate her, and to compel her to bear children. What should he do?

(W) offers a clear answer. The man should do whatever is needed to ensure the survival of the gene pool for *Homo sapiens.* If that includes rape and other forms of violence, so be it.

Yet there are ethical principles that point in a different direction. The women are autonomous agents. Their rights to make their own decisions should not be violated. They should not be treated as mere means, instruments for the preservation of hominid genes. Hence the man should not force them to copulate with him against their will.

It is easy to construct any number of similar examples. Suppose, for example, that we come to know that unless the world population is cut to a tenth of its present size, *Homo sapiens* will become extinct twenty generations hence. Assume further that any delay will make solution of the population problem impossible. It will not do to sterilize the living; most of them have to be killed. Unfortunately, the large majority of the human population refuses to go along voluntarily with schemes for the termination of their lives. What are those in power to do?

When we think about examples like these, it is no help to remind ourselves that our DNA was derived from many people and will be dispersed among many people in whatever future generations there will be. At stake are the relative values of the right to existence of future generations and the right to self-determination of those now living. The biological facts of reproduction do not give us information about that relationship. I shall return to this point shortly. It signals a crucial failure of the type of "scientific ethics" that Wilson hopes to develop.

Wilson's other attempts to advance substantive moral principles fare no better. In fact, one of them—the third— does remarkably worse. Wilson believes that we shall come to regard "universal human rights" as a primary value. Waiving any worries we might have about exactly what rights are to be regarded as universal, let us consider the alleged biological basis for this principle. According to Wilson, the important fact is that we are mammals; thus our society is built "on the mammalian plan" (1978, p. 199). The natural question is *"What* mammalian plan?"—for, as should be clear from the discussions of earlier chapters, mammalian societies are highly diverse. Moreover, we can only marvel at the claim that the "mammalian imperative" (p. 199) counsels against the perpetuation of inequities. The societies of elephant seals, langurs, lions, and hamadryas baboons offer no such comforting indications. The example thus seems to combine the use of the naturalistic fallacy in argument for a vague principle with some peculiarly selective biology.

I conclude that the ambitious projects—(C) and (D)— end in failure. I want to end my discussion of pop sociobiological ventures into ethics by emphasizing one important feature in competent discussions of ethical issues that is entirely absent from Wilson's treatment. Recognizing this feature will enable us to see clearly why the maxims of the new scientific ethics are so naive; it will also shed some light on the problem of objectivity in ethics.

Pop sociobiology is completely insensitive to the issue of how the competing interests of different individuals are to be treated. The insensitivity becomes apparent when we reflect on Wilson's "cardinal values" and imagine situations in which people would be forced to make large personal sacrifices to promote those "values." In my scenarios for exposing the dubious nature of Wilson's principle (W), I was able to exploit the absence of any perspective from which the rights and duties of particular people can be assessed.

One part of the problem of ethical objectivity turns on precisely this issue. I have my feelings about the way I want the world to be. You have yours. There will undoubtedly be conflicts. Is there any set of principles for resolving such conflicts that all people ought to acknowledge? Is there an impartial perspective, a point of view from which the values and goals of others should enter into the decisions of a moral agent? The notion of ethical objectivity may appear somewhat less mysterious when we think of the possibility that there may be a *right way* for a person to recognize the inclinations of others and to give those inclinations their due in any conflict with selfish desires. The task of arriving at ethically correct decisions no longer appears as one of conforming to ethereal entities (abstract values); rather, it involves recognizing the existence of a standard beyond personal wishes, a standard in which the wishes of others are given their place.

In an extremely oversimplified way, this approach identifies the problem that Rawls sees as central to ethical theory. Rawls suggests that

> the objectivity or subjectivity of moral knowledge turns, not on the question whether ideal value entities exist or whether moral judgments are caused by emotions or whether there is a variety of moral codes the world over, but simply on the question: does there exist a reasonable method for validating and invalidating given or proposed moral rules and those decisions made on the basis of them? (1951, p. 177)

Rawls's suggestion meets skeptical challenges to the notion of ethical objectivity at an early stage of the argument. The task of exhibiting the objectivity of ethics is that of showing that there is the possibility of giving reasons for or against moral rules or particular decisions, *reasons that are valid for all parties.*

Rawls attempts to carry out this task by suggesting that the principles that govern the resolution of differences in the desires and interests of different people are those that would be accepted by rational beings placed in a hypothetical situation that Rawls calls "the original position." I shall not elaborate the details; the basic idea is that the beings in the original position have some knowledge of human motivation but must reach their decisions from behind a "veil of ignorance." Most importantly, they do not know in advance their own particular positions in the society whose arrangements are determined by their decisions. Rawls's thesis is that the principles of justice are those that would be reached by rational agents proceeding on the basis of this mixture of knowledge and ignorance.

Wilson's assessment of this proposal exposes the depth of his misunderstanding of it and of the important questions to which Rawls is responding: "While few will disagree that justice as fairness is an ideal state for disembodied spirits, the conception is in no way explanatory or predictive with reference to human beings" (1975a, p. 562). The criticism turns on the idea that Rawls's account of justice as fairness must be inadequate because it is not imbued with the biological knowledge that Wilson claims as the foundation for his own theory. Yet even if we were to suppose that pop sociobiologists have fathomed all the hypothalamic imperatives, the problem Rawls addresses would remain untouched. There would still arise an important set of issues that refused Wilson's biologicization. Can we find a set of reasons that are valid for all parties in a clash of interests? If so, how do we specify such reasons? Has Rawls succeeded in giving a method for discovering the reasons? Plumb the hypothalamic-limbic system as we may, the answers to these questions will not be forthcoming.

Rawls's original and profound suggestions provide one way of responding to the challenge that moral "correctness" is an utterly mysterious notion. (In his recent work Rawls has explicitly addressed one issue that might continue to appear vexing: "Why should the conclusions reached by parties in an ideal situation, the original position, prove binding on actual people?" See Rawls 1980 for an attempt to answer this question. Similar inquiries are undertaken with great thoroughness in Darwall 1983.) I sketch some of Rawls's ideas only for the purpose of showing how pop sociobiological ventures relate to serious studies in moral theory. The same point can be made by appealing to very different approaches to the foundations of ethics (see, for example, the lucid discussion in Singer 1981, which is also designed to expose the limitations of pop sociobiological ethics). What is needed is not a recapitulation of what contemporary ethicists—and some of their predecessors—have said, but the construction of a perspective from which the character of their enterprise can be appreciated.

That perspective reveals what is missing from the "ethical theories" promised by Wilson and his followers. A central task for any system of ethics is the construction of the impartial perspective. With its emphasis on the dictates of neural systems that have allegedly been fashioned to maximize the inclusive fitness of the individuals who possess them, pop sociobiological "ethics" lacks any theory of the resolution of conflicts. To the extent that people can be viewed as maximizing their own inclusive fitness through cooperation with others, apparent conflicts of interest may be diagnosed as situations in which all the parties maximize their inclusive fitness by coordinating their behavior. Yet there are innumerable situations—among them some of the most troubling—in which the reproductive interests of individuals do clash. For these situations pop sociobiology has nothing to offer. There is no higher standpoint than the dictates of the hypothalamus. There is no impartial perspective. There is only the conflict.

M. *Ruse*

Evolutionary Ethics: A Phoenix Arisen

ABSTRACT. Evolutionary ethics has a (deservedly) bad reputation. But we must not remain prisoners of our past. Recent advances in Darwinian evolutionary biology pave the way for a linking of science and morality, at once more modest yet more profound than earlier excursions in this direction. There is no need to repudiate the insights of the great philosophers of the past, particularly David Hume. So humans' simian origins really matter. The question is not whether evolution is to be linked to ethics, but how.

We humans are modified monkeys, not the favored creation of a benevolent God, on the sixth day. The time has therefore come to face squarely our animal nature, particularly as we interact with others. Admittedly, so-called evolutionary ethics has a bad reputation. However, the question is not whether evolution is connected with ethics, but how. Fortunately, thanks to recent developments in biological science, the way is now becoming clear.

I begin this discussion with a brief historical introduction to the topic. Then I move to the core of my scientific and philosophical case. I conclude by taking up some central objections.

Social Darwinism

In 1859 Charles Darwin published his *On the Origin of Species by Means of Natural Selection.* In that work he argues that all organisms (including ourselves) came through a slow, natural process of evolution. Also, Darwin suggested a

Reprinted with permission of the publisher, "Evolutionary Ethics: A Phoenix Arisen," *Zygon* 21 (1986): 95–112.

mechanism: more organisms are born than can survive and reproduce; this leads to competition; the winners are thus "naturally selected," and hence change ensues in the direction of increased "adaptiveness." It is hardly true that Darwin, or even science generally, brought about the death of Christianity; but after the *Origin* increasing numbers turned from the Bible towards evolution, in some form, for moral insight and guidance (Ruse 1979a; Russett 1976). The product was generally known as social Darwinism, the traditional form of evolutionary ethics—although, as many have noted, despite its name, it owed its genesis more to that general man of Victorian science, Herbert Spencer, than to Darwin himself (Russett 1976).

A full moral system needs two parts. On the one hand, you must have the "substantival" or "normative" ethical component. Here, you offer actual guidance as in, "Thou shalt not kill." On the other hand, you must have (what is known formally as) the "metaethical" dimension. Here, you are offering foundations or justification as in, "That which you should do is that which God wills." Without these two parts, your system is incomplete (Taylor 1978).

To the social Darwinians, the metaethical foundations they sought lay readily at hand. They exist in the perceived nature of the evolutionary process. Supposedly, we have a progression from simple to complex, from amoeba to man, from (as Spencer happily pointed out) savage to Englishman (Spencer 1852; 1857). This progress is a good thing and conveys immediate worth. We need no further justification of what ought to be. And now, at once, we have the substantival directives of our system. Morally, we should aid and promote—and not hinder—the evolutionary process. Furthermore, if, as was supposedly claimed by Darwin and certainly echoed by Spencer, the evolutionary process begins with a bloody struggle for existence and concludes with the triumph of the fittest, then so be it. Our obligation is to prize the strong and successful and to let the weakest go to the wall (Ruse 1985).

Of course, as many pointed out—most splendidly Darwin's great supporter and ardent co-evolutionist, Thomas Henry Huxley (1901)—none of this will do. Metaethically speaking, evolution simply is not progressive (Williams 1966). Apart from anything else, it branches all over the place, making it quite impossible to offer true assessments of top and bottom, higher and lower, better and worse. Among today's organisms, venereal disease thrives, whereas the great apes stand near extinction. Is gonorrhea really superior to the chimpanzee? And, following up the metaethical inadequacies, at the substantival level, if anything is false, social Darwinism is false. Morality does not consist in walking over the weak and the sick, the very young and the very old. Someone who tells you otherwise is an ethical cretin.

Social Darwinism (and, so many concluded, any kind of evolutionary ethics) is wrong—not just mistaken but fundamentally misguided. Why? The answer was pinpointed by such philosophers as David Hume (in the eighteenth century) and G. E. Moore (in the twentieth century). Hume (1978) noted that you simply cannot go straight from talk of facts (like evolution) to talk of morals and obligations, from "is" language to "ought" language.

> In every system of morality, which I have hitherto met with, I have always remark'd, that the author proceeds for some time in the ordinary way of reasoning, and establishes the being of a God, or makes observations concerning human affairs, when of a sudden I am surpriz'd to find, that instead of the usual copulations of propositions, is, and is not, I meet with no proposition that is not connected with an ought, or an ought not. This change is imperceptible; but is, however, of the last consequence. For as this ought, or ought not, expresses some new relation or affirmation, 'tis necessary that it shou'd be observ'd and explain'd; and at the same time that a reason should be given, for what seems altogether inconceivable, how this new relation can be a deduction from others, which are entirely different from it. (Hume 1978, p. 469)

Then, in 1903, Moore backed up this point, in his *Principia Ethica,* arguing that all who would derive morality from the physical world stand convicted of the "naturalistic fallacy." Explicitly Moore noted that the evolutionary ethicizer is a major offender, as he goes from talk of the facts and process of evolution to talk of what one ought (or ought not) do.

At all levels, therefore, traditional evolutionary ethics ground to a complete stop. It promoted a grotesque distortion of true morality and could do so only because its foundations were rotten (Flew 1967). So matters have rested for three-quarters of a century. Now, however, the time has come for the case to be reopened. Let us see why.

The Evolution of Morality

We must begin with the science, most particularly with the evolution of the human moral sense or capacity. In fact, as Darwin pointed out, contrary to the Spencerian interpretations of the evolutionary process, although the process may start with competition for limited resources—a struggle for existence (more strictly, struggle for reproduction) this certainly does not imply that there will always be fierce and ongoing hand-to-hand combat. Between members of the same species most particularly, much more personal benefit can frequently be achieved through a process of cooperation—a kind of enlightened self-interest, as it were (Darwin 1859; 1871). Thus, for instance, if my conspecific and I battle until one is totally vanquished, no one really gains, for even the winner will probably be so beaten and exhausted that future tasks will overwhelm. Whereas, if we cooperate, although we must share the booty, there will be no losers and both will benefit (Trivers 1971; Wilson 1975; Dawkins 1976; Ruse 1979b).

All such cooperation for personal evolutionary gain is known technically as "altruism." I emphasize that this term is rooted in metaphor, even though now it has the just-given formal biological meaning. There is no implication that evolutionary "altruism" (working together for biological payoff) is inevitably associated with moral altruism (where this is the original literal sense, implying a conscious being helping others because it is right and proper to do so). The connection is no more than that between the physicist's notion of "work" and what you and I do in the yard on Saturday afternoons when we mow the grass.

However, just as mowing the lawn does involve work in the physicist's sense, so also today's students of the evolution of social behavior ("sociobiologists") argue that moral (literal) altruism might be one way in which biological (metaphorical) "altruism" could be achieved (Wilson 1978; Ruse and Wilson 1986). Furthermore, they argue that in humans, and perhaps also in the great apes, such a possibility is a reality. Literal, moral altruism is a major way in which advantageous biological cooperation is achieved. Humans are the kinds of animals which benefit biologically from cooperation within their groups, and literal, moral altruism is the way in which we achieve that end (Lovejoy 1981).

There was no inevitability in altruistic inclinations having developed as one of the human adaptations. Judging from what we know of ourselves and other animals, there were a number of other ways in which biological "altruism" might have been effected (Lumsden and Wilson 1983). Most obviously, humans could have gone the route of the ants. They are highly social, having taken "altruism" to its highest pitch through what one might call "genetic hardwiring." Ants are machine-like, working in their nests according to innate dispositions, triggered by chemicals (pheromones) and the like (Wilson 1971).

There are great biological advantages to this kind of functioning: it eliminates the need for learning, it cuts down on the mistakes, and much more. Unfortunately, however, this is all bought at the expense of any kind of flexibility. If circumstances change, individual ants cannot respond. This does not matter so much in the case of ants, since (biologically speaking) they are cheap to produce. Regretfully, humans require significant biological investment, and so apparently the production of "altruism" through innate, unalterable forces, poses too much of a risk.

Since the ant option is closed, we humans might theoretically have achieved "altruism" by going right to the other extreme. We might have evolved superbrains, rationally calculating at each point if a certain course of action is in our best interests. "Should I help you prepare for a difficult test? What's in it for me? Will you pay me? Do I need help in return? Or what?" Here, there is simply a disinterested calculation of personal benefits. However, we have clearly not evolved this way. Apart from anything else, such a superbrain would itself have high biological cost and might not be that efficient. By the time I have decided whether or not to save the child from the speeding bus, the dreadful event has occurred (Lumsden and Wilson 1981; Ruse and Wilson 1986).

It would seem, therefore, that human evolution has been driven towards a middle-of-the-road position. In order to achieve "altruism," we are altruistic! To make us cooperate for our biological ends, evolution has filled us full of thoughts about right and wrong, the need to help our fellows, and so forth. We are obviously not totally selfless. Indeed, thanks to the struggle for reproduction, our normal disposition is to look after ourselves. However, it is in our biological interests to cooperate. Thus we have evolved innate mental dispositions (what the sociobiologists Charles Lumsden and Edward O. Wilson call "epigenetic rules") inclining us to cooperate, in the name of this thing which we call morality (Lumsden and Wilson 1981). We have no choice about the morality of which we are aware. But, unlike the ants, we can certainly choose whether or not to obey the dictates of our conscience. We are not blindly locked into our courses of action like robots. We are inclined to behave morally but not predestined to such a policy.

This, then, is the modern (Darwinian) biologist's case for the evolution of morality. Our moral sense, our altruistic nature, is an adaptation—a feature helping us in the struggle for existence and reproduction—no less than hands and eyes, teeth and feet. It is a cost-effective way of getting us to cooperate, which avoids both the pitfalls of blind action and the expense of a superbrain of pure rationality.

Substantive Ethics

But what has any of this to do with the questions that philosophers find pressing and interesting? Let us grant the scientific case sketched in the last section. What now of substantival ethics, and most particularly what of metaethics? If we think that what has just been said has any relevance to foundations, then surely we violate Hume's law and smash into the naturalistic fallacy, no less than does the Spencerian.

Turning first to the moral norms endorsed by the modern evolutionist, there is little to haunt us from the past. As we have just seen, the whole point of today's approach is that we transcend a rugged struggle for existence—in thought and deed. Of course, humans are selfish and violent at times. This has been admitted. But, no less than the moralist, the evolutionist denies that this darker side to human beings has anything to do with moral urges. What excites the evolutionist is the fact that we have feelings of moral obligation laid over our brute biological nature, inclining us to be decent for altruistic reasons.

What is the actual content (speaking substantivally) of a modern evolutionary ethic? At this point we turn to philosophers for guidance! After all, these are the people whose intent it is to uncover the basic rules which govern our ethical lives. The evolutionist may modify or even reject the philosophers' claims; but, given the central (empirical) hypothesis that normal, regular morality is that which our biology uses to promote "altruism," the presumption must be that the findings of the philosophers will tell much.

In fact, there is little need for apprehension. Claims of some of today's leading thinkers sound almost as if they were prepared expressly to fill the evolutionist's bills—a point which these thinkers themselves have acknowledged. In particular, let me draw your attention to the ideas of John Rawls, whose *A Theory of Justice* deservedly holds its place as the major work in moral philosophy of the last decade. Rawls writes:

> The guiding idea is that the principles of justice for the basic structure of society are . . . the principles that free and rational persons concerned to further their own interests would accept in an initial position of equality as defining the fundamental terms of their association. These principles are to regulate all further agreements; they specify the kinds of social cooperation

> that can be entered into and the forms of government that can be established. This way of regarding the principles of justice I shall call justice as fairness. (Rawls 1971, p. 11)

How exactly does one spell out these principles that would be adopted by "free and rational persons concerned to further their own interests"? Here, Rawls invites us to put ourselves behind a "veil of ignorance," as it were. If we knew that we were going to be born into a society and that we would be healthy, handsome, wise, and rich, we would opt for a system which favors the fortunate. But we might be sick, ugly stupid, and poor. Thus, in our ignorance, we will opt for a just society, governed by rules that would best benefit us no matter what state or post we might have in that society.

Rawls argues that, under these conditions, a just society is seen to be one which, first, maximizes liberty and freedom, and, second, distributes society's rewards so that everyone benefits as much as possible. Rawls is not arguing for some kind of communistic, totally equal distribution of goods. Rather, the distribution must help the unfortunate as well as the fortunate. If you could show that the only way to get statewide, good quality medical care is by paying doctors twice as much as anyone else, then so be it.

I need hardly say how readily all of this meshes with the evolutionary approach. For both the biologist and the Rawlsian, the question is that of how one might obtain right action from groups of people whose natural inclination is (or rather, of whom one would expect the natural inclination to be) that of looking after themselves. In both cases the answer is found in a form of enlightened self-interest. We behave morally because, ultimately, there is more in it for us than if we do not.

Where the evolutionist picks up and goes beyond the Rawlsian is in linking the principles of justice to our biological past, via the epigenetic rules. This is a great bonus, for Rawls himself admits that his own analysis is restricted to the conceptual level. He leaves unanswered major questions about origins. "In justice as fairness the original position of equality corresponds to the state of nature in the traditional theory of the social contract. This original position is not, of course, thought of as an actual historical state of affairs, much less as a primitive condition of culture. It is understood as a purely hypothetical situation characterized so as to lead to a certain conception of justice" (Rawls 1971, p. 12).

This is all very well. But, "purely hypothetical situations" are hardly satisfying. Interestingly, as hinted above, Rawls himself suggests that biology might be important.

> In arguing for the greater stability of the principles of justice I have assumed that certain psychological laws are true, or approximately so. I shall not pursue the question of stability beyond this point. We may note however that one might ask how it is that human beings have acquired a nature described by these psychological principles. The theory of evolution would suggest that it is the outcome of natural selection; the capacity for a sense of justice and the moral feelings is an adaptation of mankind to its place in nature. (Rawls 1971, pp. 502–503)

This is precisely the evolutionist's approach. There is no need to suppose hypothetical contracts. Natural selection made us as we are.

Foundations—Metaethics

I expect that many traditional philosophers will feel able to go this far with the evolutionist. But now the barriers will come up. The argument will run like this: the evolution of ethics has nothing to do with the status of ethics. I may be kind to others because my biology tells me to be kind to others and because those protohumans who were not kind to others failed to survive and reproduce. But is it right that I be kind to others? Do I really, objectively, truly have moral obligations? To suppose that the story of origins tells of truth or falsity is to confuse causes with reasons. In a Spencerian fashion, it is to jumble the way things came about with the way things really are.[1] Since Rawls has been quoted as an authority, let us recall what he says at the end of his speculations on the evolution of morality: "These remarks are not intended as justifying reasons for the contract view" (Rawls 1971, p. 504).

This is a powerful response, but today's evolutionary ethicist argues that it misses entirely the full force of what biology tells us. It is indeed true that you cannot *deduce* moral claims from factual claims (about origins). However, using factual claims about origins, you can give moral claims the only foundational *explanation* that they might possibly have. In particular, the evolutionist argues that, thanks to our science we see that claims like "You ought to maximize personal liberty" are no more than subjective expressions, impressed upon our thinking because of their adaptive value. In other words, we see that morality has no philosophically objective foundation. If it is just an illusion, fobbed off on us to promote biological "altruism."

This is a strong claim, so let us understand it fully. The evolutionist is no longer attempting to derive morality from factual foundations. His/her claim now is that there are no foundations of any sort from which to derive morality—be these foundations evolution, God's will or whatever. Since, clearly, ethics is not nonexistent, the evolutionist locates our moral feelings simply in the subjective nature of human psychology. At this level, morality has no more (and no less) status than that of the terror we feel at the unknown— another emotion which undoubtedly has good biological adaptive value.

Consider an analogy. During the First World War, many bereaved parents turned to spiritualism for solace. Down the Ouija board would come the messages: "It's alright Mum. I've gone to a far better place. I'm just waiting for you and Dad." I take it that these were not in fact the words of the late Private Higgins, speaking from beyond. Rather they were illusory—a function of people's psychology as they projected their wishes. (We can, I think, discount universal fraud.)

The moral to be drawn from this little story is that we do not need an further justificatory foundation for "It's alright Mum" than that just given. At this point, we do not need a reasoned underpinning to the words of reassurance. ("Why is it alright?" "Because I'm sitting on a cloud, dressed in a bedsheet, playing a harp.") What we need is a causal explanation of why the bereaved "heard" what they did. The evolutionist's case is that something similar is very true of ethics. Ultimately, there is no reasoned justification for ethics in the sense of foundations to which one can appeal in reasoned argument. All one can offer is a causal argument to show why we hold ethical beliefs. But once such an argument is offered, we can see that this is all that is needed.

In a sense, therefore, the evolutionist's case is that ethics is a collective illusion of the human race, fashioned and maintained by natural selection in order to promote individual reproduction. Yet, more must be said than this. Obviously, "Stamping on small children is wrong," is not, really illusory like "It's alright Mum, I'm okay!" However, we can easily show why the analogy breaks down at this point. Morality is a shared belief (or set of beliefs) of the human race, unlike the messages down the Ouija board. Thus, we can distinguish between "Love little children," which is certainly not what we would normally call illusory, and "Be kind to cabbages on Fridays," which certainly is what we would normally call illusory. We all (or nearly all) believe the former but not the latter.

Perhaps we can more accurately express the evolutionist's thesis by drawing back from a flat assertion that ethics is illusory. What is really important to the evolutionist's case is the claim that ethics is illusory inasmuch as it persuades us that it has an objective reference. This is the crux of the biological position. Once it is grasped everything falls into place.

This concession about the illusory status of ethics in no way weakens the evolutionist's case. Far from it! If you think about it, you will see that the very essence of an ethical claim, like "Love little children," is that, whatever its true status may be, we think it binding upon us *because we think it has an objective status.* "Love little children" is not like "My favorite vegetable is spinach." The latter is just a matter of subjective preference. If you do not like spinach, then nothing ensues. But we do not take the former (moral) claim to be just a matter of preference. It is regarded as objectively binding upon us—whether we take the ultimate source of this objectivity to be God's will, or (if we are Platonists) intuited relations between the forms, or (like G. E. Moore) apprehension of nonnatural properties, or whatever.

The evolutionist's claim, consequently, is that morality is subjective—it is all a question of human feelings or sentiments—but he/she admits that we "objectify" morality, to use an ugly but descriptive term. We think morality has objective reference even though it does not. Because of this, a causal analysis of the type offered by the evolutionist is appropriate and adequate, whereas a justification of moral claims in terms of reasoned foundations is neither needed nor appropriate.

Furthermore, completing the case, the evolutionist points out that there are good (biological) reasons why it is part of our nature to objectify morality. If we did not regard it as binding, we would ignore it. It is precisely because we think that morality is more than mere subjective desires, that we are led to obey it.[2]

Reciprocation

This completes the modern-day case for evolutionary ethics. A host of questions will be raised. I will concentrate on two of the more important. First, let us turn to a substantival question.

Many of the queries at this level will be based on misunderstandings of the evolutionist's position. For instance, although the evolutionist is subjectivist about ethics, this does not in any sense imply that he/she is a relativist— especially not a cultural relativist. The whole point about the evolutionary approach to ethics is that morality does not work unless we are all in the game (with perhaps one or two cheaters—so-called, criminals or sociopaths). Moreover, we have to believe in morality; otherwise it will not work. Hence, the evolutionist looks for shared moral insights, and cultural variations are dismissed as mere fluctuations due to contingent impinging factors.

Analogously, there is no question of simply breaking from morality if we so wish. Even though we have insight into our biological nature, it is still *our* biological nature. We can certainly do immoral things. We do them all the time. But, a policy of persistently and consistently breaking the rules can only lead to internal tensions. Plato had a good point in the *Republic* when he argued that only the truly good person is the truly happy person, and the truly happy person is the one whose parts of the personality ("soul") function harmoniously together.

A much more significant question, on which I will focus, concerns the question of reciprocation. No one should be misled into thinking that the evolutionist proclaims the virtues (moral or otherwise) of selfishness or that the evolutionist's position implies that, as a matter of contingent fact, we are totally selfish. It has been admitted that human beings have a tendency towards selfishness; but, you did not need an evolutionist to tell you that. What is surprising is that we are not totally selfish. Humans have genuinely altruistic feelings towards their fellows. The fact that, according to the evolutionist, we are brought to literal, moral altruism by our genes acting in our biological self-interests says nothing against the genuineness of our feelings. Would you doubt the goodness of Mother Theresa's heart, were you told that she was strictly disciplined as a child? Nevertheless, while this is indeed all true, a nagging doubt remains. Let us look for a moment at the actual causal models proposed by sociobiologists in order to explain the evolution of altruism. First, it is suggested that kin selection is important. Relatives share copies of the same genes. Hence, inasmuch as a relative reproduces, you yourself reproduce vicariously, as it were. Therefore, help given to relatives leading to survival and reproduction rebounds to your own benefit. Second, there is *reciprocal altruism*. Simply, if I help you (even though you be no relative), then you are more likely to help me—and conversely. We both gain together, whereas apart we both lose.[3]

Now, surely, with both of these mechanisms, the possibility of genuine altruism seems precluded. With kin selection, the rewards come through your relatives' reproduction, so there is no need for crude overt returns. But, would not mere nonmoral love do all that is needed? I love my children, and I help them not because it is right but because I love them. As Immanuel Kant (1959) rightly points out, unless you are actually heeding the call of duty, there is no moral credit. A mother happily suckling her baby is not performing a moral act.

In the case of reciprocal altruism, the problems for the evolutionary ethicist are even more obvious. You do something in hope of return. This is not genuine altruism but a straight bargain. There is nothing immoral in such a transaction. If I pay cash for a kilo of potatoes, there is no wrongdoing. But there is nothing moral in such a transaction, either. Morality means going out on a limb, because it is right to do so. Morality vanishes if you hope for payment.

The evolutionist has answers to these lines of criticism—answers which strengthen the overall position. First, it is indeed true that much we do for our family stems from love, without thought of duty. But, only the childless would think moral obligations never enter into intrafamilial relations. Time and again we have to drive ourselves on, and we do it because it is right. Without the concepts of right and wrong, we would be much less successful parents (uncles, aunts, etc.) than we are. Humans require so much child care that they make the case for a biological backing to morality particularly compelling. If parental duties were left to feelings of kindliness, the system would break down. (I am sure there has been a feedback causal process at work here. Because we have a moral capacity, child care could be extended; and extensive child care needs set up selective pressure towards increased moral awareness.)

Second, it is agreed that reciprocal altruism would fail if there were no returns—or ways of enforcing returns. However, it is not necessary to suppose that such reciprocation requires a crude demand of returns for favors granted. Apart from anything else, morality is clearly more like a group insurance policy than a person-to-person transaction. I help you, but do not necessarily expect you personally to help me. Rather, my help is thrown into the general pool, as it were, and then I am free to draw on help as needed.

Furthermore, enforcement of the system comes about through morality itself! I help you, and I can demand help in return, not because I have helped you or even because I want help, but because it is *right* that you help me. Reciprocation is kept in place by moral obligations. If you cease to play fair, then before long I and others will chastise you or take you out of the moral sphere. We do not do this because we do not like you but because you are a bad person or too "sick" to recognize the right way of doing things. Morality demands that we give freely, but it does not expect us to make suckers of ourselves. (What about Jesus' demand that we forgive seven times. seventy times? The moral person responds that forgiveness is one thing, but that complacently letting a bad act occur four-hundred and ninety times borders on the criminally irresponsible. We ought to put a stop to such an appalling state of affairs.[4])

Thus far there should be little in the evolutionist's approach to normative ethics, properly understood, which would spur controversy. But, let me conclude this section by pointing to one implication which will certainly cause debate. Many moralists argue that we have an equal obligation to all human beings, indifferently as to relationship acquaintance, nationality, or whatever (Singer 1972). In principle, my obligations to some unknown child in (say) Ethiopia are no less than to my own son. Nevertheless, although many (most?) would pay lip service to some such view as this, my suspicion is that, sincerely meant, this doctrine makes the evolutionist decidedly queasy. Biologically, our major concern has to be towards our own kin, then to those in at least some sort of relationship to us (not necessarily a blood relationship), and only finally to complete strangers. And, feelings of moral obligation have to mirror biology.

I speak tentatively now. You could argue that biology gives us an equal sense of obligation towards all and that this sense is then filtered across strong (nonmoral) feelings of warmth towards our own children, followed by diminishing sentiments towards nonrelatives, ending with a natural air of suspicion and indifference towards strangers. But my hunch is that the care we must bestow on our children is too vital to be left to chance, and therefore we expect to find, what we do in fact find, namely that our very senses of obligation vary. Therefore, whatever we may sometimes say, truly we have a stronger feeling of moral obligation towards some people than towards others.

It is perhaps a little odd to speak thus hesitantly about our own feelings, including moral feelings. You might think that one should be able to introspect and speak definitively. However, matters are not always quite this simple, particularly when (as now) we are faced with a case where our technology has outstripped our biology and our consequent morality. A hundred years ago it would have made little sense to talk of moral obligations to Ethiopians. Now we know about Ethiopians and, at least at some level, we can do something for them. But what should we do for them? Within the limits of our abilities, as much, for each one as for each one of our own children? I suspect that most people would say not. I hasten to add that no evolutionist says we have no obligations to the world's starving poor. The question is whether we have a moral obligation to beggar our families and to send all to Oxfam.

In closing this section, let me at least note that, over this matter of varying obligations, the evolutionist takes no more stringent a line than does Rawls. Explicitly, Rawls treats close kin as a case meriting special attention, and as he himself admits it is far from obvious that his theory readily embraces relations with the Third World (Rawls 1980). It is not intuitively true that, even hypothetically, we were in an original position with the people of Africa—or India, or China. Hence, although the evolutionist certainly does not want to hide behind the cloth of the more conventional moral philosopher, he can take comfort from the fact that he is in good company.

Objectivity

We turn now to metaethical worries. The central claim of the evolutionist is that ethics is subjective, a matter of feelings or sentiment, without genuine objective referent. What distinguishes ethics from other feelings is our belief that ethics is objectively based, and it is because we think this that ethics works.

The most obvious and important objection to all of this is that the evolutionist has hardly yet really eliminated the putative objective foundation of morality. Of course, ethics is in some way subjective. How could it not be? It is a system of beliefs held by humans. But this does not in itself deny that there is something more. Consider, analogously, the case of perception. I see the apple. My sensations are subjective, and my organs of vision (eyes) came through the evolutionary process, for excellent biological reasons. Yet, no one would deny that the apple is independently, objectively real. Could not the same be true of ethics? Ultimately, ethics resides objectively in God's will, or some such thing. (Nozick [1981] pursues a line of argument akin to this.)

Let us grant the perception case although, parenthetically, I suspect the evolutionist might well have some questions about the existence of a real world beyond the knowing subject. The analogy with ethics still breaks down. Imagine two worlds, identical except that one has an objective ethics (whatever that might mean) and one does not. Perhaps, in one world God wants us to look after the sick, and in the other He could not care less what we do. The evolutionist argues that, in both situations, we would have evolved in such a way as to think that, morally, we ought to care for the sick. To suppose otherwise, to suppose that only the world of objective ethics has us caring about the sick, is to suppose that there are extra scientific forces at work, directing and guiding the course of evolution. And this is a supposition which is an anathema to the modern biologist (Ruse 1982).

In other words, in the light of what we know of evolutionary processes, the objective foundation has to be judged redundant. But, if anything is a contradiction in terms, it is a redundant objective morality: "The only reason for loving your neighbor is that God wants this, but you will think you ought to love your neighbor whether or not God wants it." In fact, if you take seriously the notion that humans are the product of natural selection, the situation is even worse than this. We are what we are because of contingent circumstances, not because we necessarily had to be as we are. Suppose, instead of evolving from savannah-living primates (which we did), we had come from cave dwellers. Our nature and our morality might have been very different. Or, take the termites (to go to an extreme example from a human perspective). They have to eat each other's feces, because they lose certain parasites, vital for digestion, when they molt. Had humans come along a similar trail, our highest ethical imperatives would have been very strange indeed.

What this all means is that, whatever objective morality may truly dictate, we might have evolved in such a way as to miss completely its real essence. We might have developed so that we think we should hate our neighbors, when really we should love them. Worse than this even, perhaps we really should be hating our neighbors, even though we think we should love them! Clearly, this possibility reduces objectivity in ethics to a mass of paradox.

But does it? Let us grant that the evolutionist has a good case against the person who would argue that the foundations of morality lie in sources external to us humans, be these sources God's will, the relations of Platonic forms, nonnatural properties, or whatever. However, there is at least one well-known attempt to achieve objectivity (of a kind) without the assumption of externality. I refer, of course, to the metaethical theorizing of Immanuel Kant (1949; 1959). He argued that the supreme principle of morality, the so-called categorical imperative, has a necessity quite transcending the contingency of human desires. It is synthetic *a priori,* where by this Kant meant that morality is a condition which comes into play, necessarily, when rational beings interact. He argued that a disregard of morality leads to "contradictions," that is to a breakdown in social functioning. Thus, we see that morality is not just subjective whim but has its being in the very essence of rational interaction. To counter an example offered above, we could not have evolved as pure haters, because such beings simply could not interact socially.

Since, more than once in this paper, the evolutionist has invoked the ideas of Rawls in his own support, a critic might reasonably point out that (having left matters dangling in *A Theory of Justice),* more recently Rawls has tried explicitly to put morality on a Kantian foundation. At a general level he writes as follows: "What justifies a conception of justice is not its being true to an order antecedent to and given to us, but its congruence with our deeper understanding of ourselves and our aspirations, and our realization that, given our history and the traditions embedded in our public life, it is the most reasonable doctrine for us" (Rawls 1980, p. 519). Then, spelling matters out a little more, Rawls claims that: "[A] Kantian doctrine interprets the notion of objectivity in terms of a suitably constructed social point of view that is authoritative with respect to all individual and associational points of view. This rendering of objectivity implies that, rather than think of the principles of justice as true, it is better to say that they are the principles most reasonable for us, given our conception of persons as free and equal, and fully cooperating members of a democratic society" (Rawls 1980, p. 554). Thus, in some way we try to show both that morality is reasonable and that it is more than a matter of mere desire or taste, like a preference for vegetables.

Responding to the Kantian/Rawlsian, so-called constructivist position, the evolutionist will want to make two points. First, there is much in the position with which he/she heartily sympathizes! Both constructivist and evolutionist agree that morality must not be sought outside human beings, and yet both agree that there is more to morality than mere feelings. Additionally, both try to make their case by pointing out that morality is the most sensible strategy for an individual to pursue. Being nice pays dividends—although, as both constructivist and evolutionist point out, one behaves morally for good reasons, not because one is consciously aware of the benefits.

Second, for all of the sympathy, the evolutionist will feel compelled to pull back from the full conclusions of the constructivist position. The evolutionist argues that morality (as we know it) is the most sensible policy, as we humans are today. However, he/she draws back from the constructivist claim that (human-type) morality must be the optimal strategy for *any* rational being. What about our termite-humans, for instance? They might be perfectly rational. Possibly, the response will be that the termite-humans' sense of obligation to eat rather strange foodstuffs is covered by a prohibition against suicide, which Kant certainly thinks follows from the categorical imperative. Hence, the constructivist admits that one's distinctive (in our case, human) nature gives one's actual morality a correspondingly distinctive appearance; but he/she argues that underlying the differences is a shared morality. The principle is the same as when everyone (including the evolutionist) explains differences in cultural norms as due to special circumstances, not to diverse ultimate moral commitments (Taylor 1958).

Yet, the evolutionist continues the challenge. If the constructivist argues that the only thing which counts is rational beings working together and that their contingent nature is irrelevant, then it is difficult to see why morality necessarily emerges at all. Suppose that we had evolved into totally rational beings, like the above-mentioned superbrains, and that we calculated chances, risks, and benefits at all times. We would be neither moral not immoral, feeling no urges of obligation at all.

Obviously, we are not like this. Apparently, therefore, we must take account of a being's contingent nature—no matter how rational it may be—in order to get some kind of morality. But this is the thin end of the wedge for moralities other than human morality. Think, for instance, how we might patch up the society of pure haters so that a kind of morality could emerge—and this is a kind quite different from ours. Suppose that it is part of our nature to hate others, and that we think we have an obligation to hate others. A Kantian "contradiction," that is, breakdown in sociality, might still be avoided and cooperation achieved, because we know that others hate us and so we feel we had better work warily together to avoid their wrath. If this sounds farfetched, consider how today's supposed superpowers function. Everything would be perfectly rational and could work (after a fashion). Yet, there would be little that we humans would recognize as "moral" in any of this.

Of course, you might still point out that such a society of pure haters would end up with rules much akin to those that the constructivist endorses, about liberty and so forth. But these rules would not be moral in any sense. They would be, explicitly, rules of expediency, of self-interest. I give you liberty not because I care for you, or respect you, or think I ought to treat you as a worthwhile individual. I hate your gut! And, I think I *ought* to hate you. I give you liberty simply because it is in my consciously thought-out interests to do so. This may be a sensible, prudent policy. It is not a moral policy.

The evolutionist concludes, against the constructivist, that our morality is a function of our actual human nature and that it cannot be divorced from the contingencies of our evolution. Morality, as we know it, cannot have the necessity or objectivity sought by the Kantian and Rawlsian.

Conclusion

Our biology is working hard to make the evolutionist's position seem implausible. We are convinced that morality really is objective, in some way. However, if we take modern biology seriously, we come to see how we are children of our past. We learn what the true situation really is. Evolution and ethics are at last united in a profitable symbiosis, and this is done without committing all of the fallacies of the last century.

Notes

1. Versions of this argument occur in Raphael (1958), Quinton (1966), Singer (1972), and—I blush to say it—Ruse (1979b).

2. See Murphy (1982) for more on the argument that a causal explanation might be all that can be offered for ethics, and Mackie (1977) for discussion of "objectification" in ethics.

3. These two mechanisms are discussed in detail in Ruse (1979b). They are related to human behavior, in some detail, in Wilson (1978).

4. This criticism assumes that the Christian is obligated to forgive endlessly, without response. Modern scholarship suggests that this is far from Jesus' true message. See Betz (1985) for more on this point, and Mackie (1978) for more on the sociobiologically inspired criticism that Christianity makes unreasonable demands on us. This latter line of argument obviously parallels that of Sigmund Freud in *Civilization and its Discontents* (1961).

References

Betz, D. 1985. *Essays on the Sermon on the Mount.* Philadelphia: Fortress Press.

Darwin, C. 1859. *On the Origin of Species by Means of Natural Selection.* London: John Murray.

———. 1871. *The Descent of Man.* London: John Murray.

Dawkins, R. 1976. *The Selfish Gene.* Oxford: Oxford University Press.

Flew, A. G. N. 1967. *Evolutionary Ethics.* London: Macmillan.

Freud, S. 1961. *Civilization and its Discontents.* In vol. 21 of *Complete Psychological Works of Sigmund Freud,* ed. J. Strachey, pp. 64–145. London: Hogarth Press. First published 1929–30.

Hume, D. 1978. *A Treatise of Human Nature.* Oxford: Clarendon Press.

Huxley, T. H. 1901. *Evolution and Ethics, and Other Essays.* London: Macmillan.

Kant, I. 1949. *Critique of Practical Reason,* trans. L. W. Beck. Chicago: University of Chicago Press.

———. 1959. *Foundations of the Metaphysics of Morals,* trans. L. W. Beck. Indianapolis: Bobbs-Merrill.

Lovejoy, O. 1981. "The Origin of Man." *Science* 211: 341–350.

Lumsden, C. J. and E. O. Wilson. 1981. *Genes, Mind and Culture: The Coevolutionary Process.* Cambridge, Mass.: Harvard University Press.

———. 1983. *Promethean Fire.* Cambridge, Mass.: Harvard University Press.

Mackie, J. L. 1977. *Ethics: Inventing Right and Wrong.* Harmondsworth, England: Penguin.

———. 1978. "The Law of the Jungle." *Philosophy* 53: 553–573.

Moore, G. E. 1903. *Principia Ethica.* Cambridge: Cambridge University Press.

Murphy, J. G. 1982. *Evolution, Morality, and the Meaning of Life.* Totowa, N.J.: Rowman and Littlefield.

Nozick, R. 1981. *Philosophical Explanations.* Cambridge, Mass.: Harvard University Press.

Quinton, A. 1966. "Ethics and the Theory of Evolution." In *Biology and Personality,* ed. I. T. Ramsey. Oxford: Blackwell.

Raphael, D. D. 1958. "Darwinism and Ethics." In *A Century of Darwin,* ed. S. A. Barnett, pp. 355–378. London: Heinemann.

Rawls, J. 1971. *A Theory of Justice.* Cambridge, Mass.: Harvard University Press.

———. 1980. "Kantian Constructivism in Moral Theory." *Journal of Philosophy* 77: 515–572.

Ruse, M. 1979a. *The Darwinian Revolution: Science Red in Tooth and Claw.* Chicago: University of Chicago Press.

———. 1979b. *Sociobiology: Sense or Nonsense?* Dordrecht, Holland: Reidel.

———. 1982. *Darwinism Defended: A Guide to the Evolution Controversies.* Reading, Mass.: Addison-Wesley.

———. 1985. *Taking Darwin Seriously: A Naturalistic Approach to Philosophy.* Oxford: Blackwell

———. and E. O. Wilson. 1986. "Darwinism as Applied Science," *Philosophy.*

Russett, C. E. 1976. *Darwin in America.* San Francisco: W. H. Freeman.

Singer, P. 1972. "Famine, Affluence, and Morality." *Philosophy and Public Affairs* 1: 229–243.

———.1981. *The Expanding Circle: Ethics and Sociobiology.* New York: Farrar, Straus, and Giroux.

Spencer, H. 1852. "A Theory of Population, Deduced from the General Law of Animal Fertility." *Westminster Review* 1: 468–501.

———. 1857. "Progress: Its Law and Cause." *Westminster Review.* Reprinted in *Essays: Scientific, Political, and Speculative.* 1868.1: 1–60. London: Williams and Norgate.

Taylor, P. W. 1958. "Social Science and Ethical Relativism." *Journal of Philosophy* 55: 32–44.

———. 1978. *Problems of Moral Philosophy.* Belmont, Calif.: Wadsworth.

Trivers, R. L. 1971. "The Evolution of Reciprocal Altruism." *Quarterly Review of Biology* 46: 35–57.

Williams, G. C. 1966. *Adaptation and Natural Selection.* Princeton, N.J.: Princeton University Press.

Wilson, E. O. 1971. *The Insect Societies.* Cambridge, Mass.: Belknap Press.

———. 1975. *Sociobiology: The New Synthesis.* Cambridge, Mass.: Harvard University Press.

———. 1978. *On Human Nature.* Cambridge, Mass.: Harvard University Press.

R. J. Richards

A Defense of Evolutionary Ethics

ABSTRACT: From Charles Darwin to Edward Wilson, evolutionary biologists have attempted to construct systems of evolutionary ethics. These attempts have been roundly criticized, most often for having committed the naturalistic fallacy. In this essay, I review the history of previous efforts at formulating an evolutionary ethics, focusing on the proposals of Darwin and Wilson. I then advance and defend a proposal of my own. In the last part of the essay, I try to demonstrate that my revised version of evolutionary ethics: (1) does not commit the naturalistic fallacy as it is usually understood; (2) does, admittedly, derive values from facts; but (3) does not commit any fallacy in doing so.

I. Introduction

"The most obvious, and most immediate, and most important result of the *Origin of Species* was to effect a separation between truth in moral science and truth in natural science," so concluded the historian of science Susan Cannon (1978, p. 276). Darwin had demolished, in Cannon's view, the truth complex that joined natural science, religion, and morality in the Nineteenth Century. He had shown, in Cannon's terms, "whatever it is, 'nature' isn't any good" (1978, p. 276). Those who attempt to rivet together again ethics and science must, therefore, produce a structure that can bear no critical weight. Indeed, most contemporary philosophers suspect that the original complex cracked decisively because of intrinsic logical flaws, so that any effort at reconstruction must necessarily fail. G. E. Moore

Reprinted by permission of Kluwer Academic Publishers, "A Defense of Evolutionary Ethics," *Biology and Philosophy* 1 (1986): 265–293, © 1986 D. Reidel Publishing Company.

believed those making such an attempt would perpetrate the "naturalistic fallacy," and he judged Herbert Spencer the most egregious offender. Spencer uncritically transformed scientific assertions of fact into moral imperatives. He and his tribe, according to Moore, fallaciously maintained that evolution, "while it shews us the direction in which we *are* developing, thereby and for that reason shews us the direction in which we *ought* to develop" (1903, p. 46).

Those who commit the fallacy must, it is often assumed, subvert morality altogether. Consider the self-justificatory rapacity of the Rockefellers and Morgans at the beginning of this century, men who read Spencer as the prophet of profit and preached the moral commandments of Social Darwinism. Marshall Sahlins warns us, in his *The Use and Abuse of Biology*, against the most recent consequence of the fallacy, the ethical and social preachments of sociobiology. This evolutionary theory of society, he finds, illegitimately perpetuates Western moral and cultural hegemony. Its parentage betrays it. It came aborning through the narrow gates of Nineteenth-Century *laissez faire* economics: "Conceived in the image of the market system, the nature thus culturally figured has been in turn used to explain the human social order, and vice versa, in an endless reciprocal interchange between social Darwinism and natural capitalism. Sociobiology . . . is only the latest phase in this cycle" (1976, p. xv). An immaculately conceived nature would remain silent, but a Malthusian nature urges us to easy virtue.

The fallacy might even be thought to have a more sinister outcome. Ernst Haeckel, Darwin's champion in Germany, produced out of evolutionary theory moral criteria for evaluating human "Lebenswerth." In his book *Die Lebenswunder* of 1904, he seems to have prepared instruments for Teutonic horror:

> Although the significant differences in mental life and cultural conditions between the higher and lower races of men is generally well known, nonetheless their respective Lebenswerth is usually misunderstood. That which raises men so high over the animals—including those to which they are closely related—and that which gives their life infinite worth is culture

and the higher evolution of reason that makes men capable of culture. This, however, is for the most part only the property of the higher races of men; among the lower races it is only imperfectly developed—or not at all. Natural men (e.g., Indian Vedas or Australian negroes) are closer in respect of psychology to the higher vertebrates (e.g., apes and dogs) than to highly civilized Europeans. Thus their individual Lebenswerth must be judged completely differently (1904, pp. 449–450).

Here is science brought to justify the ideology and racism of German culture in the early part of this century: sinning against logic appears to have terrible moral consequences.

But was the fault of the American industrialists and German mandarins in their logic or in themselves? Must an evolutionary ethics commit the naturalistic fallacy, and is it a fallacy after all? These are questions I wish here to consider.

Social Indeterminacy of Evolutionary Theory

Historians, such as Richard Hofstadter, have documented the efforts of the great capitalists, at the turn of the century, to justify their practices by appeal to popular evolutionary ideas. John D. Rockefeller, for instance, declared in a Sunday sermon that "the growth of a large business is merely a survival of the fittest." Warming to his subject, he went on: "The American Beauty rose can be produced in the splendor and fragrance which bring cheer to its beholder only by sacrificing the early buds which grow up around it. This is not an evil tendency in business. It is merely the working-out of a law of nature and a law of God" (quoted in Hofstadter 1955, p. 45). More recently, however, other historians have shown how American progressives (Banister 1979) and European socialists (Jones 1980) made use of evolutionary conceptions to advance their political and moral programs. For instance, Enrico Ferri, an Italian Marxist writing at about the same time as Rockefeller, sought to demonstrate that "Marxian socialism . . . is only the practical and fruitful complement in social life of that modern scientific revolution, which . . . has triumphed in our days, thanks to the labours of Charles Darwin and Herbert Spencer" (1909, p. xi). Several important German socialists also found support for their political agenda in Darwin: Eduard Bernstein argued that biological evolution had socialism as a natural consequence (1890–91); and August Bebel's *Die Frau und der Sozialismus* (1879) derived the doctrine of feminine liberation from Darwin's conception. Rudolf Virchow had forecast such political uses of evolutionary theory when he warned the Association of German Scientists in 1877 that Darwinism logically led to socialism (Kelly 1981, pp. 59–60).

While Virchow might have been a brilliant medical scientist, and even a shrewd politician, his sight dimmed when inspecting the finer lines of logical relationship: he failed to recognize that the presumed logical consequence of evolutionary theory required special tacit premises imported from Marxist ideology. Add different social postulates, of the kind Rockefeller dispensed along with his dimes, and evolutionary theory will demonstrate the natural virtues of big business. Though, as I will maintain, evolutionary theory is not compatible with every social and moral philosophy, it can accommodate a broad range of historically representative doctrines. Thus, in order for evolutionary theory to yield determinate conclusions about appropriate practice, it requires a mediating social theory to specify the units and relationships of concern. It is therefore impossible to examine the "real" social implications of evolutionary theory without the staining fluids of political and social values. The historical facts thus stand forth: an evolutionary approach to the moral and social environment does not inevitably support a particular ideology.

Those apprehensive about the dangers of the naturalistic fallacy may object, of course, that just this level of indeterminacy—the apparent ability to give witness to opposed moral and social convictions—shows the liability of any wedding of morals and evolutionary theory. But such objection ignores two historical facts: first, that moral barbarians have frequently defended heinous behavior by claiming that it was enjoined by holy writ and saintly example—so no judgment about the viability of an ethical system can be made simply on the basis of the policies that it has been called upon to support; and, second, that several logically different systems have traveled under the name "evolutionary ethics"—so one cannot condemn all such systems simply because of the liabilities of one or another. In other words, we must examine particular systems of evolutionary ethics to determine whether they embody any fallacy and to discover what kinds of acts they sanction.

Elsewhere I have described the moral systems of several evolutionary theorists and have attempted to assess the logic of those systems (Richards, 1987), so I won't rehearse all that here. Rather, I will draw on those systems to develop the outline of an evolutionary conception of morals, one, I believe, that escapes the usual objections to this approach. In what follows, I will first sketch Darwin's theory of morals, which provides the essential structure for the system I wish to advance, and compare it to a recent and vigorously decried descendant, the ethical ideas formulated by Edward Wilson in his books *Sociobiology* (1975) and *On Human Nature* (1978). Next I will describe my own revised version of an evolutionary ethics. Then I will consider the most pressing objections brought against an ethics based on evolutionary theory. Finally, I will show how the proposal I have in mind escapes these objections.

II. Darwin's Moral Theory

In the *Descent of Man* (1871), Darwin urged that the moral sense—the motive feeling which fueled intentions to perform altruistic acts and which caused pain when duty was ignored—be considered a species of social instinct (1871, chs. 2, 3, 5; Richards 1982; 1987, ch. 5). He conceived social instincts as the bonds forming animal groups into social wholes. Social instincts comprised behaviors that nurtured offspring, secured their welfare, produced cooperation among kin, and organized the clan into a functional unit. The principal mechanism of their evolution, in Darwin's view, was community selection: that kind of natural selection operating at levels of organization higher than the individual. The degree to which social instincts welded together a society out of its striving members depended on the species and its special conditions. Community selection worked most effectively among the social insects, but Darwin thought its power was in evidence among all socially dependent animals, including that most socially advanced creature, man.

In the *Descent*, Darwin elaborated a conception of morals that he first outlined in the late 1830s (Richards 1982). He erected a model depicting four over-lapping stages in the evolution of the moral sense. In the first, well-developed social instincts would evolve to bind proto-men into social groups, that is, into units that might continue to undergo community selection. During the second stage, creatures would develop sufficient intelligence to recall past instances of unrequited social instincts. The primitive anthropoid that abandoned its young because of a momentarily stronger urge to migrate might, upon brutish recollection of its hungry offspring, feel again the sting of unfulfilled social instinct. This, Darwin contended, would be the beginning of conscience. The third stage in the evolution of the moral sense would arrive when social groups became linguistically competent, so that the needs of individuals and their societies could be codified in language and easily communicated. In the fourth stage, individuals would acquire habits of socially approved behavior that would direct the moral instincts into appropriate channels—they would learn how to help their neighbors and advance the welfare of their group. So what began as crude instinct in our predecessors, responding to obvious perceptual cues, would become, in Darwin's construction, a moral motive under the guidance of social custom and intelligent decision. As the moral sense evolved, so did a distinctively human creature.

Under prodding from his cousin Hensleigh Wedgwood, Darwin expanded certain features of his theory in the second edition of the *Descent*. He made clear that during the ontogenesis of conscience, individuals learned to avoid the nagging persistence of unfulfilled social instinct by implicitly formulating rules about appropriate conduct. These rules would take into account not only the general urgings of instinct, but also the particular ways a given society might sanction their satisfaction. Such rules, Darwin thought, would put a rational edge on conscience and, in time, would become the publicly expressed canons of morality. With the training of each generation's young, these moral rules would recede into the very bones of social habits and customs. Darwin, as a child of his scientific time, also believed that such rational principles, first induced from instinctive reactions, might be transformed into habits, and then infiltrate the hereditary substance to augment and reform the biological legacy of succeeding generations.

Darwin's theory of moral sense was taken by some of his reviewers to be but a species of utilitarianism, one that gave scientific approbation to the morality of selfishness (Richards 1987, ch. 5). Darwin took exception to such judgments. He thought his theory completely distinct from that of Bentham and Mill. Individuals, he emphasized, acted instinctively to avoid vice and seek virtue without any rational calculations of benefit. Pleasure may be our sovereign mistress, as Bentham painted her, but some human actions, Darwin insisted, were indifferent to her allure. Pleasure was neither the usual motive nor the end of moral acts. Rather, moral behavior, arising from community selection, was ultimately directed to the vigor and health of the group, not to the pleasures of its individual members. This meant, according to Darwin, that the criterion of morality—that highest principle by which we judge our behavior in a cool hour—was not the general happiness, but the general good, which he interpreted as the welfare and survival of the group. This was no crude utilitarian theory of morality dressed in biological guise. It cast moral acts as intrinsically altruistic.

Darwin, of course, noticed that men sometimes adopted the moral patterns of their culture for somewhat lower motives: implicitly they formed contracts to respect the person and property of others, provided they received the same consideration; they acted, in our terms, as reciprocal altruists. Darwin also observed that his fellow creatures glowed or smarted under the judgments of their peers; accordingly, they might betimes practice virtue in response to public praise rather than to the inner voice of austere duty. Yet men did harken to that voice, which they understood to be authoritative, if not always coercive.

From the beginning of his formulation of a moral theory, in the late 1830s, Darwin recognized a chief competitive advantage of his approach. He could explain what other moralists merely assumed: he could explain how the moral criterion and the moral sense were linked. Sir James Mackintosh, from whom Darwin borrowed the basic framework of his moral conception, declared that the *moral sense* for right conduct had to be distinguished from the *criterion* of moral behavior. We instinctively perceive murder as vile, but in a cool moment of rational evaluation, we can also weigh the disutility of murder. When a man jumps into the river to save a drowning child, he acts impulsively and without deliberation, while those safely on shore may rationally evaluate his behavior according to the criterion of virtuous behavior. Mackintosh had no satisfactory account of the usual coincidence between motive and criterion. He could not easily explain why impulsive actions might yet be what moral deliberation would recommend. Darwin believed he could succeed where Mackintosh failed; he could provide a perfectly natural explanation of the linkage between the moral motive and the moral criterion. Under the aegis of community selection, men in social groups evolved sets of instinctive responses to preserve the welfare of the community. This common feature of acting for the community welfare would then become, for intelligent creatures who reacted favorably to the display of such moral impulses, an inductively derived but dispositionally encouraged general principle of appropriate behavior. What served nature as the criterion for selecting behavior became the standard of choice for her creatures as well.

Wilson's Moral Theory

In his book *On Human Nature* (1978) Edward Wilson elaborated a moral theory that he had earlier sketched in the concluding chapter of his massive *Sociobiology* (1975). Though Wilson's proposals bear strong resemblance to Darwin's own, the similarity appears to stem more from the logic of the interaction of evolutionary theory and morals than from an intimate knowledge of his predecessor's ethical views. Wilson, like Darwin, portrays the moral sense as the product of natural selection operating on the group. In light of subsequent developments in evolutionary theory, however, he more carefully specifies the unit of selection as the kin, the immediate and the more remote. The altruism evinced by lower animals for their offspring and immediate relatives can be explained, then, by employing the Hamiltonian version— i.e., kin selection—of Darwin's original concept of community selection. Also like Darwin, Wilson suggests that the forms of altruistic behavior are constrained by the cultural traditions of particular societies. But unlike Darwin, Wilson regards this "hard-core" altruism, as he calls it, to be insufficient, even detrimental to the organization of societies larger than kin groups, since such altruism does not reach beyond blood relatives. As a necessary compromise between individual and group welfare, men have adopted implicit social contracts; they have become reciprocal altruists.

Wilson calls this latter kind of altruism, which Darwin also recognized, "soft-core," since it is both genetically and psychologically selfish: individuals agree mutually to adhere to moral rules in order that they might secure the greatest amount of happiness possible. Though Wilson deems soft-core altruism as basically a learned pattern of behavior, he conceives it as "shaped by powerful emotional controls of the kind intuitively expected to occur in its hardest forms" (1978, p. 162). He appears to believe that the "deep structure" of moral rules, whether hard-core or soft, express a genetically determined disposition to employ rules of the moral form. In any case, the existence of such rules ultimately can only have a biological explanation, for "morality has no other demonstrable ultimate function" than "to keep human genetic material intact" (1978, p. 167).

Wilson's theory has recently received vigorous defense from Michael Ruse (1984). Ruse endorses Wilson's evaluation of the ethical as well as the biological merits of soft-core altruism: "Humans help relatives without hope or expectation of the ethical return. Humans help nonrelatives insofar as and only insofar as they anticipate some return. This may not be an anticipation of immediate return, but only a fool or a saint (categories often linked) would do something absolutely for nothing" (p. 171).

Ruse argues that principles of reciprocal altruism have become inbred in the human species and manifest themselves to our consciousness in the form of feelings. The common conditions of human evolution mean that most men share feelings of right and wrong. Nonetheless, ethical standards, according to Ruse, are relative to our evolutionary history. He believes we cannot justify moral norms through other means: "All the justification that can be given for ethics lies in our evolution" (1984, p. 177).[1]

A Theory of Evolutionary Ethics

The theory I wish to advocate is based on Darwin's original conception and has some similarities to Wilson's proposal. It is theory, however, which augments Darwin's and differs in certain respects from Wilson's. For convenience I will refer to it as the revised version (or RV for short). RV has two distinguishable parts, a speculative theory of human evolution and a more distinctively moral theory based on it. Evolutionary thinkers attempting to account for human mental, behavioral, and, indeed, anatomical traits usually spin just-so stories, projective accounts that have more or less theoretical and empirical support. Some will judge the evidence I suggest for my own tale too insubstantial to bear much critical weight. My concern, however, will not be to argue the truth of the empirical assertions, but to show that if those assertions are true they adequately justify the second part of RV, the moral theory. My aim, then, is fundamentally logical and conceptual: to demonstrate that an ethics based on presumed facts of biological evolution need commit no sin of moral logic, rather can be justified by using those facts and the theory articulating them.

RV supposes that a moral sense has evolved in the human group. "Moral sense" names a set of innate dispositions that, in appropriate circumstances, move the individual to act in specific ways for the good of the community. The human animal has been selected to provide for the welfare of its own offspring (e.g., by specific acts of nurture and protection); to defend the weak; to aid others in distress; and generally to respond to the needs of community members. The individual must learn to recognize, for instance, what constitutes more subtle forms of need and what specific responses might alleviate distress. But, so RV proposes, once different needs are recognized, feelings of sympathy and urges to remedial action will naturally follow. These specific sympathetic responses and pricks to action together constitute the core of the altruistic attitude. The mechanism of the initial evolution of this attitude I take to be kin selection, aided, perhaps, by group selection on small communities.[2] Accordingly, altruistic motives will be strongest when behavior is directed toward immediate relatives. (Parents, after all, are apt to sacrifice considerably more for the welfare of their children than for complete strangers.) Since natural selection has imparted no way for men or animals to perceive blood kin straight off, a variety of perceptual cues have become indicators of kin. In animals it might be smells, sounds, or coloring that serve as the imprintable signs of one's relatives. With men, extended association during childhood seems to be a strong indicator. Maynard Smith, who has taken some exception to the evolutionary interpretation of ethics, yet admits his mind was changed about the incest taboo (1978). The reasons he offers are: (1) the deleterious consequences of inbreeding; (2) the evidence that even higher animals avoid inbreeding; and (3) the phenomenon of kubbutzim children not forming sexual relations. Children of the kibbutz appear to recognize each other as "kin," and so are disposed to act for the common good by shunning sex with each other.

On the basis of such considerations, RV supposes that early human societies consisted principally of extended kin groups, of clans. Such clans would be in competition with others in the geographical area, and so natural selection might operate on them to promote a great variety of altruistic impulses, all having the ultimate purpose of serving the community good.

Men are cultural animals. Their perceptions of the meaning of behaviors, their recognition of "brothers," their judgments of what acts would be beneficial in a situation—

all of these are interpreted according to the traditions established in the history of particular groups. Hence, it is no objection to an evolutionary ethics that in certain tribes—whose kin systems only loosely recapitulate biological relations—the natives may treat with extreme altruism those who are only cultural but not biological kin.[3] In a biological sense, this may be a mistake; but on average the cultural depiction of kin will serve nature's ends.

RV insists, building on Darwin's and Wilson's theories, that the moral attitude will be informed by an evolving intelligence and cultural tradition. Nature demands we protect our brother, but we must learn who our brother is. During human history, evolving cultural traditions may translate "community member" as "red Sioux," "black Mau Mau," or "White Englishman," and the "community good" as "sacrificing to the gods," "killing usurping colonials," or "constructing factories." But as men become wiser and old fears and superstitions fade, they may come to see their brother in every human being and to discover what really does foster the good of all men.

RV departs from Wilson's sociobiological ethics and Ruse's defense of it, since they regard reciprocal altruism as the chief sort, and "keeping the genetic material intact" (Wilson 1978, p. 167) as the ultimate justification. Reciprocal altruism, as a matter of fact, may operate more widely than the authentic kind; it may even be more beneficial to the long-term survival of human groups. But this does not elevate it to the status of the highest kind of morality, though Wilson and Ruse suggest it does. And while the evolution of authentic altruistic motives may serve to perpetuate genetic stock, that only justifies altruistic behavior in an empirical sense, not a moral sense. That is, the biological function of altruism may be understood (and thus justified) as a consequence of natural selection, but so may aggressive and murderous impulses. Authentic altruism requires a moral justification. Such justification, as I will undertake below, will show it morally superior to contract altruism.

The general character of RV may now be a little clearer. Its further features can be elaborated in a consideration of the principal objections to evolutionary ethics.

III

Systems of evolutionary ethics, of both the Darwinian and the Wilsonian varieties, have attracted objections of two distinct kinds: those challenging their adequacy as biological theories and those their adequacy as moral theories. Critics focusing on the biological part have complained that complex social behavior does not fall obviously under the direction of any genetic program, indeed, that the conceptual structure of evolutionary biology prohibits the assignment of any behavioral pattern exclusively to the genetic program and certainly not behavior that must be responsive to complex and often highly abstract circumstances (i.e., requiring the ability to interpret a host of subtle social and linguistic signs) (Gould 1977, pp. 251–259; Burian 1978; Lewontin, Rose, and Kamin 1984, pp. 265–290). A present-day critic of Darwin's particular account might also urge that the kind of group selection his theory requires has been denied by many recent evolutionary theorists (Williams 1966, pp. 92–124), and that even of those convinced of group selection (e.g., Wilson), a number doubt it has played a significant role in human evolution. And if kin selection, instead of group selection of unrelated individuals, be proposed as the source of altruism in humans, a persistent critic might contend that human altruistic behavior is often extended to non-relatives. Hence kin selection cannot be the source of the ethical attitude (Mattern 1978; Lewontin et al. 1984, p. 261).

Within the biological community, the issues raised by these objections continue to be strenuously debated. So, for instance, some ethologists and sociobiologists would point to very intricate animal behaviors that are, nonetheless, highly heritable (Wilson 1975a; Eibl-Eibesfeldt 1970) and Ernst Mayr has proposed that complex instincts can be classified as exhibiting a relatively more open or a more closed program: the latter remain fairly impervious to shifting environments, while the former respond more sensitively to changing circumstances (1976). Further, different animal species show social hierarchies of amazing complexity (e.g., societies of low-land baboons) and display repertoires of instinctive behaviors whose values are highly context dependent (e.g., the waggle-dance of the honey bee, which specifies direction and distance of food sources). This suggests the likelihood that instinctual and emotional responses in humans can be triggered by subtle interpretive perception (e.g., the survival responses of fear and flight can be activated by a stranger who points a gun at you in a Chicago back alley). Cross-cultural studies, moreover, have evinced similar patterns of moral development, which could be explained, at least in part, as the result of a biologically based program determining the sequence of moral stages that individuals in conventional environments follow (Wilson 1975a, pp. 562–563). Further, recent impressive experiments have shown that group selection may well be a potent force in evolution (Wade 1976; 1977). Finally, some anthropologists have found kin selection to be a powerful explanation of social behavior in primitive tribes (Chagnon and Irons 1979). How these issues will eventually fall out, however, is not immediately my concern, since only developing evolutionary theory can properly arbitrate them. At this time we can say, I believe, that the objections based on a particular construal of evolution seem not to be fatal to an evolutionary ethics—and this admission suffices for my purposes.

Concerning the other class of objections, those directed to the distinctively moral character of evolutionary ethics, resolution does not have to wait, for the issues are factually mundane, though conceptually tangled. Against the moral objections, I will attempt to show that the evolutionary approach to ethics need abrogate no fundamental meta-ethical principles. For the sake of getting to the conceptual difficulties, I will assume that the biological objections concerning group and kin selection and an evolutionary account of complex social behavior have been eliminated. With this assumption, I can then focus on the question of the moral adequacy of an evolutionary ethics.

The objections to the adequacy of the distinctively moral component of evolutionary ethics themselves fall into two classes: objections to the entire framework of evolutionary ethics and objections based on the logic or semantics of the conceptual relations internal to the framework. For convenience I will refer to these as *framework questions* and *internal questions*. Questions concerning the framework and the internal field overlap, since some problems will be transitive— i.e., a faulty key principle may indict a whole framework. The interests of clarity may, however, be served by this distinction. Another helpful distinction is that between ethics as a descriptive discipline and ethics as an imperative discipline. The first will try to give an accurate account of what ethical principles people actually use and their origin: this may be regarded as a part of social anthropology. The latter urges and recommends either the adoption of the principles isolated or that they be considered *the ethically adequate principles*. The former kind of theory will require *empirical justification*, the latter *moral justification*.

Let me first consider some important internal challenges to both the empirical and moral justification of evolutionary ethics. It has been charged, for instance, that the concept of "altruism" when used to describe a soldier bee sacrificing its life for the nest has a different meaning than the nominally similar concept that describes the action of a human soldier who sacrifices his life for his community (Burian 1978; Mattern 1978; Alper 1978). It would be illegitimate, therefore, to base conclusions about human altruism on the evolutionary principles governing animal altruism. Some critics further maintain that the logic of the concept's role in sociobiology and in any adequate moral system must differ, since the biological usage implies genetic selfishness, while the moral use implies unselfishness.[4] I do not believe these are lethal objections. First, the term "altruism" does not retain a univocal meaning even when used to describe various human actions. Its semantic role in a description of parents' saving for their children's education surely differs from its role in a description of a stranger's jumping into a river to save a drowning child. Nonetheless the many different applications to human behavior and the several applications to animal behavior intend to pick out a common feature, namely that the action is directed to the welfare of the recipient and cost the agent some good for which reciprocation would not normally be expected. Let us call this "action altruism." We might then wish to extend, as sociobiologists are wont to do, the description "altruistic" to the genes that prompt such action, but that would be by causal analogy only (as when we call Tabasco "hot" sauce). Hence the explanation of human or animal "action altruism" by reference to "selfish genes" involves no contradiction; for the concept of "genetic selfishness" is antithetic neither to "action altruism"—since it is not applied to the same category of object—nor to "genetic altruism," for they are implicitly defined to be compatible by sociobiologists. It is only antithetic to clarity of exposition. For the real question at issue in applying the concepts of (action) altruism and (action) selfishness is whether the agent is motivated principally to act for the good of another or himself. Of course, one could, as a matter of linguistic punctiliousness, refrain from describing any animal behavior or genetic substrate as "altruistic." The problem would then cease to be semantic and become again one of the empirical adequacy of evolutionary biology to account for similar patterns of behavior in men and animals.

Though some varieties of utilitarianism denominate behavior morally good if it has certain consequences, the evolutionary ethics that I am advocating regards an action good if it is intentionally performed from a certain kind of motive and can be justified by that motive. I will assume as an empirical postulate that the motive has been established by community or kin selection. The altruistic motive encourages the agent to attended to the needs of others, such needs as either biology or culture (or both) interpret for the agent. Aristotelian-Thomistic ethics, as well as the very different Kantian moral philosophy, holds that action from appropriate motives, not action having desirable consequences, is necessary to render an act moral. The common-sense moral tradition sanctions the same distinction; that tradition prompts us, for example, to judge those Hippocratic physicians who risked their lives during the Athenian plague as moral heros—even though their therapies just as often hastened the deaths of their patients. The Hippocratics acted from altruistic motives—ultimately to advance the community good (i.e., the health and welfare of the group), proximately to do so through certain actions directed, unfortunately, by invincibly defective medical knowledge.

This non-consequentialist feature of RV leads, however, to another important internal objection. It suggests that either animal altruism does not stem from altruistic motives, or that animals are moral creatures (since moral creatures are those who act from moral motives) (Mattern 1978). Yet if animal altruism does not arise from altruistic motives and thus is only nominally similar to human altruism, then there is no reason to postulate community selection as the source of both and we cannot, therefore, use evidence from animal behavior to help establish RV. Thus either the evolutionary explanation of morals is deficient or animals are moral creatures. But no system that renders animals moral creatures is acceptable. Hence the evolutionary explanation is logically deficient.

To answer this objection we must distinguish between altruistic motives and altruistic (or moral) intentions. Though my intention is to write a book about evolutionary theories of mind, my motive may be either money (foolish motive that), prestige, professional advancement, or something of a higher nature. Human beings form intentions to act for reasons (i.e., motives), but animals presumably do not. We may then say that though animals may act from altruistic motives, they can neither form the intention of doing so, nor can they justify their behavior in terms of its motive. Hence they are not moral creatures. Three conditions, then, are necessary and sufficient for denominating an action moral: (1) it is performed from an altruistic (or moral) motive; (2) the agent intended to act from the motive; and (3) the agent could justify his action by appeal to the motive.

The distinction between motives and intentions, while it has the utility of overcoming the objection mentioned, seems warranted for other reasons as well. Motives consist of cognitive representations of goals or goal directed actions coupled with positive attitudes about the goal (e.g., the Hippocratic physician wanted to reinstate a humoral balance so as to effect a cure). Appeal to the agent's motives and his beliefs about the means to attain desired goals (e.g., the physician believed continued purging would produce a balance) provides an explanation of action (e.g., that the physician killed his patient by producing a severe anemia). Intentions, on the other hand, should not be identified with motives or beliefs, though they operate on both. Intentions are conscious acts that recruit motives and beliefs to guide behavior (e.g., the physician, motivated by commitment to the Oath, intended to cure his patient through purging). Intentions alone may not adequately explain action (e.g., the physician killed his patient because he intended to cure him!). Intentions, however, confer moral responsibility, while mere motives only furnish a necessary condition for the ascription of responsibility. To see this, consider Sam, a man who killed his mistress by feeding her spoiled pate. Did he murder her? Before the court, Sam planned to plead that yes, he had the motive (revenge for her infidelity) and yes, he knew spoiled pate would do it, but that in giving her the pate he nonetheless did not intend to kill her. He thought he could explain it by claiming that his wife put him in an hypnotic trance that suppressed his moral scruples. Thus, though he acted on his desire for revenge, he still did not intend to kill his erstwhile lover. Sam's lawyer suggested a better defense. He should plead that though he had the motive and knew that spoiled pate would do her in, yet he did not intend to kill her since he did not know this particular pate was spoiled. The moral of this sordid little example is threefold. First, simply that motives differ from intentions. Second, that for moral responsibility to be attributed, motives must not only be marshalled (as suggested by the second defense), but consciously marshalled (as suggested by the first defense). And finally, that conscious marshalling of motives and beliefs allows a justification of action (or in their absence, an excuse) by the agent (as suggested by both defenses).

The charge that RV would make animals moral creatures is thus overturned. For we assume that animals, though they may act from altruistic motives, cannot intend to do so. Nor can they justify or defend their behavior by appeal to such motives. Generally we take a moral creature to be one who can intend action and justify it.

In addition to these several objections to specific features of the internal logic and coherence of RV (and other similar systems of evolutionary ethics), one important objection attempts to indict the whole framework by pointing out that the logic of moral discourse implies the agent can act freely. But if evolutionary processes have stamped higher organisms with the need to serve the community good, this suggests that ethical decisions are coerced by irrational forces—that men, like helpless puppets, are jerked about by strands of their DNA. There are, however, four considerations that should defuse the charge that an evolutionary construction of behavior implies the denial of authentic moral choice. First, we may simply observe that the problem of compatibility of moral discourse and scientific discourse (which presumes, generally, that every event, at least at the macroscopic level, has a cause) is hardly unique to evolutionary ethics. Most every ethical system explicitly or implicitly recognizes the validity of causal explanations of human behavior (which explanatory efforts imply the principle that every event has a cause). Hence, this charge is not really a challenge to an evolutionary ethics, but to the possibility of meaningful ethical discourse quite generally. Nonetheless, let us accept the challenge and move to a second consideration. Though evolutionary processes may have resulted in sets of instinctual urges (e.g., to nurture children, alleviate obvious distress, etc.) that promote the welfare of the community, is this not a goal at which careful ethical deliberation might also arrive? Certainly many moral philosophers have thought so. Moreover, an evolutionary account of why men generally act according to the community good does not invalidate a logically autonomous argument which concludes that this same standard is the ultimate moral standard. The similar case of mathematical reasoning is instructive. Undoubtedly we have been naturally selected for an ability to recognize the quantitative aspects of our environment. Those protomen who failed to perform simple quantitative computations (such as determining the closest tree when the saber-tooth charged) have founded lines of extinct descendants. A mathematician who concedes that this brain has been designed, in part at least, to make quantitative evaluations need not discard his mathematical proofs as invalid, based on a judgment coerced by an irrational force. Nor need the moralist (Fried 1978). Third, the standard of community good must be intelligently applied. Rational deliberation must discover what actions in contingent circumstances lead to enhancing the community welfare. Such choices are not automatic but the result of improvable reason. Finally, the evolutionary perspective indicates that external forces do not conspire to wrench moral acts from a person. Rather, man is ineluctably a moral being. Aristotle believed that men where by nature moral creatures. Darwin demonstrated it.

I wish now to consider one final kind of objection to an evolutionary ethics. It requires special and somewhat more extended treatment, since its force and incision have been thought to deliver the coup de grace to all Darwinizing in morals.

IV. RV Escapes the Usual Form of the Naturalist Fallacy

G. E. Moore first formally charged evolutionary ethicians—particularly Herbert Spencer—with committing the naturalistic fallacy (1903, pp. 46–58). The substance of the charge had been previously leveled against Spencer by both his old friend Thomas Huxley (1893) and his later antagonist Henry Sidgwick (1902, p. 219). Many philosophers subsequently have endorsed the complaint against those who would make the Spencerean turn. Bertrand Russell, for instance, thumped it with characteristic *elan:*

> If evolutionary ethics were sound, we ought to be entirely indifferent as to what the course of evolution may be, since whatever it is is thereby proved to be the best. Yet if it should turn out that the Negro or the Chinaman was able to oust the European, we should cease to have any admiration for evolution; for as a matter of fact our preference of the European to the Negro is wholly independent of the European's greater prowess with the Maxim gun. (quoted by Flew 1967, p. 44)

Anthony Flew glosses this passage with the observation that "Russell's argument is decisive against any attempt to define the ideas of right and wrong, good and evil, in terms of a neutrally scientific notion of evolution" (1967, p. 45). He continues in his tract *Evolutionary Ethics* to pinpoint the alleged fallacy: "For any such move to be sound, [i.e., "deducing ethical conclusions directly from premises supplied by evolutionary biology"] the prescription in the conclusion must be somehow incapsulated in the premises; for, by definition, a valid deduction is one in which you could not assert the premises and deny the conclusion without thereby contradicting yourself" (1967, p. 47). Flew's objection is, of course, that one could jolly well admit all the declared facts of evolution, but still logically deny any prescriptive statement purportedly drawn from them.

This objection raises two questions for RV: Does it commit the fallacy as here expressed? and Is it a fallacy after all? I will endeavor to show that RV does not commit this supposed fallacy, but that even if at some level it derives norms from facts, it would yet escape unscathed, since the "naturalist fallacy" describes no fallacy.

There are two ways in which evolutionary ethics has been thought to commit the naturalist fallacy.[5] Some versions of evolutionary ethics have represented the current state of our society as ethically sanctioned, since whatever has evolved is right. Haeckel believed, for instance, that evolution had produced a higher German culture which could serve as a norm for judging the moral worth of men of inferior cultures. Other versions of evolutionary ethics have identified certain long-term trends in evolution, which they *ipso facto* deem good; Julian Huxley, for example, held efforts at greater social organization were morally sanctioned by the fact that a progressive integration has characterized social evolution (1947, p. 136). But RV (and its parent, Darwin's original moral theory) prescribes neither of these alternatives. It does not specify a particular social arrangement as being best; rather, it supposes that men will seek the arrangement that appears best to enhance the community good. The conception of what constitutes such an ideal pattern will change through time and over different cultures. Nor does this theory isolate a particular historical trend and enshrine that. During long periods in our prehistory, for instance, it might have been deemed in the community interest to sacrifice virgins, and this ritual might in fact have contributed to community cohesiveness and thus have been of continuing evolutionary advantage. But RV does not sanction thereafter the sacrifice of virgins, only acts that, on balance, appear to be conducive to the community good. As the rational capacities of men have evolved, the ineffectiveness of such superstitious behavior has become obvious. The theory maintains that the criterion of morally approved behavior will remain constant, while the conception of what particular acts fall under the criterion will continue to change. RV, therefore, does not derive ethical imperatives from evolutionary facts in the usual way.

But does RV derive ethical norms from evolutionary facts in some way? Unequivocally, yes. But to see that this involves no logically—or morally—fallacious move requires that we first consider more generally the roles of factual propositions in ethics.

Empirical Hypotheses in Ethics

Empirical considerations impinge upon ethical systems both as *framework* assumptions and as *internal* assumptions. In analyzing ethical systems, therefore, framework questions or internal questions may arise. Framework questions, as indicated above, concern the relationship of the ethical system to other conceptual systems and, via those other systems, to the worlds of men and nature. They stimulate such worries as: Can the ethical system be adopted by men in our society? How can such a moral code be justified? Must ethical systems require rational deliberation before an act can be regarded as moral? Internal questions concern the logic of the moral principles and the terms of discourse of a given ethical system. They involve such questions as: Is abortion immoral in this system? What are the principles of a just war in this system? Some apparent internal questions—such as, "What is the justification for fostering the community good?"—are really framework questions—to wit, "How can this system, whose highest principle is 'foster the community good,' be justified?" The empirical ties an ethical framework has to the worlds of men and nature are transitive: they render the internal principles of the system ultimately dependent upon empirical hypotheses and assumptions.

Every ethical system fit for men includes at least three kinds of empirical assumptions (or explicit empirical hypotheses) regarding frameworks and, transitively, internal elements. First, every ethical system recommended for human adoption makes certain framework assumptions about man's nature—i.e., about the kind of creatures men are such that they can heed the commands of the system. Even the austere ethics of Kant supposes human nature to be such, for instance, that intellectual intuitions into the noumenal realm are foreclosed; that behavior is guided by maxims; that human life is finite; that men desire immortality, etc. An evolutionary ethics also forms empirical suppositions about human nature, ones extracted from evolutionary theory and its supporting evidentiary base. Consequently, no objection to RV (or any evolutionary ethics) can be made on the grounds that it requires empirical assumptions—all ethical systems do.

A second level of empirical assumption is required of a system designed for culturally bound human nature: connections must be forged between the moral terms of the system—e.g., "goods," "the highest good," etc.—and the objects, events, and conditions realized in various human societies. What are goods (relative and ultimate) in one society (e.g., secular Western society) may not be in another (e.g., a community of Buddhists monks). In one sense these are internal questions of how individual terms of the system are semantically related to characterizations of a given society's attitudes, observations, and theoretical knowledge (e.g., the virtue of sacrificing virgins, since that act produces life-giving crops; the evil of thermonuclear war, since it will likely destroy all human life; etc.). But quickly these become framework questions. So, the question of what a society deems the highest good may become the question of justifying a system whose ultimate moral principle is, for example, "Seek the sensual pleasure of the greatest number of people." Since the interpretation of moral terms will occur during a particular stage of development, it may be that certain acts sanctioned by one society's moral system might be forbidden by ours, yet still be, as far as we are concerned, moral. That is, we may be ready not only to make the analytic statement that "The sacrifice of virgins was moral in Inca society," but also to judge the Inca high priest as a good and moral man for sacrificing virgins. Such judgment, of course, would not relieve us of the obligation to stay, if we could, the priest's hand from plunging in the knife.

A third way in which empirical assumptions enter into framework questions regards the methods of justifying the system and its highest principles. Consider an ethical system that has several moral axioms, of the kind we might find adopted in our own society: e.g., lying is always wrong; abortion is immoral; adultery is bad, etc. If asked to justify these precepts, someone might attempt to show that they conformed to a yet more general moral canon, such as the Golden Rule, the Ten Commandments, the Greatest Happiness Principle, etc. But another common sort of justification might be offered. Appeal might be made to the fact that moral authorities within our society have condemned or praised certain actions. Such an appeal, of course, would be empirical. Yet the justifying argument would meet the usual criterion of validity, if the contending parties implicitly or explicitly agreed on a meta-moral inference principle such as "Conclude as sound ethical injunctions what moral leaders preach." Principles of this kind—comparable to Carnap's "meaning postulates"—implicitly regulate the entailment of propositions within a particular community of discourse.[6] They would include rules that govern use of the standard logical elements (e.g., "and," "or," "if . . ., then," etc.) as well as the other terms of discourse. Thus in a community of analytic philosophers, the rule "From 'a knows x,' conclude 'x'" authorizes arguments of the kind: "Hilary knows we are not brains in vats, so we are not brains in vats." In a particular community, the moral discourse of its members could well be governed by a meta-moral inference principle of the sort mentioned. Such an inference rule would justify the argument from moral authority, because the interlocutors could not assert the premise (e.g., "Moral leaders believe abortion is wrong") and deny the conclusion (e.g., "Abortion is wrong") without contradiction. In this case, then, one would have a perfectly valid argument that derived morally normative conclusions from factual propositions. The cautious critic, however, might object that this argument does not draw a moral conclusion (e.g., "Abortion is wrong") solely from factual premises (e.g., "Moral leaders believe abortion is wrong"), but also from the meta-moral inference principle, which is not a factual proposition—hence, that I have not shown a moral imperative can be derived from factual premises alone. Moreover, so the critic might continue, the inference principle actually endorses a certain moral action (e.g., shunning abortion) and thus incorporates a moral imperative—consequently that I have assumed a moral injunction rather than deriving it from factual premises. This two pronged objection requires a double defense, one part that examines the role of inference principles, the other that analyzes what such principles enjoin.

The logical structure of every argument has, implicitly at least, three distinguishable parts: (1) one or more premises; (2) a conclusion; and (3) a rule or rules that permit the assertion of the conclusion on the basis of the premises. The inference rule, however, is not 'from which' a conclusion is drawn, but 'by which' it is drawn. If rules were rather to be regarded as among the premises from which the conclusion was drawn, there would be no principle authorizing the move from premises to conclusion and the argument would grind to a halt (as Lewis Carroll's tortoise knew). Hence, the first prong of the objection may be bent aside.

The second prong may also be diverted. An inference principle logically only endorses a conclusion on the basis of the premises—i.e., it enjoins not a moral act (e.g., shunning abortion) but an epistemological act (e.g., accepting the proposition "Abortion should be shunned"). Once we are convinced of the truth of a proposition, we might, of course, act in light of it; but that is an entirely different matter—at least logically. These two considerations, I believe, take the bite out of the objection.

We have just seen how normative conclusions may be drawn from factual premises. This would be an internal justification if the contending parties initially agreed about inference principles. However, they may not agree, and then the problem of justification would become the framework issue of what justifies the inference rule. It would also turn out to be a framework question if the original challenge were not to an inference rule, but to a cardinal principle (e.g., the Greatest Happiness, the Golden Rule, etc.) that was used as the axiom whence the moral theorems of the system were derived. To meet a framework challenge, one must move outside the system in order to avoid a circularly vicious justification. When philosophers take this step, they typically begin to appeal (and ultimately must) to common-sense moral judgments. They produce test cases to determine whether a given principle will yield the same moral conclusions as would commonly be reached by individuals in their society. In short, frameworks, their inference rules, and their principles are usually justified in terms of intuitively clear cases—i.e., in terms of matters of fact. Such justifying arguments, then proceed from what people as a matter of fact believe to conclusions about what principles would yield these matters of fact.

This method of justifying norms is not confined to ethics. It is also used, for example, in establishing "modus ponens" as the chief principle of modern logic: i.e., modus ponens renders the same arguments valid that rational men consider valid. But this strategy for justifying norms utilizes empirical evidence, albeit of a very general sort. Quite simple the strategy recognizes what William James liked to pound home: that no system can validate its own first principles. The first principles of an ethical system can be justified only by appeal to another kind of discourse, an appeal in which factual evidence about common sentiments and beliefs is adduced. (It is at this level of empirical appeal, I believe, that we can dismiss Wilson's suggestion that contract altruism—i.e., "I'll scratch your back, if and only if you'll scratch mine"—is the highest kind. For most men would declare an action non-moral if done only for personal gain. I will discuss the relation of this kind of empirical strategy to RV in a moment.)

The contention that the inference principles or cardinal imperatives of a moral system can ultimately be justified only by referring to common beliefs and practices seems degenerately relativistic. To what beliefs, to what practices, to what men shall we appeal? Should we look to the KKK for enlightenment about race relations? Further, even if the argument were correct about the justification of logical rules by appeal to the practices of rational men, the same seems not to hold for moral rules, because persons differ far less in their criteria of logical soundness. The analogy between logical imperatives and moral imperatives thus appears to wither. These objections are potent, though I believe they infect all attempts to justify moral principles (Gewirth 1982, pp. 43–45). In the case of evolutionary ethics, however, I think the prognosis is good. I will take up the last objection first and then turn to the first to sketch an answer that will be completed in the final section of this essay.

The last objection actually grants my contention that logical inference rules or principles are justified by appeal to beliefs and practices; presumably the objection would then be deflated if a larger consensus were likely in the case of moral justification. The second objection, then, either accepts my analysis of justificatory procedures or it amounts to the first objection that appeal to the beliefs and practices of men fails to determine the reference class and becomes stuck in the moral muck of relativism. My sketchy answer to the second objection, which will be filled in below, is simply that the reference class is moral men (just as in logical justification it is the class of rational men) and that we can count on this being a rather large class because evolution has produced it so (just as it has produced a large class of rational creatures). Indeed, one who cannot comprehend the soundness of basic moral principles, along with one who cannot comprehend the soundness of basic logical principles, we regard as hardly a man. Moreover, we have evolved, so I contend, to recognize and approve of moral behavior when we encounter it (just as we have evolved to recognize and approve of logical behavior). Those protohuman lineages that have not had these traits selected for, have not been selected at all. This does not mean, of course, that every infant slipping fresh out of the womb will respond to others in altruistic ways or be able to formulate maxims of ethical behavior. Cognitive maturity must be reached before the individual can become aware of the signs of human need and bring different kinds of response under a common description—e.g., altruistic or morally good behavior. Likewise, maturity and cultural transmission must complement the urges for logical consistency that nature has instilled. We should not, therefore, be misled by the KKK example. Most Klansmen are probably quite moral people. They simple have unsound beliefs about, among other things, different races, international conspiracies, etc. Our chief disagreement with them will not be with their convictions about heeding the community good, but with their beliefs about what leads to that good.

This brief discussion of justification of ethical principles indicates how the concept of justification must, I believe, be employed. "To justify" means "to demonstrate that a proposition or system of propositions conforms to a set of acceptable rules, a set of acceptable factual propositions, or a set of acceptable practices." The order of justification is from rules to empirical propositions about beliefs and practices. That is, if rules serving as inference principles or the rules serving as premises (e.g., the Golden Rule) of a justifying argument are themselves put to the test, then they must be shown to conform either to still more general rules or to empirical propositions about common beliefs and practices. Barring an infinite regress, this procedure must end in what are regarded as acceptable beliefs or practices. Aristotle, for instance, justified the forms of syllogistic reasoning by showing that they made explicit the patterns employed in argument by rational men. Kant justified the categorical imperative and the postulates of practical reason by demonstrating, to his satisfaction, that they were the necessary conditions of common moral experience: that is, he justified normative principles by showing that their application to particular cases reproduced the common moral conclusions of eighteenth century German burgers and Pietists.

If this is an accurate rendering of the concept of justification, then the justification of first moral principles and inference rules must ultimately lead to an appeal to the beliefs and practices of men, which of course is an empirical appeal. So moral principles ultimately can be justified only by facts. The rebuttal, then, to the charge that at some level evolutionary ethics must attempt to derive its norms from facts is simply that every ethical system must. Consequently, either the naturalistic fallacy is no fallacy, or no ethical system can be justified. But to assert that no ethical system can be justified is just to say that ultimately no reasons can be given for or against an ethical position, that all ethical judgments are nonrational. Such a view sanctions the canonization of Hitler along with St. Francis. Utilizing, therefore, the common rational strategy of appealing to common beliefs and practices to justify philosophical positions, we must reject the idea that the 'naturalistic fallacy' is a fallacy.

The Justification of RV as an Ethical System

RV stipulates that the community welfare is the highest moral good. It supposes that evolution has equipped human beings with a number of social instincts, such as the need to protect offspring, provide for the general well-being of members of the community (including oneself), defend the helpless against aggression, and other dispositions that constitute a moral creature. These constitutionally imbedded directives are instances of the supreme principle of heeding the community welfare. Particular moral maxims, which translate these injunctions into the language and values of a given society, would be justified by an individual's showing that, all things considered, following such maxims would contribute to the community welfare.

To justify the supreme principle, and thus the system, requires a different kind of argument. I wish to remind the reader, however, that I will attempt to justify RV as a moral system *under the supposition that it correctly accounts for all the relevant biological facts.* I will adopt the forensic strategy that several good arguments make a better case than one. I have three justifying arguments.

First Justifying Argument. The first argument is adapted from Alan Gewirth who, I believe, has offered a very compelling approach to deriving an "ought" from an "is." He first specifies what the concept of 'ought' means (i.e., he implicitly indicates the rule governing its deployment in arguments). He suggests that it typically means: "necessitated or required by reasons stemming from some structured context" (1982, p. 108). Thus in the inference "It is lightning, therefore it ought to thunder," the "ought" means, he suggests, "given the occurrence of lightning, it is required or necessary that thunder also occur, this necessity stemming from the law-governed context of physical nature" (1982, p. 108). Here descriptive causal laws provide the major (unexpressed) premise of the derivation of "ought" from "is." The practical sphere of action also presents structured contexts. So, for example, as a member of the University, I ought to prepare my classes adequately. Now Gewirth observes that derivation of a practical ought, such as the one incumbent on a university professor, requires first that one accept the structured context. But then, he contends, only hypothetical 'ought's are produced: e.g., If I am a member of the University, then I ought to prepare classes adequately. Since nothing compels me to become a member of the University, I can never be categorically enjoined: "Prepare classes adequately." Gewirth further argues that if one decides to commit oneself to the context, e.g., to university membership, then the derivation of 'ought' will really be from an obligation assumed, that is from one 'ought' to another 'ought.' He attempts to overcome these obstacles by deriving 'ought's from a context that the person cannot avoid, cannot choose to accept or reject. He claims that the generic features of human action impose a context that cannot be escaped and that such a context requires the agent regard as good his freedom and well-being. From the recognition that freedom and well-being are necessary conditions of all action, the agent can logically derive, according to Gewirth, the proposition "I have a right to freedom and basic well-being." This 'rights' claim, which indeed implies "I ought to have freedom and well-being," can only be made if the agent must grant the same right to others. Since the claim depends only on what is required for human agency and not on more particular circumstances, Gewirth concludes that every one must logically concede the right to any other human agent.

Gewirth's derivation of 'ought' from 'is' has been criticized by Alisdair MacIntyre among other. MacIntyre simply objects that because I have a need for certain goods does not entail that I have a right to them, i.e., that others are obliged to help me secure them (1981, pp. 64–65). This, I believe, is a sound objection to Gewirth's formulation. Gewirth's core position, however, can be preserved, if we recognize that a generally accepted moral inference principle sanctions the derivation of rights-claims from empirical claims about needs common to all men. Anyone who doubts the validity of such an inference principle need only perform the empirical test mentioned above (i.e., consult the kind of inferences most men actually draw). Yet even if we granted the force of MacIntyre's objection to Gewirth, the evolutionary perspective permits a similar derivation, though without the objectionable detour through human needs. Evolution provides the structured context of moral action: it has consituted men not only to be moved to act for the community good, but also to approve, endorse, and encourage others to do so as well. This particular formation of human nature does not impose an individual need, not something that will be directly harmful if not satisfied; hence, the question of a logical transition from an individual (or generic) need to a right does not arise. Rather, the constructive forces of evolution impose a practical necessity on each man to promote the community good. We must, we are obliged to heed this imperative. We might attempt to ignore the demand of our nature by refusing to act altruistically, but this does not diminish its reality. The inability of men to harden their consciences completely to basic principles of morality means that sinners can be redeemed. Hence, just as the context of physical nature allows us to argue "Since lightening has struck, thunder ought to follow," so the structured context of human evolution allows us to argue *"Since each man*

*has evolved to advance the community good, each ought to act
altruistically."*

Two important objections might be lodged at this junc-
ture. First, that just because evolution has outfitted men
with a moral sense of commitment to the community welfare, this fact *ipso sole* does not impose any obligation. After
all, evolution has installed aggressive urges in men, but
they are not morally obliged to act upon them. A careful
RVer will respond as follows. An inborn commitment to the
community welfare, on the one hand, and an aggressive
instinct, on the other, are two greatly different traits. In the
first, the particular complex of dispositions and attitudes
produced by evolution (i.e., through kin and group selection
in my version) leads an individual to behave in ways that
we can generally characterize as acting for the community
good; in the second, the behavior cannot be so characterized. Moral 'ought'-propositions are not sanctioned by the
mere fact of evolutionary formation of human nature, but
by the fact of the peculiar formation of human nature we
call "moral," which has been accomplished by evolution.
(The evolutionary formation of human nature according to
other familiar biological relations might well sanction such
propositions as "Since he has been constituted an aggressive
being by evolution, he ought to react hostilely when I punch
him in the nose.")

The second objection points out what appears to be a
logical gap between the structured context of the evolutionary constitution of man and an 'ought'-proposition. Even if
it is granted that evolution has formed human nature in a
particular way, call it the "moral way" (the exact meaning
of which must yet be explored), yet what justifies concluding
that one 'ought' to act altruistically? What justified the move,
of course, is an inference principle to the effect: "From a
particular sort of structured context, conclude that the activity appropriate to the context ought to occur." Gewirth, in
his attempt to show that moral "ought"s can be derived
from "is"s, depends on such a rule; and significantly,
MacIntyre's response does not challenge it. Indeed, MacIntyre
employs another such inference rule, which Gewirth would
likely endorse: i.e., "From 'needs'-propositions alone one may

not conclude to 'claims'-propositions." All meta-level discussions, all attempts to justify ethical frameworks depend on such inference rules, whose ultimate justification can only be their acceptance by rational and moral creatures.

Second Justifying Argument. The second justifying argument amplifies the first. It recognizes that evolution has formed a part of human nature according to the criterion of the community good (i.e., according to the principles of kin and group selection). This we call the moral part. The justification for the imperative advice to a fellow creature "Act for the community good" is therefore: "Since you are a moral being, constituted so by evolution, you ought act for the community good." To bring a further justification for the imperative would require that the premise of this inference be justified, which would entail furnishing factual evidence as to the validity of evolutionary theory (including RV). And this, of course, would be ultimately to justify the moral imperative by appeal to empirical evidence. The justifying argument, then, amounts to: *the evidence shows that evolution has, as a matter of fact, constructed human beings to act for the community good; but to act for the community good is what we mean by being moral. Since, therefore, human beings are moral beings—an unavoidable condition produced by evolution—each ought act for the community good.* This second justifying argument differs from the first only in stressing: (1) that ultimate justification will require securing the evidentiary base for evolutionary theory and the operations of kin and group selection in forming human nature; and (2) that the logical movement of the justification is from—(a) the empirical evidence and theory of evolution, to (b) man's constitution as an altruist, to (c) identifying being an altruist with being moral, to (d) concluding that since men so constituted are moral, they morally ought promote the community good.

Three points need to be made about this second justifying argument in light of these last remarks, especially those under number (2). To begin, the general conclusion reached—i.e., "Since each human being is a moral being, each ought act for the community good"—does not beg the question of deriving moral imperatives from evolutionary facts. The connection between being human and being moral is contingent, due to the creative hand of evolution: it is because, so I allege, that creatures having a human frame and rational mind also underwent the peculiar processes of kin and group selection that they have been formed 'to regard and advance the community good' and approve of altruism in others. (There is a sense, of course, in which a completely amoral person will be regarded as something less than human.) Having such a set of attitudes and acting on them is what we mean by being moral.[7] Further, given our notion of what it is to be moral, it is a factual question as to whether certain activity should be described as "moral behavior."

The second point is an evolutionary Kantian one and refers back to the previous discussion on the nature of justification. If challenged to justify altruism as being a moral act in reference to which 'ought'-propositions can be derived, a defender of RV will respond that the objecter should consult his own intuitions and those commonly of men. If the evolutionary scenario of RV is basically correct, then the challenger will admit his own intuitions confirm that he especially values altruistic acts, that spontaneously he recognizes the authority of the urge to perform them, and that he would encourage them in others—all of which identifies altruistic behavior with moral behavior. But if he yet questions the reliability of his own intuitions or if he fails to make the identification (because his own development has been devastatingly warped by a wicked aunt), then evidence for evolutionary theory and kin and group selection must be adduced to show that men generally (with few exceptions) have been formed to approve, endorse, and encourage altruistic behavior.

The third point glosses the meaning of "ought." In reference to structured contexts, "ought to occur," "ought to be," "ought to act," etc. typically mean "must occur," "must be," "must act, *provided there is no interference.*" Structured contexts involve causal processes. Typically "ought" adds to "must" the idea that perchance some other cause might disrupt the process (e.g., "Lightening has flashed, so it ought to thunder, that is, it must thunder, provided that no sudden vacuum in the intervening space is created, that there is an ear around to transduce movement of air molecules into nerve potentials, etc."). In the context of the evolutionary constitution of human moral behavior, "ought" means that the person must act altruistically, provided he has assessed the situation correctly and a surge of jealousy, hatred, greed, etc. does not interfere. The "must" here is a causal "must"; it means that in ideal conditions—i.e., perfectly formed attitudes resulting from evolutionary processes, complete knowledge of situations, absolute control of the passions, etc.—altruistic behavior would necessarily occur in the appropriate conditions. When conditions are less than ideal—when, for example, the severe stress of war causes an individual, to murder innocent civilians—then we might be warranted in expressing another kind of 'ought'-proposition: e.g., under conditions of brutalizing war, some soldiers ought to murder non-combatants. In such cases, of course, the "ought" is not a moral ought; it is not a moral ought because the 'ought'-judgment is not formed in recognition of altruism as the motive for behavior. In moral discourse, expressions of 'ought'-propositions have the additional function of encouraging the agent to avoid or reject anything that might interfere with the act. The "ought" derived from the structured context of man's evolutionary formation, then, will be a moral ought precisely because the activities of abiding the community good and approving of altruistic behavior constitute what we mean and (if RV is correct) must mean by "being moral."

This second justifying argument recognizes that there are three kinds of instances in which moral imperatives will not be heeded. First, when a person misconstrues the situation (e.g., when a person, without warrant, takes the life of another, because he didn't know the gun was loaded and, therefore, could not have formed the relevant intention). But here, since the person has misunderstood the situation, no moral obligation or fault can be ascribed. The second case occurs when a person does understand the moral requirements of the situation, but refuses to act accordingly. This is analogous to the case when we say thunder ought to have followed lightening, though did not (because of some intervening cause). The person who so refuses to act on a moral obligation will not be able, logically, to justify his action, and will be called a sinner. Finally, there is the case of the person born morally deficient, the sociopath who robs, rapes, and murders without a shadow of guilt. Like the creature born without cerebral hemispheres, the sociopath has been deprived of what we have come to regard as an essential organ of humanity. We do not think of him as a human being in the full sense. RV implies that such an individual, strange as it seems, cannot be held responsible for his actions. He cannot be held morally guilty for his crimes, since he, through no fault of his own, has not been provided the equipment to make moral decisions. This does not mean, of course, that the community should not be protected from him, nor that it should permit his behavior to go unpunished; indeed, community members would have an obligation to defend against the sociopath and inflict the kind of punishment that might restrain unacceptable behavior.

Third Justifying Argument. The final justifying argument for RV is second order. It shows RV warranted because it grounds other of the key strategies for justifying moral principles. Consider how moral philosophers have attempted to justify the cardinal principles of their systems. Usually they have adopted one of three methods. They might, with G. E. Moore, proclaim that certain activities or principles of behavior are intuitively good, that their moral character is self-evident. But such moralists have no ready answer to the person who might truthfully say, "I just don't see it, sorry." Nor do they have any way to excluding the possibility that a large number of such people exist or will exist. Another strategy is akin to that of Kant, which is to assert that men have some authentic moral experiences, and from these an argument can be made to a general principle in whose light their moral character is intelligible. But this tactic, too, suffers from the liability that men may differ in their judgments of what actions are moral. Finally, there is the method employed by Herbert Spencer. He asks of someone proposing another principle—Spencer's was that of greatest happiness—to reason with him. The outcome should be—if

Spencer's principle is the correct one—that the interlocutor will find either that actions he regards as authentically moral do not conform to his own principle, but to Spencer's, or that his principle reduces to or is another version of Spencer's principle. But here again, it is quite possible that the interlocutor's principle will cover all the cases of action he describes as moral, but will not be reducible to Spencer's principle. No reason is offered for expecting ultimate agreement in any of these cases.

All three strategies suppose that one can find near-universal consent among men concerning what actions are moral and what principles sanction them. Yet no way of conceptually securing such agreement is provided. And here is where RV obliges: it shows that the pith of every man's nature, the core by which he is constituted a social and moral being, has been created according to the same standard. Each heart must resound to the same moral cord, acting for the common good. It may, of course, occur that some men are born deformed in spirit. There are psychopaths among us. But these, the theory suggests, are to be regarded as less than moral creatures, just as those born severely retarded are thought to be less than rational creatures. But for the vast community of men, they have been stamped by nature as moral beings. RV, therefore, shows that the several strategies used to support an ultimate ethical principle will, in fact, be successful, successfully showing, of course, that the community good is the highest ethical standard. But for RV to render successful several strategies for demonstrating the validity of the highest ethical principle is itself a justification.

In this defense of evolutionary ethics, I have tried to do three things—to demonstrate that if we grant certain empirical propositions, then my revised version (RV) of evolutionary ethics: (1) does not commit the naturalistic fallacy as it is usually formulated; (2) does, admittedly, derive values from facts; but (3) does not commit any fallacy in doing so. The ultimate justification of evolutionary ethics can, however, be accomplished only in the light of advancing evolutionary theory.

Notes

I am grateful to my colleagues Alan Gewirth and Robert DiSalle, who tried to warn me off bad arguments.

1. I am in sympathy with the spirit of Ruse's defense of Wilson, though, as will be indicated below, I take exception to a major conclusion concerning the moral primacy of reciprocal altruism and certain aspects of the justification of the system he advances.

2. The usual models of group selection assume that individual selection and group selection work at cross-purposes, that, for instance, the individual must pay a high price for altruistic behavior (e.g., bees' disemboweling themselves by stinging enemies; risking one's life to save a drowning child, etc.). But in most familiar cases, individuals perform altruistic acts at little practical cost. In a hostile environment, those small tribal groups populated by altruists and co-operators would have a decided advantage. Cheating would not likely become widespread, since the advantage would be quite small and the possible cost quite high (e.g., ostracism of the individual or death of the tribe). Under such circumstances group selection, especially on tribes laced with relatives, might well become a force to install virtuous behavior. For an analysis of the problematic assumptions of most group selection models, see Wade (1978).

3. This is largely the objection of Marshall Sahlins to the sociobiology of human behavior (1976).

4. Playing on the apparent reduction of altruistic behavior to genetic selfishness and then to selfishness simply, Lewontin et al. complain: "by emphasizing that even altruism is the consequence of selection for reproductive selfishness, the general validity of individual selfishness in behaviors is supported. . . . Sociobiology is yet another attempt to put a natural scientific foundation under Adam Smith" (1984, p. 264).

5. In an early discussion of evolutionary ethics, Ruse (1979, pp. 199–204) affirmed that any evolutionary ethics must commit the naturalist fallacy, and admitted that the two characteristics mentioned in the text produce the most potent objections to evolutionary ethics: without begging the question, we would have no way of specifying what trends or what aspects of the evolutionary process should constitute the moral standard.

6. For a consideration of inference principles of the kind mentioned, see Carnap (1956, pp. 222–232), Sellars (1948), and McCawley (1981, p. 46).

7. Gewirth (1982, pp. 82–83) endorses the following criteria as establishing a motive as moral: the agent takes it as prescriptive; he universalizes it; he regards it as over-riding and authoritative; and it is formed

of principles that denominate actions might simply because of their effect on other persons. These criteria are certainly met in altruistic behavior described by RV.

References

Alper, J. 1978. "Ethical and Social Implications." In M. Gregory, A. Silvers, and D. Sutch, eds., *Sociobiology and Human Nature.* San Francisco: Jossey-Bass.

Ayer, A. 1936. *Language, Truth and Logic.* London: Gollancz.

Baier, A. 1975. "Intention, Practical Knowledge, and Representation." In M. Brand and D. Walton, eds., *Action Theory.* Boston: Reidel.

Baier, K. 1978. "Moral Reasons," *Midwest Studies in Philosophy* 3: 62–73.

———. 1958. *The Moral Point of View.* Ithaca, N.Y.: Cornell University Press.

Banister, R. 1979. *Social Darwinsim: Science and Myth in Anglo-American Social Thought.* Philadelphia: Temple University Press.

Barlow, G., and Silverberg, J., eds. 1980. *Sociobiology: Beyond Nature/Nurture.* Boulder Colo.: Westview Press.

Barnett, S. 1980. 'Biological Determinism and the Tasmanian Native Hen." In Montagu (1980).

Bebel, A. 1879. *Die Frau und der Sozialismus.* Stuttgart Dietz.

Bernstein, E. 1890–1891. "Ein Schüler Darwin's als Vertheidiger des Sozialismus." *Die Neue Zeit* 9: 171–177.

Burian, R. 1978. "A Methodological Critique of Sociobiology." In Caplan (1978).

Cannon, S. 1978. *Science in Culture: The Early Victorian Period.* New York: Science History Publications.

Caplan, A. 1980. "A Critical Examination of Current Sociobiological Theory." In Barlow (1980).

Caplan, A., ed. 1978. *The Sociobiology Debate.* New York: Harper.

Carnap, R. 1956. *Meaning and Necessity.* Chicago: University of Chicago Press.

Cela-Conde, C. 1984. "Nature and Reason in the Darwinian Theory of Moral Sense." *History and Philosophy of the Life Sciences* 6: 3–24.

Chagnon, N., and Irons, W., eds. 1979. *Evolutionary Biology and Human Social Behavior: An Anthropological Perspective.* North Scituate, Mass.: Duxbury Press.

Crook, J. 1980. *The Evolution of Human Consciousness.* Oxford: Clarendon Press.

Darwall, S. 1983. *Impartial Reason.* Ithaca, N.Y.: Cornell University Press.

Darwin, C. 1871. *The Descent of Man and Selection in Relation to Sex,* 2 vols. London: Murray.

————. 1936. *The Descent of Man and Selection in Relation to Sex.* New York: Modern Library.

Eibl-Eibesfeldt, I. 1970. *Ethology: the Biology of Behavior.* New York: Holt, Reinhart and Winston.

Ferri, E. 1909. *Socialism and Positive Science,* trans. E. Harvey. London: Independent Labour Party.

Feyerabend, P. 1975. *Against Method.* London: New Left Books.

Feinberg, J. 1980. "Legal Moralism and Freefloating Evils." *Pacific Philosophical Quarterly* **61**: 122–55.

Flew, A. 1967. *Evolutionary Ethics.* London: Macmillan.

Frankena, W. 1939. "The Naturalistic Fallacy." *Mind* **48**: 464–77.

Fried, C. 1978. "Biology and Ethics: Normative Implications." In Stent (1978).

Gauthier, D. 1978. "Economic Rationality and Moral Constraints." *Midwest Studies in Philosophy* **3**: 75–96.

————. 1967. "Morality and Advantage." *Philosophical Review* **76**: 460–475.

Gewirth, A. 1985. "Rights and Virtues." *Review of Metaphysics* **38**: 739–762.

————. 1983. The Rationality of Reasonableness." *Synthese* **57**: 225–247.

————. 1982. *Human Rights: Essays on Justification and Applications.* Chicago: University of Chicago Press.

————. 1978. *Reason and Morality.* Chicago: University of Chicago Press.

Gibbard, A. 1982. "Human Evolution and the Sense of Justice." *Midwest Studies in Philosophy* **7**: 31–46.

Gould, S. 1980. "Sociobiology and the Theory of Natural Selection." In Barlow (1980).

———. 1978. "Sociobiology and Human Nature: A Potpanglossian Vision." In Montagu (1980).

———. 1977. "Biological Potential vs. Biological Determinism." In *Ever Since Darwin.* New York: Norton.

Haeckel, E. 1904. *Die Lebenswunder: Gemeinverständliche Studien oder Biologische Philosophie.* Stuttgart: Kröner.

Hare, R. 1984. *Moral Thinking.* Oxford: Oxford University Press.

———. 1963. *Freedom and Reason.* Oxford: Clarendon Press.

Hofstadter, R. 1955. *Social Darwinism in American Thought,* rev. ed. Boston: Beacon Press.

Huxley, J. 1943. "Evolutionary Ethics." In *Touchstone for Ethics,* 1893–1943. New York: Harper, 1947.

Huxley, T. 1893. "Evolution and Ethics." In *Collected Essays,* vol. 9. New York. D. Appleton, 1902.

Jones, G. 1980. *Social Darwinism and English Thought.* New Jersey: Humanities Press.

Kelly, A. 1981. *The Descent of Darwin: the Popularization of Darwinism in Germany,* 1860–1914. Chapel Hill: University of North Carolina Press.

Kern, L., Mirels, H., and Hinshaw, V. 1983. "Scientists' Understanding of Propositional Logic." *Social Studies of Science* 13: 131–146.

Kohlberg, L. 1981. *The Philosophy of Moral Development.* New York: Harper and Row.

Kort, F. 1983. "An Evolutionary-Neurobiological Explanation of Political Behavior and the Lumsden-Wilson 'Thousand-Year Rule,'" *Journal of Social and Biological Structures* 6: 219–230.

Lewontin, R., Rose, S., and Kamin, L. 1984. *Not in Our Genes: Biology, Ideology, and Human Nature.* New York: Pantheon.

Lumsden, C., and Wilson, E. 1981. *Genes, Mind and Culture.* Cambridge, Mass.: Harvard University Press.

MacIntyre, Alistair. 1981. *After Virtue.* Notre Dame, Ind.: University of Notre Dame Press.

Mattern, R. 1978. "Altruism, Ethics, and Sociobiology." In Caplan (1978).

Mayr, E. 1976. "Behavior Programs and Evolutinary Strategies." In *Evolution and the Diversity of Life.* Cambridge, Mass.: Harvard University Press.

McCawley, J. 1981. *Everything that Linguists Have Always Wanted to Know about Logic.* Chicago: University of Chicago Press.

Montagu, A. ed. 1980. *Sociobiology Examined.* Oxford: Osford University Press.

Moore, G. 1903. *Principia Ethica.* Cambridge: Cambridge University Press.

Nagel, T. 1979. *Mortal Questions.* Cambridge: Cambridge University Press.

————. 1970. *The Possibility of Altruism.* New York: Oxford University Press.

Prior, A. 1949. *Logic and the Basis of Ethics.* Oxford: Claredon Press.

Richards, R. 1987. *Darwin and the Emergence of Evolutionary Theories of Mind and Behavior.* Chicago: University of Chicago.

————. 1982. "Darwin and the Biologizing of Moral Behavior." In W. Woodward and M. Ash, eds. *The Problematic Science: Psychology in Nineteenth-Century Thought.* New York: Praeger.

Ruse, M. 1984. "The Morality of the Gene." *Monist* **67**: 167–199.

————. 1979. *Sociobiology: Sense or Nonsense?* Dordrecht: D. Reidel.

Sahlins, M. 1976. *The Use and Abuse of Biology.* Ann Arbor: University of Michigan Press.

Schilcher, F. von, and Tennant, N. 1984. *Philosophy, Evolution and Human Nature.* London: Routledge and Kegan Paul.

Searles, J. 1964. "How to Derive 'Ought' from 'Is'." Philosophical Review **73**: 43–58.

Sellars, W. 1948. "Concepts as Involving Laws and Inconceivable without Them." *Philosophy of Science* **15**: 287–315.

Sidgwick, H. 1902. *Lectures on the Ethics of T.H. Green, Mr. Herbert Spencer, and J. Martineau.* London: Macmillan.

Simon, H. 1983. *Reason in Human Affairs.* Stanford: Stanford University Press.

Singer, P. 1981. *The Expanding Circle.* Oxford: Clarendon Press.

Smith, J. 1978. "The Concepts of Sociobiology." In Stent (1978).

Stent, G., ed. 1978. *Morality as a Biological Phenomenon.* Berkeley: University of California Press.

Suppes, P. 1985. "Davidsons's Views on Psychology as a Science." In B. Vermazen and M. Hintikka, eds. *Essays on Davidson: Actions and Events.* New York: Oxford University Press.

Thomas, L. 1985. "Human Nature, Love, and Morality: The Possibility of Altruism." In J. Fetzer, ed. *Sociobiology and Epistemology*. Boston: D. Reidel.

———. 1983. "Morality, the Self, and Our Natural Sentiments." In I. Irani and G. Myers, eds. *Emotion: Philosophical Studies*. New York: Haven Publications.

———. 1982. "Law, Morality, and Our Psychological Nature." In M. Bradie and D. Braybrooke, eds. *Social Justice*. Bowling Green, Ohio: Bowling Green University Press.

Toulmin, S. 1960. *The Place of Reason in Ethics*. Cambridge: Cambridge University Press.

Trigg, R. 1985. *Understanding Social Science*. Oxford: Blackwell.

———. 1982. *The Shaping of Man: Philosophical Aspects of Sociobiology*. Oxford: Blackwell.

———. 1980. *Reality at Risk: A Defense of Realism in Philosophy and the Sciences*. Brighton: Harvester Press.

Trivers, R. 1985. *Social Evolution*. Menlo Park, Cal.: Benjamin/Cummings.

———. 1971. "The Evolution of Reciprocal Altruism." *Quarterly Review of Biology* **46**: 35–57.

Wade, M. 1978. "A Critical Review of the Models of Group Selection." *Quarterly Review of Biology* **53**: 101–114.

———. 1977. "An Experimental Study of Group Selection." *Evolution* **31**: 134–153.

———. 1976. "Group Selection among Laboratory Populations of Tribolium." *Proceedings of the National Academy of Sciences* **73**: 4604–4607.

Williams, G. 1966. *Adaptation and Natural Selection*. Princeton: Princeton University Press.

Wilson, E. 1978. *On Human Nature*. Cambridge, Mass.: Harvard University Press.

———. 1975. *Sociobiology*. Cambridge, Mass.: Harvard University Press.

F. J. Ayala

The Biological Roots of Morality

ABSTRACT: The question whether ethical behavior is biologically determined may refer either to the *capacity* for ethics (i.e., the proclivity to judge human actions as either right or wrong), or to the moral norms accepted by human beings for guiding their actions. My theses are: (1) that the capacity for ethics is a necessary attribute of human nature; and (2) that moral norms are products of cultural evolution, not of biological evolution.

Humans exhibit ethical behavior by nature because their biological makeup determines the presence of the three necessary, and jointly sufficient, conditions for ethical behavior: (i) the ability to anticipate the consequences of one's own actions; (ii) the ability to make value judgments; and (iii) the ability to choose between alternative courses of action. Ethical behavior came about in evolution not because it is adaptive in itself, but as a necessary consequence of man's eminent intellectual abilities, which are an attribute directly promoted by natural selection.

Since Darwin's time there have been evolutionists proposing that the norms of morality are derived from biological evolution. Sociobiologists represent the most recent and most subtle version of that proposal. The sociobiologists' argument is that human ethical norms are sociocultural correlates of behaviors fostered by biological evolution. I argue that such proposals are misguided and do not escape the naturalistic fallacy. The isomorphism between the behaviors promoted by natural selection and those sanctioned by moral norms exists only with respect to the consequences of the behaviors; the underlying causations are completely disparate.

Introduction

Ethics is a human universal. People have moral values, i.e., they accept standards according to which their conduct is

Reprinted by permission of Kluwer Academic Publishers, "The Biological Roots of Morality," *Biology and Philosophy* (1987): 235–252, © D. Reidel Publishing Company.

judged either right or wrong, good or evil. The particular norms by which moral actions are judged vary to some extent from individual to individual, and from culture to culture (although some norms, like not to kill, not to steal, and to honor one's parents are widespread and perhaps universal), but value judgments are passed in all cultures. This universality raises the question whether the moral sense is part of human nature, one more dimension of our biological make-up; and whether ethical values may be the product of biological evolution, rather than simply given by religious and cultural traditions.

Aristotle and other philosophers of classical Greece and Rome, as well as Thomas Aquinas and the scholastics, held that we are ethical beings by nature. Man is not only *homo sapiens,* but also *Homo Moralis.* But biological evolution adds the important diachronic dimension. We do not attribute ethical behavior to animals (at least not to all animals and not to the same extent as to humans). Even if we would agree with Aristotle and Aquinas, the following questions would remain: When did the capacity for ethical behavior come about? And why did it evolve? Is it a simple by-product of other attributes (intelligence, for example) or was it specifically promoted as a direct target of natural selection?

Moral Evaluations and Moral Norms

The question whether ethical behavior is biologically determined may refer to either one of the following two issues: (1) Is the capacity for ethics—the proclivity to judge human actions as either right or wrong—determined by the biological nature of human beings? (2) Are the systems or codes of ethical norms accepted by human beings biologically determined?

The first question is more fundamental; it asks whether or not the biological nature of man is such that humans are necessarily inclined to make moral judgments and to accept ethical values, to identify certain actions as either right or wrong. Affirmative answers to this first question do not necessarily determine what the answer to the second question should be. Independent of whether or not humans are necessarily ethical, it remains to be determined whether particular moral prescriptions are in fact determined by the biological nature of man, or whether they are chosen by society, or by individuals. Even if we were to conclude that people cannot avoid having moral standards of conduct, it might be that the choice of the particular standards used for judgment would be arbitrary. The need for having moral values does not necessarily tell us what the moral values should be, like the capacity for language does not determine which language we shall speak.

The thesis that I will propose is that humans are ethical beings by their biological nature; that humans evaluate their behavior as either right or wrong, moral or immoral, as a consequence of their eminent intellectual capacities that include self-awareness and abstract thinking. These intellectual capacities are products of the evolutionary process, but they are distinctively human. Thus, I will maintain that ethical behavior is not causally related to the social behavior of animals, including kin and reciprocal "altruism."

A second thesis, which I will put forward is that the moral norms according to which we evaluate particular actions as either morally good or morally bad (as well as the grounds that may be used to justify the moral norms) are products of cultural evolution, not of biological evolution. The norms of morality belong, in this respect, to the same category of phenomena as the political and religious institutions, or the arts, sciences, and technology. The moral codes, like these other products of human culture, are often consistent with the biological predispositions of the human species, and of other animals. But this consistency between ethical norms and biological tendencies is not necessary or universal: it does not apply to all ethical norms in a given society, much less in all human societies.

Moral codes, like any other cultural systems, depend on the existence of human biological nature and must be consistent with it in the sense that they could not counteract it without promoting their own demise. Moreover, the acceptance and persistence of moral norms is facilitated whenever they are consistent with biologically conditioned human behaviors. But the moral norms are independent of such behaviors in the sense that some norms may not favor, and may hinder, the survival and reproduction of the individual and its genes, which survival and reproduction are the targets of biological evolution. Discrepancies between accepted moral rules and biological survival are, however, necessarily limited in scope or would otherwise lead to the extinction of the groups accepting such discrepant rules.

Three Necessary and Sufficient Conditions For Ethical Behavior

The question whether ethical behavior is determined by our biological nature must be answered in the affirmative. By "ethical behavior" I understand the urge *to judge* human actions as either good or bad, rather than *good behavior* (i.e., choosing to do what is perceived as good instead of what is perceived as evil). Humans exhibit ethical behavior by nature because their biological constitution determines the presence in them of the three necessary, and jointly sufficient, conditions for ethical behavior. These conditions are: (i) the ability to anticipate the consequences of one's own actions; (ii) the ability to make value judgments; and (iii) the ability to choose between alternative courses of action. I shall briefly examine each of these abilities and show that they exist as a consequence of the eminent intellectual capacity of human beings.

The ability to anticipate the consequences of one's own actions is the most fundamental of the three conditions required for ethical behavior. Only if I can anticipate that pulling the trigger will shoot the bullet, which in turn will strike and kill my enemy, can the action of pulling the trigger be evaluated as nefarious. Pulling a trigger is not in itself a moral action; it becomes so by virtue of its relevant consequences. My action has an ethical dimension only if I do anticipate these consequences.

The ability to anticipate the consequences of one's actions is closely related to the ability to establish the connection between means and ends; that is, of seeing a mean precisely as mean, as something that serves a particular end or purpose. This ability to establish the connection between means and their ends requires the ability to anticipate the future and to form mental images of realities not present or not yet in existence.

The ability to establish the connection between means and ends happens to be the fundamental intellectual capacity that has made possible the development of human culture and technology. The evolutionary roots of this capacity may be found in the evolution of the erect position, which transformed the anterior limbs of our ancestors from organs of locomotion into organs of manipulation. The hands thereby gradually became organs adept for the construction and use of objects for hunting and other activities that improved survival and reproduction, i.e., that increased the reproductive fitness of their carriers. The construction of tools depends not only on manual dexterity, but in perceiving them precisely as tools, as objects that help to perform certain actions, that is, as means that serve certain ends or purposes: a knife for cutting, an arrow for hunting, an animal skin for protecting the body from the cold. Natural selection promoted the intellectual capacity of our biped ancestors, because increased intelligence facilitated the perception of tools as tools, and therefore their construction and use, with the ensuing amelioration of biological survival and reproduction.

The development of the intellectual abilities of our ancestors took place over three million years or longer, gradually increasing the ability to connect means with their ends and, hence, the possibility of making ever more complex tools serving remote purposes. The ability to anticipate the future, essential for ethical behavior, is therefore closely associated with the development of the ability to construct tools, an ability that has produced the advanced technologies of modern societies and that is largely responsible for the success of mankind as a biological species. From its obscure beginnings in Africa, mankind has spread over the whole earth except the frozen wastes of Antarctica, and has become the most numerous species of mammal. Numbers may not be an unmixed blessing but they are a measure of biological success.

The second condition for the existence of ethical behavior is the ability to make value judgments, to perceive certain objects or deeds as more desirable than others. Only if I can see the death of my enemy as preferable to his survival (or vice versa) can the action leading to his demise be thought as moral. If the alternative consequences of an action are neutral with respect to value, the action cannot be characterized as ethical. The ability to make value judgments depends on the capacity for abstraction, i.e., on the capacity to perceive actions or objects as members of general classes. This makes it possible to compare objects or actions with one another and to perceive some as more desirable than others. The capacity for abstraction requires an advanced intelligence such as it exists in humans and apparently in them alone.

The third condition necessary for ethical behavior is the ability to choose between alternative courses of actions. Pulling the trigger can be a moral action only if I have the option not to pull it. A necessary action beyond our control is not a moral action: the circulation of the blood or the process of food digestion are not moral actions. Whether there is free will is a question much discussed by philosophers and this is not the appropriate place to review the arguments. I only will advance two considerations which are common sense evidence of the existence of free will. One is our personal experience, which indicates that the possibility to choose between alternatives is genuine rather than only apparent. The second consideration is that when we confront a given situation that requires action on our part, we are able mentally to explore alternative courses of action, thereby extending the field within which we can exercise our free will. In any case, if there were no free will, there would be no ethical behavior; morality would only be an illusion. The point that I want to make here is, however, that free will is dependent on the existence of a well developed intelligence, which makes it possible to explore alternative courses of action and to choose one or another in view of the anticipated consequences.

In summary, ethical behavior is an attribute of the biological make-up of humans and, hence, is a product of biological evolution. But I see no evidence that ethical behavior developed because it was adaptive in itself. I find it hard to see how *evaluating* certain actions as either good or evil (not just choosing some actions rather than others, or evaluating them with respect to their practical consequences) would promote the reproductive fitness of the evaluators. Nor do I see how there might be some form of "incipient" ethical behavior that would then be promoted by natural selection. The three necessary conditions for there being ethical behavior are manifestations of advanced intellectual abilities. It rather seems to me that the target of natural selection was the development of these advanced intellectual capacities. This was favored by natural selection because the construction and use of tools improved the strategic position of our biped ancestors. Once bipedalism evolved and tool-using and tool-making became possible, those individuals more effective in these functions had a greater probability of biological success. The biological advantage provided by the design and use of tools persisted long enough so that intellectual abilities continued to increase, eventually yielding the eminent development of intelligence that is characteristic of *homo sapiens*.

The Evolution of Information Processing and the Question of Animal Ethics

The development of human intellectual abilities may be seen as one terminus of a process that is evolutionarily continuous and gradual. An evolutionary trend particularly apparent in animal lineages, is a gradual increase in the ability to obtain and process information about the external environment. This ability is adaptive because it allows the organism to react flexibly to the environmental conditions (Ayala 1982a). A most rudimentary ability to gather and process information about the environment can be detected in certain single-celled organisms. A paramecium follows a sinuous path as it swims, ingesting the bacteria that it encounters. Whenever it meets unfavorable conditions, such as unsuitable acidity or salinity in the water, the paramecium checks its advance, turns, and starts in a new direction. This reaction is purely negative: the paramecium does not seek its food or a favorable environment but simply avoids unsuitable conditions. A greater ability to process information about the environment occurs in the single-celled alga Euglena, which has a sensitive spot by means of which it can orient itself towards the direction of light. Euglena's motions are directional; it not only avoids unsuitable environments, but it actively seeks suitable ones. An amoeba represents further development in the same direction; it reacts to light by moving away from it and also actively pursues food particles.

The ability to gather and process information about the environment has not increased through time in all evolutionary lineages. Today's bacteria are not more advanced in this respect than their ancestors of one billion years ago. In many evolutionary lineages some limited progress took place in the early stages, without further advances through the rest of their histories. In general, animals are more advanced by this standard than plants; vertebrates are more advanced than invertebrates; mammals more advanced than reptiles, which are more advanced than fish (see Ayala, 1982a, p. 12, for more details).

Vertebrates are able to obtain and process much more complicated signals and to produce a much greater variety of responses than invertebrates, including the insects and other anthropods. In animals in general, the ability to obtain and process information about the environment is rooted in the nervous system and in the brain, which integrates the sensorial signals transmitted by the nerves and coordinates the appropriate responses. The vertebrate brain has an enormous number of associative neurons with an extremely complex arrangement. Among the vertebrates, progress in the ability to obtain and to deal with environmental information is correlated with an increase in the size of the cerebral hemispheres and with the appearance and development of the neopallium. The neopallium is an organ involved in association and coordination of all kinds of impulses from all receptors and brain centers. The neopallium appeared first in the reptiles. In the mammals it has expanded to become the cerebral cortex, which covers most of the cerebral hemispheres. The larger brain of vertebrates compared with invertebrates permits them also to have a large amount of neurons committed to information storage or memory. The relative size and absolute complexity of the brain, and in particular of the cerebral cortex, reach a maximum in humans, who have a much greater capacity than any other organisms to perceive the environment and to integrate, coordinate, and react flexibly to what is perceived. The extraordinary development of the brain has endowed humans with intellectual powers that make possible abstraction and self-awareness, i.e., the objectivation of the thinking subject, the ability of an individual to perceive itself as an object.

The question that arises is whether the capacity for ethical behavior, which as I have argued is associated with the advanced development of intelligence, might not also be present at least in a rudimentary fashion in other animals, in proportion to the development of their intelligence. My answer is negative (see also Stent, 1978). Certain animals exhibit behaviors analogous with those resulting from ethical actions in humans, such as the loyalty of dogs or the appearance of compunction when they are punished. But such behaviors are either genetically determined or elicited by training ("conditioned responses"). Genetic determination and not moral evaluation is also what is involved in the "altruistic" behavior of some animals. In my view, none of the three necessary conditions for ethical behavior obtains in animals.

The capacity for ethics is an outcome of gradual evolution, but it is an attribute that only exists when the underlying attributes (i.e., the intellectual capacities) reach an advanced degree. The necessary conditions for ethical behavior only come about after the crossing of an evolutionary threshold. The approach is gradual, but the conditions only appear when a degree of intelligence is reached such that the formation of abstract concepts and the anticipation of the future are possible. Thresholds occur in other evolutionary developments—for example, in the origins of life, multicellularity, and sexual reproduction—as well as in the evolution of abstract thinking and self-awareness. Thresholds also occur in the inorganic world; for example, water heats gradually, but at 100°C boiling begins and the transition from liquid to gas suddenly starts.

Moral Norms: Religious and Evolutionary Proposals

I have answered in the affirmative the first of the two questions I posed. Ethical behavior is rooted in the biological make-up of man. I have also proposed that ethical behavior did not evolve because it was adaptive in itself, but rather as the indirect outcome of the evolution of eminent intellectual abilities. Now I turn to the second question: whether our biological nature also determines which ones are the moral norms or ethical codes that human beings must obey. My answer, is negative. The moral norms according to which we decide whether a particular action is either right or wrong are not specified by biological evolution but by cultural evolution. The premises of our moral judgments are received from religious and other social traditions.

I hasten to add, however, that moral systems, like any other cultural activities, cannot long survive if they run outright contrary to our biology. The norms of morality must be consistent with biological nature, because ethics can only exist in human individuals and in human societies. One might therefore also expect, and it is the case, that accepted norms of morality will often promote behaviors which increase the biological adaptation of those who behave according to them. But this is neither necessary nor indeed always the case.

Before going any further, it seems worthwhile to consider briefly the proposition that the justification of the codes of morality derives from religious convictions and only from them. There is no necessary, or *logical*, connection between religious faith and moral principles, although there usually is a motivational, or psychological connection. What I mean by this is that religious beliefs do explain why people accept particular ethical norms, because they are motivated to do so by their religious convictions. But in following the moral dictates of his religion, an individual is not rationally justifying the moral norms that he accepts. It may, of course, be possible to develop such rational justification; for example, when a set of religious beliefs contains propositions about human nature and the world from which the ethical norms can be logically derived. But in this case, the logical justification of the ethical norms does not come from religious faith as such, but from a particular conception of the world; it is the result of philosophical analysis grounded on certain premises. Theologians in general, and Christian theologians in particular, do often propose to justify their ethics on rational foundations concerning human nature. A notable example is the theory of "Natural Law" of Saint Thomas Aquinas, for long the most influential Christian theologian. I shall add that the motivational connection between religious beliefs and ethical norms is the decisive one for the religious believer. But this is true in general: most people, religious or not, accept a particular moral code for social reasons, without trying to justify it rationally by means of a theory from which the moral norms can be logically derived.

There are many theories concerned with the rational grounds for morality, such as deductive theories that seek to discover the axioms or fundamental principles that determine what is morally correct on the basis of direct moral intuition; or theories like logical positivism or existentialism, that negate rational foundations for morality, reducing moral principles to emotional decisions or to other irrational grounds. After the publication of Darwin's theory of evolution by natural selection, philosophers as well as biologists have attempted to find in the evolutionary process the justification for moral norms. The common ground to all such proposals is that evolution is a natural process that achieves goals that are desirable and thereby morally good; indeed it has produced man. Proponents of these ideas see that only the evolutionary goals can give moral value to human action: whether a human deed is morally right depends on whether it directly or indirectly promotes the evolutionary process and its natural objectives.

Herbert Spencer was perhaps the first philosopher seeking to find the grounds of morality in biological evolution. More recent attempts include those of the distinguished evolutionists J. S. Huxley (1947, 1953) and C. H. Waddington (1960) and of Edward O. Wilson (1975, 1978), founder of Sociobiology as an independent discipline engaged in discovering the biological foundations of all social behavior.

In *The Principles of Ethics* (1893), Spencer seeks to replace the Christian faith as the justification for traditional ethical values with a natural foundation. Spencer argues that the theory of organic evolution implies certain ethical principles. Human conduct must be evaluated, like any biological activity whatsoever, according to whether it conforms to the life process; therefore, any acceptable moral code must be based on natural selection, the law of struggle for existence. According to Spencer, the most exalted form of conduct is that which leads to a greater duration, extension, and perfection of life; the morality of all human actions must be measured by that standard. Spencer proposes that, although exceptions exist, the general rule is that pleasure goes with that which is biologically useful, whereas pain marks what is biologically harmful. This is an outcome of natural selection—thus, while doing what brings them pleasure and avoiding what is painful, organisms improve their chances for survival. With respect to human behavior, we see that we derive pleasure from virtuous behavior and pain from evil actions, associations which indicate that the morality of human actions is also founded on biological nature.

Spencer proposes as the general rule of human behavior that anyone should be free to do anything that he wants, so long as it does not interfere with the similar freedom to which others are entitled. The justification of this rule is found in organic evolution: the success of an individual, plant or animal, depends on its ability to obtain that which it needs. Consequently, Spencer reduces the role of the state to protect the collective freedom of individuals to do as they please. This *laissez faire* form of government may seem ruthless, because individuals would seek their own welfare without any consideration for others' (except for respecting their freedom), but Spencer believes that it is consistent with traditional Christian values. It may be added that, although Spencer sets the grounds of morality on biological nature and on nothing else, he admits that certain moral norms go beyond that which is biologically determined; these are rules formulated by society and accepted by tradition.

Social Darwinism, in Spencer's version or in some variant form, was fashionable in European and American circles during the latter part of the nineteenth century and the early years of the twentieth, but it has few or no distinguished intellectual followers at present. Spencer's critics include the evolutionists J. S. Huxley and C. H. Waddington who, nevertheless, maintain that organic evolution provides grounds for a rational justification of ethical codes. For Huxley, the standard of morality is the contribution that actions make to evolutionary progress, which goes from less to more "advanced" organisms. For Waddington, the morality of actions must be evaluated by their contribution to human evolution.

Huxley and Waddington's views are based on value judgments about what is or is not progressive in evolution. Contrary to Huxley's proposal, there is nothing objective in the evolutionary process itself (i.e., outside human considerations; see Ayala, 1982a) that makes the success of bacteria, which have persisted as such for more than two billion years and in enormous numbers, less desirable than that of the vertebrates, even though the latter are more complex. Nor are the insects, of which more than one million species exist, less desirable or less successful from a purely biological perspective than humans or any other mammal species. Waddington fails to demonstrate why the promotion of human biological evolution by itself should be the standard to measure what is morally good.[1]

A more fundamental objection against the theories of Spencer, Huxley and Waddington—and against any other program seeking the justification of a moral code in biological nature—is that such theories commit the 'naturalistic fallacy" (Moore, 1903), which consists in identifying what "is" with what "ought to be." This error was pointed out already by Hume ([1740] 1978, p. 469):

> In every system of morality which I have hitherto met with I have always remarked that the author proceeds for some time in the ordinary way of reasoning . . . when of a sudden I am surprised to find, that instead of the usual copulations of propositions, *is* and *is not,* I meet with no proposition that is not connected with an *ought* or *ought not.* This change is imperceptible; but is, however, of the last consequence. For as this *ought* or *ought not* expresses some new relation or affirmation, it is necessary that it should be observed and explained; and at the same time a reason should be given, for what seems altogether inconceivable, how this new relation can be a deduction from others, which are entirely different from it.

The naturalistic fallacy occurs whenever inferences using the terms "ought" or "ought not" are derived from premises that do not include such terms but are rather formulated using the connections "is" or "is not." An argument cannot be logically valid unless the conclusions only contain terms that are also present in the premises. In order to proceed logically from that which "is" to what "ought to be," it is necessary to include a premise that justifies the transition between the two expressions. But this transition is what is at stake, and one would need a previous premise to justify the validity of the one making the transition, and so on in a regression *ad infinitum.* In other words, from the fact that something *is* the case, it does not follow that it *ought to be* so in the ethical sense; *is* and *ought* belong to disparate logical categories.

Because evolution has proceeded in a particular way, it does not follow that that course is morally right or desirable. The justification of ethical norms on biological evolution, or on any other natural process, can only be achieved by introducing value judgments, human choices that prefer one rather than other object or process. Biological nature is in itself morally neutral.

It must be noted, moreover, that using natural selection or the course of evolution for determining the morality of human actions may lead to paradoxes. Evolution has produced the smallpox and AIDS viruses. But it would seem unreasonable to accuse the World Health Organization of immorality because of its campaign for total eradication of the smallpox virus; or to label unethical the efforts to control the galloping spread of the AIDS virus. Human hereditary diseases are conditioned by mutations that are natural events in the evolutionary process. But we do not think it immoral to cure or alleviate the pain of persons with such diseases. Natural selection is a natural process that increases the frequency of certain genes and the elimination of others, that yields some kinds of organisms rather than others; but it is not a process moral or immoral in itself or in its outcome, in the same way as gravity is not a morally-laden force. In order to consider some evolutionary events as morally right and others wrong, we must introduce human values; moral evaluations cannot be reached simply on the basis that certain events came about by natural processes.

Sociobiology: Altruism and Inclusive Fitness

Edward O. Wilson (1975, p. 562) has urged that "scientists and humanists should consider together the possibility that the time has come for ethics to be removed temporarily from the hands of the philosophers and biologicized." Wilson, like other sociobiologists (Barash 1977; Wilson 1978; Alexander 1979; see also Ruse 1986a), sees that sociobiology may provide the key for finding a naturalistic basis for ethics. Sociobiology is the "systematic study of the biological basis of all forms of social behavior in all kinds of organisms" (Wilson, in the Foreword to Barash 1977) or, in Barash's concise formulation, "the application of evolutionary biology to social behavior" (1977, p. ix). Its purpose is "to develop general laws of the evolution and biology of social behavior, which might then be extended in a disinterested manner to the study of human beings" (Wilson ibid.). The program is ambitious: to discover the biological basis of human social behavior, starting from the investigation of the social behavior of animals.

The sociobiologist's argument concerning normative ethics is not that the norms of morality can be grounded in biological evolution, but rather that evolution predisposes us to accept certain moral norms, namely those that are consistent with the "objectives" of natural selection. It is because of this predisposition that human moral codes sanction patterns of behavior similar to those encountered in the social behavior of animals. The sociobiologists claim that the agreement between moral codes and the goals of natural selection in social groups was discovered when the theories of kin selection and reciprocal altruism were formulated. The commandment to honor one's parents, the incest tabu, the greater blame usually attributed to the wife's adultery than to the husband's, the ban or restriction of divorce, are among the numerous ethical precepts that endorse behaviors that are also endorsed by natural selection, as has been discovered by sociobiology.

The sociobiologists reiterate their conviction that science and ethics belong to separate logical realms; that one may not infer what is morally right or wrong from a determination of how things are or are not in nature. In this respect they avoid committing the naturalistic fallacy. According to Wilson, "To devise a naturalistic description of human social behavior is to note a set of facts for further investigation, not to pass a value judgment or to deny that a great deal of the behavior can be deliberately changed if individual societies so wish" (in Barash, 1977, p xiv). Barash (1977, p. 278) puts it so: "Ethical judgments have no place in the study of human sociobiology or in any other science for that matter. What is biological is not necessarily good." And Alexander (1979, p. 276 asks what is it that evolution teaches us about normative ethics or about what we *ought* to do, and responds "Absolutely nothing."

There is nevertheless some question as to whether the sociobiologists are always consistent with the statements just quoted. Wilson (1975, p. 564), for example, writes that "the requirement for an evolutionary approach to ethics is self-evident. It should also be clear that no single set of moral standards can be applied to all human populations, let alone all sex-age classes within each population. To impose a uniform code is therefore to create complex, intractable moral dilemmas." Moral pluralism is, for Wilson, "innate." Biology, then, helps us at the very least to decide that certain moral codes (e.g., all those pretending to be universally

applicable) are incompatible with human nature and therefore unacceptable. This is not quite an argument in favor of
the biological determinism of ethical norms, but it does
approach determinism from the negative side: because the
range of valid moral codes is delimited by the claim that
some are not compatible with biological nature.

Wilson goes, however, further when he writes: "Human
behavior—like the deepest capacities for emotional response
which drive and guide it—is the circuitous technique by which
human genetic material has been and will be kept intact.
Morality has no other demonstratable ultimate function" (Wilson, 1978, p. 167, my italics). How is one to interpret this
statement? It is possible that Wilson is simply giving the
reason why ethical behavior exists at all; his proposition
would be that humans are prompted to evaluate morally
their actions as a means to preserve their genes, their biological nature. But this proposition is erroneous. Human
beings are by nature ethical beings in the sense I have
expounded earlier: they judge morally their actions because
of their innate ability for anticipating the consequences of
their actions, for formulating value judgments, and for free
choice. Human beings exhibit ethical behavior by nature
and necessity, rather than because such behavior would help
to preserve their genes or serve any other purpose.

Wilson's statement may alternatively be read as a justification of human moral codes: the function of these would
be to preserve human genes. But this would entail the naturalistic fallacy and, worse yet, would seem to justify a morality that most of us detest. If the preservation of human
genes (be those of the individual or of the species) is the
purpose that moral norms serve, Spencer's Social Darwinism
would seem right; racism or even genocide could be justified
as morally correct if they were perceived as the means to
preserve those genes thought to be good or desirable and to
eliminate those thought to be bad or undesirable. There is
no doubt in my mind that Wilson is not intending to justify
racism or genocide, but this is one possible interpretation of
his words.

I shall now turn to the sociobiologists' proposition that
natural selection favors behaviors that are isomorphic with

the behaviors sanctioned by the moral codes endorsed by most humans.

Evolutionists had for years struggled with finding an explanation for the apparently altruistic behavior of animals. When a predator attacks a herd of zebras, these will attempt to protect the young in the herd, even if they are not their progeny, rather than fleeing. When a prairie dog sights a coyote, it will warn other members of the colony with an alarm call, even though by drawing attention to itself this increases its own risk. Examples of altruistic behaviors of this kind can be multiplied.

Altruism is defined in the dictionary I happen to have at hand *(Webster's New Collegiate,* 2nd ed.) as "Regard for, and devotion to, the interests of others." To speak of animal altruism is not to claim that explicit feelings of devotion or regard are present in them, but rather that animals act for the welfare of others at their own risk just as humans are expected to do when behaving altruistically. The problem is precisely how to justify such behaviors in terms of natural selection. Assume, for illustration, that in a certain species there are two alternative forms of a gene ("alleles"), of which one but not the other promotes altruistic behavior. Individuals possessing the altruistic allele will risk their life for the benefit of others, whereas those possessing the non-altruistic allele will benefit from altruistic behavior without risking themselves. Possessors of the altruistic allele will be more likely to die and the allele will therefore be eliminated more often than the non-altruistic allele. Eventually, after some generations, the altruistic allele will be completely replaced by the nonaltruistic one. But then how is it that altruistic behaviors are common in animals without the benefit of ethical motivation?

One major contribution of sociobiology to evolutionary theory is the notion of "inclusive fitness." In order to ascertain the consequences of natural selection it is necessary to take into account a gene's effects not only on a particular individual but on all individuals possessing that gene. When considering altruistic behavior, one must take into account not only the risks for the altruistic individual, but also the benefits for other possessors of the same allele. Zebras live in herds where individuals are blood relatives. An allele prompting adults to protect the defenseless young would be favored by natural selection if the benefit (in terms of saved carriers of that allele) is greater than the cost (due to the increased risk of the protectors). An individual that lacks the altruistic allele and carries instead a non-altruistic one, will not risk its life, but the non-altruistic allele is partially eradicated with the death of each defenseless relative.

It follows from this line of reasoning that the more closely related the members of a herd or animal group typically are, the more altruistic behavior should be present. This seems to be generally the case. We need not enter here into the details of the quantitative theory developed by sociobiologists in order to appreciate the significance of two examples. The most obvious is parental care. Parents feed and protect their young because each child has half the genes of each parent: the genes are protecting themselves, as it were, when they prompt a parent to care for its young.

The second example is more subtle: the social organization and behavior of certain animals like the honeybee. Worker bees toil building the hive and feeding and caring for the larvae even though they themselves are sterile and only the queen produces progeny. Assume that in some ancestral hive, an allele arises that prompts worker bees to behave as they now do. It would seem that such an allele would not be passed on to the following generation because such worker bees do not reproduce. But such inference is erroneous. Queen bees produce two kinds of eggs: some that remain unfertilized develop into males (which are therefore "haploid," i.e., carry only one set of genes); others that are fertilized (hence, are "diploid," carry two sets of genes) develop into worker bees and occasionally into a queen. W. D. Hamilton (1964) demonstrated that with such a reproductive system daughter queens and their worker sisters share in two-thirds of their genes, whereas daughter queens and their mother share in only one-half of their genes. Hence, the worker bee genes are more effectively propagated by workers caring for their sisters than if they would produce and care for their own daughters. Natural selection can thus explain the existence in social insects of sterile casts, which exhibit a most extreme form of apparently altruistic behavior by dedicating their life to care for the progeny of another individual (the queen).

Sociobiologists point out that many of the moral norms commonly accepted in human societies sanction behaviors also promoted by natural selection (which promotion becomes apparent only when the inclusive fitness of genes is taken into account). Examples of such behaviors are the commandment to honor one's parents, the incest tabu, the greater blame attributed to the wife's than to the husband's adultery, the ban or restriction on divorce, and many others. The sociobiologists' argument is that human ethical norms are sociocultural correlates of behaviors fostered by biological evolution. Ethical norms protect such evolution-determined behaviors as well as being specified by them.

I believe, however, that the sociobiologists' argument is misguided and does not escape the naturalistic fallacy (see Ayala 1980 and Ayala 1982b for more extensive discussion). Consider altruism as an example. Altruism in the biological sense (altruism[b]) is defined in terms of the population genetic consequences of a certain behavior. Altruism[b] is explained by the fact that genes prompting such behavior are actually favored by natural selection (when inclusive fitness is taken into account), even though the fitness of the behaving individual is decreased. But altruism in the moral sense (altruism[m]) is explained in terms of motivations: a person chooses to risk his own life (or incur some kind of "cost") for the benefit of somebody else. The isomorphism between altruism[b] and altruism[m] is only apparent: an individual's chances are improved by the behavior of another individual who incurs a risk or cost. The underlying causations are completely disparate: the ensuing genetic benefits in altruismb; regard for others in altruism[m].[2]

The discrepancy between biologically determined behaviors and moral norms and, therefore, a radical flaw in the sociobiologists' argument for a naturalistic foundation for ethics, is enhanced by three additional considerations that I shall briefly enunciate. The first observation is that our biological nature may *predispose us* to accept certain moral precepts, but it does not constrain us to accept them, nor to behave according to them. The same eminent intellectual abilities discussed above that make ethical behavior possible and necessary, and in particular free will, also give us the power to accept some moral norms and to reject others, independently of any natural inclinations. A natural predisposition may influence our behavior, but influence and predisposition are not the same as constraint or determination.

This observation deserves attention because authors such as Konrad Lorenz (1963) and Robert Ardrey (1966) have presented aggression and the territorial "imperative" as natural tendencies, which might therefore be futile to try to resist. Whether or not aggression and the territorial imperative are ingrained in our genes is neither obvious nor needs to be explored here. What needs to be said, however, is (1) that the morality of the behaviors in question is to be assessed in any case by the accepted norms of morality and not by recourse to biological evidence, and (2) that if such tendencies or imperatives would exist, people would still have the possibility and the duty of resisting them (even at the expense of a fitness reduction) whenever they are seen as immoral (Dobzhansky 1973).

A second observation is that some norms of morality are consistent with behaviors prompted by natural selection, but other norms are not so. The commandment of charity: "Love thy neighbor as thyself," often runs contrary to the inclusive fitness of the genes, even though it promotes social cooperation and peace of mind. If the yardstick of morality were the multiplication of genes, the supreme moral imperative would be to beget the largest possible number of children and (with lesser dedication) to encourage our close relatives to do the same. But to impregnate the most women possible is not, in the view of most people, the highest moral duty of a man.

The third consideration is that moral norms differ from one culture to another and even "evolve" from one time to another. Many people see nowadays that the Biblical injunction: "Be fruitful and multiply" has been replaced by a moral imperative to limit the number of one's children. No genetic change in human populations accounts for this inversion of moral value. Moreover, an individual's inclusive fitness is still favored by having many children.

Moral norms are not determined by biological processes, but by cultural traditions and principles that are products of human history. The evaluation of moral codes or human actions must take into account biological knowledge. But for deciding which moral codes should be accepted, biology alone is palpably insufficient.

References

Alexander, R. D. 1979. *Darwinism and Human Affairs*. Seattle: University of Washington Press.

Ardrey, R. 1966. *The Territorial Imperative*. New York: Aheneum.

Ayala, F. J. 1980. *Origen y Evolucion del Hombre*. Madrid: Alianza Editorial.

———. 1982a. "The Evolutionary Concept of Progress." In G. A. Almond et al., eds., *Progress and Its Discontents*, pp. 106–124. Berkeley: University of California Press.

———. 1982b. "La Naturaleza Humana a la Luz de la Evolucion." *Esludios Filosoficos* 3, no. 1: 397–441.

Barash, D. P. 1977. *Sociobiology and Behavior*. New York: Elsevier.

Dobhansky, T. 1962. *Mankind Evolving*. New Haven, Conn.: Yale University Press.

———. 1973. "Ethics and Values in Biological and Cultural Evolution." *Zygon* 8, no. 26: 1–281.

Hamilton, W. D. 1964, 'The Genetical Evolution of Social Behavior." *Journal of Theoretical Biology* 7: 1–51

Hume, D. [1740] 1978. *Treatise of Human Nature*. Oxford: Oxford University Press.

Huxley, J. S. 1953. *Evolution in Action*. New York: Harper.

Huxley, T. H., and J. S. Huxley. 1947. *Touchstone for Ethics*. New York: Harper.

Lorenz, K. 1963. *On Aggression*. New York: Harcourt, Brace and World.

Moore, C. E. 1903. *Principia Ethica*. Cambridge: Cambridge University Press.

Ruse, M. 1986a. *Taking Darwin Seriously: A Naturalistic Approach to Philosophy*. Oxford: Basil Blackwell.

———. 1986b. "Evolutionary Ethics: A Phoenix Arisen." *Zygon* 21: 95–112.

——— and E. O. Wilson. 1986. "Moral Philosophy as Applied Science," *Philosophy*.

Simpson, G. G. 1949. *The Meaning of Evolution*. New Haven, Conn.: Yale University Press.

———. 1969. *Biology and Man*. New York: Harcourt, Brace and World.

Spencer, H. 1893. *The Principles of Ethics*. London.

Stent, G. S., ed. 1978. *Morality as a Biological Phenomenon*. Berlin: Dahlem.

Waddington, C. H. 1960. *The Ethical Animal*. London: Allen and Unwin.

Wilson, E. O. 1975. *Sociobiology, the New Synthesis*, Cambridge: Belknap.

———. 1978. On *Human Nature*. Cambridge, Mass.: Harvard University Press.

Notes

This article is based on a paper presented at the International Symposium on Biological Models of Human Action, Palma de Mallorca, Spain, 16–18 December 1985.

1. For an incisive criticism of Huxley's notion of biological progress, see Simpson (1949). Huxley's and Waddington's efforts to discover in biological evolution the foundations of ethical norms have been refuted by Simpson (1969) and Dobzhansky (1962, 1973).

2. The two disparate meanings of altruism are well distinguished by Ruse (1986a; 1986b; Ruse and Wilson, 1986) who in his recent writings has become an ardent proponent of the sociobiologists' thesis concerning the foundations of ethics. Ruse uses quotation marks ("altruism") to signify altruism in the biological sense and to differentiate it from moral altruism (which he writes without the quotation marks). Ruse has articulated perhaps more clearly than anybody else a sociobiological explanation or the evolution of the moral sense; namely that the moral sense—our proclivity to evaluate certain actions as good and others as evil—has evolved so that we behave in ways that improve our fitness, but do not do so in a way that is immediately obvious. Humans tend to be selfish because that usually serves best our fitness. Yet, there are situations where

the (inclusive) fitness of our genes is enhanced by cooperation rather than selfishness; examples are cases of "altruistic" behavior similar to those of adult zebras protecting the young in the herd or to the warning cry of a prairie dog. Natural selection has tricked humans into exhibiting such non-obviously (biologically) beneficial behavior by prompting us to evaluate such behavior as morally right, which in turn has necessitated the evolution of the moral sense. In Ruse's own words (1986b, pp. 97–99): "All such cooperation for personal evolutionary gain is known technically as 'altruism.' I emphasize that this term is rooted in metaphor, even though now it has the just-given biological meaning. There is no implication that evolutionary 'altruism' (working together for biological pay-off) is inevitably associated with moral altruism. . . . [Sociobiologists] argue that moral (literal) altruism might be one way in which biological (meta-phorical) 'altruism' could be achieved. . . . Literal, moral altruism is a major way in which advantageous biological cooperation is achieved. . . . In order to achieve 'altruism,' we are altruistic! To make us cooperate for our biological ends, evolution has filled us full of thoughts about right and wrong, the need to help our fellows, and so forth." This is all the explicit interpretation of Wilson's statement that I quote in the article ("Human behavior . . . is the circuitous technique by which human genetic material has been and will be kept intact. Morality has no other demonstrable ultimate function"). This justification of the evolution of the moral sense is in my view misguided. I have argued that we make moral judgments as a consequence of our eminent intellectual abilities, not as an innate way for achieving biological gain. I have also argued that the sociobiologists' position may be interpreted as requiring also that the preferred norms of morality be those that achieve biological gain (because that is, in their view, why the moral sense evolved at all). This, in turn, would justify social attitudes that many of us (sociobiologists included) would judge morally obtuse and even heinous.

George C. Williams

Huxley's Evolution and Ethics in Sociobiological Perspective

ABSTRACT. T. H. Huxley's essay and prolegomena of 1894 argued that the process and products of evolution are morally unacceptable and act in opposition to the ethical progress of humanity. Modern sociobiological insights and studies of organisms in natural settings support Huxley and justify an even more extreme condemnation of nature and an antithesis of the naturalistic fallacy: what is, in the biological world, normally ought not. Modern biology also provides suggestions on the origin of the human moral impulse and on tactics likely to be effective in the combat against nature urged by Huxley.

Let us understand, once for all, that the ethical progress of society depends, not on imitating the cosmic process, still less on running away from it, but in combating it.

Thomas H. Huxley

Thomas Huxley first presented "Evolution and Ethics" as his Romanes Lecture in 1893. The published version and "Prolegomena" first appeared in 1894. They have been favorites among anthologists and have excited comment ever since. In my view most of the better known comments (e.g., Dewey 1900; Julian Huxley 1947; Waddington 1971) would have been better left unsaid. Their main errors have been ably rectified by D. Daiches Raphael (1958) and Anthony G. N. Flew (1967), who make it clear that Thomas Huxley's views were far more tenable than those of twentieth-century critics.

Reprinted with permission of the publisher, "Huxley's Evolution and Ethics in Sociobiological Perspective," *Zygon* (1988): 383–407.

317

I think Flew (1967, p. 50) fails in one respect. He accuses Huxley of going too far in recognizing a negative moral value in nature rather than mere moral neutrality. I also criticize Huxley on this point, but in the opposite way. I will attempt to show that Huxley did not go, far enough in his condemnation of the evolutionary process. We now have a far deeper understanding of evolution than Huxley had, and far more information on what this process has wrought. Huxley, for instance, understood nothing of forces favoring the development of nepotism or of parent-offspring and other sorts of conflict in nature. He knew little of the prevalence and violence of infanticide and cannibalism.

There are several important themes in Huxley's essay. One deals with the evolutionary origin of human ethical motivations and attitudes, and what he calls "the apparent paradox that ethical nature, while born of cosmic nature, is necessarily at enmity with its parent" (Huxley 1894, p. viii). This topic is ably discussed by Peter Singer (1981) and Richard Alexander (1987), with whom I am mostly in agreement.

Although his "paradox" is not a matter that can be ignored, I will deal here mainly with Huxley's more prominent theme, his moral evaluation of nature, succinctly summarized: "Thus, brought before the tribunal of ethics, the cosmos might well seem to stand condemned. The conscience of man revolted against the moral indifference of nature, and the microscopic atom should have found the illimitable macrocosm guilty" (Huxley 1894, p. 59). Condemnation and guilt are dubious verdicts for mere moral *indifference*. Huxley clearly implies something worse, and the inconsistency makes the statement vague and disappointing. I would prefer something more along these lines: "Thus, brought before the tribunal of ethics, the cosmos stands condemned. The conscience of man must revolt against the gross immorality of nature."

I attribute the defects of Huxley's version to two factors. The first is that despite his accomplishments Huxley was, after all, only an Englishman and no doubt afflicted with the English habit of understatement. Secondly his grasp of natural selection was inferior to that of Charles Darwin and a few other nineteenth-century biologists, (Leonard Huxley

1900, 12, 372; Mayr and Provine 1980, p. 133). No one of his generation could have appreciated our modern concept of natural selection, which can honestly be described as a process for maximizing short-sighted selfishness. Moral indifference might aptly characterize the physical universe. For the biological world a stronger term is needed.

My concept of *gross immorality* here is similar to that of pacifists who claim that war is immoral. It need not imply any intentional evil or personal accountability. Pacifists' realization that wars start for complex reasons, and seldom merely from anyone's consciously evil decision, need not make them prefer Huxley's *moral indifference* to my *immorality*. War is immoral to pacifists because it systematically produces results that they find morally repugnant.

There is a morally important difference between being struck by lightning and being struck by a rattlesnake. Only the intellectually dead could fail to see that the snake has what are clearly weapons, precisely designed and used to produce a victim. The distinction between pain and death produced by aggressive use of weapons and those produced by accident is important but is obscured when a term such as *moral indifference* is used for both. They illustrate a basic contrast between physical nature and biological nature, and one that Huxley did not fully appreciate. I grant the major difference between a morally accountable human mind and a snake mind, but this is widely appreciated, and I can more confidently discuss the difference between the behavior of a rattlesnake and that of lightning. I hope that my discussion will show, at least to those who would concede that war is or at least may be immoral, that natural selection may be worse than warfare, and worse than Huxley imagined.

Recent Understanding and Misunderstanding of Natural Selection

The process of natural selection requires the events of successes and failures: an early bird gets the worm, a later one does not; one worm gets eaten, a different one escapes. It also requires the keeping of records on such events. This means changes in gene frequency. The eating of worms by early birds and deprivation of late risers will affect bird evolution only if these processes affect gene frequencies in the bird population. Recognition of this distinction between events taking place and the record being kept had to await a thorough appreciation of the relationships among genes and genotypes and characters. Neither these relationships nor their moral implications could have been comprehended in Huxley's time. The comprehension is essential to any understanding of the role recognized by modern biology for an individual organism in Huxley's cosmic process. Its role is to transmit its genes to future generations to the maximum possible extent. This summary of current understanding of natural selection is, of course, grossly oversimplified, but perhaps adequate here. More detailed discussions are available (Dawkins 1976; Williams 1984; Williams in press).

The principles of population genetics as developed by R. A. Fisher, J. B. S. Haldane, and Sewall Wright around 1930 clarify the process by, which the genetic record is kept and elucidate the nature of that record. It is a store of information about what has succeeded at transmitting genes in the past and a prediction as to what will succeed in the future. An important implication of this advance, especially important for social behavior and its moral implications, was first recognized by William Hamilton (1964). The survival and reproduction of a relative are partly equivalent, in evolutionary effect, to one's own survival and reproduction. Hamilton proposed an expansion of Darwin's concept of fitness to include any ability to get one's own genes represented in future generations. It does not matter whether these genes are present in one's own cells or present, for genealogical reasons, in relatives. He termed this broader concept *inclusive fitness*. His key formulation was that assistance to a relative will be favored if the benefit to the relative, times the coefficient of relationship, exceeds the cost to the donor.

Consider the problem of maximizing the fitness of individual 5 (Figure 1). The distribution of her special set of genes in herself and her relatives is shown by the stippling.

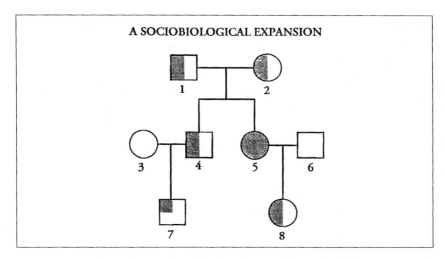

Figure 1. Hypothetical pedigree diagram, applicable to any outcrossed diploid organism with separate sexes. Males are represented by squares, females by circles mating by horizontal lines connecting males and females, offspring by verticals from the horizontals. Stippling shows the proportion of the genes in each individual that are necessarily identical with those in 5. Her fitness is measured by her ability to pass these genes to future generations. Unstippled regions represent random samples of genes on which 5 can have only random effects.

Her fitness is measured by her ability to get these genes passed on to future generations. A useful device is to consider such questions as: What is the probability that an arbitrarily chosen gene in the focal individual (5) is also present in her father (1)? In sexual reproduction half of one's genes come from one's father. So the probability is .5, and this is the coefficient of relationship of 5 to 1. The gene would be favored if it tended in any way to make 5 behave towards 1 as if his genes were half as important as hers. Her fitness will be enhanced, up to a point, by a willingness to jeopardize her own well-being to increase his.

The extent of the self-sacrifice favored would be determined by the .5 coefficient and the cost-benefit relationship, with costs and benefits measured as effects on the likelihood of transmitting genes. On the assumption of exactly equal prospects for future reproduction and an absolute certainty that 1 is 5's father, natural selection would favor her risking her life up to a .5 probability of loss, if she can surely save him by taking the risk, and if he will surely die if she does not. With conditions otherwise similar except that it is nephew 7 who is endangered, .25 would be the maximally tolerable risk.

Such *kin selection* normally deals with less than life-and-death matters. A more likely problem is whether to give a food item to a nephew (7) or a daughter (8). The daughter's coefficient of relationship is twice that of a nephew. So the nephew's potential benefit would have to exceed twice that of a daughter to justify giving it to him and depriving her. Selection thus favors nepotism towards close relatives over distant ones. In the symbolism of the diagram, the evolutionary role of individual 5 is to devote her life to the proliferation of that represented by the stippling. The agent that assigns this role to every individual is what Huxley called "a tenacious and powerful enemy" (Huxley 1894, p. 85).

I believe that this is a fair summary of the concept of kin selection, but I also realize that specialists in any subject may use common terms in uncommon and potentially misleading ways. For instance, when I discussed how an individual ought to behave towards her father, I did not mean literally that I meant how she could be expected to react to stimuli normally associated with fatherhood. Neither a wild animal nor a primitive tribesman knows anything of coefficients of relationship or of roles assigned by a tenacious and powerful enemy. A male bird can be expected to react to hatchlings in his nest according to his likely coefficient of relationship with such hatchlings. If he is indeed their father, the coefficient is at least .5, but, as discussed below, sexual infidelity and nest parasitism may be common. A sociobiologist would expect his behavior to be closely determined by the average coefficient during recent history for males in his position.

I will mention one more of the many possible misunderstandings. Even a complete kin-selection argument would still give a grossly incomplete view of the natural selection at work on social relationships. Kinship is merely one of many important factors. The individuals: diagrammed in Figure 1 must vary in many ways, not merely in kinship to the one I picked for special attention. She may have established mutually beneficial reciprocation with others, some perhaps unrelated. Her mate (6) would be an obvious example. Her sister-in-law (3) is also unrelated, but even if she has no other significance she has value (to 5) if she is helping nephew 7.

Individuals also vary in the amount of benefit they would realize from a given donation. A post-menopausal mother and adolescent daughter are equally related to each other, but it obviously makes evolutionary sense to be more generous to the girl than to the old woman. Questions such as why animals concern themselves so much more with their offspring than with equally related brothers and sisters are based on the assumption that kinship, to be important in evolution, has to be the only factor. A complete answer to such a question would have to consider the relative reliability, for adults of reproductive age, of available evidence for parenthood and that for other kinds of relationship; the reproductive potential, likely survival, and needs of recipients; needs and capabilities of prospective donors; alternatives for the investment of resources; and many other factors.

Recent Evolutionary Thought and the Morality of Huxley's Cosmic Process

It is only twenty-five years since Hamilton (1964) elucidated kinship as a factor in the evolution of social behavior, and less than that since Robert Trivers's (1971) insights on conditions for the evolution of reciprocity. Prior to these developments there was no consistent way of interpreting what animals were doing with each other. This absence of theoretical guidance and the outwardly benign appearance of some social interactions made it possible to paint a morally acceptable picture of nature. Romantically inspired naturalists found wholesome lessons in the mutual grooming of monkeys, the feeding of one bird by another, the brave self-sacrifice of worker bees for colony and queen. Such observations served as parables for moral guidance in a system that Donald Campbell (1978) called *normative biologism*. The noble-savage myth is a part of this larger complex. It persists despite abundant evidence of personal cruelty, group bigotry, and environmental destructiveness of primitive societies (Day 1953; Guthrie 1971; Speth 1983).

Romantics could deal with overt selfishness and destructiveness in nature by name changing and selective attention. Territorial disputes could be seen, not as truculent striving to garner resources for oneself at one's neighbor's expense, but as a wise program of birth control through limitation on the number of breeding territories. Verbal obfuscation is not merely practiced, but may be explicitly advocated. Objections have recently been made to accusing animals of practicing slavery, adultery, rape, or other sins (Gowaty 1982; Leacock 1980; Power 1980). The usual form of argument urges that some human practice, such as slavery, is largely determined by culture rather than genes and differs in many descriptive details from anything practiced (for example) by ants. So one must not use the term *slavery* for any kind of ant behavior.

Objections are never made to biologists' using such terms as *courtship, migration, fasting,* or many others that normally refer to culture-laden and descriptively unique human activities. The essential requirement for objection is for a term to refer to something wicked. There may even be an explicit decision not merely to relabel wickedness but to ignore it. Sarah Blaffer Hrdy found a superb example in a treatise on Antarctic penguins: "Occasionally some of the colonies are plagued by little knots of 'Hooligans' who hang about their outskirts, and should a chick go astray it stands a good chance of losing its life at their hands. The crimes that they commit are such as to find no place in this book" (Hrdy 1977b, p. 3).

Times have changed. Biologists today realize that unpleasant behavior can be important, and they are increasingly willing to study it. They often conclude that unpleasantness may be normal and adaptive, and they are also reinterpreting various seemingly benign or cooperative behavior. Armed with insights from Hamilton and Trivers they usually find that apparent generosity is limited to special situations in which it can be explained by one or more of three possible factors, none especially laudable.

The first and more prevalent is the nepotism explicitly discussed by Hamilton (1964). Cues available to a donor indicate an expected coefficient of relationship with a recipient, and the value of the aid given times the coefficient of relationship exceeds the cost. The service rendered is an investment by the donor in its own genes, as these are represented in the recipient. As the conditions differ, so does the behavior. Full sibs are nicer to each other than half sibs. Mother-love seems to be greater for offspring that are more nearly mature and therefore more likely to mature, but younger mothers are expected and found to be less loving than older ones (Andersson, Wiklund, and Rundgren 1980; Bierman and Robertson 1981).

Manipulation is the second reason why one individual may provide benefits for another. A mouse can provide nutritive benefits to a cat and when handled by the cat's paws is literally manipulated, but the term normally has a metaphorical meaning. For example, threat of physical force may substitute for force itself, as when a subordinate monkey relinquishes a feeding site to a dominant. More interesting kinds of manipulation result from deception, most obvious when practiced against another species. A snapper may swim eagerly towards the jaws of an anglerfish that deceives it with its lure. Social-insect pheromones that suppress reproduction by workers are interpreted as both a kin-selected response by workers and manipulation by the queen. *Manipulation* may imply exploitation by a manipulator, but it may be that communication within a species is usually adaptive for both sender and receiver. A hen may use vocal signals to get her chicks to behave in ways that serve her genetic interests, but obedience will usually serve a chick's interest. The same might be said for most verbal exchanges between human parents and their children. Richard Dawkins (1982) argues convincingly for the prevalence of manipulation in nature.

The third reason for one individual acting in the service of another is reciprocity. Whatever is given up by the donor costs it less than some expected repayment. Neither the expectation nor the repayment need be conscious or even behavioral. The secretions of an aphid may later repay an ant that protects it from a predator. In cooperative ventures the mutual benefits may be simultaneous. Two hyenas in a cooperative attack on a wildebeest calf defended by its mother are more than twice as likely to succeed as one acting alone (Gould 1982), and one calf can be a feast for several hyenas. A cooperative hyena may therefore eat while a loner goes hungry. In application to human behavior Darwin (1871, p. 163) called reciprocity a "low motive."

Reciprocity in nature is strictly limited by the necessity of safeguards against cheating. No matter how great the collective benefit might be from a cooperative venture, the necessary behavior will not evolve if the benefits can be enjoyed by freeloaders. It might be that a gregarious species could reduce its rate of loss to predators by having each individual warn the others with a loud call when it sights an enemy. This would in no way assure favorable selection for calling. If the call attracts the notice of the predator it may increase the caller's likelihood of being the victim. This cost would not be borne by a silent freeloader that merely seeks its own safety on seeing a predator. It would survive better than the callers so that sounding the alarm would not be favored.

This sort of reasoning has led students of animal behavior to prefer kin selection over reciprocity as an explanation for known alarm calls, and predictions based on the kin-selection model have been borne out in recent studies. Alarm calls of various sciurid rodents are given mainly by those age-sex categories most likely to have close kin nearby, and the actual presence of individuals with a coefficient of relationship of .25 or more (grandchildren, nephews, aunts) increases the likelihood of calling (Dunford 1977; Sherman 1980). Animals sound alarms to warn close relatives. If such benefits also benefit the group as a whole, that is an incidental consequence of selection for nepotism and has no bearing on the evolution of alarm calls in gregarious animals.

It could work the other way around, with alarm calls being important in the evolution of gregariousness. If my neighbors shout at their children when they see a bear approaching, it behooves me to stay close enough to hear their alarm calls. The more such neighbors I have, the greater my safety. I should stay with them if I can, and encourage them to stay with me. More important is the *selfish herd* factor formulated by Hamilton (1971). The advantage comes from maximizing competition for the bad things in life. If I were a Christian in the Flavian Amphitheater, I would want as many Christian companions as I could muster to share the attention of the lions. Perhaps the best technical term would be the *St. Ignatius Strategy,* after the Bishop of Antioch who was the earliest on record to make use of this principle. Various groups of animals seem to use it more successfully than St. Ignatius did (S. A. Altmann 1974; Kaufmann 1974).

As a general rule today a biologist seeing one animal doing something to benefit another assumes either that it is manipulated by the other individual or that it is being subtly selfish. Its selfishness would always be defined in relation to its single ultimate interest, the replication of its own genes. Nothing resembling the Golden Rule or other widely preached ethical principle is operating in living nature. It could scarcely be otherwise. Evolution is guided by a force that maximizes genetic selfishness.

Even if it turns out that natural selection among (as opposed to within) populations is more potent than is admitted by current orthodoxy, it would make little difference for a moral evaluation of Huxley's cosmic process. If some populations are consistently better than others at maintaining themselves and giving rise to new populations, they achieve their success by causing the extinction of less favored groups. To claim that this is morally superior to natural selection at the level of competing individuals would imply, in its human application, that systematic genocide is morally superior to random murder. There is no level of inclusiveness of selected entities at which the survival of the fittest is morally acceptable. The morally acceptable goal in relation to survival has to be "the fitting of as many as possible to survive" (Huxley 1894, p. 83).

Examples of the Triumph of Selfishness

Until now I have mainly discussed phenomena that seem benign, such as sharing food with relatives, or sounding an alarm that warns others of danger. Now I will deal with behavior that is not only selfish in some theoretical sense but patently pernicious. Only the morally and intellectually dishonest could label it otherwise. My intent is to present representative phenomena in straightforward fashion, not put on a horror show. More clinically detailed or melodramatic accounts are available (Gargett 1978; Dillard 1974). Scientific writing is supposed to be free of emotion, but occasionally the emotional trauma of observing some routine destruction sneaks into the technical literature, as in the fragment of field notes on ground squirrels published by Paul Sherman (1981), and Hrdy's (1977b) admission that her own tears were among the problems to be overcome in pursuit of data on family life in langurs.

Kin selection does not assure that relations between relatives will be friendly, nor need a mutually advantageous coalition like that between mates be really amicable. Trivers (1974) was the first to perceive the near universality of conflict within the family. He showed that evolution favors offspring that try to get more than their fair share of resources from parents. Any success in this attempt is achieved at a cost to parents and other offspring. The same evolutionary process favors parents that try for maximal reproductive success per unit of expenditure. They can achieve this by a precise optimum compromise between numbers of offspring and benefits to each. If the parents succeed, it means that each young gets less than its own optimum allotment.

Trivers discussed this conflict mainly for weaning. There comes a time in the development of a litter of kittens when weaning is in the best interests of the mother, but continued nursing is best for each kitten. The kitten ideal is to continue nursing but not have its litter mates do so. Members of nuclear families have coefficients of relationship of 0.5, not 1.0, and this means partly different genetic interests and different individual optima. A result is the noisy weaning conflict often observed in mammalian family life. Even in primates and other mammals that normally have one young at a time, the conflict can be intense (J. Altmann 1980). Continued nursing may delay the next pregnancy or reduce nutritive reserves on which the mother depends for survival to the next breeding season. Thus successive young are ultimately in conflict with each other just like litter mates. Only mammals can have a weaning conflict, but analogous strife can be found in all groups in which parents provide services for developing offspring. Joanna Burger (1981) describes the lively dissention over termination of parental feeding of young in herring gull colonies.

Conflict between mates or potential mates is often bellicose. Recent accounts of reproductive behavior in wild animals are tales of sexual intrigue full of deception, desertion, strife, and sometimes lethal violence. Conflict arises because of basic physiological differences between males and females in most species (Trivers 1972). A female may need to mate with a male to produce offspring, but one mating may be enough to fertilize all the eggs she has or all she can produce in a breeding season. Mating once with the best male available can be a better strategy than mating once with the best and once with the second best. The female can be expected to try to optimize her choice of male and the timing, locality, and all other circumstances that might influence the ultimate success of the eggs to be fertilized. For the male, reproductive success may be largely a matter of how many females he can inseminate. He can be expected to make use of every available opportunity to fertilize eggs and to seek out or try to produce such opportunities. The common outcome is for males to spend much time and effort in mating attempts that females just as persistently avoid. A tank full of guppies is a scene of endless conflict between males and females. Such is the power of romantic self-deception that many people find such displays attractive. Mating conflict exacts a high cost for survival and well being in many species (Daly 1978).

The possibility of cuckoldry gives another dimension to male-female conflict for species in which fertilization is internal and males contribute to the care of offspring. A female songbird may be fertilized, willingly or unwillingly, by a neighbor rather than her apparent mate, or her mate may die or desert. Her best strategy is then to behave as if she has a full complement of fertilizable eggs and allow herself to be courted and won by a suitable male. He could still sire a fraction of her clutch but would waste part of his parental investment on another male's offspring and raise fewer of his own than he otherwise might. The result is an evolutionary arms race between a female's ability to deceive and a male's ability to detect deception. Many details of courtship in birds have recently been interpreted as a dialog based on male suspicion and female representations of fidelity. An essential part of courtship may be a male's effort to sequester and monitor his mate long enough to minimize the possibility of cuckoldry. Evidence for such interpretations is provided by swallows (Beecher and Beecher 1979), bluebirds (Gowaty 1982; Power and Donner 1980), and doves (Lumpkin 1983).

There may be benefits to a female in undetected adultery with one or more of her mate's rivals. A female mouse can perhaps make the rival less likely to kill her young later on (Elwood and Ostermeyer 1984). Adultery can also be a safeguard against a mate's sterility. If a male bird has a 10 percent probability of being partly or entirely sterile, a strictly monogamous mate has a 10 percent probability of losing all or part of her brood. Insemination by two males would reduce the hazard to 1 percent. That females often copulate with males other than their mates has been shown by surgically sterilizing males. About half of the mates of sterilized redwing blackbirds studied by Thomas A. Roberts and James J. Kennelly (1980) produced fertilized eggs, and similar observations have been made in many other species (McKinney, Cheng, and Bruggers 1984).

These observations need not indicate adaptive bet hedging by females, a possibly costly tactic. Actual or suspected adultery may expose a female to rejection or even violent attack by her mate (Barash 1980), and it may be that much of the illegitimacy results from rape. Even a brief absence of her mate may make a female vulnerable to rape by neighboring males in the goose colony studied by Mineau and Cooke (1979). An unguarded female mallard may be attacked so persistently by gangs of males that she drowns

(Barash 1977). Joanna Burger and C. G. Beer (1982) observed 162 males that succeeded in mounting unwilling females in a gull colony, and many more that did not succeed. Apparent rape has been documented in eighty-one species of birds (McKinney, Cheng, and Bruggers 1984).

In some insects it would appear that females mate only as a result of male violence (Parker 1979), and in some sharks it appears that mating takes place only after injurious attack by males (Pratt 1979). Rape occurs in turtles (Berry and Shine 1980) and newts (Verrell 1982), and homosexually in a parasitic worm. The male victim may later find it difficult to fertilize a female with his own sperm (Abele and Gilchrist 1977).

The concept of rape would most clearly include mating as a result of threat or actual violence by males. A more theoretically useful definition would include any circumvention of mate-choice mechanisms used by females. By this definition it would be of common occurrence in plants (Janzen 1977; Wilson and Burley 1983). In animals it should include the use of deception and stealth. A subordinate male frog may hide near a calling dominant. A female attracted to the caller may be intercepted and mounted and have her eggs fertilized by the unwanted subordinate (Forester and Lykens 1986). Subordinate male sunfish may lurk about the nests of dominants, sometimes with the color and behavior of females. They may then dart into the nest of a spawning pair, release a cloud of semen, and flee any attack by the dominant male (Dominey 1980; Gross 1979). Similar phenomena in diverse species are reviewed by Anthony Arak (1984).

Related phenomena occur in species with internal fertilization. For example, James Farr (1980) showed that by a combination of stealth and speed a male guppy may sometimes circumvent attempts at rejection by females. Even in species in which mating does not normally occur without female consent, an incapacitated female may be quickly inseminated. Male fruit flies mate more readily with anesthetized females than with active ones, and fish hybrids can be produced routinely by presenting males of one species with anesthetized females of another (Bowden 1969).

Besides adultery and rape, just about every other kind of sexual behavior that has been regarded as sinful can be found abundantly in nature. Brother-sister matings are the rule in many species (Hamilton 1967). Masturbation is common in mammals (Beach 1964), and especially common in juvenile male marmosets whose mothers are in heat (Hershkovitz 1977). Males may mount obviously pregnant females or other inappropriate objects (S. A. Altmann 1962). Homosexual behavior is common in a wide variety of vertebrates (Beach 1978), and perhaps homosexual preference (Weinrich 1980).

The killing of other members of the same species is a frequent phenomenon in a wide variety of forms and contexts. Simple cannibalism is the commonest and can be expected in all animals except strict vegetarians (Polis 1981). It is a general rule among fishes. Aquarium keepers find that speedy separation of young from adults is needed to prevent consumption of the young in many species. The phenomenon is widespread in nature, an extreme example provided by the walleye (Cuff 1980). Stomachs of large walleye contained smaller ones, which had eaten still smaller ones, for at least a fourfold cycle of cannibals within cannibals.

Conspecific destruction can also take special forms in fishes, several shown by the mottled sculpin (Downhower and Brown 1981). Large males are better egg guarders than small ones, and females prefer them, but if there is too great a difference in size he may find her more tempting as a meal than as a mate. Egg guarding is a stress for males, because it does not allow productive foraging. The required fast is justified only if it results in a certain minimum of hatched young. If the male gets only a single clutch of eggs and no more for a few days, he may eat them and abandon the attempt to reproduce that year. If he gets a succession of clutches from different females, and is sufficiently hungry after a long bout of egg guarding, he may eat the last batch instead of waiting for them to hatch. The eating of eggs or young in other individuals' nests is common in many fishes (Keenleyside 1972; Rohwer 1978) and amphibians (Crump 1983).

Sherman (1981) showed that about 8 percent of the young in a colony of ground squirrels are killed by members of their own species. A male may raid a nest to kill and eat one of the young. A female may raid the nest of a competitor and kill all the young but not eat them, Nearly half the litters in a prairie dog colony were victimized by infanticide, sometimes by close relatives (Hoogland 1985). Cannibalism among insects is common, often the eating of young or of mates or potential mates (Buskirk, Frolich, and Ross 1984; Eichwort 1973; O'Neil and Evans 1981).

Destruction of the young of rivals can be a major source of mortality in birds (Picman 1977; Trail, Strahl, and Brown 1981). Destruction of one of a pair of young, with consumption of the victim, is frequent in birds of prey (Stinson 1979), and this killing may be by a brother or sister. Valerie Gargett (1978) recorded hundreds of attacks by a larger black eagle chick against a smaller nest mate over a period of three days, when the smaller finally died of its wounds and starvation. An authoritative compendium on infanticide in the animal kingdom is now available (Hausfater and Hrdy 1984). It is now generally realized that infanticide rates of some primitive human populations were sufficient for important demographic consequences (section 5 in Hausfater and Hrdy).

Mammalian infanticide may evolve as a male adaptation to female reproductive physiology because lactation may inhibit ovulation. For a male's reproduction the essential resource is an ovulating female. A female deferring ovulation while nursing another male's young is only a potential resource. She can be changed from potential to actual by the death of the unweaned infant. For females such young are of highest importance because with a bit more investment they can be turned into self-feeding juveniles. So the death of the young would be a major loss for the female but only a minor gain in time for the male. Unfortunately such issues are not settled by any principles of justice or net costs and benefits, but strictly on a might-makes-right basis.

Hrdy (1977a; 1977b) describes dramatic examples of this sort of male-female conflict for a monkey that often lives in groups of related adult females, their young, and one temporarily dominant male. Males keep such harems only so long as they can avoid being deposed by rivals. Sooner or later some rival will succeed in defeating any currently privileged male and in taking over his mates. When this happens there is an immediate conflict between the new male and any female with an unweaned infant. The sooner the infant stops nursing, the sooner its mother will turn into a valuable resource, and the only way to get it to stop nursing is to kill it. This is not always an easy task. The male is bigger and stronger than the female, and can kill an infant with one efficient bite into the skull, but he may fail despite repeated attempts. A female's motivation to protect her infant may be greater than his desire to kill it, and it may be necessary for him to fight both the mother and one or more other relatives of the infant. Members of the harem are closely related, and a grandmother or aunt or older half-sister has half as much at stake in the infant's survival as the mother has. Kin selection results in the formation of coalitions of related females in opposition to infanticidal males.

In the absence of ideology, only nepotism can produce such a coalition, and never anything analogous to feminism or an urge for justice or group welfare. If infanticide by a male raises his fitness even slightly, it is in a mother's interest to have her son practice it if and when he succeeds in taking a harem from some other mother's son. There is no way for the female sex to constitute a group for which group selection could produce any kind of change. If she loses her infant, the mother quickly comes into estrus and accepts her infant's killer as the father of her next offspring.

Many conspecific killings result from contests over resources, a common event among insects (Parker 1979). The disputed resource is most often a female ready to reproduce. In large mammals with horns or antlers, death or debilitating injury from fighting over females may claim 5 to 10 percent of adult males every breeding season (Clutton-Brock et al. 1979; Wilkinson and Shank 1976). Death from strife among neighbors tends to be recorded for any wild animal population carefully observed for a thousand hours or more (Wilson 1975). Consider for comparison the annual homicide rate of 0.0003 for Houston, apparently the most murderous of major American cities (*World Almanac and Book of Facts* 1983, p. 966). It would be necessary to keep ten Houston residents under continuous observation for three centuries to make it likely that one murder would be seen.

Males of our own and most other mammalian species are more likely than females to kill or injure others of their own kind, but competition among females may not be so much of lesser intensity as of greater subtlety. They commonly deprive each other of resources in various ways, aggressively interfere with each others' courtship, attack each others' young, and actively aggravate male competition when it serves their interests (Silk et al. 1981; Wasser and Barash 1983).

Losses from sexual conflict may go far beyond direct results to participants. Males in combat may accidentally injure or kill females or young in such diverse animals as seals (LeBoeuf 1974) and dung flies (Parker 1979). Bright colors useful in attracting females or intimidating rivals may attract predators. This is certainly true in many fishes (Endler 1978) and insects. Elaborate sexual and competitive behaviors also increase vulnerability either by their conspicuousness or the inattention of participants. George Schaller (1972, p. 243) found that predation by lions was especially high on fighting warthogs or courting reedbucks. Merlin Tuttle and Michael Ryan (1981) noted that a predatory bat used frogs' mating calls to locate such prey. Other losses are less dramatic but real. In many species a large size is advantageous for males in winning females, but is deleterious in other respects. Myron Baker and Stanley Fox (1978) found that larger male grackles were especially vulnerable to a chemical eradication technique.

Such observations support the common assumption that females more closely approximate the engineering optima for a species but that males compromise these optima with requirements of sexual competition. Adult male modifications may go far beyond scaling for larger size. Antlers and horns are nutritionally expensive structures, and there may be major structural modifications related to the offensive use of these weapons and to withstanding violent collisions with rivals (Schaffer 1968). Russell Lande's (1980) calculations support the recently common assumption that increased effectiveness in sexual competition can increase the likelihood of extinction. The consistently higher human male rates of mortality and morbidity measure the price of features useful in sexual rivalry.

Many of the unpleasant phenomena reviewed above have been described only recently. They are likely to be impressive only if unexpected as a result of the blindness of romanticism. None are really needed for the argument being advanced. The inescapable arithmetic of predation and parasitism should be enough to show that nature is morally unacceptable. This should be so even if some romantic fictions were really true, which they are not. It is sometimes claimed, for example, that predators take only what they need and avoid unnecessary killing. The excess carnage in attacks by bluefish or swordfish on fish schools are a well known example of wasteful predation (Bigelow and Schroeder 1953). Foxes raiding gull colonies often kill far more prey than they use (Kruuk 1976). Prehistoric Indians would sometimes drive bison herds off cliffs and then only harvest foetuses. Andrew Sih (1980) and Jeffrey Lucas (1985) argue the general importance of individual optima of wastefulness.

The survival of one organism is possible only at great cost to others. The moral message in this obvious fact has been recognized by many philosophers and humanists, despite the general prevalence of romanticism. Tennyson (In Memoriam, p. 55) confessed to a confusion and pessimism about Nature when

> That I, considering everywhere
> Her secret meaning in her deeds,
> And finding that of fifty seeds
> She often brings but one to bear,

He must have realized that one-in-fifty would be extraordinarily favorable odds for all but a small minority of the world's species.

Prospects for Morality in an Immoral World

Huxley viewed the cosmic process as an enemy that must be combated. Mine is a similar but more extreme position, based on the more extreme contemporary view of natural selection as a process for maximizing selfishness. If the enemy is worse than Huxley thought, the more urgent is the need for biological understanding. As Singer (1981, p. 168) stated it in precisely this context, "The more you know about your opponent, the better your chances of winning." Inadequate knowledge is likely to lead to counterproductive tactics, as Donald Symons (1979) noted for feminist issues.

Modern insights may help resolve Huxley's (1894, p. viii) paradox. How could the maximization of selfishness produce an organism often capable of advocating, and occasionally practicing, charity towards strangers and even towards animals? Huxley dealt only sketchily with this problem, but anticipated that biology would someday ". . . arrive at an understanding of the aesthetic faculty . . ." that makes people want a society that ". . . demands self-restraint; in place of thrusting aside, or treading down, all competitors, it requires that the individual shall not merely respect, but shall help his fellows; its influence is directed, not so much to the survival of the fittest, as to the fitting of as many as possible to survive" (Huxley 1894, pp. 80–82).

A number of recent sociobiologists have concerned themselves with Huxley's paradox, most notably Alexander (1987). Not surprisingly, all invoke kin-selected altruism and adaptations for taking advantage of reciprocation. They attempt to show why such factors operating in stone-age society should produce attitudes that favor the development, in modern societies, of broadly inclusive ethical systems. A similar attempt is made by Singer (1981), a philosopher admirably knowledgeable on modern evolutionary theory. He proposes that the human capacity for reasoned argument constantly imposes a necessity for publicly presentable justification of personal action. If the chief of the Eastern Mohawks wants to achieve a trade agreement with his Western counterpart, he must be able to argue convincingly that the agreement would benefit all Mohawks. Some such need led Plato to urge consideration of the welfare of all Greeks, not merely of all Athenians (Singer 1981, p. 117). As the necessity for dealing with an ever broader range of groups arises, comparably expanded ethical systems must be advocated and followed.

As Singer's ever expanding circle of consideration reaches individuals of negligible relationship or likelihood of reciprocation it puts an altruist into ever more basic conflict with Huxley's cosmic process. This combat being urged, between the "microscopic atom" and the "illimitable macrocosm" may seem a bit one-sided. Is not Annie Dillard showing a pathetic megalomania when she exclaims "I came from the world, I crawled out of a sea of amino acids, and now I must whirl around and shake my fist at that sea and cry shame!" (Dillard 1974, p. 177). Are Huxley and Dillard perhaps like Job's neighbors urging him to rebel against oppression by an arbitrarily malicious, all-powerful, and omniscient god?

No, not omniscient. The evolutionary process is immensely powerful and oppressive, but unlike Job's god it is abysmally stupid. It can reliably maximize current selfishness at the level of the gene, but is blind to future macroscopic consequences of current action. It does not have the sense to realize that mechanisms evolved for practicing unfair nepotism or making self-seeking deals with others can be subverted in the interests of broad altruism. All through evolutionary history there have been such changes with important future consequences entirely unrelated to the selfishness that brought them about.

I will mention two of many possible examples. Manipulation was designed in the service of selfishness, but can play a positive role in human society. Anyone who makes an anonymous donation of money or blood or other resource, as a result of some public appeal, is biologically just as much a victim of manipulation as someone whose self-sacrifice serves the interests of a tyrant. In his otherwise enlightened treatment of ethics and sociobiology Singer (1981) misses the role of manipulation in philanthropy and social activism. He maintains that the prevalence of anonymous blood donation shows an altruism in human nature that defies evolutionary interpretation. It is indeed correct that truly altruistic acts cannot be favored by selection, but the ability to induce others to behave altruistically certainly can be.

My second example is anatomical. The subtle and versatile engineering of the human hand was fully appreciated by Galen about 1800 years ago (May 1968). In the last million years it has been modified by selection for precise manipulation of objects, but such selection could only be brought to bear on an organ already adapted to grasping and rotation. This earlier stage was produced by selection for special sorts of arborial locomotion, such as brachiation, which demands an ability to turn the body with a hand holding an overhead limb. The production of an organ capable of turning doorknobs was made possible as an incidental consequence of selection to be better than one's neighbors at swinging through the trees.

The helping hand of the Good Samaritan and the motivation for its use raise no question on the malice or power of natural selection. They merely show that Huxley's tenacious and powerful enemy is a mindless fool. The stupidity of the enemy is the one advantage enjoyed by those who would follow Huxley's banner into combat. It is hardly a cause for complacency. The enemy is in fact powerful and tenacious, and we need all the help we can get to overcome billions of years of selection for selfishness.

If biology can aid our understanding of our enemy it could be of great value. A key insight is the need to be suspicious of attitudes that arise from the biology of family life and group loyalties. They are based on narrow genetic self-interest and must be there to serve the enemy's cause, not ours. As Singer states it: "Discovering biological origins for our intuitions should make us skeptical about thinking of them as self-evident moral axioms. . . . Far from justifying principles that are shown to be 'natural,' a biological explanation is often a way of debunking the lofty status of what seemed a self-evident moral law" (Singer 1981, pp. 70–71). In natural selection there may be a parallel to the doctrine of original sin as a partial explanation for human misconduct. This was noted by Huxley (1894, p. 27) and more recently by Campbell (1975, pp. 103–104) and Harry Power (1981, p. 17).

Human speech is so effective a form of communication that once evolved it gave rise to a system of information transfer to rival the transmission of genes in reproduction. It made elaborate teaching possible, and it enormously augmented a purely cultural evolutionary process. The mechanism of cultural evolution is fundamentally different from that of genetic transmission, but the resulting evolutionary processes have many formal features in common. The transmission of cultural information by verbal messages or direct imitation can be followed, like genes, by phenotypic effects on recipient individuals. Recognizable cultural elements (Dawkins's *memes*) can wax and wane in a population, and such quantitative effects can be treated by mathematical devises not very different from those of population genetics (Cafalli-Sforza and Feldman 1981).

A meme (e.g., a new song, food fad, religious cult) will spread wherever society provides a favorable environment for its spread. There is an obvious analogy with selection acting on a gene. Perhaps the natural selection of memes is a bit less deplorable than that of genes. Human beings are not as stupid as nature. They can sometimes anticipate the social effects of adopting a meme.

But ultimately the ethical problems are much the same. The one necessary and sufficient reason for a meme spreading in a human population is that it is good at getting itself spread. It is not necessary that it enhance the biological fitness or perceived well-being of its practitioners nor that it increase general prosperity. I am sure that cigarette smoking has spread more rapidly through many populations in recent decades than have many sound public health practices. Richard Dawkins (1976) identifies the natural selection of memes as another aspect of the tenacious and powerful enemy.

In its recognition of the evolutionary importance of manipulation and the added potential received from language, biology can add its voice to the chorus of warnings on the dangers of propaganda. Both the ability to use propaganda and an inclination to be suspicious of it were designed by natural selection to spread selfish genes in tribal microcosms. In its boundless stupidity this evolutionary process incidentally designed machinery capable of dealing with the question of whether a message is one of help or harm for what we really want for the macrocosm. We can use abilities developed for petty intrigue to deal with sermons coming from the pulpit, activists' (or sociobiologists') tracts, or manipulation by politicians on television screens. People can now espouse remote and inclusive ideals far removed from the selfishness that gave rise to the power to do so. It is understandable that people in the novel civic environments of the last few millennia will have aspirations for the dictatorship of the proletariat, or the triumph of the master race, or the saving of souls. Because such strivings are not directly favored by natural selection, I have hope that some such cause can provide the humane artifice that can save humanity from human nature.

Modern biology also helps us identify ourselves as apt soldiers for Huxley's army and clarifies the distinction between ourselves and the enemy. Each of us at conception received a unique genotype that never existed before. Unless there is an early division of the embryo it will never be duplicated. This genotype has no significance in evolution beyond its brief and minor influence on rates of increase and decrease of the component genes. It is of the utmost personal significance because it directs individual development and controls vital functions. In these processes each gene interacts in various ways with the rest of the genotype and with environmental conditions. On the average, a gene must produce results favorable to its own replication, but the particular interactions in our own development were unique and unpredictable and may deviate markedly from average effects. We are all special genotypically besides having unique individual histories that give us our own personal collections of memories and experience that constitute the self. There is no conceivable justification for any personal concern with the interests (long-term average proliferation) of the genes we received in the lottery of meiosis and fertilization. As Huxley was the first to recognize, there is every reason to rebel against any tendency to serve such interest.

Gunther Stent (1979) objects that Dawkins's concept of rebelling against one's own genes is a meaningless contradiction. He apparently missed the relevance of major technologies (hair dyeing, tonsillectomy, etc.) based on such rebellion. They are directed at individuals' perceptions of flaws in the development controlled by the genes in the special association of their own genotypes. The combat urged by Huxley and refined by Dawkins is against the much less personal multi-generational effects of our genes, and this is even less of a contradiction. It is what Joseph Lopreato (1981, p. 124) meant when he proposed that the goal of moral striving should be the "ultimate negation of the commandment of natural selection" which is very much in the spirit of Huxley's (1894, p. 63) urging that we "refuse any longer to be the instruments of the evolutionary process. . . ."

Like Huxley and everyone else, I have my opinions on what the world ought to be like and on the best ways of moving towards that goal. Huxley did not write his essay to champion his particular view of utopia, and my purpose is merely to update Huxley's message and to characterize the enemy more clearly than was possible in Huxley's time. The updated program for the betterment of the human condition is a twofold attack on the natural enemy and any institutional enemies favored by cultural evolution. In Dawkins's words (1976, p. 215), we must " . . . rebel against the tyranny of the selfish replicators."

References

Abele, Lawrence G., and Sandra Gilchrist. 1977. "Homosexual Rape and Sexual Selection in Acanthocephalan Worms," *Science* 197: 81–83.

Alexander, Richard D. 1987. *The Biology of Moral Systems* (Chicago: Aldine de Gruyter).

Altmann, Jeanne. 1980. *Baboon Mothers and Infants* (Cambridge, Mass.: Harvard University Press).

Altmann, Stuart A. 1962. "A Field Study of the Sociobiology of the Rhesus Monkey, *Macaca Mullata*," *Annals of the New York Academy of Sciences* 102: 338–435.

————. 1974. "Baboons, Space, Time and Energy," *American Zoologist* 14: 221–248.

Andersson, Malthe, Christer G. Wiklund, and Helen Rundgren. 1980. "Parental Defense of Offspring: A Model of an Example," *Animal Behavior* 28: 536–542.

Arak, Anthony. 1984. "Sneaky Breeders," in *Producers and Scroungers: Strategies of Exploitation and Parasitism,* ed. C. J . Barnard, pp. 154–194 (New York: Chapman and Hall).

Baker, Myron Charles, and Stanley F. Fox. 1978. "Differential Survival in Common Grackles Sprayed with Turgitol," *American Naturalist* 112: 675–682.

Barash, David P. 1977. "Sociobiology of Rape in Mallards *(Anas platyrhynchos):* Responses of the Mated Male," *Science* 197: 788–789.

Beach, Frank A. 1964. "Biological Bases for Reproductive Behavior," in *Social Behavior and Organization Among Vertebrates,* ed. W. Etkin, pp. 117–142 (Chicago: University of Chicago Press).

————. 1978. "Sociobiology and Interspecific Comparisons of Behavior," in *Sociobiology and Human Nature,* ed. M. S. Gregory, A. Silvers, and D. Sutch, pp. 116–135 (Chicago: University of Chicago Press).

Beecher, Michael D., and I. M. Beecher. 1979. "Sociobiology of Bank Swallows: Reproductive Strategy of the Male," *Science* 205: 1282–1285.

Berry, James F., and Richard Shine. 1980. "Sexual Size Dimorphism and Sexual Selection in Turtles (order Testudines)," *Oecologia* 44: 185–191.

Bierman, Gloria C., and Raleigh J. Robertson. 1981. "An Increase in Parental Investment during the Breeding Season," *Animal Behavior* 29: 487–489.

Bigelow, Henry B., and William C. Schroeder. 1953. "Fishes of the Gulf of Maine," *Fishery Bulletin,* 53 (Washington, D.C.: U.S. Government Printing Office).

Bowden, Bradley S. 1969. "A New Method for Obtaining Precisely Timed Inseminations in Viviparous Fishes," *Progressive Fish Culturist* 31: 229–230.

Burger, Joanna. 1981. "On Becoming Independent in Herring Gulls: Parent-Young Conflict," *American Naturalist* 117: 444–456.

———— and C. G. Beer. 1975. "Territoriality in the Laughing Gull (*L. atricilla*)," *Behaviour* 55: 301–320.

Buskirk, Ruth, Cliff Frolich, and K. C. Ross. 1984. "The Natural Selection of Sexual Cannibalism," *American Naturalist* 123: 612–625.

Campbell, Donald T. 1978. "Social Morality Norms as Evidence of Conflict Between Biological Human Nature and Social System Requirements," *Dahlem Konferenzen, Life Science Research Report* 9: 75–92.

Cavalli-Sforza, L. L., and Marcus W. Feldman. 1981. *Cultural Transmission and Evolution: A Quantitative Approach* (Princeton, N.J.: Princeton University Press).

Clutton-Brock, T. H., S. D. Albon, R. M. Gibson, and F. E. Guinness. 1979. "The Logical Stag: Adaptive Aspects of Fighting in Red Deer (*Corvus elaphus* L)." *Animal Behavior* 27: 21 1–225.

Crump, Martha L. 1983. "Opportunistic Cannibalism by Amphibian Larvae in Temporary Aquatic Environments," *American Naturalist* 121: 281–289.

Cuff, Wilfred R 1980. "Behavioral Aspects of Cannibalism in Larval Walleye, *Stizostedion vitreum*," *Canadian Journal of Zoology* 58: 1504–1507.

Daly, Martin. 1978. "The Cost of Mating," *American Naturalist* 112: 771–774.

Darwin, Charles. 1871. *The Descent of Man and Selection in Relation to Sex* (London: John Murray; reprinted 1981 by Princeton University Press).

Dawkins, Richard. 1976. *The Selfish Gene* (Oxford: Oxford University Press).

———. 1982. *The Extended Phenotype* (Oxford: W. H. Freeman & Co).

Day, Gordon M. 1953. "The Indian as an Ecological Factor in the Northeastern Forest," *Ecology* 34: 329–346.

Dewey, John. [1900] 1954. "Evolution and Ethics," *Scientific Monthly* 78: 57–66.

Dillard, Annie. 1974. *Pilgrim at Tinker Creek* (New York: Harper's Magazine Press).

Dominey, Wallace J. 1980. "Female Mimicry in Male Bluegill Sunfish—A Genetic Polymorphism?" *Nature* 284: 546–548.

Downhower, Jerry F., and Luther Brown. 1981. "The Timing of Reproduction and Its Behavioral Consequences for Mottled Sculpins, *Cottus bairdi*," in *Natural Selection and Social Behavior*, ed. R. D. Alexander and D. W. Tinkle, pp. 78–95 (New York: Chiron Press).

Dunford, Christopher. 1977. "Kin Selection for Ground Squirrel Alarm Calls," *American Naturalist* 111: 782–785.

Eichwort, Kathleen R. 1973. "Cannibalism and Kin Selection in *Labidomera clivicollis* (Coleoptera: Chrysomelidae)," *American Naturalist* 107: 452–453.

Elwood, Robert W., and Malcolm C. Ostermeyer. 1984. "Does Copulation Inhibit Infanticide in Male Rodents?" *Animal Behavior* 32: 293–294

Endler, John A. 1978. "A Predator's View of Animal Color Patterns," *Evolutionary Biology* 11: 319–364.

Farr, James A. 1980. "The Effects of Sexual Experience and Female Receptivity on Courtship-Rape Decisions in Male Guppies, *Poecilia reticulata* (Pisces: Poeciliidae)," *Animal Behavior* 28: 1195–1201.

Flew, Anthony G. N. 1967. *Evolutionary Ethics* (London: Macmillan).

Forester. Don C., and David V. Lykens. 1986. "Significance of Satellite Males in a Population of Spring Peepers *(Hyla crucifer).*, *Copeia* 1986: 719–724.

Gargett, Valerie. 1978. "Sibling Aggression in the Black Eagle of the Matapos Rhodesia," *Ostrich* 49: 57–63.

Gould, James. 1982. *Ethology: The Mechanisms and Evolution of Behavior* (New York: W. W. Norton).

Gowaty, Patricia Adair. 1982. "Sexual Terms in Sociobiology: Emotionally Evocative and, Paradoxically, Jargon," *Animal Behavior* 30: 630–631.

Gross, Mart R. 1979. "Cuckoldry in Sunfishes *(Lepomis:* Centrarchidae)." *Canadian Journal of Zoology* 57: 1507–1509.

Guthrie, Daniel A. 1971. "Primitive Man's Relationship to Nature," *BioScience* 21: 721–723.

Hamilton, William D. 1964. "The Genetical Evolution of Social Behavior. I and II." *Journal of Theoretical Biology* 7: 1–52.

———. 1967. "Extraordinary Sex Ratios," *Science* 156: 477–488.

———. 1971. "Geometry for the Selfish Herd," *Journal of Theoretical Biology* 31: 295–311.

Hausfater, Glenn and Sarah Blaffer Hrdy. 1984. *Infanticide: Comparative and Evolutionary Perspectives* (Chicago: Aldine).

Hershkovitz, Philip. 1977. *Living New World Monkeys (Platyrhini).* Vol. 1 (Chicago: University of Chicago Press).

Hoogland, John L. 1985. "Infanticide in Prairie Dogs Affects 47 Percent of Litters," *Science* 230: 1037–1040.

Hrdy, Sarah Blaffer. 1977a. "Infanticide as a Primate Reproductive Strategy," *American Scientist* 65: 40–55.

―――. 1977b. *The Langurs of Abu* (Cambridge, Mass.: Harvard University Press).

Huxley, Julian. 1947. *Evolution and Ethics* (London: Pilot Press).

Huxley, Leonard. 1900. *Life and Letters of Thomas Henry Huxley* (Edinburgh: D. Appleton and Co.).

Huxley, Thomas H. 1894. *Evolution and Ethics and Other Essays* (New York: D. Appleton).

Janzen, Daniel H. 1977. "A Note on Optimal Mate Selection by Plants," *American Naturalist* 111: 365–371.

Kaufmann, John H. 1974. "The Ecology and Evolution of Social Organization in the Kangaroo Family (Macropodidae)," *American Zoologist* 14: 51–62.

Keenleyside, Miles H. A. 1972. "Intraspecific Intrusions into Nests of Spawning Long-Ear Sunfish (Pisces: Centrarchidae)," *Copeia* 1972: 272–278.

Kruuk, Hans. 1976. "The Biological Function of Gulls' Attraction Towards Predators." *Animal Behavior* 24: 146–153.

Lande, Russell. 1980. "Sexual Dimorphism, Sexual Selection, and Adaptation in Polygenic Characters," *Evolution* 34: 292–305.

Leacock, Eleanor. 1980. "Social Behavior, Biology and the Double Standard," American *Association for the Advancement of Science Selected Symposium* 35: 465–488.

LeBoeuf, Burney J. 1974. "Male-Male Competition and Reproductive Success in Elephant Seals," *American Zoologist* 14: 163–176.

Lopreato, Joseph. 1981. "Toward a Theory of Genuine Altruism in *Homo sapiens,*" *Ethology and Sociobiology* 2: 113–126.

Lucas, Jeffrey R. 1985. "Partial Prey Consumption by Antlion Larvae," *Animal Behavior* 33: 945–958.

Lumpkin, Susan. 1983. "Female Manipulation of Male Avoidance of Cuckoldry Behavior in the Ring Dove," in *Social Behavior of Female Vertebrates,* ed. S. K. Wasser, pp. 91–112 (New York: Academic Press).

McKinney, Frank, Kimberly M. Cheng, and David J. Bruggers. 1984. "Sperm Competition in Apparently Monogamous Birds," in *Sperm Competition and the Evolution of Avian Mating Systems,* ed. Robert L. Smith, pp. 523–545. (New York: Academic Press).

May, Margaret Talmadge. 1968. *Galen on the Usefulness of the Parts of the Body* (Ithaca; N.Y.: Cornell University Press).

Mayr, Ernst, and Will Provine. 1980. *The Evolutionary Synthesis* (Cambridge, Mass.: Harvard University Press).

Mineau, Pierre, and Fred Cooke. 1979. "Rape in the Lesser Snow Goose," *Behaviour* 70: 280–291.

O'Neill, Kevin M., and Howard E. Evans. 1981. "Predation on Conspecific Males by Females of the Beewolf *Philanthus basilaris* Cresson (Hymenoptera: Sphecidae)," *Journal of the Kansas Entomological Society* 54: 553–556.

Parker, Geoffrey A. 1979. "Sexual Selection and Sexual Conflict," in *Reproductive Competition in Insects,* ed. M. S. Blum and N. A. Blum, pp. 123–126 (New York: Academic Press).

Picman, Jaroslav. 1977. "Intraspecific Nest Destruction in the Long-Billed Marsh Wren, *Telmatodytes palustris palustris,*" *Canadian Journal of Zoology* 55: 1997–2003

Polis, Gary A. 1981. "The Evolution and Dynamics of Intraspecific Predation," *Annual Review of Ecology and Systematics* 12: 225–251.

Power, Harry W. 1980. "On Bluebird Cuckoldry and Human Adultery," *American Naturalist* 116: 705–709.

———. 1981. "The Question of Altruism," *Sociobiology* 6: 7–21.

——— and C. G. P. Doner. 1980. "Experiments on Cuckoldry in the Mountain Bluebird," *American Naturalist* 116: 689–704.

Pratt, Harold L., Jr. 1979. "Reproduction in the Blue Shark, *Prionace glauca.*" *Fishery Bulletin, U.S.* 77: 445–470.

Raphael, D. Daiches. 1958. "Darwinism and Ethics," in *A Century of Darwin,* ed. S. A Barnet, pp. 334–359 (London: Heinemann Educational Books).

Roberts, Thomas A., and James J. Kennelly. 1980. "Variation in Promiscuity Among Red-Winged Blackbirds," *Wilson Bulletin* 92: 110–112.

Rohwer, Sievert, 1978. "Parent Cannibalism of Offspring and Egg Raiding as a Courtship Strategy," *American Naturalist* 112: 429–440

Schaffer, William M. 1968. "Intraspecific Combat and the Evolution of the Caprini," *Evolution* 22: 817–825.

Schaller, George B. 1972. *The Serengeti Lion* (Chicago: University of Chicago Press).

Sherman, Paul W. 1980. "The Limits of Ground Squirrel Nepotism," *American Association for the Advancement of Science, Selected Symposium* 35: 505–544.

———. 1981. "Reproductive Competition and Infanticide in Belding's Ground Squirrels and Other Mammals," in *Natural Selection and Social Behavior,* ed. R. D. Alexander and D. W. Tinkle, pp. 311–331 (New York: Chiron Press).

Sih, Andrew. 1980. "Optimal Foraging: Partial Consumption of Prey," *American Naturalist* 116: 281–290.

Silk, Joan B., C. B. Clark-Wheatley, P. S. Rodman, and Amy Samuels. 1981. "Differential Reproductive Success and Facultative Adjustment of Sex Ratios Among Captive Female Bonnet Macaques *(Macaca radiata),*" *Animal Behavior* 29: 1106–1120.

Singer, Peter. 1981. *The Expanding Circle* (New York: Farrar, Straus, and Giroux).

Speth, John D. 1983. *Bison Kills and Bone Counts* (Chicago: University of Chicago Press).

Stent, Gunther S. 1979. "Introduction: The Limits of the Naturalistic Approach to Morality," *Dahlem Konferenzen, Life Sciences Research Reports* 9: 13–21.

Stinson, Christopher H. 1979. "On the Selective Advantage of Fratricide in Raptors," *Evolution* 33: 1219–1225.

Symons, Donald. 1979. *The Evolution of Human Sexuality* (New York: Oxford University Press).

Trail, Pepper W., Stuart D. Strahl, and Jerram L. Brown. 1981. "Infanticide in Relation to Individual and Flock Histories in a Communally Breeding Bird, the Mexican Jay *(Aphelocoma ultramarina),*" *American Naturalist* 118: 72–82.

Trivers, R. L. 1971. "The Evolution of Reciprocal Altruism, "*Quarterly Review of Biology* 46: 35–57.

Trivers, Robert L. 1971. "The Evolution of Reciprocal Altruism," *Quarterly Review of Biology* 46: 35–57.

———. 1972. "Parental Investment and Sexual Selection," in *Sexual Selection and the Descent of Man 1871–1971,* ed. B. Campbell. 136–179 (Chicago: Aldine).

———. 1974. "Parent-Offspring Conflict," *American Zoologist* 14: 249–264.

Tuttle, Merlin D. and Michael J. Ryan. 1981. "Bat Predation and the Evolution of Frog Vocalizations in the Neotropics," *Science* 214: 677–78.

Verrell, Paul. 1982. "The Sexual Behavior of the Red-Spotted Newt. *Notophthalmus viridescens*," *Animal Behavior* 30: 1244–1236.

Wasser, Samuel K. and David P. Barash. 1983. "Reproductive Suppression among Female Mammals: Implications for Biomedicine and Sexual Selection Theory," *Quarterly Review of Biology* 48: 513–538.

Weinrich, James D. 1980. "Homosexual Behavior in Animals: A New Review of Observations from the Wild, and Their Relationship to Human Sexuality," in *Medical Sexology: The Third International Congress.* ed. R. Forleo & W. Pasini. 288–295 (Littleton, Mass.: PSG Publishing).

Wilkinson, Paul F. and Christopher C. Shank. 1976. "Rutting-Fight Mortality among Musk Oxen on Banks Island, Northwest Territories, Canada," *Animal Behavior* 24: 756–758.

Williams, George C. 1984. "A Defense of Reductionism in Evolutionary Biology," *Oxford Surveys in Evolutionary Biology* 2: 1–27.

———. 1989. "A Sociobiological Expansion of *Evolution and Ethics,*" in Evolution and Ethics. J. Paradis and G. C. Williams. 179–214 (Princeton, N.J.: Princeton University. Press).

Wilson, Mary F. and Nancy Burley. 1983. *Mate Choice in Plants* (Princeton, N.J.: Princeton University Press).

Wilson, Edward O. 1975. *Sociobiology: The New Synthesis* (Cambridge, Mass.: Harvard University Press).

World Almanac and Book of Facts. 1983. New York: Newspaper Enterprise Association.

Alexander Rosenberg

The Biological Justification of Ethics:
A Best-Case Scenario

Social and behavioral scientists—that is, students of human nature—nowadays hardly ever use the term 'human nature'. This reticence reflects both a becoming modesty about the aims of their disciplines and a healthy skepticism about whether there is any one thing really worthy of the label 'human nature'.

For some feature of humankind to be identified as accounting for our 'nature', it would have to reflect some property both distinctive of our species and systematically influential enough to explain some very important aspect of our behavior. Compare: molecular structure gives the essence or the nature of water just because it explains most of its salient properties. Few students of the human sciences currently hold that there is just one or a small number of such features that can explain our actions and/or our institutions. And even among those who do, there is reluctance to label their theories as claims about 'human nature'.

Among anthropologists and sociologists, the label seems too universal and indiscriminate to be useful. The idea that there is a single underlying character that might explain similarities threatens the differences among people and cultures that these social scientists seek to uncover. Even economists, who have explicitly attempted to parlay rational choice theory into an account of all human behavior, do not claim that the maximization of transitive preferences is 'human nature'.

I think part of the reason that social scientists are reluctant to use 'human nature' is that the term has traditionally

Reprinted with permission of the publisher, "The Biological Basis of Ethics: A Best Case Scenario," *Social Philosophy and Policy* (1989) 8: 86–101.

labeled a theory with normative implications as well as descriptive ones. Any one who propounds a theory of human nature seems committed to drawing conclusions from what the theory says *is* the case to what *ought* to be the case. But this is just what twentieth-century social scientists are reluctant to do. Once the lessons of David Hume and G. E. Moore were well and truly learned among social scientists, they surrendered the project (associated with the 'moral sciences' since Hobbes) of deriving 'ought' from 'is'.[1]

The few scientists who have employed the term 'human nature' do draw evaluative conclusions from their empirical theories. The best recent examples of such writers are sociobiologists like E. O. Wilson, eager to extend the writ of evolutionary biology to include both the empirical study of humans and the foundations of their moral philosophy.[2]

It is relatively easy to offer a review and philosophical critique of the excesses that are bound to creep into evolutionary biologists' attempts to transcend the traditional limits of their discipline. But more useful than still another catalog of sociobiological foibles would be a sympathetic examination of the best we might hope for from the application of evolutionary biology to traditional questions about moral philosophy. Of all the intellectual fashions of the late twentieth century, it has the best claim to provide an account of human nature in the scientist's sense of 'nature', for it is undeniable that every aspect of humanity has been subjected to natural selection over blind variation literally since time immemorial. If any one thing has shaped us it is evolution, and if any piece of science is going to shed light on ethical issues, sociobiology—the application of Darwinian theory to human affairs—will. Therefore, my aim will be to identify the minimal conditions under which evolutionary biology *might* be able to tell us something about traditional issues in moral philosophy. If the rather strong assumptions evolutionary biology requires to shed light on these issues fail to obtain, then—as our best guess about human nature—biology will have no bearing on moral philosophy. This, in fact, is my strong suspicion. Nevertheless, I herewith attempt to put together the best case scenario for the ethical significance of evolutionary biology.

I. The Possible Projects

There are several sorts of insights evolutionary biology might be supposed to offer about human nature and its relation to morality. One among them is uncontroversial and beyond the scope of moral philosophy. Like any scientific theory, evolutionary biology may well provide factual information that, together with independent normative principles, helps us make ethical decisions. It may uncover hitherto unnoticed means we can employ in meeting ethically established ends. It may even identify subsidiary goals that we need to meet in order to attain other intrinsic goals. For example, there are plain facts (about, for example, ecology, genetic diversity, and the importance to us of preserving threatened species) which biology reveals and which can be combined with moral standards into hypothetical imperatives governing human action.

More controversially, evolutionary biology may reveal constraints and limitations on human behavior that our ethical prescriptions will have to take account of. If 'ought' implies 'can', the contrapositive will be valid too: 'can't' should imply 'need not'. Like other scientific theories, evolutionary biology may help fill in the list of what we (nomologically) cannot do. However, for a theory of human nature to have ramifications for moral philosophy itself, it will have to do more than any of these things.

The most impressive accomplishment for a theory of human nature would be the derivation of particular moral principles, like the categorical imperative or the principle of utility, from biological facts about human beings. Slightly less impressive would be to derive from such facts our status as moral *agents* and *subjects*, or to establish on the strength of our biology the *intrinsic value* of human life. A derivation of agency or intrinsic value is equivalent to deriving the generic conclusion that there is some normative principle or other governing our actions. Such a derivation would be less impressive because it would leave open the question of which moral principles about agents or objects of intrinsic value were the right ones. Still less impressive but significant in its own right would be the derivation of some important component or condition or instance of morally praiseworthy conduct—like cooperation, altruism, or other-regarding behavior—as generally obligatory. To be significantly interesting the derivation need not be deductive, but it cannot be question-begging: it cannot begin from assumptions with substantial normative content. Otherwise, it will be open to the charge that these assumptions are doing all the real work, and that the biological theory makes no distinctive contribution to the derivation.

The possibility of this project, of deriving agency and/or value (or, equivalently, deriving the existence of some moral principle or other), rests on two preconditions. The first is that we can derive 'ought' from 'is': that there is some purely factual, empirical, contingent, strictly biological property of organisms, which could underwrite, explain, or justify their status as agents or loci of intrinsic value. The second is that this property is *common and peculiar* to *all Homo sapiens*, so that it will count as constituting our nature.

That the first of these two preconditions for deriving morality from human nature cannot be realized seems to me to be at least as widely held a view as any other claim in moral philosophy or metaethics. Accordingly, I will not offer new arguments to supplement the observations of Hume and Moore. I recognize, however, that the more sophisticated sociobiologists are perfectly aware of these strictures on moral justification. Among sociobiologists, those who nevertheless go on to attempt to derive some normative claims from biological findings do Moore and Hume the courtesy of noting and rejecting their arguments.[3]

But even if we grant the sociobiologist's claim that the derivation of 'ought' from 'is' has not yet been totally excluded, there remains a second precondition required by the project of deriving morality from human nature. And the failure of this condition is something on which all evolutionary biologists should be in agreement.

Humans are supposed to be moral agents. This is what distinguishes us from moral subjects, like animals, and from morally neutral objects. Now, for some biological property of human beings to ground our status as the unique set of moral agents (in our biosphere at least), that property will have to be as widely distributed among human beings as the moral property it grounds, and it will have to be peculiar to humans as well. For if it is not restricted to humans there will be other subjects with equal claim to the standing of moral agents. The trouble is that if modern evolutionary biology teaches anything, it shows that there are no such properties common and peculiar to each member of a species. If there were, taxonomy would be a much easier subject. And since there are none, what evolutionary biology in fact shows is that there is no such thing as *the* unique human nature, any more than there is beaver nature or dodo-bird nature or *E. coli* nature.

Population genetics and molecular biology have shown that, up and down the entire range of living things, there are no interesting *essential* properties—no properties which will explain a range of behavior in the way that, say, molecular structure explains most of what a chemical compound does. It is not that modern biology has yet to find such essential properties, which give the nature of a species. Rather, evolutionary and genetic theory *requires* that biological species have no such common and peculiar essential properties.

Gradual evolution by natural selection requires vast amounts of *variation* within and between species. This variation is provided by mutation genetic drift, immigration, emigration, and most of all by genetic recombination in the sexual reproduction of offspring. The result is that there are no *essential* (suites of) phenotypes. Neither the typical nor average nor mean nor median values of the heritable phenotypes which face selection are their *natural, essential* values. They do not constitute the normal traits of members of a species, from which differences and divergences might count as deviations, disturbances, defects, or abnormalities. Of course there are biological properties common to every member of a species. For example, all *Homo sapiens* engage in respiration. But then so does every other organism we know about. Similarly, there are some biologically-based properties peculiar to individual humans—self-consciousness, speech, a certain level of intelligence, opposable thumbs, absence of body fur, etc. But these properties are plainly not distributed universally among humans, nor would the lack of any one of them be enough to deprive someone of membership in our moral community who was otherwise endowed with it. There is no human nature in the sense in which 'natures' are identified in modern science.

It might well be supposed that there is some complex combination of properties—say, self-consciousness *cum* opposable thumbs *cum* a disjunction of blood-types—that is sufficient for moral agency. But the project of grounding agency in (and only in) human nature requires that this complex combination of properties be necessary for agency as well as sufficient for it, and that it be universal among *Homo sapiens*. For consider, how could a property *restricted* in its instantiation only to some members of a class provide the basis for a property *common* to all members of the class: how can we derive 'All As are Cs' from 'Some As are Bs' and 'All Bs are Cs'? Doubtless, a philosopher can solve this problem by cooking up some gruesome gerrymandered relational property. For example, one could define property C as the property of being a member of a class some of whose members have property B. Then the derivation is trivial. But, clearly, being a moral agent is not a relational property— not at any rate, if it derives solely from the nature of the individual human. And this makes the logical problem a grave one for those who seek to derive agency from human nature.

Deriving a particular moral principle, or even the generic status of moral agency, from human nature alone—at least as evolutionary biology understands it—is not a feasible project, even if we could derive 'ought' from 'is'.

A third potential project for the biological account of human nature is that of *explanation*: telling a plausible story about how a particular moral principle or 'morality' in general, or some important precondition or component of it, emerged in the evolution of *Homo sapiens*.

The qualification "plausible" cannot be emphasized too strongly here. The most we can expect of any evolutionary account of chronology is plausibility: that the narrative will be consistent with evolutionary theory and with such slim data as may be available. The reason is that the problem of explaining the emergence of morality is similar to (but even more difficult than) that faced by, say, the task of explaining the disappearance of the dinosaur. There is a saying in paleontology: "The fossil record shows at most that evolution occurred elsewhere." In the case of explaining the evolution of behavior, there are no bones, no "hard parts" left to help us choose among competing explanations. The most we can hope for is plausibility.

This raises the question of how much a merely plausible story is worth, what it is good for, and why we should want it for more than its entertainment value. The question is particularly pressing in moral philosophy and metaethics. For it is not clear that even a well-confirmed explanation for the emergence of aspects of morality from human nature has any relevance to the concerns of philosophers. It would be a genetic fallacy to infer that a particular normative conclusion was right, justified, or well grounded—or, for that matter, that it was wrong, unjustified, or groundless—from a purely causal account of its origins.

If, however, we could parlay the explanation for the emergence of aspects of morality from human nature into an argument about why it is rational to be moral, then for all its evidential weakness, the causal story would turn out to have some interest. It would address a traditional question in moral philosophy: why should I be moral? There may be some reason to think such a strategy will work. For natural selection is an optimizing force for individuals,[4] and so is self-interest. Explanations in evolutionary biology proceed by nationalizing an innovation as advantageous for an organism's survival. Egoistic justification does something quite similar. Like evolutionary explanation, it rationalizes actions as means to ends.

This, I think, is the only interesting project in moral philosophy or metaethics for a biological approach to human nature. In what follows, I sketch the outlines of such a project. I should note two things about my sketch. First, little that follows is original. Mostly, I have plucked insights from a bubbling cauldron of sociobiological and evolutionary theorizing. Second, I am by no means optimistic that this project of rationally justifying morality can succeed, even in part. My aim is to identify the strictures it will have to satisfy if it stands a chance of succeeding.

II. Natural Selection, Blind Variation, Fitness Maximization

If the theory of natural selection is right, then the overriding fact about us is that we are all approximate fitness-maximizers. Of course, this is not a special feature of people. Indeed, it is the most widely distributed property of biological interest that there is. Every organism in every reproducing species is an approximate fitness-maximizer, for natural selection selects for fitness maximization *uber haupt*. All the phenotypes that have been selected for in the course of evolution have this in common. And if the theory is correct, then over time, given constant environments, successive generations of organisms are better approximations to fitness-maximization than their predecessors. This is what adaptation consists in.

What exactly is fitness-maximization? This is a vexed question in the philosophy of biology. For present purposes it will suffice to adopt the following definitions: x is fitter than y if, over the long run, x leaves more fertile offspring than y. Thus, an organism maximizes its fitness if it leaves the largest number of fertile offspring it can over the long run. It will be convenient if we define 'offspring' in a special way: an offspring will count as one complete set of an organism's genes. Therefore, the result of asexual reproduction is one offspring, but the result of sexual reproduction is half an offspring, since each child bears only one-half the genes of each of its parents. Note that, by this means of reckoning offspring, if a childless woman's brother has one child, the woman has a quarter of an offspring. Thus five fertile nieces and nephews make for greater fitness than one child: 5/4 > 1. This means that nature, in its relentless search for fitness- maximizing organisms, sometimes selects for fewer children and more offspring.

Nature selection has made us *approximate* fitness-maximizers, not perfect ones. There are several reasons for this.

To begin with, nature selects for fitness-maximization only indirectly, by seeking adaptive phenotypes: among giraffes it selects for long necks, among cheetahs for great foot speed, among chameleons for mimicry, and among eagles for eyesight. But each of these is selected because it makes for the survival and the well-being of the organisms endowed with it. And survival, along with well-being, are in turn necessary conditions for reproductive success. Mere survival is not enough; an organism must be healthy enough to reproduce and ensure the survival of its offspring. But the point is that except where selection operates directly on the organs of reproduction, birth, feeding, and protection, every other piece of an organism's equipment is selected for direct effect on survival and well-being, and through them for indirect effects on fitness. This means that much of what nature selects may not look like it bears on reproduction and fitness.

In its culling of these properties that bear indirectly on fitness, natural selection puts a premium on quick and dirty solutions to the problem of fitness-maximization. It prefers these cheap, imperfect solutions to slow but sweet ones that may do the job better but take a long time to emerge. Nature recognizes Keynes's maxim that in the long run we are all dead, and it acts on this maxim before it's too late. Thus, all organisms are at best approximate, jury-rigged, only intermittent fitness-maximizers. As genetic recombination and the other sources of phenotypic novelty turn up variations, the best among them out-reproduce the others. But the best may not be very good on any absolute scale. It need only be good enough to survive and outlive the other variants among which it emerges.

Selection operates on what variation provides. It has no power to call forth solutions to problems of adaptation, only to pick and choose among those that recombination and mutation may offer. Here is a nice example (with thanks to Daniel Dennett). Fish need to be able to recognize predators. But fish do not have very sophisticated predator recognition capacities; they have not evolved the sort of cognitive capacities for discriminating other fish, let alone telling friend from foe. Yet in the presence of predators they invariably startle, turn, and flee. Of course they also respond this way to all fish, not just the predatory ones. Indeed, present a fish with any bilaterally symmetrical stimulus and it will emit this flight response. The reason is that selection has resulted in the emergence of a relatively simple solution to the predator detection problem: bilateral symmetry detection. This is not a very discriminating capacity, but at least it is within the cognitive powers of a fish, and it works well enough at predator detecting. Its defects are obvious—the fish wastes energy fleeing non-predators. But in its environment the cost of this imperfection is low enough, and without it fish would not have lasted long enough to give rise to those species cognitively powerful enough to do the job of predator recognition any better.

There is a related reason why natural selection leads to the evolution only of approximate fitness-maximizers. Environments change, and organisms must survive in an environment that manifests wide extremes, and they must survive when one environment is displaced by another environment. Such conditions put a premium on being a jack of many trades instead of a master of one. An environment of great uniformity lasting over epochs of geological length provides selection with the opportunity to winnow successive variations to remarkable degrees of perfection. Consider the human eye, which is the result of a series of adaptations to a solar spectrum that has remained constant for almost the whole of evolutionary history. Such fine-tuning, however, gives hostages to fortune. For when an environment changes, there is too little variation in the received phenotype for selection to operate on. A phenotype that maximizes fitness perfectly in one environment is so closely adapted to it that it may not retain enough variation to survive in any other environment.

Since we are the products of selection over changing environments, we are only approximate fitness-maximizers. Nature has produced us by selecting from what was immediately available for shaping to insure short-term survival. Doubtless, in its impatience nature has nipped in the bud potential improvements in our own species and in its predecessors. For the moment the only moral of this part of the story, for moral philosophy, is this: merely showing that altruism or other well-established patterns of morally praise-worthy action are strictly incompatible with monomaniacal, perfect, complete fitness-maximization is a poor argument for the claim that human behavior has become exempt from evolutionary selection. For we are not perfect fitness-maxi-mizers. Natural selection has shaped us for only approxi-mate fitness-maximization in the environments in which *Homo sapiens* has evolved. Approximate fitness maximiza-tion leaves a great deal of room for non-adaptive altruism and other selfless actions.

III. Parameters, Strategies, and the Maximization of Fitness

Now, among approximate fitness-maximizers, what sort of social behavior should evolve? This is a problem that arises with the advent of selection for living in family groups, which of course obtained long before *Homo sapiens* emerged. Until this point fitness maximization is, in the game theorist's terms, 'parametric', not 'strategic'. Which behavior is maxi-mizing depends only on the environment, which provides parameters fixed *independently* of which behavior the organ-ism is going to emit. But when organisms interact, which behavior one emits may be a function of what the other is going to do. So which behavior is fitness-maximizing will depend on how other organisms behave. This means that the optimal behavior is one that reflects a *strategy*, which takes account of the prospective behavior of other organ-isms. When social interaction emerges, fitness-maximiza-tion becomes a strategic problem.

This does not mean that, once groups emerge, organ-isms begin to calculate and select strategies based on recog-nition of the strategies of other organisms. It means something much less implausible. It means that those be-haviors will emerge as fitter which, as a matter of fact, are coordinated with one another in the way they would have been, had they been the result of reflection and deliberation. This is because there is enough time for fitness differences between the rarer but *fortuitously* coordinated behavioral phenotypes and more common uncoordinated ones to pile up and select the coordinated ones.

Coordinated behaviors are sometimes cooperative ones; they are other-regarding, involving putting oneself at the mercy (or, at least, at the advantage) of another. Thus, they constitute a significant component of morality. The emergence of coordinated behaviors makes one sort of scenario for the emergence of morality tempting. This is the *group selection* scenario, according to which nature selected societies and groups because their institutions, including their moral rules, are more adaptive for the group as a whole. On this model, selection proceeds at the level of the individual (for individual fitness-maximization) and at the level of the group (for group survival and growth). The idea that evolution might lead to the emergence of morality by selecting for groups that manifest moral rules and against groups that retain a state of nature is, on the face of it, more attractive than trying to find a story of how morality might have emerged at the level of the individual. For the fitness-maximizing individual is concerned only with maximizing its offspring; it is ready to sacrifice others to this end. The fact that there are so many immoral and amoral people around makes implausible the notion that morality emerged among *Homo sapiens* the way opposable thumbs did—as an individual response to the selection of individual organisms. But the emergence of morality as a group institution is at least compatible with the observed degree of moral imperfection among individuals. Selection at the level of the group does not require uniformity among the individuals who compose it; no championship team has ever had the best players in the league at every (or even any) position (cf. New York Mets, 1969).

So, one way to reconcile other-regarding cooperative behavior with monomaniacal evolutionary egoism is to locate selection for cooperative institutions at the level of the group and selection for individual fitness-maximization at the level of the individual. If the forces selecting for the adaptation of groups are independent of those selecting for the adaptation of individuals, then those groups within which cooperation, promise-keeping, property, fidelity, etc. emerged, for whatever reason, might do better, last longer, or have larger, healthier populations than those groups which lacked such virtuous institutions. Thus, morality is explained as an evolved holistic social constraint on individual selfishness.

This is a nice idea, but one which evolutionary biology must exclude. For no matter how much better off a society with ethical institutions might be than one without them, such a society is seriously unstable, and in the evolutionary long haul must fall victim to its own niceness. The reason is that selection at the level of the group and the level of the individual are never independent enough to allow for the long-term persistence of a moral majority and an immoral minority. In fact, they aren't independent at all. The latter will eventually swamp the former.

Consider a society of perfectly cooperative altruistic organisms, genetically programmed never to lie, cheat, steal, rape, or kill, but in which provisions for detection and elimination of organisms who do not behave in this manner are highly imperfect (as in our own society). Since everyone is perfectly cooperative, the society needs no such provision. Now suppose that a genetically programmed scoundrel emerges within this society (never mind how—it might be through mutation, recombination, immigration, etc.). By lying, cheating, stealing, raping, and otherwise free-riding whenever possible (recall the detection and enforcement mechanisms are imperfect), the scoundrel does far better than anyone else, both in terms of well-being, and in terms of eventual fitness-maximization. He leaves more offspring than anyone else. If his anti-social proclivities are hereditary, then in the long run his offspring will come to predominate in the society. Eventually, 100 percent of its membership will be composed of scoundrels and its character as a cooperative group will long since have disappeared.

Evolutionary game theorists have provided a useful jargon to describe this scenario: a group with a morally desirable other-regarding strategy is not "evolutionarily stable": left alone, it will persist, but it can be "invaded" even by a small number of egoists—who will eventually overwhelm it and convert the society into one bereft of other-regarding patterns of interaction. By contrast, a society composed wholly of fitness-maximizing egoists is an "evolutionarily stable" one: a group of such egoists cannot be successfully invaded by some other, potentially nicer pattern of behavior. Its members will all, one after another, play the nice guys for suckers and outbreed and ultimately extinguish them.

The trouble, then, with group-selectionist explanations of the emergence of morality is that a group of other-regarders might do better than a group of selfish egoists, but it is vulnerable to invasion by one such egoist, an invasion which evolutionary theory tells us must always eventually occur—since nature is always culling for improvements in individual fitness-maximization. Whether from within or without, scoundrels will eventually emerge to put an end to other-regarding groups by converting them into societies of fitness-maximizers.

If morality is to emerge from the nature of organisms as approximate fitness-maximizers, it will have to happen at the level of individual selection. And it will have to be selection for optimizing behavior in the context of "strategic" interaction, where the optimum behavior of each organism depends on the behavior of other organisms. The trouble is that game theorists have increasingly come to suspect that there is no optimal strategy under these circumstances. If this is right, then there is none for evolution to choose, and no way for moral institutions to evolve from the strategic interactions of fitness-maximizers.

The problem of an optimal strategy for nature to select is easily illustrated in the children's game of Rock, Paper and Scissors. In this game, kids pick one of the three choices. Rock breaks scissors and so beats it, scissors cut paper and so beats it, but paper covers rock and so beats it Whether your choice wins depends on what the other kid picked, and no choice is better than any other. In an evolutionary situation like this, no strategy ever comes to predominate. Of course, if you know what your competitor will pick, you can always win. But what the other kid picks is going to depend on what he thinks you will pick. So, you have to know what he thinks you will pick in order to pick the best strategy, and so on backwards *ad infinitum*. There is no end to the calculation problem, and therefore no optimal strategy in the rock-paper-scissors game. Game theorists have labeled the problem of this sort of game with no finite solution—no best strategy for any player—"the problem of common knowledge." In principle, the problem of having to infinitely iterate calculations about what other players will do bedevils most strategic games.

While the problem of common knowledge cannot affect organisms which are incapable of making calculations about the strategies of others, it can affect the evolution of fitness-maximizing strategies. As nature selects the best among competing strategies for fitness-maximization, it must eventually face contexts in which the best strategy for an organism to play depends on what other strategies are available to be played by other organisms. If the game theorist can prove that, in the long run, there is no single best strategy—even with rational calculation on the part of the players—then we can expect natural selection to do no more than produce a motley of equally good or bad strategies that compete with one another, at best gaining temporary ascendancy in a random sequence. In other words, natural selection will produce nothing but noise, disorder, no real pattern in the behavior of fitness-maximizers who face strategic competition as opposed to parametric optimization problems.

It seems safe to assume that *Homo sapiens* has not in fact suffered this fate. For the most part, our interactions do show a pattern, and an other-regarding, cooperative one at that. Morality is the rule and not the exception (and not just one among a series of cyclically succeeding patterns of behavior). It must follows, therefore, that evolution has not led us (or our evolutionary forebearers) down the cul-de-sac of the problem of common knowledge. But, if game theorists are right, almost the only way evolution could have avoided this sort of chaos is for other-regarding principles of conduct to have emerged in parametric contexts, and then to be evolutionarily stable, un-invadable when these contexts became strategic.

IV. Kin-Selection and Uncertainty

For a fitness-maximizing organism, interactions with off-spring are close to being parametric. For, almost no matter what children and kin do to you, if you act in their interests, the result will increase your fitness. The fitness-maximizing strategy for an organism is therefore to act so as to maximize the fitness of its offspring. Thus, in selecting for fitness-maximization, nature will encourage organisms whose genetically encoded dispositions include sharing and cooperating, and even unreciprocated altruism towards kin—children, siblings, even parents. For these strategies are likely to increase one's offspring, no matter how they respond to you. This sort of kin-altruism is evolutionarily stable and un-invadable. A short-sighted, selfish organism, who behaves as though its own survival or that of its children counted for its fitness, would end up with fewer offspring over the long haul. For sometimes it would look out for number one (or number one's kids) when sacrificing itself or a child would result in the survival of a larger number of offspring (recall, that under sexual reproduction, a child is only half an off-spring). In selecting for fitness, nature will select for "inclusive fitness" and "kin selection" will emerge. Kin selection is something we can count on emerging long before *Homo sapiens* appears. It becomes an adaptive strategy as soon as the number of genetic offspring begins to exceed the number of children. (Recall, three nephews carry more of an individual's genes than, one child.)

When *Homo sapiens* emerges, therefore, we are already beyond Hobbes's state of nature. Cooperation, altruism, and other-regarding behavior generally is already established inside both the nuclear and the extended family. Indeed, it is likely to already have been established a bit beyond this. Consider that individuals do not wear name tags or carry their genealogy on their sleeves for others to examine before deciding whether an interaction will be parametric or strategic. There are, of course, clear signs of kinship that even animals with limited recognition powers can use: odor, proximity to a nest or region. And there are clear signs of xenonimity—strangerness. But there is always a large area of uncertainty in between, a range of interactions in which two organisms just can't tell with any more than a certain moderate level of probability whether they are kin or not. This will be more true for males and their putative offspring than for females. Given the nature of procreation and gestation in many mammalian species—and especially in *Homo sapiens*—the male can never be as certain as the female that the young in his family are his offspring—i.e., that they share some of his genes. Unless the female is under constant and perfect surveillance during the critical period, the question of whose sperm fertilized her ovum must always be a matter of some doubt. Beyond the relation between mother and child, the degree of consanguinity between any two organisms is always a matter of probabilities, and doubts about kinship are easier to raise than to allay.

Under conditions of uncertainty about kinship, what is the optimal strategy for a fitness-maximizer? Game theory tells us that the rational thing to do is to apportion the degree of one's other-regarding behavior to the strength of the evidence of consanguinity. In the long run, as natural selection operates, it must favor this strategy as well. Even in cases where the available positive evidence of consanguinity (subtle similarities of smell, coat color, shape of beak, pitch of mating call, etc.) is difficult to detect, one can expect nature to select for cooperation and other-regarding behavior between kin, provided only that it has enough time to fine-tune the detection mechanisms. Considering the job it has done in optimizing the eye for vision within the time constraint of four million years, it may seem reasonable to suppose it can fine-tune kin-selection strategies as well. And if everyone turns out probably to be closely enough related to everyone else, then natural selection might be expected by itself to produce other-regarding behavior up to levels of frequency that match the probability of universal consanguinity. Here we have the emergence of morality, or at least a crucial aspect of it, without having to solve the problems common knowledge makes for strategic games.

However, the amount of other-regarding behavior that might in fact be fitness-maximizing just because of the fact that we are all each other's seventh cousin hardly seems sufficient to explain the emergence and persistence of moral conduct. The problem with this neat explanation is that we have no independent idea of whether the payoffs (in more offspring) for being other-regarding are really great enough when the probability of being related falls to the level that obtains between you and me. And there doesn't seem to be any easy way to find out. In short, our explanation isn't robust enough. It rests on a certain variable taking on a very limited range of values, one within which we have no reason to think it falls. We need a better explanation for the emergence and persistence of other-regarding behavior than kin selection and the uncertainty of relatedness can give us. It's all right to start with kin selection, but we need an explanation that carries other-regarding conduct into the realm of strategic interactions among fitness maximizers unlikely to be kin.

To do this, we need to help ourselves to another brace of healthy assumptions about morality and game theory. First, let us accept without argument that the institutions of morality are public goods: they cannot be provided to one consumer without being provided to all others, so that any one consumer has an incentive to understate the value of the good to him and so decline to pay its full value provided he is confident that others will pay enough to provide it. Certainly, the institution of generalized cooperation is like this. No one can count on it unless everyone can, and we all have an incentive to understate its value to us whenever we are asked to pay our fair share to maintain it. Moreover, fitness-maximizers have an incentive to cheat, to decline to cooperate, if they can get away with it undetected or unpunished. But if everyone knows this. and everyone knows that everyone knows this, etc., then the institution of cooperation will break down because of our common knowledge. The public good is lost, and every one is worse off. The prisoner's dilemma graphically illustrates this problem of the provision of public goods. Individual rational agents have an incentive to be free-riders, to decline to cooperate. The result is a non-optimal equilibrium in which no cooperation is visible. The natural selection version of this collapse from the fortuitous provision of public goods to a non-optimal equilibrium takes time, as individual defectors emerge through recombination or mutation and out-reproduce co-operators.

The second assumption we need is that most of our morally relevant interactions are moves in an indefinitely long sequence of prisoner's dilemma games. This seems a not unreasonable assumption: honoring moral obligations is not a one-shot, all-or-nothing affair. It is a matter of repeated interactions largely among the same individuals. Interactions with strangers are by definition less frequent than with people we have interacted with and will interact with in the future. Now, one important fruit of the joint research of game theorists and evolutionary biologists has been the conclusion that, even among strangers, being a free-rider (always declining to cooperate, always taking advantage) is not the fitness-maximizing strategy in an it-erated prisoner's dilemma. Rather, the best strategy is what is known as "tit-for-tat": that is, for optimal results one should cooperate on the initial occasion for interaction, and on each subsequent occasion do what the other player did on the last round. This strategy will maximize fitness even when everyone knows that everyone else is employing this strat-egy. For even on the assumption that there is complete common knowledge of what strategies will be chosen, tit-for-tat remains the best strategy. Once in place, it assures cooperation even among unrelated fitness-maximizers. It circumvents the common knowledge problem.

V. Ethics—Quick and Dirty

There is one rather serious obstacle to natural selection's helping itself to this strategy: the problem of getting it into place. For tit-for-tat cannot invade and overwhelm the strat-egy of narrow selfishness that is required by strict fitness-maximization. In a group of organisms that never cooperate, anyone playing tit-for-tat will be taken advantage of at least once by every other player. This advantage is enough to prevent tit-for-tat players eventually swamping selfishness. In fact, it may be enough of an advantage for tit-for-tat to be driven to extinction by the strategy of selfishness every time it appears as a strategy for interaction.

This is where nature's preference for the quick and dirty, *approximate* solution to the problem of selecting for fitness-maximization comes in. Our approximate fitness-maximizers' optimum strategy involves other-regarding behavior with kin, and selfishness with others. How will fitness be maximized in the borderline area where kinship and its absence are difficult or impossible to determine? When the only choice for an organism is to cooperate or decline to do so, how does it behave? By flipping a coin weighted to reflect the evidence for kinship, and doing as the coin indicates? A few pages back I derided this suggestion, though we cannot put it past nature to have evolved a device within us that has this effect. On the other hand, nature will prefer quick and dirty solutions to mathematically elegant ones, provided they are cheap to build, early to emerge, and do the job under a variety of circumstances, etc. If tit-for-tat is almost as good a strategy for fitness-maximization in cases of uncertainty as employing the probability calculus and far easier for nature to implement, then on initial encounters under uncertainty about kinship, individuals playing this strategy will cooperate. But this means they will cooperate therafter as well. Thus, interactions at the borderline come to have the character of interactions within the family; parties to any and every interactive situation will generally cooperate.

Now suppose that among organisms genetically programmed to be other-regarding within the family and to play tit-for-tat at the borderlines, one or more individuals emerge with a new variation: their genome is programmed to encourage tit-for-tat always and everywhere, or at least whenever interacting with strangers. Interaction with selfish strangers will be costly to such organisms and should lead to their extinction. But suppose such interaction is rare. Furthermore, suppose (as seems reasonable) that the strategy of always playing tit-for-tat is otherwise an adaptive one, with advantages over other more complex strategies, especially for organisms lacking complex cognitive and calculational powers. For the cost of maintaining and using a storage system for kin and non-kin may be greater than the cost of being taken for a sucker in just the first round of an indefinitely iterated interaction. This will likely be true when the chances of meeting a stranger are extremely low, as they will be in the earlier stages of the evolution of mammalian species living in family groups. It is, in general, easy to imagine scenarios that make tit-for-tat the best over-all strategy under most circumstances in a given environment. But this means that natural selection for approximate fitness-maximization among individuals has led to the emergence of cooperative, other-regarding strategies. It has solved the problem of providing public goods to individual organisms geared always and only to look out for themselves and their kin. If ethical institutions are, after all public goods, then we have explained how they might emerge among approximate fitness-maximizers.

Of course, this entire story applies to us only to the extent that we are approximate fitness-maximizers. This is not hard to show. In fact, if anything, it's too easy to show. For the story does not include any indication of how good an approximation to perfect fitness-maximization is required for the emergence of other-regarding strategies. Even if it did, we have no idea of whether *Homo sapiens* is in fact a good enough fitness-maximizer for this scenario actually to obtain. For these reasons, the claim that we are in fact approximate fitness-maximizers will have vanishingly small empirical content. But then empirical content was never the strong point of any evolutionary theory, and is of little interest in moral philosophy anyway.

That we are fitness-maximizers to some degree of approximation goes without saying. After all, the only alternative to being an approximate fitness-maximizer is being extinct. And how did nature shape us for fitness maximization? What phenotypical properties of *Homo sapiens* did it shape in this direction? Well, the quickest and dirtiest way of making us approach fitness-maximization is to make us *approximate utility-maximizers*, to shape us into systems organized to maximize our well-being, by linking well-being to the avoidance of discomfort, pain, and distress, and the attainment of comfort, pleasure, and feelings of security. The reason is obvious: an organism's reproductive potential is, *ceteris paribus*, a function of its well-being So, in order to select for fitness-maximization, nature will select for organisms that by-and-large maximize their well-being. The by-and-large clause reflects the fact that there are certain departures from utility-maximization that nature will select for too. For example, it will select for organisms that sacrifice their own well-being to offspring, especially after they have passed the age of optimal procreation. Or, equivalently, nature will select for preference structures that make kin altruism pleasing to the individual This, is, a quick and dirty solution to the problem of programming kin-selection, one which corresponds to the philosopher's claim that altruism is just the reflection of a perverse preference structure.

If the quick and dirty solution to the problems of designing an approximate fitness-maximizer is to design an approximate utility-maximizer, then our merely plausible explanation for the emergence of morality or of one important component of it may have another role to play. It may turn out to be a part of a (weak) justification of morality, or at least of one important component of it. One traditional question of interest to moral philosophers is that of how to convince the rational egoist to be moral, how to show the egoist that being moral is in his interest. Nowadays this problem is often set forth as that of showing how morality could be part of a strategy that maximizes individual utility. In its own way, natural selection provides reason to suppose that morality is part of a utility- maximizing strategy, and our story provides a plausible scenario for how this might have happened.

It is clear that nature began selecting for utility-maximizers long before it began selecting for other-regarding cooperators. For one thing, maximizing well-being is a strategy to be found across the phylogenetic spectrum; it doubtless characterized our ancestors long before the rearing of offspring in nuclear or extended families and the emergence of social groups made other-regarding cooperation possible and necessary. Having laid down very early in evolution approximate utility-maximization as a quick and dirty strategy for approximating fitness-maximization, nature is unlikely ever to "rip it out" and start over. This means that when it lays down other strategies, they will at least have to be compatible with utility maximizing. It is much more likely that the new strategy will be new ways to maximize utility under new circumstances. But if cooperation and other-regarding behavior generally is nature's way of most efficiently maximizing utility, then it should be good enough for us. That is, in our own calculations and reflection on how to maximize our utilities, we should expect to come eventually to the same conclusion which it has taken nature several geological epochs to arrive at. Both rational agents and nature operate in accordance with principles of instrumental rationality; they both seek the most efficient means to their ends. Since nature's end (approximate fitness-maximization) is served by our ends (approximate utility-maximization), our means and nature's will often coincide.

VI. Conclusion

It's a nice story, and it seems to have a moral for moral philosophy. I think it is absolutely the best biology can do by way of shedding light on anything worth calling 'human nature' and drawing out its implications for matters of interest to moral philosophers. But before taking any comfort in it at all, we need to recall and weigh the hostages to fortune it leaves—the many special assumptions about us and about the nature of moral conduct that it requires just to get off the ground: to begin with the idea that just because one is cooperative or other-regarding, one has attained the status of a moral agent or some important precondition to it. Then there are the claims about humankind as approximate fitness-maximizers. Even if you accept this view of 'human nature', as I do, you are committed to a level of fitness-maximization that you cannot specify beyond saying it is high enough to allow for the scenario I have tried to unfold. Then you have to find a way to draw the force or circumvent the difficulty of the problem of strategic games, in which there seem to be no stable equilibria in the behavior of fitness-maximizers, let alone equilibria that underwrite any part of morality. (And you can't call upon group selection to help solve this problem.) Then you have to buy into the theory of kin-selection and its application to conditions of uncertainty. This is one of the smaller gnats to strain on, given the independent evolutionary evidence for kin-selection. But the trouble is that it will not suffice when interactions begin to transcend the family. At this point, we need to assimilate morality further to strategies of choice to be analyzed by the tools of economics and game theory. Finally, we need to be able to fudge our account enough to say that morality emerges because we are not perfect fitness-maximizers, since the best nature can do is make us approximate utility-maximizers.

But perhaps the most difficult consequence of this story to swallow is this: if nature had been able to do any better, morality might never have emerged at all.

Notes

1. David Hume, *A Treatise of Human Nature,* ed. L. A. Selby-Bigge (Oxford: Clarendon Press, 1888), bk.11; G.F Moore, *Principia Ethica* (London: Routlege and Kegan Paul, 1907).

2. E. O. Wilson, *On Human Nature* (Cambridge, Mass.: Harvard University Press, 1978).

3. Ibid., ch. 1; R. Alexander, *Darwinism and Human Affairs* (Seattle: University of Washington Press, 1979).

4. As is explained below, natural selection cannot operate to optimize the properties of groups, as opposed to individual. See section II.

William A. Rottschaefer and David Martinsen

Really Taking Darwin Seriously: An Alternative to Michael Ruse's Darwinian Metaethics

ABSTRACT: Michael Ruse has proposed in his recent book *Taking Darwin Seriously* and elsewhere a new Darwinian ethics distinct from traditional evolutionary ethics, one that avoids the latter's inadequate accounts of the nature of morality and its failed attempts to provide a naturalistic justification of morality. Ruse argues for a sociobiologically based account of moral sentiments, and an evolutionarily based causal explanation of their function, rejecting the possibility of ultimate ethical justification. We find that Ruse's proposal distorts, overextends and weakens both Darwinism and naturalism. So we propose an alternative Darwinian metaethics that both remedies the problems in Ruse's proposal and shows how a Darwinian naturalistic account of the moral good in terms of human fitness avoids the naturalistic fallacy and can provide genuine, even if limited, justifications for substantive ethical claims. Thus, we propose to really take Darwin seriously.

Evolutionary ethics is dead and rightfully buried. But Darwinian ethics is born again in sociobiology and deservedly so. So contends philosopher and historian of biology Michael Ruse in a series of recent publications (Ruse 1984; 1986a; 1986b; 1987; and Ruse and Wilson 1986). Although efforts to revive interest in an ethics based in sociobiology, the study of animal and human social behavior, have been almost unanimously rejected, the recent publications of sociobiologist Richard Alexander (1987), historian and philosopher of biology Robert Richards (1986a; 1987) and Ruse's own work manifest a resurgence of interest in the relationships between evolutionary theory and ethics. In this essay

Reprinted by permission of Kluwer Academic Publishers, "Really Taking Darwin Seriously: An Alternative to Michael Ruse's Darwinian Metaethics," *Biology & Philosophy* 5 (1990):149–173 © 1990 D. Reidel Publishing Company.

we examine Ruse's claims for a Darwinian ethics based on sociobiology. Is there life there, and is it worth nourishing, or are Ruse's efforts merely attempts to revive a corpse?

Ruse distinguishes the proposals of Darwin about evolutionary theory and ethics from those of Spencer and the Social Darwinians, for instance, Sumner, as well as the twentieth century attempts to connect biology and ethics by Julian Huxley, Dobzhansky and Waddington. Darwinian ethics is a different breed than these traditional evolutionary ethics (TEE) (1986b, pp. 73–93). Ruse himself had not always believed this. Indeed in his earlier work on the issue (1979), though sympathetic to the scientific findings and potential of sociobiology, he found the efforts of people like E. O. Wilson (Lumsden and Wilson 1981; Wilson 1975; 1978) to link the new discipline with ethics unsuccessful. But now he has seen the light (1986b, pp. 93–101). It's not that he finds all of Wilson's substantive proposals completely acceptable now. Unfortunately, some of them are of the doomed evolutionary sort, modelled as they are, in Ruse's view, on a Spencerian approach. But Ruse finds in sociobiology, particularly the proposals of Wilson, hints of a radically different sort of approach to the decisive metaethical issues about the nature of morality and the ultimate justification of moral principles (1986b, pp. 68–70; 213–217; 250–252).

Using these hints, Ruse contends that the nature of morality is best grasped by examining what he calls our biologically based "moral sentiments". These sentiments prescribe altruistic actions of us all. By freely following their dictates, we not only act morally but increase our evolutionary prospects. However, Ruse contends that since the values toward which these sentiments incline us are illusory, Darwinian ethicists need not fear committing the naturalistic fallacy (NF), thus avoiding the nemesis of all TEE. Darwinian ethicists do not mistakenly identify facts with values, the definitional form of the fallacy, since, in Ruse's view, there are no objective values. Nor do they attempt to justify normative claims on the basis of factual evolutionary assertions, the derivational form of the fallacy, because, in Ruse's view, Darwinian metaethics (DME) can only provide a causal explanation of morality, not a justification.

It is these crucial metaethical issues about the nature of the moral sentiments and moral justification that we shall address in assessing Ruse's attempt to take Darwin seriously in thinking about our moral life. We agree with Ruse about both the importance of a naturalistic approach, which takes seriously the results of our best scientific theories for the resolution of metaethical questions, and the central role that evolutionary biology should play in such a naturalistic approach. However we shall argue that Ruse distorts, over-extends and weakens a Darwinian contribution to understanding the moral sentiments—one founded in the modern synthesis and sociobiology—only to salvage a manque account of the nature of morality. We shall then propose an alternative Darwinian view of the moral sentiments that corrects these problems by adhering more closely to a Darwinian and naturalistic perspective than does Ruse. Finally, we shall examine Ruse's concerns about avoiding NF. We argue that Ruse, by abandoning the objectivity of values and denying the possibility of ethical justification, has needlessly cast aside both a robust naturalism and Darwinism in order to avoid that fallacy.[1] We suggest an alternative understanding of the gap between fact and value, and show how, with that understanding, a Darwinian metaethics can maintain both the objectivity of values and the possibility of a naturalistic justification of morality without committing NF. In sum, we shall contend that Ruse fails to take Darwin seriously enough and that by taking Darwin more seriously, our proposal leads to more adequate answers than does Ruse's to the questions about morality's nature and justification.

The Nature of the Moral Sentiments

Ruse claims to have found the immediate inspiration for his philosophical conversion to the plausibility of biologically based naturalistic ethics in E. O. Wilson's work and its ultimate source in Darwin himself. We are not convinced that Ruse's Wilson bears much resemblance to the ethical positions of Wilson himself Nor do we believe that Ruse has nourished his new production sufficiently in Darwinian soil.

However, we realize that it was not Ruse's intention simply to describe Darwin's views but to use the hypothesis of moral sentiments, explicated by Wilson in terms of epigenetic rules, to develop a Darwinian account of ethics. We take that to be an account based on the best of current evolutionary theory including human sociobiology. It is this Darwin that Ruse urges us to take seriously and whom we believe Ruse himself has not taken seriously enough. Although we are not as confident about the empirical support for human sociobiology as Ruse is (Kitcher 1985; Kitcher et al. 1987), we shall for the most part grant Ruse his empirical case for the existence of genetically based dispositions to act altruistically, and focus on the adequacy of his interpretation of these dispositions both for understanding the moral sentiments and for meeting the challenges of the naturalistic fallacy.

Ruse takes it as a given that the nature of morality cannot be adequately accounted for without showing moral claims to be altruistic in content and to have the formal characteristics of prescriptivity, universality and objectivity. As Ruse puts it, moral injunctions to act altruistically are "laid upon me and all of us externally" (1986b, pp. 68–70; 213–217; 250–252). Ruse contends that some of our genetically based cognitive and behavioral dispositions meet these requisites of morality and so deserve to be called moral sentiments. Moral sentiments are, according to Ruse, genetically based dispositions to approve of and perform certain altruistic actions and to disapprove of and refrain from other, selfish actions (1984, pp. 173–174; 1986a, pp. 97–99; 1986b, pp. 221, 222; and Ruse and Wilson 1986, pp. 180–185). Sibling incest avoidance, care for one's children, helping kin and cooperating with non-relatives are some examples provided by Ruse. Even though these dispositions as adaptations work for the genetic advantage of the individual or her relatives, their content is genuinely moral. Ruse does not deny the existence of pure altruism, dispositions and actions that benefit a non-relative recipient more than the actor; but he does not require the altruism that he makes a characteristic of morality to be without genetic advantage for the altruist. Of course, Ruse realizes

that genuinely moral action requires knowledge and freedom. But that poses no problem for a Darwinian. The moral
sentiments are the dispositional bases, the raw materials,
for such genuinely moral action. However, unlike normal
feelings, whether selfish or altruistic, moral sentiments are
not mere likes or dislikes, wants or desires, they are genuinely prescriptive, that is, they have in Ruse's terms the
character of being laid upon one. But not just one, *everyone*. So they also have the mark of universal prescriptivity.
Thus the moral sentiments possess the modalities of
prescriptivity and universality rightly demanded, in Ruse's
view, by objectivists. Moreover, as genetically in-built dispositions of our human nature they manifest the dependence on human nature required by subjectivists but without
the shortcoming of being mere likes or dislikes. In addition,
moral sentiments manifest an "air of objectivity", of something thrust upon us externally (1984, pp. 190–192; 1986a,
pp. 101–103; 1986b, p. 253). Without this appearance of
objectivity, moral sentiments would not have their motivating power. Nevertheless, since, in Ruse's view, there are
no objective values, this sense of objectivity is illusory.
Because good Darwinians acknowledge the illusoriness of
objective values, while maintaining their motivating power
through the appearance of external imposition, they can
take full advantage of objectivist insights into the nature
of moral demands without committing their errors. Moreover, this denial of the objectivity of values also enables
Darwinians to avoid the TEE's error of committing NF.

The Distortion of Darwinism

Although we agree with Ruse that altruistic actions that
ultimately benefit the altruist genetically can belong in the
moral realm, we nevertheless contend that Ruse has unduly
limited the scope of morality by confining it to other-regarding dispositions and actions. According to Ruse, moral sentiments are to be distinguished from feelings since some of
the latter are selfish and all of them lack universal
prescriptivity (1986b, pp. 250–251). We believe this distinction between moral sentiments and feelings is problematic.

For although altruistic behavior generally belongs to the moral realm, it does not constitute that realm in its entirety. Self-regarding behavior need not be either amoral or immoral (Murphy, 1982, pp. 84–88).[2] For instance, protecting oneself from harm or maintaining one's health are usually morally right and obligatory activities that achieve moral goods for the individual. So such self-regarding feelings as fear for, and anger in defense of, one's safety, to the extent that they are genetically in-built, could be classified with respect to content as moral sentiments. Ruse mentions the issue of duties toward oneself, but does not seem to recognize its significance for the issues of the nature of moral sentiments and the content of morality (1986, p. 217). He argues that the basis of rights can be found in reciprocal altruism. Thus he implicitly allows for the moral rightness of the indirectly self-regarding behavior contained in the assertion of rights. But if it is right for me to urge that others acknowledge my right to sufficient food to survive, it is *a fortiori* right for me to seek directly for myself food sufficient for survival. Consequently, the sentiments that incline me to such action belong to the moral realm. Thus we believe that Ruse has given an incomplete account of the content of moral sentiments. As a consequence Ruse has distorted DME.

The Overextension of Darwinism

But even if we grant to Ruse that altruistic behavior of either the kin or reciprocal sort constitutes the content of moral sentiments, his claim that moral sentiments, unlike altruistic feelings, possess the formal characteristics of prescriptivity and universality is also problematic. We believe that Ruse has overextended his Darwinian bases by attributing to moral sentiments the full-fledged moral modalities of prescriptivity and universality. Ruse suggests that, during childhood, biologically based epigenetic rules lead automatically to the development of what he calls moral sentiments which possess both the content and structure of morality. Although Ruse often focuses on the experiences of the moral agent, it seems that he uses the prescriptivity and universality of moral discourse as criteria for identifying the features of morality that in his view the moral sentiments possess. We take the full-fledged manifestations of prescriptivity and universality to be those manifested in moral discourse. These, we will argue, are primarily the results of learning and reasoning rather than simply emerging in child development under the guidance and constraints of relatively fixed epigenetic rules.

Ruse maintains that moral sentiments must be distinguished from altruistic feelings because the former are prescriptive and the latter are not. He points out, for instance, that we distinguish between feelings of love for our children that lead us to want to take care of them and the moral sentiment that prescribes that we do. Ruse characterizes this prescriptivity metaphorically. It has the aspect of being laid upon one. Ruse seems to be appealing to our conscious experience of the difference between feeling morally compelled and merely wanting to do something. Similarly, Ruse claims that a person experiences moral sentiments as something laid upon everyone, not merely herself, but everyone in her moral community. Ruse does not intend to claim that all moral norms apply to everyone nor that they apply to everyone in the same way (1985, pp. 68–69). Nor does he believe that we have a biologically based disposition to make *all* humans the beneficiary of our moral actions; such a disposition, in Ruse's view, is the result of culture. Rather, he means that in having moral sentiments we and all others in our moral community feel required to do and refrain from doing certain actions, and believe that all others in similar circumstances are also so obliged and feel that way. (Of course it is another matter whether we act on such sentiments.) We suspect that for most people these experiences of inclination and duty are phenomenologically distinct. But such phenomenological distinctions do not allow us to draw any conclusions about their causal origins.

Moral experiences, even though widely shared, do not reveal to us whether moral sentiments derive primarily from nature or from nurture. For example, the behavior of parental care for children is a common one across cultures. From that we can conclude that there is a behavioral disposition on the part of parents to care for their children. Is that disposition primarily due to nature or to nurture? Using a notion analogous to Kitcher's of "precluded state" (1985, p. 27), we can say that a disposition is primarily the result of nature if it is an "included state". By an included state we mean that for a given genotype (or collection of genotypes) there is virtually no possible environment in which that state fails to appear. So we can claim that the behavioral disposition to care for one's children is primarily due to nature, if in all or most current and past environments, as well as other conceivable environments in which human life seems to be viable, parental child care manifests itself. It is clear that under these stringent requirements, we can not yet—and may never—be able to answer our question. However, we can weaken these requirements by assuming that current environments are sufficiently similar to past and other possible environments. One might then claim that there is enough evidence to conclude that a behavioral disposition for child care on the part of parents is primarily due to nature. But that evidence is not sufficient to make Ruse's case for a moral sentiment of child care. Behavioral evidence reveals only a behavioral disposition, a tendency to perform certain actions in specific situations. Let us distinguish between such a *bare disposition* and both a *cognitive/emotional disposition* and *moral disposition.* A cognitive/emotional disposition can manifest itself in subjective feelings and cognitive states and is reportable intersubjectively. A moral disposition has the features of the cognitive/emotional disposition as well as the features ascribed to moral sentiments by Ruse. If parents possess a moral disposition, they report that they feel morally obliged to care for their children and by that intend that these feelings have the characteristics of full-fledged prescriptivity and universality proper to moral norms and principles. What Ruse, therefore, needs to make his case for the primacy of nature in the origin of moral sentiments is *evidence* that moral sentiments are moral dispositions and that such sentiments are included states. But Ruse has failed to provide this evidence, either in the case of parental care or, his favorite example, the avoidance of sibling incest. Ruse seems to think that the phenomenon of incest avoidance is especially supportive for his position.

> We are going beyond the evidence as we argue that (in the human case) the way in which selection spurs us into biologically advantageous social action is by infusing our pertinent innate dispositions, our epigenetic rules, with a sense of moral obligation. However, we do now have a strong hypothesis—an hypothesis made yet more plausible when we recollect that the incest barrier, undoubtedly of biological value, is backed by a forceful sense of right and wrong. It is not just that you do not want to sleep with your sister/brother, but that you feel you should not. (Ruse 1985, p. 235)

Ruse has provided no evidence for this claim about moral dispositions nor, as far as we can determine, for any of the other examples of moral sentiments that he discusses.

In fact, the evidence for the development of conscience in children seems to indicate that different modes of parental moral training affect the type of conscience their children develop (Hoffman 1970; 1988; Raddke-Yarrow, Zahn-Waxler, and Chapman 1983). In a major review of theories of moral development, Hoffman (1988), argues that the evidence shows that the achievement of moral internalization, the ability to act on the basis of what is believed to be morally right, especially in situations of conflict with one's self interest, depends markedly on the kind of childrearing techniques used by parents. He distinguishes three types of childrearing techniques, power assertive, love withdrawal, and inductive. Only the latter shows correlation with moral internalization and Hoffman contends that there is good reason to think that the relationship is a causal one. In inductive techniques, parents point out to their children the beneficial and harmful effects of their actions on others in a manner appropriate to their ages. The use of power assertive and love withdrawal methods seem to produce children who act on the bases of the fear of punishment or the avoidance of anxiety. Internalization in the social psychological literature is usually investigated and discussed in the context of moral conflict between an individual's desires and the demands of morality. Although this is not the only context of moral action—consider, for instance, the person who has two conflicting moral demands—it is a prominent one and one that Ruse often envisages. Thus Ruse's account of the origin of moral sentiments in this kind of moral context appears to fail. Moreover, if it does not provide a suitable causal account of a such a significant portion of moral agency, the adequacy of his entire account becomes problematic. Be that as it may, there is reason to think that the prescriptivity and universality of the feelings associated with moral sentiments, in at least the conflict situations of concern to internalization theories, are differentially affected by the environment of moral training that the child experiences (even within the same culture!). On that basis we surmise that the dispositions that Ruse calls the moral sentiments do not constitute included states, even in the weakened version. In other words, the full-fledged prescriptivity and universality experienced and expressed in these situations is primarily the result of a certain kind of moral training not present in all or even most environments. So we conclude that these features of the moral sentiments are primarily due to nurture and not to nature.

Darwin (1871) argued that, as with other social species of animals, humans inherit basic social instincts, desires, for example, to help others and to be approved of by others. But in his view the development of a full blown moral sense, or conscience, requires a great deal more: "Ultimately our moral sense or conscience becomes a highly complex sentiment—originating in the social instincts, largely guided by the approbation of our fellow men, ruled by reason, self-interest . . . and confirmed by instruction and habit" (p. 178). In discussing Darwin's notion of the moral sense, Murphy (1982) provides for a way to understand the differences between the formal characteristics of prescriptivity and universality that we associate with morality in the full-fledged sense and what Darwin refers to as social instincts. In his interpretation of Darwin, Murphy distinguishes between primary desires (normal feelings) and secondary desires (moral feelings), desires about desires. Kitcher (1985) and others have also made extensive use of this distinction, introduced by Frankfurt (1971), to explicate a soft determinist account of freedom and moral responsibility. The second-level desires (and beliefs) regulate the first-level ones. Their prescriptivity and universality derive from this regulatory function and have the full-fledged character associated with norms and moral principles. The first-level desires and beliefs have only an analogue of those formal characteristics. Some of these first-level desires and beliefs may be the result of biologically based epigenetic rules. These, we believe, are properly designated moral sentiments. Ruse's characterization of moral sentiments, however, is more closely akin to Murphy's second-level desires and beliefs. But the second-level moral desires and beliefs are more plausibly understood to be primarily the result of learning processes, whether of imitation or symbolic learning and reasoning, including the inductive moral training discussed by Hoffman.

Moreover, if we take Ruse's characterization of prescriptivity as laid upon one literally, then from a Darwinian perspective normal and moral altruistic feelings do not seem to differ. For the characterization indicates a kind of probabilistic causal determination, an inclination to behave in a certain way. If both moral sentiments and feelings are the products of our genes and natural selection, both are laid upon us in the same way and both promote survival and reproduction.

Ruse tells us that moral sentiments are sometimes necessary to get the evolutionary job done (1986b, pp. 250–251). What he has in mind are cases of conflict between duty and selfishness or cases when more is asked of us than even our altruistic feelings are able to achieve. But these distinctions do not seem to call for a distinction in kind. A simpler and more empirically supportable position is to make no distinction in kind between moral and normal feelings. Normal feelings, whether self-regarding or other-regarding, incline us toward actions that generally promote survival and reproduction. And if reproduction and survival have required altruism, then evolution has shaped us so that altruistic inclinations are sufficiently strong in situations of conflict with selfish feelings that they win out often enough. On this account, prescriptivity and universality, at the level of moral sentiments, do not have the full-fledged phenomenological sense of being morally bound, but rather refer to both a behavioral inclination and whatever cognitive and motivational components that are associated with the genetically based analogues of this phenomenological sense. Nor need these inclinations include the notion that all in the moral community are bound as I feel that I am.

Thus we agree with Ruse that, as Darwin believed, humans possess biologically based altruistic dispositions. But we do not believe that he has provided sufficient evidence to show that these dispositions have the full-fledged moral modalities of prescriptivity and universality that are associated with the experiences of obligation and duty. These, we contend, are due to the acquisition of moral norms and principles. In our view, moral sentiments possess only a proto-prescriptivity and universality, deriving ultimately from their association with fitness and reproductive success, and of the same sort that attaches to any genetically based cognitive and behavioral disposition. The full-fledged prescriptivity and universality that Ruse ascribes to the moral sentiments belong rather to something like the Darwinian moral sense and are primarily the result of social/cultural learning. Thus we believe that Ruse has overextended his Darwinian base in explicating the prescriptivity and universality of moral sentiments.

The Weakening of Darwinism

In Ruse's view moral sentiments give us not only the sense of something imposed upon one, and all, but also of something forced upon us externally. Ruse believes that the first two perceptions are accurate but the last, though absolutely necessary, is illusory. Yet it is their apparent objectivity that really makes moral sentiments effective (1986b, p. 253). If that is so, and if moral sentiments are designed to win out over our selfish feelings and to supplement our altruistic feelings, we might expect that feelings would not even have the appearance of objectivity. They would clearly be subjective. But, on the contrary, they appear to be objective. Both feelings and moral sentiments seem to be externally imposed. Some things appear to be morally good or desirable in themselves. And some actions appear to be right or desirable in themselves. So I feel obliged or am desirous because of something about the objects of my obligations or desires. Aside from the phenomenological point, both feelings and moral sentiments are externally imposed by natural and social environmental selective forces acting on genetic variation. From a Darwinian perspective these causal factors, together with the moral sentiments themselves, are the sources of the goodness or desirability of objects. Thus, both phenomenologically and causally, values seem to be objective. Why, then, does Ruse hold that a Darwinian metaethician must think otherwise?[3]

Ruse is working with two distinct but related senses of both objectivity and subjectivity (1986b, pp. 213–217; 250–252). Values are objective either (1) if they exist independently of humans in some non-physical way or (2) if they are externally imposed. Values are subjective either (1) if without human nature there is no right or wrong or (2) if there is no source of morality independent of human nature. First, we should notice that the objectivity of external imposition does not imply the objectivity of non-physical independence. Nor does the denial of the latter imply the lack of external imposition. Values may be independent of human nature in a physical way and externally imposed. Indeed, this seems to be a plausible naturalistic position. Thus Ruse's rejection of Platonic, theistic, and Moorean accounts of values as independent of human nature in a non-physical fashion is not sufficient to support his contention that moral sentiments are not objective in the sense of being externally imposed (1986b, pp. 213–216). Second, with regard to subjectivity, we should note that the second sense of subjective, if taken to mean that human nature is a necessary and sufficient condition for constituting what is moral, is not implied by the first sense. Morality can be a function of human nature without being constituted by it. So Ruse's acceptance of subjectivism on the basis that both it and DME make morality a function of human nature is not enough to establish the claim that DME is subjectivist in the sense that morality is constituted by human nature.

Nor is morality's being subjective in the first sense of being a function of human nature incompatible with morality being objective in the second sense of being externally imposed. Thus Ruse cannot argue for the illusory character of values on the basis of their subjectivity. It is not clear to us that Ruse intends to do this. But it is clear, on Ruse's account, though we are not sure he recognizes it, that morality can be both a function of human nature and externally imposed, thus both subjective (sense # 1) and objective (sense # 2). Moreover, there seems to be no reason for the Darwinian to claim that the evolutionary forces that constitute human nature are not externally imposed and thus objective. Even if we consider the human genetic make-up as internal to human nature, the social and natural environmental selective forces are not. Only if morality is constituted by human nature, could one argue that it is not objective in either sense of the term. But to claim that morality is constituted by human nature contradicts Ruse's account of the moral sentiments. Human nature is a necessary, but not a sufficient, condition for the existence of moral sentiments since on the Darwinian account human nature itself depends on both genetic and selective environmental factors. Thus the claim that moral sentiments are illusory in the sense that they appear to be externally imposed but are not in fact so does not follow either from Ruse's acceptance of subjectivism nor his rejection of objectivism.[4]

But surely Ruse would respond that he is not denying the reality of the moral sentiments nor the evolutionary forces that created them. He is merely denying the objectivity of the values toward which these moral sentiments propel us. Food, shelter, clothing, warmth, and companionship are among these natural and social selective forces. They seem to be real enough. But are they objectively valuable? More precisely, do they possess objective moral properties? What prevents a Darwinian naturalist from holding that they do? Ruse addresses this question directly only once, as far as we can determine, and claims that an affirmative answer is a clear instance of NF (1984, p. 191). This blunt rejection of objective moral properties seems to put the philosophical cart before the scientific horse. A Darwinian naturalist ethicist, it seems to us, has prior commitments to naturalism and Darwinism. If these commitments lead her to claim, for instance, that food, shelter, and companionship have objectively valuable properties, then she must face Hume's Law straightforwardly. Ruse believes that he can do an "end run around Hume's Law" (1986b, p. 265). He seems rather to be running away from the line of scrimmage toward his own goal line. He avoids NF by giving up a robust Darwinian naturalism.

But, perhaps the situation is not as disastrous for Ruse as we have portrayed it. What Ruse might have in mind is that just as we attribute colors to objects, even though they are not really colored, so too we attribute objective value to objects and states of affairs even though they do not possess moral properties (Goldman 1987). There are indications that Ruse does have this notion of the illusory character of values in mind in his discussion of the Humean ancestry of Darwinian ethics (1987, p. 428; 1986b, pp. 261–269). So even though objects may have certain causal properties which along with normal perceptual conditions and normal perceivers generate the perception of colors and claims that objects are colored, we know now that colors are not in any straightforward sense of the term properties of objects. So too Ruse might want to argue that even though objects and states of affairs normally incite in the moral person by means of the moral sentiments judgments about values and morally right actions, these objects and situations do not possess properties of goodness or rightness. Food does, indeed, have causal properties that promote the health of the person who eats it and thus his or her survival and reproduction. It is good for the person in that sense. But it does not possess the property of goodness.

At most this response eliminates a straightforward objectivism about moral properties. It does not accomplish Ruse's goal of making values subjective in the sense of denying the existence of moral properties. In the case of colors, the realist can argue not only that there are objective sources for, but also objective referents of, the perception of colors. Micro-physical surface characteristics and electromagnetic radiation are the realities with which our visual perceptual system indirectly puts us in contact. Objectivity has not been abandoned; rather, naive realism has been replaced by scientific realism. Similarly, in the case of moral properties, a Darwinian can argue not only that there are objective sources for, but also objective referents of, the perception of values. But she need not claim that the moral sentiments are directly revelatory of the nature of the value properties of, for instance, food or companionship. Scientific accounts of these objective value properties and their causal sources may supplement or replace common-sense assessments. But their objectivity need not be denied.

A robust Darwinian has a general characterization of these properties which derives directly from evolutionary theory. They are the properties of the natural and social environment to which the person is adapted and in terms of which one can claim that the person is fit. As such they are relational properties. Just as fitness is a relational property of an individual organism so too are moral properties. Both terms of the relation are necessary and both terms can be denominated morally because of the relation. One term of that relation is, indeed, the human subject and his or her moral sentiments and actions. The other is the natural and social environment. For a robust Darwinian the terms of the relations and the relations are objective either from a common-sense or a scientific realist perspective or both. Thus there seem to be no reasons for either a naturalist or a Darwinian to make values illusory. A robust Darwinian does not need to weaken her Darwinism in the fashion Ruse does in order to present an adequate naturalistic account of the nature of morality.

To sum up, our position is that Ruse has distorted Darwinism in order to account for the content of the moral sentiments and overextended it to provide an adequate analysis of its prescriptive and universal modalities. By including self-regarding as well as other-regarding actions in the content of the moral sentiments we have remedied this distortion. Ruse's overextension of the Darwinian base can be fixed by attributing only an analogue of universal prescriptivity to the moral sentiments. Specific kinds of moral training are required for the full-fledged sense of universal prescriptivity that we might associate with Darwin's moral sense. In addition, Ruse has unnecessarily weakened his Darwinian bases by arguing for the illusory character of the values aimed at by the moral sentiments. Neither his rejection of objectivist metaethics nor his acceptance of subjectivist metaethics precludes the existence of moral properties and the objectivity of values. Indeed, there are good Darwinian and naturalistic reasons for maintaining that values are objective.

The Objective Nature of Morality and the Definitional Form of the Naturalistic Fallacy

From Ruse's perspective our argument for the objectivity of values is merely an attempt to raise the evolutionary ethical corpse over the eternal curse of Hume's Law. To identify the objects of moral sentiments or certain of their properties with moral goodness flies in the face of the definitional form of NF which prohibits the definition of moral properties in terms of natural properties. Indeed, Ruse believes that he has succeeded metaethically where TEE has failed previously because he has found a way to link the Darwinian naturalistic view of things to our fundamental understanding of morality and its explanation without committing NF. The key to his own success, Ruse believes, is the realization that the objectivity of values is in fact illusory. But we have argued that Ruse's contention that values are only apparently objective is not based on Darwinian principles. So Ruse's proposed end run round Hume's Law is really a retreat toward the Darwinians' own goal line. Ruse, we believe, gives up or surely weakens Darwinian naturalistic metaethics in order to avoid NF. But does our contention that values are objective put us on a collision course with Hume's Law?

We agree with Ruse (1986b, pp. 86–90) that there is something to the distinction between fact and value, but contend that a distinction can be maintained without resorting to Ruse's radical solution of making values illusory. A plausible interpretation of the distinction between fact and value and of the point of the Humean and Moorean injunctions, though not necessarily intended by those authors, is an anti-reductionist one: moral properties ought not to be reduced to non-moral properties (Edel 1980; Campbell and Pargetter 1986; and Ball 1988). And if moral properties are not to be identified with non-moral properties, they cannot be defined in terms of these properties. Consequently, the definitional form of the naturalistic fallacy is avoided.

Thus a robust Darwinian naturalist contends that some moral properties are biologically emergent relational properties of things and states of affairs, on the one hand, and human subjects, their moral sentiments, beliefs, actions and practices, on the other. These properties supervene on the other natural properties of persons and things (Campbell and Pargetter 1986). Moral properties are properties of the other natural properties of persons and things just as, for instance, biological fitness is a supervenient property of organisms (Sober 1984, pp. 48–51; and Cooper 1988, p. 208). Fitness is itself a measure of the chances an organism has for surviving and reproducing (Sober 1984, pp. 39–44). Understood as a dispositional property, its causal bases lie in the adaptive traits of the organism which has been selected for in a given environment (Sober 1984, pp. 196–211). But there is no single adaptation and environmental feature that makes for fitness in, for instance, antelopes or hawks. Nor, to use a different example, is there a single specification of chemical bondings that constitutes the dispositional property of malleability in clay and in dough. Similarly, moral goodness and rightness can be said to supervene on natural characteristics. Such diverse properties and states as pleasure, happiness, knowledge, and friendship can all be characterized as morally good and the action right that they might prompt or from which they might result. But no one of these natural properties can be identified with goodness and rightness. For each in proper circumstances can be both a source and a result of moral goodness and rightness. And each could, when associated with another property, pleasure with maliciousness, for instance, be morally evil and morally wrong.[5] Thus there seems to be good reason for not identifying moral goodness and rightness with any particular natural quality. Yet we have a way to understand them as objective properties of persons and things. Consequently, the robust Darwinian can avoid the definitional form of NF.

Indeed, Ruse (1986b, pp. 262–272; 1985) implicitly supports a notion of supervenience in his critique of Kant's thesis of a single morality for all rational persons. Moreover, it seems that he must make use of the doctrine of supervenience or be himself charged with committing the definitional form of NF. For Ruse claims that both the actions based on moral sentiments and the moral sentiments themselves are generally morally right even though ultimately they lack justification. Ruse, then, must show what natural, but subjective, property of the agent constitutes moral rightness. Otherwise, he is forced to deny that even the moral sentiments and the actions they inspire are morally right. A minimalist Darwinian can appeal to the supervenience of the subjective moral realm with respect to the various natural properties that constitute the moral sentiments and moral action. Thus, given Ruse's desire to avoid NF in its definitional form he must, if he is to avoid total ethical skepticism, invoke the doctrine of supervenience. And in so doing, he has in principle allowed for not merely a minimalist Darwinian account of moral properties but also for the robust one we are proposing. What, then, is the moral realm according to our robust account? And how can the moral sentiments be called morally good, the actions they incite morally right, and the goods they achieve moral?

In the first instance, the moral realm is the realm of conscious and free human actions concerning the moral good. Actions that achieve the moral good are morally right and the things and states of affairs they achieve are morally good. Consequently the moral realm is not only biologically but also culturally emergent. How do we make a connection, then, with the evolutionarily emergent? First, the robust Darwinian includes among the multiple moral goods those things and states of affairs that normally promote human adaptations, fitness, and survival and reproduction (S/R). Secondly, following the lead of Ruse, she appeals to the moral sentiments as genetically in-built cognitive, motivational and behavioral tendencies which as adaptations produce fitness and S/R. So, it is in part by means of the moral sentiments that humans discover the properties of things and states of affairs that promote their biological— and moral—ends and are motivated by the recognition of their value to possess these things and bring about these states of affairs. However, both the cognitive and the motivational content of the Rusean moral sentiments is, in our view, minimal and contrast sharply with that of the Darwinian moral sense which includes social cultural learning and reasoning. The moral sentiments, therefore, are merely the raw materials upon which socio-cultural learning and reasoning work and from which, with learning and reasoning, moral action ensues.

The moral attributes of a person's actions are distinguished generally from adaptations, the traits that promote human fitness, by the mode of their achievement. Although both fitness and moral properties are natural relational properties and supervene on other natural properties, the latter are achieved by the conscious, free activity of the person; the former is the result of genetic variation and natural selection. But, insofar as the moral sentiments, as adaptations brought about by genetic variation and natural selection, facilitate actions that are morally right and lead to states of affairs and objects that can be considered morally good, these sentiments themselves are morally good. This extension of the attribution of moral goodness to the moral sentiments is parallel to the familiar extension of moral rightness and goodness from actions to patterns of human activity, habitual ways of acting and their dispositional bases, thus enabling the discussion of moral virtues and character. Similarly, we can distinguish adaptive goods, those which generally make for human fitness and which are attained without conscious, free activity from those same goods as moral goods where their mode of realization or attainment is through conscious, free activity. These latter are the primary instantiations of moral goods. But these same goods, as objects of the moral sentiments, can be denominated as moral goods in a secondary, derivative sense. Thus we are claiming that part of human moral value is constituted by the relational triad of moral sentiments, as evolutionary adaptations, the objects to which they incline us, and the fitness that their achievement entails.

But why might a Darwinian naturalist want to postulate objective moral properties in things and states of affairs? So what if they can be understood as distinct from, because supervenient on, natural properties! Are they really necessary? There are two lines of argument that we will sketch briefly for postulating such properties. First, if humans possess moral sentiments as evolutionary adaptations and if they continue to promote fitness, both of which claims Ruse makes, then the Darwinian needs to maintain that there are selective factors that are causally responsible, along with genetic factors, for the maintenance of these moral sentiments. So, for instance, it is the particular properties of such environmental features as human social interactions that help maintain the adaptive actions of child care and the forming of friendships. And it is these adaptations that promote fitness and S/R. To deny the objectivity of these features of human social interactions seems to deny their causal role and thus to render the presence of the assumed adaptations inexplicable on Darwinian natural selectionist terms. Secondly, the particular adaptations we are discussing are cognitive, motivational, and behavioral dispositions to perform certain actions. On this basis it is arguably plausible, with respect to both the cognitive and the motivational aspects involved, that humans by means of these dispositional capacities recognize what is biologically valuable for them and are motivated to achieve or realize these valuable objects or states of affairs. On the level of conscious moral activity we find that people often explain why they did what they did in terms of an action being the right thing to do in the circumstances. In addition, they justify their moral judgments and beliefs about actions on the basis of their perceptions of the situation itself and what was going on in the situation (Railton 1986; Sturgeon 1984; 1986). Such common-sense realism is, of course, open to scrutiny (Harman 1977), but is not implausible. We believe that there is reason to extend it to actions that are facilitated by moral sentiments and to the beliefs and motivations that in part constitute moral sentiments.

But even if we avoid the clutches of the definitional form of NF, will not any attempt to justify moral actions and moral sentiments on the basis of our Darwinian metaethical claims about the objectivity of values fall into the deadly embrace of the derivational form of that fallacy?

The Justification of Morality and the
Derivational Form of the Naturalistic Fallacy

Justifications of morality are concerned with assessments of motivations, actions and beliefs. Our focus is ethical beliefs or claims. We take a naturalistic justification of ethical claims to be the use of empirical premises to provide adequate reasons for holding ethical conclusions. Empirical reasons are ones deriving directly or indirectly from our ordinary or refined perceptual capacities or the scientific theories based on these capacities. We distinguish two sorts of cognitivist naturalistic justification of ethical claims. The first holds that moral beliefs can be true or false depending on the presence of good-making and right-making characteristics, moral properties, in things. Call this objectivist naturalism and, when Darwinian principles are relied on, robust Darwinian ethical naturalism (RDEN). A second approach maintains that moral beliefs can be true or false, but they are so on the basis of whether they belong to the best coherent justificatory system available for the practices, conventions and principles that we happen to embrace. Call this second approach intersubjectivist naturalism and when Darwinian principles are involved minimalist Darwinian ethical naturalism (MDEN). RDEN and MDEN are two forms of cognitivist naturalism since they assert the possibility of truth or falsity for ethical claims. There are, of course, non-cognitivist forms.

By restricting Darwinian connections with ethics to causal links and maintaining that ultimate moral principles deriving from our biologically based moral sentiments are ultimately unjustifiable, Ruse has offered us an impoverished Darwinian metaethics. A MDEN involves no appeal to objective moral properties and seems perfectly compatible with Ruse's position on the illusoriness of objective values.

Indeed, some of Ruse's own arguments for substantive Darwinian ethical principles seem close to MDEN, for instance,
his appeals to a reflective equilibrium between ethical principles and the moral sentiments (Ruse, 1986b, pp. 76; 241).
Thus it does not follow from Ruse's rejection of the objectivity of values that he must give up all ultimate justification
of basic substantive ethical principles. But since several MDEN
positions have been developed elsewhere recently, we shall
not pursue further this alternative to Ruse's position (D.
Campbell, 1978; R. Campbell, 1984).[6] Rather, we shall sketch
an RDEN. However, we note that even if RDENs prove to be
flawed, Ruse's impoverished, non-justificational DME is not
the only alternative left to us. MDENs remain a viable alternative.

Ruse, we suppose, would have at least three objections
to our attempt to use Darwinian principles in a robust fashion to provide ultimate justifications for morals. First, our
proposal commits NF because it is merely an effort to resus-
citate TEEs, which are notorious for their failure in this regard. Second, attempts to justify substantive ethical claims
using Darwinian principles are bound to fail since they
confuse explanatory causes with justificatory reasons. Third,
such alleged justifications assume without warrant the objective goodness of human S/R. We contend that all these
objections fail and that Darwinian principles can provide
genuine, though limited, justifications for moral sentiments
and the principles based on them. Because of limitations of
space, we shall not directly address the challenge that our
proposal is a reincarnated TEE. We believe that there are
significant differences between our proposal and TEEs. No
matter whether our proposal is another TEE, we shall argue
that it does not commit the derivational form of NF.

Are we caught in the derivational form of NF? Given
our earlier account of the supervenience of moral properties,
the answer should be obvious. We can follow Frankena's
(1976) formula for avoiding NF by using some naturalistically formulated justificatory moral premises.[7] We have
adopted a non-reductionistic account of the moral realm,
according to which the moral properties of persons and
things, moral rightness and goodness, are distinct from

natural non-moral properties because they supervene on the latter. So the justificatory principles we appeal to can support basic substantive moral principles in a non-fallacious manner because these principles are themselves moral principles. We derive oughts from oughts and values from values, and postulate that among basic human values is the value of human fitness leading to S/R. On that basis we argue that the activities toward which the moral sentiments as fitness-inducing adaptations incline us can often be morally justified.

But this leads us to a second Rusean objection: Would not such a proposed justification confuse explanatory causes with justificatory reasons? Ruse contends that Darwinian metaethicists can explain moral sentiments but cannot justify them (1984, pp. 185–194; 1986a, p. 102; 1986b, pp. 256–258). Darwinian explanations of moral sentiments require evolutionary causal accounts of moral sentiments and these are available in terms of how moral sentiments promote S/R; but metaethical justifications would require evolutionarily based justificatory reasons for the moral goodness and rightness of moral sentiments. But none such are available and evolutionary explanatory causes are not suited to the job of serving as justificatory reasons since there is a fundamental distinction between causes and reasons.

How much would the invocation of the causes/reasons distinction assist Ruse? Not much. There doesn't seem to be much reason to insist upon a fundamental distinction between causes and reasons especially for a Darwinian and naturalist. Indeed, Ruse (1987) seems to have abandoned the distinction but without, it appears, realizing the implications of doing so for his claim that evolutionary theory can only explain, but not justify, moral sentiments. Regardless, it seems beyond dispute now that the original bases for making a fundamental distinction between actions based on reasons and behaviors based on causes—that actions are logically related to the reasons that accounted for them, but causes are not so related to the events they produce—is not tenable (Scarrow 1981). So we can reject the consequences of such a view, namely that the sciences are confined to the empirical investigation of the contingent connections be-

tween causes and effects while some other sort of investigation, conceptual analysis, perhaps, displays the necessary
relationships between reasons and human behavior. Indeed,
reasons (considered as wants/desires and beliefs) can be
causes of actions (Scarrow 1981). In the ordinary sense of a
factor which produces something, reasons are a factor, certainly not the only factor, in the effecting of action. Moreover, in the sense of necessary and sufficient conditions for
an action, reasons are necessary conditions for actions. And
reasons can be appealed to in order to predict and explain
actions. On the other hand, causes can serve as reasons. The
case of perception seems to be a clear one. We can appeal
to both a well-functioning perceptual system, normal perceptual circumstances, and the causal operation of the object of perception on our perceptual system in order not only
to explain a perception but to justify a perceptual claim
(Kitchener 1987; Kornblith 1985). Thus, it seems to us that
the Darwinian naturalist, in her appeal to genetic variation
and natural selective forces to account for moral sentiments,
can provide not only a causal explanation of these sentiments but a reasoned justification for them.

How would this justification go? What makes an action
good in the most fundamental sense in a DME, what justifies it, is that it promotes human adaptations and, thereby,
fitness leading normally to S/R. That is its ultimate justification. A person who appeals to the ultimate Darwinian
metaethical principle to justify his or her action is using
that principle as a justificatory reason. That reason can move
the person to act if she has adopted in a consistent manner
a Darwinian ethics. And it can be used to justify her actions.
Moreover, *ex hypothesi*, natural selection and genetic variation cause the moral sentiments which may motivate the
moral action that promotes these ends. Thus the Darwinian
can also appeal to moral sentiments as a justificatory reason since these sentiments as adaptations, would be reliable
mechanisms for the discernment of the moral ends involved.
Consequently, the Darwinian can appropriate on the level
of conscious-free activity what can also motivate on the level
of Rusean moral sentiments without the intervention of moral
reasoning and freedom.

But even if it is granted that our proposed justification is not fallacious because it neither commits the derivational form of NF nor because it confuses explanatory causes with justificatory reason, how good a justification is it? Does it not assume without warrant the objective value of S/R? Our appeal to the value of S/R, and thus to human fitness and the biological adaptations that promote it, is necessarily limited for both extrinsic and intrinsic reasons. First, the intrinsic reasons. What constitutes human fitness is intrinsically indeterminate in at least two important ways. Human fitness does not, for instance, determine the particular biological goods whose achievement enable it. Although we must have food and protection from cold in order to be fit, the particular foodstuffs and type of clothing are not specified merely biologically. They are determined primarily by culture. In addition, the scope of human fitness as a moral value does not seem to be determined biologically. It is not clear to us that the evolutionarily based value of human fitness includes all humans; but this is a controversial point that we cannot pursue here.[8]

Secondly, human fitness is extrinsically limited as a value in several ways. The Darwinian naturalist need not claim that human fitness is the only, nor necessarily the highest, of a variety of naturalistically identifiable values. She is a value pluralist. She holds that in addition to the primarily biologically based value of human fitness there are other, primarily culturally based human values, for instance, science, mathematics and art. Furthermore, she can claim that there are other non-human biological values, for instance, the continued existence and flourishing of non-human organisms. The former supposition, that there are primarily culturally based human values is, we believe, non-controversial and perfectly compatible with both Darwinism and naturalism. The postulation of nonhuman biological values is controversial (Calicott 1984). We make it only to clarify our position and cannot argue for it here.

But granting both the intrinsic indeterminateness of the value of human fitness and its extrinsic limitations by other, primarily cultural human values and biological, non-human values, human S/R is a necessary condition for both cultural human values and culturally specified biological human values. (It goes without saying that at present there is a severe conflict between some human values and the fitness of other organisms.) Thus we believe that the value of human fitness can serve a justificatory role for the value of the objects of the moral sentiments and must, as a necessary condition for other above-mentioned values, be presupposed as valuable in any justification of these values, or actions based on these values. As such, human S/R is not a mere instrumental value, that is, one that can be set aside in the achievement of some goal. So in this narrowly conceived fashion our claim about the value of human fitness and S/R is not, it seems to us, completely unwarranted. For their value is supported both by the fact that they are necessary conditions for the achievement of what we deem to be intrinsically, or, at least, independently valuable, and because they are often valued in themselves.

Thus we believe that our DME provides a way to understand how appeals to human fitness, including human S/R, can function in the justification of moral actions without committing the derivational form of NF. In addition, we believe that such justifications have *prima facie* adequacy. But this brings us to a final objection. Someone may object that our claim about the justificatory role for the value of human S/R is either circular or both trivial and unnecessary. Indeed, we grant that the charge of circularity is not without merit, given our limited discussion of justification. Our contention, however, is that, as with other causal theoretical justification, the seeming circularity—instances leading to theory which is then reciprocally confirmed by those very instances—is not necessarily vicious. The decisive test is whether the theory is fruitful both in generating further predictive implications that are themselves confirmed and in explaining phenomena otherwise left unexplained or not as well explained by other competing theories. Indeed, the value of human S/R does lead to the explanation and justification of some value phenomena, for instance, human sociality and the general ordering of value priorities, phenomena which seem to be less well explained and justified in other value theories. For example, contractual theories of society seem less plausible than the evolutionary one. And the general preference to fulfill needs for food, warmth and companionship before fulfilling those for learning for its own sake are better explained on the basis of an evolutionary ethical theory. Thus we believe that the charge of circularity is not *prima facie* destructive of our position.

It might still be argued that such a normative Darwinian justification is both trivial and unnecessary since it merely restates what we know full well without it by means of common-sense ethical perceptions. We believe that this would be the case only if the account of the evolutionary good merely reiterated the common-sense insight that the flourishing of humans is good, but, in fact, it does more than that. Evolutionary theory refines the claim and can, indeed, help specify more precisely the form of that flourishing, given, for instance, various environmental/populational pressures. In addition, the fact that our DME is in agreement with common-sense ethical insight lends it some support. However, since most ethical theories, even some non-naturalistic theories, reflect common-sense ethical insight and thus are confirmed by it, Darwinian ethics does not receive decisive support from it over these other theories. But those theories as a group are supported over ethical theories that might hold that human extinction in support of certain ideals is better than a human existence that compromises these ideals, the "better-dead-than-Red" class of ethical theories.

Finally, we believe that Ruse's understanding of the derivational form of the fallacy may reveal that he has misconceived naturalistic justification. Ruse seems to demand of those who seek a justification the kind of foundationalist account so beloved of both the rationalist and empiricist epistemological traditions. On this view, justification cannot proceed unless one has certainty about one's premises, whether that certainty is achieved rationalistically or empirically. Ruse's skepticism seems premised on the inability to attain such certainty about intrinsic goods. Ruse seems to reason that unless we have established that human S/R is objectively intrinsically good, then none of the means to these goods are objectively intrinsically good either. So we have to give up the objectivity of our moral sentiments, both individually and collectively. This is a very high price to pay, too high, we believe. An approach much more compatible with the scientific naturalism that Ruse seems to espouse is to conceive of justification as a fallible process. Indeed, Ruse himself seems to embrace this kind of fallibility in his account of Darwinian epistemology (Ruse 1986b, p. 206). On this score, then, the Darwinian ultimate principle of moral justification, formulated realistically, i.e., in terms of the intrinsic goodness of human adaptations, fitness and S/R, can be considered a tentative, incomplete principle that serves both to explain why some of the physical things and states of affairs that we accurately perceive to be morally good are so, and to justify actions attempting to secure or realize them.

Conclusion

We have examined Michael Ruse's proposals for a naturalistic, Darwinian metaethics and have found them wanting both from a naturalistic and a Darwinian perspective. In particular, Ruse has distorted Darwinism in his account of the nature of the moral sentiments by restricting the content of morality to other-regarding actions, and has overextended his Darwinian bases in order to account for the universal and prescriptive form of morality. These faults in his account of moral sentiments can be remedied by showing that a genuinely Darwinian view would include self-regarding actions in their content and must involve not only moral sentiments but Darwin's moral sense, which includes considerable learning and moral reasoning, in order to account for the universality and prescriptivity of morality. In addition, Ruse has unnecessarily weakened his Darwinian roots in attempting to avoid NF. In order to avoid the definitional and derivational forms of NF, he has denied both the objectivity of the values toward which the moral sentiments incline us, and the possibility of any justification of the actions based on these moral sentiments. We have accepted Ruse's view that the point of NF is to remind us of a genuine separation of fact and value. But that separation can be preserved without relinquishing naturalistic and Darwinian principles, something we contend Ruse has done. Thus we have opted to avoid the naturalistic fallacy by using evolutionary theory to interpret values as emergent natural properties, refusing to reduce them to non-moral natural properties. Human adaptations, fitness and its usual consequences of survival and reproduction become the central features of a biologically based human moral good. Although this good is limited both intrinsically insofar as it is indeterminate about specific biological goods and extrinsically insofar as there are both culturally based human goods and biological non-human goods, it can be used to provide not only a partial causal explanation of the activities prompted by Ruse's moral sentiments and Darwin's moral sense, but also a partial justification of these actions. We conclude that Ruse's metaethics has failed because he has not taken Darwin seriously enough. A stronger, more competitively viable Darwinian metaethics can be achieved by doing just that, really taking Darwin seriously.

References

Alexander, R. 1987. *The Biology of Moral Systems.* New York: Adline de Gruyter.

Ball, S. 1988. "Reductionism in Ethics and Science: A Contemporary Look at G. E. Moore's Open Question Argument." *American Philosophical Quarterly* 25: 197–214.

Brink, D. 1984. "Moral Realism and the Skeptical Arguments from Disagreement and Queerness." *Australasian Journal of Philosophy* 62: 111–125.

———. 1989. *Moral Realism and the Foundations of Ethics.* New York: Cambridge University Press.

Calicott, J. 1984. "Non-Anthropocentric Value Theory and Environmental Ethics." *American Philosophical Quarterly* 21: 299–309.

Campbell, D. 1978. "Social Morality as Evidence of Conflict Between Biological Human Nature and Social Requirement." In G. Stent, ed., *Morality as a Biological Phenomenon,* pp. 75–92. Berlin: Abakon Verlagsgesellschaft.

Campbell, J, and Pargetter, R. 1986. "Goodness and Fragility." *American Philosophical Quarterly* 23: 155–165.

Campbell, R. 1984. "Sociobiology and the Possibility of Ethical Naturalism." In D. Copp and D. Zimmerman, eds., *Morality, Reason and Truth*, pp. 270–296. Totowa, N.J.: Rowan and Allanheld.

Churchland, P. M., and Hooker, C. 1985. *Images of Science: Essays on Realism and Empiricism with a Reply from Bas C. van Fraassen*. Chicago: University of Chicago Press.

Cooper, G. 1988. "Fitness and Explanation." In A. Fine and J. Leplin, eds., *PSA 1988: Proceedings of the 1988 Biennial Meeting of the Philosophy of Science Association*, pp. 207–215. East Lansing, Mich.: Philosophy of Science Association.

Darwin, C. 1871. *The Descent of Man and Selection in Relation to Sex*, 2 vols., London: John Murray.

Edel. A. 1980. *Exploring Fact and Value*, Vol. 2, *Science, Ideology and Value*. New Brunswick, N.J.: Transaction Books.

Flanagan, O., Jr. 1982. "Quinean Ethics." *Ethics* 93: 56–74.

Frankena, W. 1976. "Naturalistic Fallacy." In K. Goodpaster ed., *Perspectives in Morality*. Notre Dame, Ind.: Notre Dame Press.

Frankfurt, H. 1971. "Freedom of the Will and the Concept of a Person." *Journal of Philosophy* 6S: 5–20.

Gibbard, A. 1982. "Human Evolution and the Sense of Justice." In P. French, T. Uehling, Jr., and H. Wettstein eds., *Midwest Studies in Philosophy*, Vol. 7. *Social and Political Philosophy*, pp. 31–46. Minneapolis: The University of Minnesota Press.

Goldman, A. 1987. "Red and Right." *Journal of Philosophy* 84, 349–362.

Harman, G. 1977. *The Nature of Morality*. Oxford: Oxford University Press.

Hoffman, M. 1970. "Moral Development." In P. Mussen ed., *Carmichael's Manual of Child Psychology*, 3rd ed., pp. 261–359. New York: John Wiley & Sons.

———. 1988. "Moral Development." In M. Bornstein and M. Lamb, eds., *Developmental Psychology: An Advanced Textbook*. Hillsdale, N.J.: Lawrence Erlbaum Associates.

Hooker, C. 1987. A *Realistic Theory of Science*, Albany: State University of New York Press.

Kitchener, R. 1987. "Is Genetic Epistemology Possible?" *British Journal for the Philosophy of Science* 38: 283–299.

Kitcher, P. 1985. *Vaulting Ambition: Sociobiology and the Quest of Human Nature.* Cambridge, Mass.: MIT Press.

————. et al. 1987. "Precis of Vaulting Ambition: Sociobiology and the Quest for Human Nature, Open Peer Commentary and Author's Response." *Behavior and Brain Sciences* 10: 61–100.

Kohlberg, L. 1983. *Essays in Moral Development,* Vol. 2, *The Psychology of Moral Development: The Nature of and Validity of Moral Stages.* New York: Harper and Row.

Kornblith, H., ed. 1985. *Naturalizing Epistemology.* Cambridge, Mass.: MIT Press.

Leplin, J., ed. 1984. *Scientific Realism.* Berkeley: University of California Press.

Lumsden, C., and Wilson, E. 1981. *Genes, Mind and Culture.* Cambridge Mass.: Harvard University Press.

Mackie, J. 1977. *Ethics Inventing Right and Wrong.* Harmondsworth: Penguin.

Murphy, J. 1982. *Evolution, Morality and the Meaning of Life.* Ottawa: Rowman and Littlefield.

Raddke-Yarrow, M., C. Zahn-Waxler, and M. Chapman. 1983 "Children's Prosocial Development and Behavior." in P. Mussen, ed., *Handbook of Child Psychology,* 4th ed., Vol. IV, E. Hetherington (vol. ed.), *Socialization, Personality, and Social Development,* pp. 469–546. New York: John Wiley & Sons.

Railton, P. 1986. "Moral Realism." *Philosophical Review* 95: 163–207.

Richards, R. 1986a. "A Defense of Evolutionary Ethics." *Biology and Philosophy* 1: 265–292.

————. 1986b. "Justification Through Biological Faith: A Rejoinder." *Biology and Philosophy* 1: 337–354.

————. 1987, *Darwin and the Emergence of Evolutionary Theories of Mind and Behavior.* Chicago: University of Chicago Press.

Ruse, M. 1979. *Sociobiology: Sense or Nonsense?* Dordrecht: Reidel.

————. 1984. "The Morality of the Gene." *The Monist* 67: 167–199.

————. 1985. "Is Rape Wrong on Andromeda?" in E. Regis, ed., *Extraterrestrials,* pp. 43–78, Cambridge: Cambridge University Press

————. 1986a. "Evolutionary Ethics: A Phoenix Arisen." *Zygon* 21: 95–112.

————. 1986b. *Taking Darwin Seriously.* Oxford: Basil Blackwell.

———. 1987. "Darwinism and Determinism." *Zygon* 21: 419–422.

——— and Wilson, E. 1986. "Ethics as Applied Science." *Philosophy* 61: 173–192.

Scarrow, D. 1981. "The Causality of Reason: A Survey of Some Recent Developments in the Mind-Body Problem." *Metaphilosophy* 12: 13–30.

Singer, P. 1981. *The Expanding Circle: Ethics and Sociobiology.* New York: Farrar, Strauss and Geroux.

Sober, E. 1984. *The Nature of Selection: Evolutionary Theory in Philosophical Focus.* Cambridge, Mass.: MIT Press.

Sturgeon, N. 1984. "Moral Explanation." In D. Copp and D. Zimmerman, eds., *Morality, Reason and Truth*, pp. 79–103. Totowa, N.J.: Rowan and Allanheld.

———. 1986. "Harman on Moral Explanations of Natural Facts." *Southern Journal of Philosophy* 24, Supplement: 69–78.

Wilson, E. 1975. *Sociobiology: The New Synthesis.* Cambridge, Mass.: Harvard University Press.

———. 1978. *On Human Nature.* Cambridge, Mass.: Harvard University Press.

Notes

1. We shall distinguish below between a robust Darwinian naturalism that postulates objective moral properties and a minimalist Darwinian naturalism that does not make such assumptions. Our contention is that Ruse unnecessarily relinquishes both sorts of naturalisms in order to avoid the naturalistic fallacy. Both robust and minimalist Darwinian naturalisms, as well as Ruse's own Darwinian naturalism as we interpret it, presuppose a realist account of evolutionary theory, that is, one that takes claims about the causal factors of evolution, for instance, natural selection and genetic endowment, to be capable of truth and falsity, and postulates that the terms of the theory have referential capacity. We assume that evolutionary theory is more than a conceptual device to facilitate the organization of our thoughts and enhance our predictive powers. For recent general discussions of the issue of scientific realism, sec Churchland and Hooker 1985; Hooker 1987; and Leplin, 1984.

2. Jeffrie Murphy, although very supportive of Darwin's and Wilson's accounts of the biological bases of ethics, criticizes the former for not attending enough to the properly ethical character of self-regarding activity. Thus Ruse may be closer to Darwin on this score than we are.

3. Ruse's view that values are subjective reflects Mackie's (1977) well-known stance against the objectivity of moral facts, although Ruse does not employ Mackie's arguments from moral disagreement and queerness to support his own stance. Brink (1984; 1989) addresses Mackie's arguments directly and Campbell and Pargetter (1986) set for themselves the task of meeting Mackie's call for some account of the supervenience relation between moral facts and natural facts.

4. Ruse raises the specter of metaphysical skepticism in his discussion of evolutionary epistemology and does not appear very sanguine about overcoming it (1986b, pp. 192–206). We set aside this issue since neither Darwinian nor naturalistic considerations require such radical skepticism and its acceptance seems to render a discussion of the subjectivity of values otiose by calling into question the reality of the human nature upon which Ruse builds his discussion of the subjectivity and objectivity of values.

5. It might be suggested that the dispositional property in question could be identified with the disjunction of its bases, for instance, malleability with a disjunction of the chemical bondings that constitute its various bases. Campbell and Pargetter (1986, p. 157) suggest several reasons why this is not a very promising strategy.

6. Richmond Campbell has developed such a view and Donald Campbell's hypothetical Darwinian ethics might be interpreted as a MDEN. Allan Gibbard (1982), on the other hand, has sketched a non-cognitivist account of a biologically based moral sentiment of justice.

7. Most moral philosophers in this century have taken NF very seriously. We do too, although as naturalists we contend that it can be avoided without resorting to non-naturalism. Some naturalistic philosophers, for example, Flanagan (1982) following Quine, have interpreted the difficulties raised by NF as an instance of the general problem of the underdetermination of empirical hypotheses by their supporting evidence. Although we believe that there is a way to understand our account of NF and how to avoid it that fits this interpretation, we do not agree with an anonymous referee who indicates that NF is merely the fallacy of drawing a necessary conclusion about a particular case from a statistical hypothesis.

8. Ruse's biological mentor, Wilson, makes the entire human gene pool the object of his first cardinal principle concerning values (1978, pp. 196–197). At the other extreme, Richard Alexander (1987, pp. 33–41) seems to limit the scope of human fitness as a value to a person's family and rather immediate relatives. Peter Singer (1981) seems to stand between the extremes.

John Collier and Michael Stingl

Evolutionary Naturalism and the Objectivity of Morality

ABSTRACT: We propose an objective and justifiable ethics that is contingent on the truth of evolutionary theory. We do not argue for the truth of this position, which depends on the empirical question of whether moral 1 functions form a natural class, but for its cogency and possibility. The position we propose combines the advantage of Kantian objectivity with the explanatory and motivational advantage of moral naturalism. It avoids problems with the epistemological inaccessibility of transcendent values, while avoiding the relativism or subjectivism often associated with moral naturalism. Our position emerges out of criticisms of the contemporary sociobiological views of morality found in the writings of Richard Alexander, Michael Ruse, and Robert Richards.

1. Introduction

In traditional Kantian ethics, moral values are objective only if they do not depend on any particular motivational structure. The justification of morality, on this view, can safely ignore facts about human motivation and desire, although these will, of course, be relevant for judging the moral value of particular acts. But neither fundamental moral values nor their moral force are dependent on the particular facts of the human world. Rational creatures are supposed to be able to be moved to act morally by reason alone, no matter what their desires might be. The commands of morality are thus underwritten by the commands of pure reason, which is the presumed source of objective reasons for action for

Reprinted by permission of Kluwer Academic Publishers, "Evolutionary Naturalism and the Objectivity of Morality," *Biology & Philosophy* 8: 47–60 (1993), © 1993 D. Reidel Publishing Company.

any creature with the capacity for rational thought. Naturalists typically deny the cogency of this transcendent objectivity: they believe that moral values can move us only because of causal connections to what Hume called the passions. They hold that the either or both of the explanation and justification of morality must consider certain general desires, for example, pleasure. Evolutionary naturalists believe, in particular, that morally relevant human motivation, and consequently our moral values, are significantly constrained by evolution. They are thereby distinguished from naturalists who believe that the morally significant aspects of our motivational structure are fundamentally a matter of social conditioning or personal choice.

In the current literature, there are three progressively stronger positive positions on the relevance of evolution to morality. The weakest holds only that moral behaviour and capacities can be given an evolutionary explanation in terms of adaptive processes. population genetics, and epigenetic rules, but says nothing about moral values themselves. This position is compatible with Kantian ethics. A stronger position holds that moral values themselves can be given a biological explanation. This position conflicts with Kantian ethics, rendering it either false or superfluous. An even stronger position holds that not only can evolutionary theory explain fundamental moral values, but it can also justify them. The weakest of these three positions is purely descriptive; for the sake of argument we will assume it in the rest of this paper. We will be concerned with the stronger positions, which start with evolutionary facts and end with moral values.

The strongest current position, due to Richards (1986, 1987), holds that biology can both explain and justify fundamental moral values. However, because it takes these values to be species specific, it does not give us general moral principles. After discussing and criticising the current views, we will propose a view that is explanatory, justificatory, and provides general moral principles. Our proposal implies that morality is contingent on the facts of evolution, but is specific only to a general type of creature: evolved, intelligent, and social. On our view, inherited moral instincts can be articulated, refined, and even corrected by discovering more about the true character of natural morality as it emerges according to the laws of evolution in our world. We reject the view that there are universal (categorical) moral principles or values that apply to all rational beings irrespective of their origin. We propose that in our world, and in worlds nomologically similar to ours, morality exists when there are intelligent social creatures who are products of typical evolutionary processes.[1]

2. Contemporary Sociobiological Positions on Morality

Richard Alexander (1979, 1987) has the most complete descriptive account of the biological basis of moral behaviour. Although it differs in details from other sociobiological accounts, the main patterns are similar. Adaptive processes acting on small bands of humans and proto-humans produced instincts that promoted not only individual survival, but also an overlay of nepotistic, reciprocal altruistic and true altruistic instincts capable of overriding individual interests, all in the service of the ultimate end of gene survival. As society developed, these instincts were articulated according to epigenetic rules into social conventions and laws in an increasingly complex social environment. The adaptations and implied epigenetic rules are analogous to the "universal grammar" that Chomsky proposed for language, whereas the particular social expression of these rules is, like the surface structure of language, variable from culture to culture. Moral function, like grammatical function, is determined by the deep structure, not its surface manifestation. Alexander holds in particular that our inherited behavioural adaptations constitute social atoms that combine according to the contingencies of particular cultural histories to yield functional moral systems. Our true motives are concealed from us because they are not cognitive, but are there to be discovered and enhanced as we progress towards universal beneficence. Alexander's cynicism about the selfish motives of our genetic heritage is balanced by his optimism about our capacity to discover these motives and marshall them to our (collective) benefit.

Alexander, however, believes that sociobiology can contribute only to the first task of explaining our moral instincts and behaviour. Biology can tell us how our moral sense evolved, its physiological basis, the relations between the capacities and our behaviour, and their evolutionary value. These explanations will have moral consequences, because understanding the basis of our behaviour makes it possible for us to modify it more effectively. The biological story can tell us what is good for us, but this isn't enough to create moral obligation. Alexander presumes that there are morally preferable ways for us to act independently of biology. On his view, true moral obligation arises through the interaction of biological value with independent moral ends.

Michael Ruse is a major proponent of the second position in our hierarchy (1986, 1990). He agrees that biology is not the source of moral obligation, but denies there is an objective morality that is any practical concern of ours. He argues that moral phenomena can be explained adequately by biology, and that any postulation of an additional objective morality is gratuitous, since there is nothing left over to explain. Furthermore, a transcendent objective morality, if it did exist, would be irrelevant, since it is epistemically inaccessible. We have no way of knowing, Ruse says (personal communication), that God doesn't want us to torture innocent babies. On the other hand, Ruse believes that the naturalistic fallacy rules out inferring moral imperatives from the fact that we have those values, so there is no internal, evolutionary justification of morality (Ruse 1986, pp. 256–258). By denying that moral values can be justified objectively, he commits the naturalistic fallacy. Since there is no justification of morality, there is no need to explain why, for example, obligations have moral force. Morality, on Ruse's view, is a contingent phenomenon with no objective justification. Morality is objective in the sense that our moral goods are determined by our evolution and our circumstances (Ruse and Wilson 1986,

p. 188), but these moral goods are not rationally justifiable, except inasmuch as we have species-relative and history-dependent practical justifications for our moral activity (Ruse 1984, p. 177).

Ruse offers a mischievous argument that we have nevertheless been selected for a propensity to believe that morality is objective (Ruse and Wilson 1986, p. 179; Ruse 1986, pp. 253–256). Since our moral instincts are adaptive, and their function is stronger and more secure if we believe our morality is objective, Ruse proposes that we will develop adaptations leading us to believe our morality is objective. John Mackie (1977, p. 109) and Gilbert Harman (1977) gave earlier variants of this argument in which the apparent objectivity of ethics is a social adaptation that enhances social order. These arguments tell us that we cannot rely solely on our intuitions about the truth of moral statements. They are mischievous because they question the need for an objective justification morality. Anyone who wants objective justification must show not only that satisfying the demand is epistemically possible, but also that the criteria that must be satisfied are not equally illusory. Both religious and rationalistic justifications of morality tend to beg the question on the issue. Without mischievous, there is, no doubt, a *prima facie* case for relying on our moral intuitions. But if it is even plausible that moral objectivity might be an consider the biological and sociological evidence.

But even more important for our purposes here is the positive rule [sic]. Ruse gives the mischievous argument in explaining our sense of moral obligation:

> . . . the Darwinism especially wants to keep the is/ought barrier the whole point about moral altruism is to get us to do something we would not otherwise do. Struggle and selection obviously incline one towards selfishness. . . . However, sometimes biological altruism is a good tactic, and so we need an extra push. This is to be found in the peculiar nature of biological altruism: obligation. Without a feeling of obligation, we are all going to start to cheat, and biological altruism will collapse. (1990, p. 65)

The mischievous argument indicates the source of the required obligation. Our presumed adaptation to believe our morality is objective creates an illusion of moral obligation (usually encoded in religion or other ideology) that restricts cheating: "The simple point is that unless we believe morality to be objective . . . it will not work. If everyone recognized the illusory nature of morality . . . then very soon people would start to cheat and the whole social system would collapse" (1990, p. 66). Ruse's epistemic argument against transcendent objectivism cannot be dismissed lightly. On the one hand he undermines claims that we can know what everything is to explain about morality, including our most fundamental moral intuitions, especially the intuition that we ought to act morally. The facts of our moral system, including our sense of moral objectivity, can be explained on Ruse's account without assuming transcendent objective moral values, or indeed, anything more than practical values that we have an innate propensity to think of as moral.

Robert Richards (1986, 1987), a proponent of the third position, argues (like Ruse) that ultimately all fundamental principles must be justified by reference to facts, and that, if justifying norms by facts is fallacious, there can be no justification of norms (1987, p. 620). On the other hand, he holds that the naturalistic fallacy is not a fallacy at all, and offers three justifying arguments for evolutionary ethics. Two directly address objectivity. For the sake of argument, both assume that community welfare has evolved to be the highest moral goal among humans (Richards 1987, p. 620).[2] Community welfare is a rough notion; other similarly rough moral notions could be substituted without damaging the arguments. Suitable candidates would be based in instinctive drives that can override individual interests and allow for ample variation according to particular circumstances.

Richard's first argument establishes that we have reasons to act morally. He assumes that humans are genetically constrained to hold community welfare as the highest good. On recognising this, we ought to pursue this goal in order to achieve it more effectively. This follows from the tenets of practical reason: if we have a certain goal, and that goal will most likely be reached by adopting certain methods, we should adopt those methods. Given the speculative assumption that we have evolved a goal of achieving the greater communal good (or some similar altruistic end, which he terms "moral sense"), we should try to do things that achieve this end. The "should" in this case is a moral should because of the moral context of the adaptive process—the adaptation functions in a moral context. Put simply, we have evolved so that the function of moral activity is to achieve the greater communal good. Thus moral activity is justified by its contribution to this end, and we have a practical reason to act morally. This is compatible with Ruse's position, but it gives us no reason to place moral reasons above other practical reasons, the only difference being in the context of the reasons.

Despite Richards' claim that the practical "ought" is a moral "ought" because of' the moral context (1987, p. 622), this argument does not really explain moral obligation, since we have also evolved non-moral or even immoral ends which are subject to the same practical justification. The problem is that while the argument claims that certain practical oughts are also moral oughts because of the ends they aim for, it does nothing to establish the morality of the ends themselves. Richards recognises this problem, and replies with his second argument: " . . . the evidence shows that evolution has, as a matter of fact, constructed human beings to act for the community good; but to act for the community good is what we mean by being moral. Since, therefore, human beings are moral beings . . . each ought to act for the community good" (1987, pp. 623, 624). The circumstances of evolution constrain what we could mean by "moral end" to ends evolved in moral contexts. Still, it isn't clear how meaning is tied to past adaptations. Furthermore, it is not clear that Richards hasn't simply pushed the problem with his first argument further back. The question is, why should we suppose that what we have evolved to mean by morality has anything more to do with morality itself than the fact that we have evolved into creatures with certain sorts of ends? This issue is crucial; we will return to it below. If Richards' meaning argument fails, his position reduces to Ruse's.

3. Critique of the Contemporary Positions

In the next section we will propose a position that has been overlooked in the current literature. Although the position is attractive in its own right, we introduce it by way of what we take to be crucially mistaken in each of the current positions. Examining the nature of these mistakes yields a more credible defence of our proposal. In this section we will discuss both the mistakes and what they obscure.

Alexander's story of the origins of morality is both vague and incomplete, not to mention deficient of empirical support. It is questionable whether his supposed social atoms even exist, let alone whether they can be combined in the simple way he suggests. His story of the relation between the ultimate causes of genes and the proximate motives of individual humans is confusing and conceptually muddled (for criticism, see Collier 1991 and references therein). Furthermore, Alexander commits the mistake, endemic to current sociobiology, of reading current views of morality back into the biological story, rather than letting biology speak for itself. This error is at least in part the result of a selectionist methodology that first assumes that current behaviours are optimal, and then looks for an explanation in term of prior adaptations. Alexander takes this to such an extreme that he argues that we need not look at the proximate causes of our behaviour at all in order to understand their function. Although other sociobiologists are not so blatant, their arguments commonly start with observed behaviour, give a story about how such behaviour might enhance gene survival, and conclude that the behaviour is the consequence of a genetic adaptation expressed through epigenetic rules (see, for example, Kitcher 1985, pp. 126–127 for this criticism of Wilson). Both Ruse and Richards subscribe to something close to selectionism. We reject the optimality implicit in his methodology, and hope thereby to avoid the tendency to rationalise current practice or ideals with biological fairy tales. Nonetheless, we will assume with Alexander and other sociobiologists that our morally relevant instincts are fairly complex and form the precognitive basis of concepts like altruism, beneficence and justice, which we later discover through reflection. These instincts are good for us (or for our genes) in much the same way that drinking clear fluids can be good for us.[3] Our intelligence gives us the capacity to discover these goods, but the instinct and behaviour precede the discovery.

Ruse's moral scepticism is supported independently by either his invocation of the naturalistic fallacy, or his assumption that evolution optimises adaptation (personal communication). If our adaptations are optimised, there is no basis for questioning whether or not our evolved ethical "deep structures" are correct or appropriate. Ruse's optimistic view of adaptation requires that we could not evolve moral instincts superior to the ones we have evolved, so questions about the validity or advantage of our evolved ethics are moot. We doubt that adaptation is so "fine-tuned" (Rosenberg 1991, p. 92), and argue below that the question of objective justification is genuine.

As noted above, Ruse's invocation of the naturalistic fallacy involves a problem about cheaters and free-riders, to which his mischievous argument responds. We call this problem the Political Worry.[4] On Ruse's view we are obliged to be moral only insofar as we believe ourselves to be obliged; if there are members of society who do not believe themselves to be so obliged, the social system threatens to break down. It is doubtful whether sanctions would be sufficient to meet this problem. Ruse's response to the Political Worry can be traced back through Harman (1977, p. 62) and Mackie (1977, p. 109) to Hume (Mackie 1980, pp. 71–73, 121–123, 147–150). The basic idea is that a limited amount of sympathy, together with the force of habit centred around particular conventions, can combine to produce a sense of moral obligation sufficient for broad compliance. Since this sense of obligation involves the illusion of objectivity, this hypothesis is called the "error theory". On Ruse's own account, however, there is more behind the social story than limited sympathy: there are altruistic instincts as well. If they are strong enough to override self interest, then the error is itself superfluous.

Ruse seems to think that altruism evolves in a limited form in conjunction with self-interests, and that it needs some further support. But if altruism arises as an overlay on a selfish motivational structure, then it seems likely that it must be strong enough to sometimes override selfishness, since otherwise it would not evolve. More pointedly, either altruism is strong enough to evolve by itself, or else it must evolve in conjunction with tendencies to see moral obligations as binding. The latter hypothesis is more complex, requiring two adaptations rather than one, so it is unlikely to be true. Moreover, although cheaters are likely to be found out in small social groups (like families or tribes), making cheating a poor strategy, cheating is more likely to be successful with strangers, especially strangers one will never see again. It seems likely that we have evolved cues that stimulate altruistic behaviour and repress cheating behaviour under conditions of familiarity. Since humans evolved in small groups, it seems less likely that we have biologically evolved a tendency to believe our obligations are objective. This adaptation, if general, would interfere with our ability to cheat strangers to our advantage.

In larger groups it is less likely that cues to stimulate altruism would be widely present; it is here that the Political Worry emerges with its full force. It seems unlikely that large human societies have been around long enough to allow adaptation to the absence of cues for altruistic behaviour. On the other hand, social adaptations to enhance cooperation, such as religious or aristocratic systems, could be easily associated with myths of objective justification, given the general credulity of humans. Furthermore, if a society has some degree of fairness, extension of the adaptations for cooperation that work in smaller groups becomes a possibility. A leading hypothesis of current political theory is the idea that if a society's basic structure is fair and its citizens raised to be cognisant of this fact, the strains of social commitment will be minimal (Rawls 1971). Given what we have said about small groups, this hypothesis cannot be easily dismissed. It seems likely that trust is a correlate of cooperative behaviour, and fairness is likely to inspire trust. But whether trust arises through fair means or foul, we don't need to postulate a biological propensity to objectify morality for either small or large groups.

Biology, especially sociobiology, suggests that morally relevant instincts go well beyond the minimal sympathy assumed by the social error theorists. Since the adaptations for morality probably preceded our beliefs about morality, it seems reasonable to say that we discovered rather than created our morality, and that moral progress consists in the continued articulation and development of our moral instincts as we discover more about them. The error theory, therefore, seems to be superfluous at the social as well as the biological level This implies nothing about the justification of our moral values except that we have reason to look further for why we believe them to be justified. If the error theory is false, then it is more likely that our beliefs about the objectivity of morality are true, or that we are capable of having true beliefs about the objectivity of morality.

Setting aside the Political Worry, then, we are left with what we take to be the deepest challenge to the objectivity of our beliefs about morality. The Metaphysical Worry is the concern that other species, or indeed, the human species, might have evolved with a different morality, so there may be no general moral principle, even thought there are many species capable of morality. Ruse raises this worry as follows: "For the Darwinian, what works is what counts. Had evolution taken us down another path, we might well think moral that which we now find horrific, and conversely. This is not a conclusion acceptable to the traditional objectivist" (1986, p. 254) and " . . . the ethical code of one species cannot be translated into that of another. No abstract moral principles exist outside the particular nature of individual species" (Ruse and Wilson 1986, p. 186). Both Ruse and Richards base morality solely in the products of a particular evolutionary process and see no basis for morality independent of the particular (selectionist) processes that produced it. They agree that morality is species relative. Ruse is happy with this conclusion, since he gives up any chance of objective justification. As Richards points out (1987, p. 620), this sanctions the canonisation of Hitler along with St. Francis. Richards avoids this problem, but he has a similar problem across species lines.

Evolutionary contingencies could sanction different but inconsistent fundamental moral values for different species. But if the Metaphysical Worry is enough reason to reject Ruse's position, then it seems it should be enough reason to reject Richards' as well. A satisfactory naturalistic morality needs a way to connect our moral capacities and behaviours to non-relativistic moral values.

The Metaphysical Worry is either something that must be swallowed, in which case there is a capricious element in morality and there may be equally justified yet inconsistent moralities, or else it is a serious problem, and the theories that do not resolve it are unacceptable. The following proposal suggests that evolutionary naturalism need not swallow the Metaphysical Worry, much less choke on it.

4. A Proposal for an Objective Evolutionary Ethics

A key problem with Richards' position is that if it does provide objective justification, its optimality assumption implies that there are no grounds for questioning the moral values implicit in our evolved ends. This trivialises questions of the rightness or wrongness of our evolved ends, and, as Ruse points out, trivialises the question of objective justification. There are no general standards for comparing the moral worth of different evolved ends.

On our view, the species relativism that both Ruse and Richards fall into results from their implicit assumption that our evolved moral sense is as good as it could be. If evolution is not optimal, this opens up the possibility of studying the sorts of conditions that could produce creatures with more optimal moral instincts. The conditions for this hypothetical optimality will be determined by the general conditions governing evolution for the sorts of creatures to which morality applies: intelligent social creatures. Optimal moral instincts will ground fundamental moral principles that are absolute for our world and nomologically similar worlds, but contingent on evolution. These principles are the basis of objective morality.

We thus adopt Richards' argument that the reference of moral terms is tied to the conditions under which our moral instincts evolved, but rather than tying the reference to the particular circumstances of human evolution, we believe that moral values refer to general ends produced by the effects of evolution, according to natural laws. Human cognitive connections to these natural moral kinds is by way of the particular circumstances of our evolution, much as our general idea of gold is gained by way of acquaintance with particular instances of gold, or, more aptly, our concept of vision has its roots in particular less than ideal instances of vision. Like vision. we propose that our evolved moral propensities can be less than optimal for their function, but this does not mean that we cannot imagine how these propensities could be optimised for moral function.[5] The non-optimality of our evolved moral instincts permits extension of species specific moral concepts, with the help of evolutionary theory and information about more optimal moral adaptations, which allows us to discover and formulate better and more general moral principles.

The exact process by which moral concepts acquire meaning remains an open question. A satisfactory explanation would require a naturalistic theory of meaning that locates the sense of our intuitive notions ecologically in the conditions under which they evolved. These conditions, which are reflected and preserved physiologically in our instincts, give us reasons to act. The capacity for articulating our moral intuitions in thought and language allows us to discover the meaning of moral value, and to formulate moral principles which are theories about the consequences of our innate moral sense. Knowledge of evolutionary theory and adaptive processes allows us to speculate about what our moral instincts might have been had our morality evolved more optimally. This, in turn, allows us to formulate (still as a process of empirical discovery) what general moral principles might apply to optimally evolved, intelligent, social creatures. On our proposal, moral theory is empirical, objective, correctable, and provides both individual motives for compliance which are, in addition, objective moral obligations.

Modern science, having jettisoned superstitions about a designer, is accustomed to thinking of the world as value-neutral. The presupposition seems to be that value is always in the service of some end, and that the world itself does not have any end. The world does, though, naturally produce creatures that have ends. Given the contingencies of evolution and the various demands for survival, in any intelligent creature the ends are likely to have a certain amount of consistency and harmony. Given the need of any organism for nutrients, and the advantages of sensitivity, avoidance of harm, and anticipation of the environment, it seems reasonable to expect that pleasure, avoidance of pain, and intelligence will be natural values. In highly evolved social creatures, true altruism is also likely to evolve, for a variety of well-known reasons. This function can be enhanced in intelligent creatures if it is cognitive. We should expect, therefore, that highly evolved intelligent and social creatures will have, in some more or less distorted fashion, common welfare and other mutual projects as fundamental goals. The convergence of theoretically expected natural values and our evolved moral intuitions suggests that at least sometimes our moral intuitions direct us towards objective and general values. Although only biology can tell us what moral values are likely to evolve widely, and thus be general. we can explore the structure of natural values and their consequences with our evolved ethical sense. This allows us (though it is by no means inevitable) to improve on what nature has given us.

Morality emerges, contingently and imperfectly through the evolutionary process, wherever reflective intelligent social creatures evolve. Moral progress is first biologically based, but the emergence of cognitive and reflective powers allows organisms to discover their own morality and articulate it and extend it in line with their particular moral instincts. The study of evolutionary theory allows a Copernican shift away from our imperfectly evolved (non-optimal) moral instincts to a more general and optimal moral theory. The logical, intuitive and instinctive connections to the sources of our morality insure that this objectified view of morality still gives us reason to act morally.

5. Consideration of Some Objections to Our Proposal

Objections to our proposal are either general objections against evolutionary naturalism, or are specific to our proposal. We will deal with the former briefly, the latter in more detail.

A general objection against ethical naturalism is that it is superfluous, since we can do metaethics adequately by other means, like linguistic analysis, reflective equilibrium on our intuitions, or rationalistic methods. One problem with these methods is that they run up against the error theory: the evidence they work with may be an illusion. The other problem is that even if we can get an objective ethical theory by these methods, it is unclear why such a theory could give any reason to be moral. The advantage of evolutionary theories is that they tie together motivational structures with moral principles as an inevitable consequence of their source in adaptive processes.

Another concern is that our evolved instincts may not be rich enough for a biologically based morality. This is the position of Mackie, Harman, and perhaps Hume. They believe that morality is socially constructed rather than biologically based. Our strongest reply to this is that the biological evidence suggests otherwise. Speculation aside, this question requires an empirical resolution.

The naturalistic fallacy is often supposed to undermine any form of naturalistic ethics. Although Ruse's version skirts this problem at the expense of giving up objectivity, we must answer this objection directly. On the Received View of science, explanation involves the derivation of what is to be explained from the explaining theory and auxiliary assumptions. This is a plausible necessary condition for explanation, and so it appears that evolutionary explanation of moral values must commit the naturalistic fallacy. But in a perceptive article on Moore's open question argument, Stephen Ball (1988) points out this argument applies to deductive relations only. The naturalistic fallacy presents a problem for naturalistic ethics only if it postulates a deductive relationship between ethical truths and biological theory. In the program we outlined above, however, the pattern of reasoning is not deductive, but abductive, from consequences to a possible cause. The cause, in this case, is an evolved set of fundamental values governing moral behaviour. Postulating such a cause, we can infer from its consequences some of its properties and structure. We postulate moral values to explain moral phenomena, rather than derive them. We do not explain moral values in terms of non-moral biological facts.

Another objection to our position is that there is no independent way to know what objective morality is, so we cannot compare it with our intuitions. In reply, we note that this is true for perceptions as well: "bootstrapping" is not always illegitimate. A process of reflective equilibrium informed by evolutionary theory can lead us to discover which moral intuitions we can trust, and which we cannot. We may also need to revise our opinions that certain of our values are moral values.

In the case of perception, we accept that there is at least a partial, though perhaps sometimes misleading, correspondence between our sensations and the world. Our belief in this correspondence can be justified at least in part by an evolutionary account of perception and its function. In order to get started, this justification needs to be augmented by at least *prima facie* reasons to trust our sensations, but it goes some way towards defeating naturalistic arguments against objective facts analogous to Ruse's argument against objective ethics. Although there is good biological reason for us to be predisposed to believe in the objectivity of our sensory experience, just as we are predisposed to objectify our moral intuitions, there is also good biological reason why accurate perceptions should evolve (Matthen 1988). Analogously, on our proposal, we have *prima facie* reasons to accept our moral intuitions, and then evolutionary theory tells us that these intuitions are likely to correspond at least partly to an objective morality that would be likely to evolve in the sort of creature we are.

Another objection is that our moral intuitions evolved under very special conditions, and we should expect them to be correspondingly limited in scope. This is equally true of our perceptions; there are many forms of energy to which we are not sensitive. We can, though, infer conditions we cannot perceive from those we can perceive, and this may be possible for morality as well. In any case, even if our morality is very limited in scope, and not in any sense general, this does not rule out its objectivity in its restricted domain.

A deeper objection is that there may not be any morally consistent representation of our instincts, even after a process of reflective study. Since adaptations do not need to be consistent in order to be adaptive, it is possible that we have evolved inconsistent intuitions about what is morally correct, as long as the problems caused by the inconsistencies are minimal compared to their overall biological advantages. Although inconsistencies among our fundamental moral intuitions would make discovering morality difficult, they do not rule it out altogether, since the objective basis of morality need not be just the content of our intuitions, any more than the objective basis of our perceptions needs to be the same as the phenomenal aspects of our sensory experience might immediately suggest. Physics is difficult and often counter-intuitive; a scientific ethics might be equally counter-intuitive.

The most troublesome objection for our position questions whether morality is a natural grouping or set of groupings that are subject to selection in (statistically) law-like ways. On our account, this is required both for the assumption that our morally relevant instincts are rich enough on which to found a moral system, and for our assumption that the reference of moral terms is tied to nomologically general principles through the historical connection to the circumstances of the evolution of our morally relevant instincts. The ultimate answer to this objection depends on close sociobiological studies. In the meantime, we can point out that the contingencies of life among intelligent social creatures make it nomologically likely that this sort of behaviour and its underlying motivational structures will be selected. That is at least plausible, and all we claim to establish here is plausibility.

6. Conclusion

On our proposal, the evolution of morality is not necessary; it is made likely by evolution, but not certain. Nor is moral progress necessary. It may be that we lack the cognitive capacities to fully articulate our moral instincts (especially in large societies), and it is certainly possible that other instincts will dominate, and we will end up in an immoral but self-preserving fascist dead end, or some other abomination. Furthermore, our capacity to perform the moral Copernican revolution may be restricted for reasons unknown to us. Perhaps our instincts are so restricted that this move will be prevented; we may be doomed to view the world anthropocentrically. It is even possible that we could intellectually discover an optimal ethics for creatures like us, but lack the motivation to implement it. On the other hand, the adaptive advantages of intellectual and emotional flexibility for intelligent social creatures are great, and it seems likely that any creature that has evolved morality, and the cognitive capacity to articulate it reflectively, will also have the flexibility to override the limitations of its instincts, however difficult this might be. Again, this is the point where speculation must end, and empirical study must begin.

The fundamental problem with non-naturalistic ethics is that if its objectivity is not simply an illusion, then it remains a deep mystery how we might come to have knowledge of moral values, much less be motivated by them to act. Evolutionary ethics provides solutions to such mysteries, but current versions imply that moral principles so derived must be relativistic and arbitrary. Against this implication, we propose that morality is contingent on the general facts governing evolution. On our view, morality evolves as a motivational structure in response to contingent needs felt by highly evolved, intelligent, social creatures. This evolution is imperfect, and subject to cognitive correction through consideration of what would be optimal for our sort of creature. If evolutionary theory were false, and we had been produced differently (for example, as an experiment devised by an evil genius), the basis of morality might have been quite different. As it is, morality is determined by the general facts of evolution as applied to organic, intelligent, social creatures. Evolution provides creatures like us with physiologically based moral values: motivationally effective imperatives, with nomological rather than categorical force.

Acknowledgments

John Collier was supported by a SSHRCC Canada Research Fellowship at the University of Calgary during the preparation of this paper. It also benefited from comments on earlier versions presented to the University of Calgary, the Western Canadian Philosophical Association, the Canadian Philosophical Association, the Philosophy Department of the University of Melbourne and the International Society for History, Philosophy and Social Studies in Biology. Discussions with Michael Ruse and Robert Richards, and commentary by R. A. Sharpe and an anonymous referee were also very helpful.

References

Alexander, Richard. 1979. *Darwinism and Human Affairs*. Seattle: University of Washington Press.

———. 1987. *The Biological Basis of Morality*. New York: Aldine de Gruyter.

Ball, Stephen W. 1988. "Reductionism in Ethics and Science: A Contemporary Look at G. E. Moore's Open-Question Argument." *American Philosophical Quarterly* 25: 197–212.

Collier, J. D. 1991. "Critical Notice of Richard Alexander, the Biology of Moral Systems." *Canadian Journal of Philosophy* 21: 73–88.

Gibbard, Allan. 1990. "Norms, Discussion, and Ritual: Evolutionary Puzzles." *Ethics* 100: 787–802.

Harman, Gilbert. 1977. *The Nature of Morality*. Oxford: Oxford University Press.

Kitcher, Philip. 1985. *Vaulting Ambition*. Cambridge, Mass.: MIT Press.

Mackie, J. L. 1977. *Ethics: Inventing Right and Wrong*. Harmondsworth: Penguin Books.

———. 1980. *Hume's Moral Theory*. London: Routledge and Kegan Paul.

Matthen, Mohan. 1988. "Biological Functions and Perceptual Content." *Journal of Philosophy* 85: 5–27.

Railton, Peter. 1986. "Moral Realism." *Philosophical Review* 95: 163–207.

Rawls, John. 1971. *A Theory of Justice*. Cambridge, Mass.: Harvard University Press.

Richards, Robert. 1986. "A Defense of Evolutionary Ethics." *Biology and Philosophy* 1: 265–293.

———. 1987. *Darwin and the Emergence of Evolutionary Theories of Mind and Behavior*. Chicago: University of Chicago Press.

Rosenberg, Alexander. 1991. "The Biological Justification of Ethics: A Best Case Scenario." *Social Philosophy and Policy* 8: 86–101.

Rottschaeffer, William A., and David Martinsen. 1990. "Really Taking Darwin Seriously: An Alternative to Michael Ruse's Darwinian Metaethics." *Biology and Philosophy* 5: 149–174.

Ruse, Michael. 1984. "The Morality of the Gene." *Monist* 67: 176–199.

———. 1986. *Taking Darwin Seriously*. London: Blackwell.

———. 1990. "Evolutionary Ethics and the Search for Predecessors: Kant, Hume, and All the Way Back to Aristotle?" *Social Philosophy and Policy* 8: 59–85.

——— and E. O. Wilson. 1986. "Moral Philosophy as Applied Science." *Philosophy* 61: 173–192.

Notes

1. The position we propose bears some resemblance to that of Rottschaeffer and Martinsen (1990), although our line of argument is different. One of the authors (Collier) was influenced by a paper that Rottschaeffer read several years ago at a meeting in Idaho.

2. It is important to recognise that this is only for the sake of argument. On a naturalistic account the function of morality is an empirical question just as much as is the function of circulation or vision.

3. A similar point is made by Railton (1986).

4. Gibbard (1990, p. 792) calls this the problem of allegiance, but we find our label more perspicuous in terms of the level of social

organisation at which it arises and the area of philosophy within whose jurisdiction it has traditionally fallen.

5. It is important to note here that the optimality is for moral function, not for survival. An eye that is optimised for vision is not necessarily optimal for survival. Just so with motivational structures that are optimised for moral function.

General Bibliography

Alexander, R. 1987. *The Biology of Moral Systems*. New York: Adline De Gruyter.

———. 1979. *Darwinism and Human Affairs*. Seattle: University of Washington Press.

Ball, S. 1988. "Reductionism in Ethics and Science: A Contemporary Look at G. E. Moore's Open Question Argument." *American Philosophical Quarterly* 25: 197–214.

Bischof, N. 1975. "Comparative Ethology of Incest Avoidance." In *Biosocial Anthropology*, ed. Robin Fox, pp. 37–67. London: Malaby Press.

Boehm, C. 1978. "Rational Pre-selection from Hamadryas to Homo Sapiens: The Place of Decisions in Adaptive Process." *Amer. Anthro.* (in press).

Brink, D. 1984, "Moral Realism and the Skeptical Arguments from Disagreement and Queerness." *Australasian Journal of Philosophy* 62: 111–125 .

———. 1989. *Moral Realism and the Foundations of Ethics*. New York: Cambridge University Press.

Calicott, J. 1984. "Non-Anthropocentric Value Theory and Environmental Ethics." *American Philosophical Quarterly* 21: 299–309.

Campbell, D. T. 1959. "Methodological Suggestions from a Comparative Psychology of Knowledge Processes." *Inquiry* 2: 152–182.

———. 1972. "On the Genetics of Altruism and the Counterhedonic Components in Human Culture." *J. Social Issues* 28: 21–37; reprinted in *Sympathy, Altruism and Helping*, ed. L. G. Wispe. New York: Academic Press.

———. 1974. "Evolutionary Epistemology." In *The Philosophy of Karl Popper*, ed. P. A. Schilpp, vol. 14, I. The Library of Living Philosophers. LaSalle, Ill.: Open Court Publishers.

———. 1975a. "On the Conflicts between Biological and Social Evolution and Between Psychology and Moral Tradition." *Amer. Psychol.* 30: 1103–1126.

———. 1975b. "Reintroducing Konrad Lorenz to Psychology." *In Konrad Lorenz: The Man and His Ideas*, ed. R. I. Evans. New York: Harcourt Brace Jovanovich.

————. "Social Morality as Evidence of Conflict Between Biological Human Nature and Social Requirement." In G. Stent, ed., *Morality as a Biological Phenomenon*, pp. 75–92. Berlin: Abakon Verlagsgesellschaft.

Campbell, J., and Pargetter, R. 1986. "Goodness and Fragility." *American Philosophical Quarterly* 23: 155–165.

Campbell, R. 1984. "Sociobiology and the Possibility of Ethical Naturalism." In D. Copp and D. Zimmerman, eds., *Morality, Reason and Truth*, pp. 270–296. Totowa, N.J.: Rowan and Allanheld.

Caplan, A., ed. 1978. *The Sociobiology Debate*. New York: Harper Books.

Chambers, R. 1844. *The Vestiges of the Natural History of Creation*. London: Churchill (published anonomously).

Cooper, G. 1988. "Fitness and Explanation." In A. Fine and J. Leplin, eds., *PSA 1988: Proceedings of the 1988 Biennial Meeting of the Philosophy of Science Association*, pp. 207–215. East Lansing, Mich.: Philosophy of Science Association.

Darwall, S. 1983. *Impartial Reason*. Ithaca: Cornell University Press.

Darwin, C. 1859. *On the Origin of Species by Means of Natural Selection*. London: John Murray.

————. 1871. *The Descent of Man, and Selection in Relation to Sex*, 2 vols. London: John Murray.

Darwin, E. 1794. *Zoonomia or the Laws of Organic Life*. London: Johnson.

Dawkins, R. 1976. *The Selfish Gene*. Oxford: Oxford University Press.

Desmond, A., and J. Moore. 1991. *Darwin*. New York: Warner Books.

Ebling, F. J., ed. 1969. *Biology of Ethics: Institute of Biology Symposia*; Number 18. New York: Academic Press.

Edel. A. 1980. *Exploring Fact and Value*, vol. 2, in *Science, Ideology and Value*. New Brunswick, N.J.: Transaction Books.

Erikson, E. 1966. "Ontogeny of Ritualization in Man." In *Philosophical Transactions of the Royal Society in London*, Series B, 772, 251: 337–349.

Flanagan, O., Jr. 1982. "Quinean Ethics." *Ethics* 93: 56–74.

Flew, A. G. N. 1967. *Evolutionary Ethics*. London: Macmillan.

Frankena, W. 1976. "Naturalistic Fallacy." In K. Goodpaster, ed., *Perspectives in Morality*. Notre Dame, Ind.: Notre Dame Press.

Frankfurt, H. 1971. "Freedom of the Will and the Concept of a Person." *Journal of Philosophy* 68: 5–20.

Ghiselin, M. T. 1974. *The Economy of Nature and the Evolution of Sex*. Berkeley, Los Angeles, and London: University of California Press.

Ghiselin, M. T. 1976. "Comment." *Amer. Psychol.* 31: 358–359.

Gibbard, A. 1982. "Human Evolution and the Sense of Justice." In P. French, T. Uehling, Jr., and H. Wettstein, eds., *Midwest Studies in Philosophy*, Vol. 8. *Social and Political Philosophy*, pp. 31–46. Minneapolis: University of Minnesota Press.

Goodall, J. 1974. *In the Shadow of Man*. Glasgow: Fontana Books.

Gould, S. J. 1976. "Biological Potential *vs.* Biological Determinsm," *Natural History Magazine* 85: 12–22.

———. 1978. "Sociobiology: The Art of Storytelling." *New Scientist* 80: 530–533.

——— and R. Lewontin. 1978. "The Spandrals of San Marco and the Panglossian Paradigm: A Critique of the Adaptationist Programme." *Proceedings of the Royal Society of London*, 205: 581–598.

Hamilton, W. D. 1964. "The Genetical Theory of Social Behaviour," *J. Theor. Biol.* 6: 1.

Harman, G. 1977. *The Nature of Morality.* Oxford: Oxford University Press.

Hume, D. 1739. *A Treatise of Human Nature,* books 1 and 2. London; reprinted 1978 Oxford: Clarendon Press.

———. 1740. *A Treatise of Human Nature,* Book 3. London.

———. 1751. *Enquiry Concerning the Principles of Morals.* London.

Huxley, T. H. 1901. *Evolution and Ethics, and Other Essays.* London: Macmillan.

——— and J. S. Huxley. 1947. *Evolution and Ethics.* London: Pilot Press.

Kant, I. 1949. *Critique of Practical Reason,* trans. L. W. Beck. Chicago: University of Chicago Press.

———. *Foundations of the Metaphysics of Morals,* trans. L. W. Beck. Indianapolis: Bobbs-Merrill.

Kitcher, P. 1985. *Vaulting Ambition: Sociobiology and the Quest of Human Nature.* Cambridge, Mass.: MIT Press.

——— et al. 1987. "Precis of Vaulting Ambition: Sociobiology and the Quest for Human Nature, Open Peer Commentary and Author's Response." *Behavior and Brain Sciences* 10: 61–100.

Kohlberg, L. 1969. "Stage and Sequence: The Cognitive-developmental Approach to Socialization." In D. A. Goslin (ed.) *Handbook of Socialization Theory and Research,* pp. 347–380. Chicago: Rand McNally Co.

Kohn, D., ed. 1985. *The Darwinian Heritage.* Princeton, N.J.: Princeton University Press.

Lamarck, J.-B. de. 1809. *Philosophie Zoologique.* Paris: Dentu.

LeVine, R. A., and D. T. Campbell. 1972. *Ethnocentrism: Theories of Conflict, Ethnic Attitudes and Group Behavior.* New York: Wiley.

Lewontin, R. 1972. "Testing the Theory of Natural Selection" *Nature* 236: 181–182.

———. 1978. "Adaptation." *Scientific American* 239: 213–230.

———, S. Rose, and L. Kamin. 1984. *Not in Our Genes: Biology, Ideology, and Human Nature.* New York: Pantheon Books.

Lorenz, K. A. 1941. "Kant's Lehre vom Apriorischen im Lichte gegenwartiger Biologie." *Blatter fur Deutsche Philosophie* 15: 94–125.

———. 1964. "Moral-analoges Verhalten der Tiere-Erkenntnisse heutiger Verhaltensforschung." *Universitas* 19: 43–54.

———. 1967. *On Aggression*. New York: Bantam Books.

———. 1973. *Civilized Man's Eight Deadly Sins*. New York: Harcourt Brace Jovanovich.

———. 1975. "Konrad Lorenz Responds." In *Konrad Lorenz: The Man and His Ideas*, ed. R. I. Evans, pp. 119–127. New York: Harcourt Brace Jovanovich.

Lovejoy, O. 1981. "The Origin of Man," *Science* 211:341–50.

Lumsden, C. J., and E. O. Wilson. 1981. *Genes, Mind and Culture: The Coevolutionary Process*. Cambridge, Mass.: Harvard University Press.

———. 1983. *Promethean Fire*. Cambridge, Mass.: Harvard University Press.

Mackie, J. L. 1977. *Ethics: Inventing Right and Wrong*. Harmondsworth, England: Penguin Books.

———. 1978. "The Law of the Jungle." *Philosophy* 53: 553–573.

Malthus, T. R. 1798. *An Essay on the Principle of Population*. London: Johnson (this first edition was published anonomously, the second edition of 1803 bore Malthus's name).

———. 1830 *A Summary View of the Principle of Population*. London: John Murray.

Maynard Smith, J. 1974. "The Theory of Games and the Evolution of Animal Conflicts." *J. theor. Biol.* 47: 209–221.

———. 1976a. "Group Selection." *Q. Rev. Biol.* 51: 277.

———. 1976b. "Evolution and the Theory of Games." *American Scientist* 64: 41.

——— and G. A. Parker. 1976. "The Logic of Asymmetric Contests." *Anim. Behav.* 24: 159–175.

——— and G. R. Price. 1973. "The Logic of Animal Conflict." *Nature* 246: 15–18.

Mivart, St. G. 1871a. *On the Genesis of Species*. New York: Appleton.

———. 1871b. "Darwin's *Descent of Man*." *Quarterly Review* 131: 47–90.

———. 1872. "Evolution and Its Consequences: A Reply to Professor Huxley." *The Contemporary Review* 19: 168–197.

———. 1893. "Evolution in Professor Huxley." *Nineteenth Century* 34: 198–211.

Moore, G. E. 1903. *Principia Ethica*. Cambridge: Cambridge University Press.

Murphy, J. G. 1982. *Evolution, Morality, and the Meaning of Life*. Totowa, N.J.: Rowman and Littlefield.

Nozick, R. 1981. *Philosophical Explanations*. Cambridge, Mass.: Harvard University Press.

Pugh, G. E. 1977. *The Biological Origin of Human Values*. New York: Basic Books.

Quillian, W. S. 1945. *The Moral Theory of Evolutionary Naturalism*. New Haven, Conn.: Yale University Press.

Quinn, P. 1981. *Divine Commands and Moral Requirements*. New York: Oxford University Press.

Quinton, A. 1966. "Ethics and the Theory of Evolution." In *Biology and Personality,* ed. I. T. Ramsey. Oxford: Blackwell.

Railton, P. 1986. "Moral Realism." *Philosophical Review* 95: 163–207.

Raphael, D. D. 1958. "Darwinism and Ethics." In *A Century of Darwin,* ed. S. A. Barnett, pp. 355–378. London: Heinemann.

Rawls, J. 1951. "Outline of a Decision Procedure for Ethics," *Philosophical Review* 60: 177–197.

———. 1971. *A Theory of Justice.* Cambridge, Mass.: Harvard University Press.

———. 1980. "Kantian Constructivism in Moral Theory," *Journal of Philosophy* 77: 515–572.

Richards, R. 1986a. "A Defense of Evolutionary Ethics." *Biology and Philosophy* 1: 265–292.

———. 1986b. "Justification Through Biological Faith: A Rejoinder." *Biology and Philosophy* 1: 337–354.

———. 1987. *Darwin and the Emergence of Evolutionary Theories of Mind and Behavior.* Chicago: University of Chicago Press.

Ruse, M. 1979a. *The Darwinian Revolution: Science Red in Tooth and Claw.* Chicago: University of Chicago Press.

———. 1979b. *Sociobiology: Sense or Nonsense?* Dordrecht, Holland: Reidel.

———. 1982. *Darwinism Defended: A Guide to the Evolution Controversies.* Reading, Mass.: Addison-Wesley.

———. 1984. "The Morality of the Gene." *The Monist* 67: 167–199.

———. 1985. "Is Rape Wrong on Andromeda?" In E. Regis, ed., *Extraterrestrials,* pp. 43–78. Cambridge University Press, Cambridge.

———. 1986a. "Evolutionary Ethics: A Phoenix Arisen." *Zygon* 21: 95–112.

———. 1986b. *Taking Darwin Seriously: A Naturalistic Approach to Philosophy.* Oxford: Blackwell.

———. 1987. "Darwinism and Determinism." *Zygon* 21: 419–422.

——— and E. O. Wilson. 1986. "Darwinism as Applied Science." *Philosophy.*

——— and Wilson, E. 1986. "Ethics as Applied Science." *Philosophy* 61: 173–192.

Russett, C. E. 1976. *Darwin in America.* San Francisco: W. H. Freeman.

Scarrow, D. 1981. "The Causality of Reason: A Survey of Some Recent Developments in the Mind-Body Problem." *Metaphilosophy* 12: 13–30.

Scott, J. F. 1971. *Internalization of Norms: A Sociological Theory of Moral Commitment.* Englewood Cliffs: Prentice-Hall.

Scudo, F. M., and M. Acanfora. 1985. "Darwin and Russian Evolutionary Biology." In *The Darwinian Heritage,* ed. David Kohn, pp. 731–752. Princeton, N.J.: Princeton University Press.

Searle, J. R. 1964. "How to Derive 'Ought' from 'Is'." *Philosophical Review* 73.

———. 1969. *Speech Acts.* Cambridge: Cambridge University Press.

Settle, T. 1993. " 'Fitness' and 'Altruism': Traps for the Unwary, Bystander and Biologist Alike." *Biology and Philosophy* 8: 61–83.

Sidgwick, H. 1874. *Methods of Ethics*. London: Macmillan; later editions were extensively revised: 1877, 1884, 1890, 1901, 1907.

———. 1902. *Lectures on the Ethics of T. H. Green, Mr. Herbert Spencer, and J. Martineau*. London: Macmillan.

Singer, P. 1981. *The Expanding Circle: Ethics and Sociobiology*. New York: Farrar, Straus, and Giroux.

Sober, E. 1984. *The Nature of Selection: Evolutionary Theory in Philosophical Focus*. Cambridge, Mass.: MIT Press.

———. 1988. "What Is Evolutionary Altruism?" *Canadian Journal of Philosophy* (supplementary issue) 14: 75–99.

Spencer, H. 1851. *Social Statics: Or, the Conditions Essential to Human Happiness Specified, and the First of Them Developed*. London: Chapman.

———. 1852. "A Theory of Population, Deduced from the General Law of Animal Fertility." *Westminster Review* 1: 468–501.

———. 1857. "Progress: Its Law and Cause." *Westminster Review;* reprinted in *Essays: Scientific, Political, and Speculative*. (1868). 1; pp. 1–60. London: Williams and Norgate.

———. 1893. *Principles of Ethics*. London: Williams and Norgate.

Sturgeon, N. 1984. "Moral Explanation." In D. Copp and D. Zimmerman, eds., *Morality, Reason and Truth*, pp. 79–103. Totowa, N.J.: Rowan and Allanheld.

———. 1986. "Harman on Moral Explanations of Natural Facts." *Southern Journal of Philosophy* 24, Supplement: 69–78.

Sumner, W. G. 1906. *Folkways*. Boston: Ginn.

Taylor, P. W. 1958. "Social Science and Ethical Relativism." *Journal of Philosophy* 55: 32–44.

———. 1978. *Problems of Moral Philosophy*. Belmont, Calif.: Wadsworth.

Trigg, R. 1982. *The Shaping of Man*. Oxford: Blackwell.

Trivers, R. L. 1971. "The Evolution of Reciprocal Altruism." *Quarterly Review of Biology* 46: 35–57.

Wade, M. 1978. "A Critical Review of the Models of Group Selection," *Quarterly Review of Biology* 53: 101–114.

Westermarck, E. 1907 and 1909. *Ursprung und Entwicklun der Moralbegriffe*, Vol. I and II. Leipzig: Klinkhardt.

Wickler, W. 1972. *The Biology of the Ten Commandments*. New York: McGraw-Hill.

Williams, G. C. 1966. *Adaptation and Natural Selection*. Princeton, N.J.: Princeton University Press.

Wilson, D. S. 1975a. "A Theory of Group Selection." *Proceedings of the National Academy of Sciences* USA 72, no. 1: 779–807.

———. 1975b. "Structured demes and the evolution of group-advantageous traits," *The Amer. Natur.* 110: 779–807.

———. 1980. *The Natural Selection of Populations and Communities*. Menlo Park, Calif.: Benjamin.

Wilson, E. O. 1971. *The Insect Societies*. Cambridge, Mass.: Belknap Press.

———. 1975a. *Sociobiology: The New Synthesis.* Cambridge, Mass.: Belknap Press of Harvard University Press.

———. 1975b. "Human Decency Is Animal." *The New York Times Magazine.* (Oct. 12), pp. 38–50.

———. 1978. *On Human Nature.* Cambridge, Mass.: Harvard University Press.

———. 1980a. "The Relation of Science to Theology," *Zygon.* 15: 425–434.

———. 1980b. "Comparative Social Theory," *Tanner Lecture,* University of Michigan.

Wynne-Edwards, V. C. 1962. *Animal Dispersion in Relation to Social Behaviour.* Edinburgh: Oliver and Boyd.

Zweig, A. 1959. "Tierpsychologische Beitrage zur Phylogenese der rch-Ueber-Ich-Instanzen." *Schweiz. Z. F. Psychol.,* Suppl. 37.

Notes on Contemporary Contributors

Richard D. Alexander is Donald Ward Tinkle Professor of Evolutionary Biology in the Department of Biology and is Curator of Insects in the Museum of Zoology, University of Michigan. In addition to numerous articles, he is the author of *Darwinism and Human Affairs* and *The Biology of Moral Systems*.

Francisco Ayala is Professor in the Department of Ecology and Evolutionary Biology, University of California, Irvine. In addition to numerous articles, he is the editor of *Studies in the Philosophy of Biology*, and author (with J. Valentine) of *Evolving*, and (with J. A. Kiger) of *Modern Genetics*. He is an Associate Editor of *Biology and Philosophy*.

John D. Collier is Lecturer in History and Philosophy of Science, University of Melbourne. He received his Ph.D. in 1984 from the University of Western Ontario and is the author of numerous articles.

Philip Kitcher is Professor in the Department of Philosophy, University of California, San Diego. In addition to numerous articles, he is the author of *The Nature of Mathematical Knowledge, Abusing Science*, and *Vaulting Ambition: Sociobiology and the Quest for Human Nature*.

J. L. Mackie was Reader in Philosophy and Fellow of University College, Oxford University. He was also a Fellow of the British Academy. Among his many publications are *Truth, Probability, and Paradox, The Cement of the Universe: A Study of Causation, Problems from Locke, Ethics: Inventing Right and Wrong*, and *The Miracle of Theism: Arguments For and Against the Existence of God*. He died in 1981.

David Martinsen is Professor in the Department of Biology, Lewis and Clark College.

Robert J. Richards is Professor in the Departments of History, Philosophy and Psychology, University of Chicago. In addition to numerous articles, he is the author of *Darwin and the Emergence of Evolutionary Theories of Mind and Behavior*. He is Director of the Program in History, Philosophy and Social Studies of Science and Medicine as well as Chair of the Committee on the Conceptual Foundations of Science at the University of Chicago.

Alexander Rosenberg is Professor and Director of the UHP in the Department of Philosophy, University of California, Riverside. In addition to numerous articles, he is author of *Hume and the Problem of Causation* (with T. L. Beauchamp), *Sociobiology and the Preemption of Social Science, Microeconomic Laws: A Philosophical Analysis, The Structure of Biological Science* and *Economic.*

William A. Rottschaefer is Professor in the Department of Philosophy, Lewis and Clark College. He received his Ph.D. in 1973 from Boston University.

Michael Ruse is Professor in the Departments of Philosophy and Zoology, University of Guelph. Among his numerous publications are *The Philosophy of Biology, Sociobiology: Sense or Nonsense, The Darwinian Revolution: Science Red in Tooth and Claw, Darwinism Defended, Taking Darwin Seriously.* He is editor of *Biology and Philosophy.*

Michael Stingl is Associate Professor in the Department of Philosophy, University of Lethbridge.

George C. Williams is Professor in the Department of Biology, State University of New York at Stony Brook. Among his numerous publications are *Adaptation and Natural Selection, Sex and Evolution,* and *Evolution and Ethics.*

Edward O. Wilson is Frank B. Baird, Jr. Professor of Science and Curator of Entomology in the Museum of Comparative Zoology, Harvard University. In addition to numerous articles, he is author of *The Insect Societies, Sociobiology: The New Synthesis, On Human Nature,* (with Charles Lumsden) *Genes, Mind and Culture: The Coevolutionary Process, Biophilia,* and (with Charles Lumsden) *Promethean Fire: Reflections on the Origin of Mind.*

Index

(Major or thematic occurrences of names, words or ideas)